KT-519-568

ECONOMIC GLOBALIZATION IN ASIA

Economic Globalization in Asia

Edited by
PARTHA GANGOPADHYAY
University of Western Sydney, Australia
and
MANAS CHATTERJI
Binghamton University, New York, USA

ASHGATE

© Partha Gangopadhyay and Manas Chatterji 2005

Partha Gangopadhyay and Manas Chatterji have asserted their right under the Copyright, Designs and Patents Act, 1988, to be identified as editors of this work.

Published by
Ashgate Publishing Limited
Gower House
Croft Road
Aldershot
Hampshire GU11 3HR
England

Ashgate Publishing Company
Suite 420
101 Cherry Street
Burlington, VT 05401-4405
USA

Ashgate website: http://www.ashgate.com

British Library Cataloguing in Publication Data
Gangopadhyay, Partha
    Economic globalization in Asia
    1.Globalization - Economic aspects - Asia 2.Financial
    crises - Asia - History - 20th century 3.Asia - Economic
    conditions - 1945- 4.Asia - Economic policy
    I.Title II.Chatterji, Manas, 1937-
    338.9'5

Library of Congress Cataloging-in-Publication Data
Economic globalization in Asia / by Partha Gangopadhyay and Manas Chatterji,
[editors].
        p. cm.
    Includes bibliographical references and index.
    ISBN 0-7546-4114-7
    1. Asia--Economic policy. 2. Asia--Economic conditions. 3. Asia--Foreign economic
relations. 4. International trade. 5. International economic integration. 6.
Globalization--Economic aspects. I. Chatterji, Manas,
1937- II. Gangopadhyay, Partha.

    HC412.E2175 2004
    337.5--dc22
                                                                    2004018314
    Reprinted 2006

    ISBN 0 7546 4114 7

Printed and bound by Athenaeum Press, Ltd.,
Gateshead, Tyne & Wear.

Contents

List of Contributors   vii

Preface
Matthew F. McHugh   viii

Introduction
Partha Gangopadhyay and Manas Chatterji   x

1   **The Role of Complexity Theory in International Business Strategy Development: Evidence from East and Southeast Asia**
David McHardy Reid and John Walsh   1

2   **Dynamic Changes of Japan's FDI in South Korea from 1985 to 1997**
Tsuyoshi Koizumi   15

3   **The Asian Crisis – Signals from Multinational Enterprises: Obstacles and Managerial Impediments to Foreign Direct Investment**
Frank L. Bartels and Hafiz Mirza   24

4   **International Financial Crises: Causes, Prevention and Cures**
Lawrence H. Summers   47

5   **Social Progress and the Asian Crisis**
Clive Hamilton   64

6   **The Asian Crisis and Financial and Capital Account Liberalization**
Chander Kant   78

7   **Major Causes of the Korean and Asian Economic Crises**
Chang Woon Nam   89

8   **Questioning the Explanations of the Asian Crisis**
Partha Gangopadhyay   108

9   **China Beyond the Asian Financial Crisis: A New Path of Institutional Change**
Leong H. Liew   119

10   **Problems of Globalization in India**
      Alok Ray   136

11   **Growth vs. Development: A Challenge to China for the 21st Century**
      Lilai Xu and (Late) J.C. Liu   146

12   **Globalization, Growth and Fiscal Policy: Lessons from East Asia**
      Jocelyn Horne   156

13   **Globalization, Trade Liberalization and Economic Growth:**
      The Case of Vietnam
      Binh Tran-Nam   170

14   **Decentralization and Capacity Building:**
      Selecting Modes of Training for Indonesia
      Koichi Mera   185

15   **Japan: Maturity and Stagnation?**
      Bill Lucarelli and Joseph Halevi   198

16   **Indicators and Trends in Economic Globalization**
      Stanislav Menshikov   212

17   **Some Theoretical Foundations of Russian Economic Policies**
      A. Nekipelov   229

18   **Characteristics of Small Firm Managers: Evidence from Sri Lanka**
      Jonathan Batten and Samanthala Hettihewa   248

19   **The Political Economy of Rural Health Care in India**
      Amit S. Ray and Saradindu Bhaduri   261

Index   **273**

List of Contributors

Frank L. Bartels, Nanyang Technical University, Singapore
Jonathan Batten, Macquarie University, Australia
Saradindu Bhaduri, Jawaharlal Nehru University, India
Manas Chatterji, Binghamton University, USA
Partha Gangopadhyay, University of Western Sydney, Australia
Joseph Halevi, University of Sydney, Australia
Clive Hamilton, The Australia Institute, Australia
Samanthala Hettihewa, University of Western Sydney, Australia
Jocelyn Horne, Macquarie University, Australia
Chander Kant, Seton Hall University, USA
Tsuyoshi Koizumi, Hyogo College, Japan
Leong H. Liew, Griffith University, Australia
(Late) J.C. Liu, Binghamton University, USA
Bill Lucarelli, University of Western Sydney, Australia
Matthew F. McHugh, World Bank, USA
Stanislav Menshikov, Russian Academy of Science, Russia
Koichi Mera, University of Southern California, USA
Hafiz Mirza, University of Bradford, U.K
Chang Woon Nam, Institute for Economic Research, Munich, Germany
A. Nekipelov, Russian Academy of Science, Russia
Alok Ray, Queen's University, Canada
Amit S. Ray, Jawaharlal Nehru University, India
David McHardy Reid, Rochester University of Technology, USA
Lawrence H. Summers, Harvard University, USA
Binh Tran-Nam, University of New South Wales, Australia
John Walsh, Curtain University of Technology, Australia
Lilai Xu, La Trobe University, Australia

Preface

Matthew F. McHugh

The Asian financial crisis has had a profound effect not only on the nations of that region, large and small, but on the global marketplace more generally. It is important that we understand the causes of that crisis, as well as the lessons to be learned from our experience in coping with it. Most of the papers in this diverse collection deal with recent economic developments in Asia, including their implications for institutional reform, trade, the development of the private sector, and a variety of related topics. In some cases, the scope of these papers extends beyond economics, touching upon political, social and cultural changes.

Whether the developments considered are economic, political, social, or a combination thereof, they are all occurring in the context of globalization and often at a rapid pace. This poses challenges, as well as opportunities, for policymakers and others in the mix.

As Thomas Friedman observed in his best-selling book, *The Lexus and the Olive Tree*, globalization is the international system that replaced the Cold War system. Protesters in Seattle and elsewhere may decry the system, but it is surely with us and is likely to be for some time. It is driven by powerful technologies that are integrating our societies more each day, and by the aspirations of people for a better life who see no alternative to plugging into this system. Like it or not, in economic terms, the winners in today's world will be those who understand globalization and accommodate themselves to it.

However, accommodation can be difficult, even painful. Governments must adopt free market policies that often run counter to established interests – protectionism must give way to open trade, state run enterprises need to be privatized, corruption and crony capitalism must be abandoned, banking, legal and regulatory systems need to be reformed. Government and business must be more transparent. In short, to integrate into the global marketplace, nations must put institutions, programs and policies in place that will attract and sustain private investors; the ultimate engine of growth in any society.

Globalization generates some understandable concerns. While it promotes economic growth, the benefits of this growth are not always equitable. The most vulnerable in society can be left behind. Moreover, beyond the economic consequences, globalization is often seen as bringing with it foreign values which break down traditional cultures. Muslim countries, for example, often associate globalization with Western values with which they are not particularly comfortable. These concerns need to be addressed if there is to be economic, social and political stability. There is no obvious alternative to globalization today, and societies do need to act on this reality. Those that lack the experience of financial capacity to adapt on their own deserve the help of the more fortunate, since we all have an interest in promoting growth and stability. At the same time, the stresses and inequities that accompany such rapid change need to be remedied. Many developing countries cannot yet cope with globalization unaided. The international community, through institutions like the IMF, the World Bank, and others, must help. The recent experience in Asia, and its impact elsewhere, has been instructive. It was both a crisis and an opportunity. The international community did respond and most countries, with appropriate assistance, have adopted policies, which provide hope for the future. The papers presented here reflect this experience and contribute to our knowledge of a rapidly changing, but compelling world.

Introduction

Partha Gangopadhyay and Manas Chatterji

The term globalization usually calls forth an annotation since this term is embroiled in mundane controversies. In recent years, the World Economic Forum has turned out to be a Janus with one face chanting the litany of globalization – mainly by custodians of multinational corporations, their trusted allies and beneficiaries. The other face – representing labor unions, various interest groups, rent-seekers and environmental lobbies – spits fire outside the Forum condemning globalization and inciting riots after riots. There is, however, a little consensus about what one really means by this term; the situation has been exacerbated by our efforts to fit the concept of globalization in a Procrustean bed to pursue our selfish motives. So it is of little use to take on a Socratic method to define globalization. Despite these problems, it seems unanimous that globalization purports two critical facets: one is quantitative while the other is qualitative. On the quantitative front, it is generally recognized that volumes of trans-border trade, capital and investment flows have risen spectacularly and, thereby, assumed a paramount significance towards the end of the last millennium in shaping national and global economic outcomes. Pundits still lock their horns over the question of whether such trans-border flows have been unprecedented, or otherwise. Yet there is a near consensus that economic fortunes of nations are critically enmeshed with such trans-border flows driven by multinational firms. Secondly, the reliance of nations on trans-border trade, capital and investment flows has led to the emergence of market forces as the most powerful mechanism in coordinating economic activities and allocating national income within a nation State. Consequently, the market mechanism assumed an unprecedented ascendancy that has gradually pushed national governments to peripheral activities. The main qualitative facet of globalization therefore encompasses the changing role of governments in turning the wheel of fortunes of a nation. To put it baldly, the qualitative facet characterizing globalization amounts to shrinkage of the range of gubernatorial activities that traditionally drove the economic and social dynamics of a nation. A corollary of this change is reflected in the increased vulnerability of a nation to the vagaries of market fluctuations and unpredictable changes in trans-border flows.

A transition to this global system was neither instantaneous nor painless. The global system gradually evolved from the debris of the Second World War that had been precipitated primarily by the hollowness of national and racial hubris of the 1930s. Once the spontaneous disorder of the Second World War had been crushed, the major challenge to social thinkers, economic and political architects in Europe was how to ensure an acceptable standard of living for the masses by avoiding close economic and social contacts between nations. Both these elements were rooted in the catastrophe of the War and, to some extent, also in the hungry thirties. In order to minimize interracial tensions and conflicts between nations, borders between nation states were reinforced and trans-border transactions were drastically reduced. A quick-fire industrialization of the war-ravaged European economies was considered the panacea for their economic malediction created by the War while necessary resources were made available from the United States under the Marshall plan. The endless pain, miseries and sufferings of the hungry thirties were still engraved on the memory of the people; social architects were, therefore, anxious to keep the potential evils of a possible market failure in chain. Consequently, the State was given an exalted status in the economic life of a nation. The political mandate for a strong intervention by governments came from the swelling ranks of unemployed in these economies. This was partly possible because of the weakening of interest groups and private businesses caused by ravages of the War. The fear of another war – driven by xenophobia – also necessitated the visible hand of a strong government to crush irrational and xenophobic emotions. All these changes led to the gradual dismantling of the global economy that was in its infancy by the turn of the 20th century. We call this de-internationalization.

At the conclusion of the Second World War, this process of de-internationalization started as the European nations adopted an inward-looking philosophy of national economic management driven mainly by the tenets of simple Keynesianism. The invisible hand was eclipsed by the visible hand of governments. Government interventions became all pervasive and the philosophy of fine-tuning of an economy was an accepted way of life while the formation of public capital propelled economic growth and future prosperity of these nations within reinforced borders. In this sense, market forces were accorded a secondary role as the public sector became the prime mover of an economy. While these changes took place in Western Europe in the late 1940s, the Soviet model of command economy was strengthening its hold on Eastern Europe. The Soviet model shunned the market mechanism and, instead, relied solely on the visible hand of the State as a servomechanism and also for allocation of national income. As the Cold War between the East and the West intensified, European nations became even more isolated in their pursuits of economic progress. Roughly at the same time, significant changes were afoot in former colonies of European nations: clutches of the European imperialism developed major cracks due to the Second World War and gradually Asian and African colonies attained their complete autonomy to pursue self-determination. Poverty, economic destitution, inequality and stagnation characterized the common fate of these nations. It was widely recognized that these newly emancipated economies were in great need of a social engineering to achieve three critical transitions, namely agrarian, industrial and demographic, in a relatively short span of time in order to escape the tyranny of the vicious cycle of poverty. National governments were accorded mandate in order to achieve these critical transitions. Since markets were in an inchoate stage in these countries, or simply missing, and Western nations were locked in their inward looking strive for economic progress, and cross-border transactions were severely restricted – the developing world adopted an inward looking, import-substituting and state-led growth strategy to initiate the aforementioned transitions. Limited cross-border trade and investment flows were managed through the Bretton Woods system. Thus, the late 1940s witnessed an increasingly splintered world while the *dirigisme* was fast becoming the dominant philosophy of the economics science. The world was truly de-internationalized by the early1950s. The process of de-internationalization continued unabated and possibly intensified as national governments engaged in coordination of economic activities and allocation of resources within national boundaries. The basic calculus of economic progress had a material bias since it was rooted in a commodity-centered notion that typically requires a higher material well-being to result in an improvement in the welfare of people. Material progress was soon equated with the growth of per capita national income that was taken as a proxy for an improvement in national welfare. Efforts were undertaken to outstrip the growth in population by growth in national income in the developing world.

There is no gainsaying the fact that significant economic growth and material progress were recorded both in the developing world and Western European nations during 1950s and 1960s as a direct product of the dirigisme. In the West the average standard of living improved significantly while major transitions were achieved in the developing world. Yet, within two decades from its inception, it seemed that people were getting disillusioned with the era of state-led economic progress despite its enviable track record in terms of economic indicators. There were also clear signs that the Soviet system had been graying prematurely. It started off as a general discomfiture that the dirigisme – though it may cure market failure – is prone to government failure. Unnecessary bureaucracy started bothering people as the standard of living reached its pinnacle in the West and as subjects were gradually turned into citizens in developing nations. As the world strode into the 1970s the dislike for dirigisme reached its peak as the developed world confronted the ravages of stagflation. The dirigisme was seen as a failure and also as a causal factor behind stagflation. The fine-tuning by the visible hand was interpreted as a contributory factor to the instability in the price system while all pervasive bureaucratic interventions were made responsible for choking the incentive mechanism. The dirigisme was, hence, held responsible for engendering stagnation and inflation in the developed world. In the developing world, roughly at the same time, we see the emergence of debt crises that rendered most States financially non-viable and patently unsustainable. The dirigisme, as is argued now, engendered government failure characterized by predatory activities of governments, inefficient and incompetent bureaucracy and strong influence of special interest groups and rent-seekers on bureaucracy. In 1970s it was also recognized that economic growth was seriously hampered by the limited market size caused by the de-internationalization of the globe. The fragmentation of the globe became a serious deterrence to increased specialization and division of labor. It became apparent further improvements of material well-being cannot be achieved without expanding cross-border flows of goods, services and investment. By the 1980s the developing world seemed to have learnt an important lesson from the experience of unprecedented economic successes of East Asian nations to adopt an outward looking and export-oriented strategy to provide a boost to their weakening economies. We thus witnessed a remarkable retreat of the State from the forefront of economic and social engineering in the developing world as market forces were increasingly accorded the major role to drive the material well-being of citizens. We experienced, all through the 1980s, a new wave of deregulation, decontrol and privatization as people increasingly pledged their trust in the efficiency of markets rather than in the efficacy of governments. With the collapse of the Soviet-type economic system, the pace of privatization and deregulation accelerated in the 1990s.

The litany of markets reached an unprecedented crescendo as the American economy consolidated its lead in the world market and also as East Asia and the miracle economies of Asia maintained their economic growth. By early 1990s we have inherited a new global system that gradually evolved from the previous system that was characterized by isolation and dirigisme. In the new system the role of States has been significantly diminished and supplanted by the market mechanism. Trade and investment barriers have been significantly scaled down. There is an increased trust in the efficiency of the market over the efficacy of governments as, it seems, international businesses have had the Midas touch in creating and expanding the network of successful business across the globe and, thereby, creating employment and enhancing economic and social progress. The driving force behind the economic progress in the new era is foreign direct and portfolio investment undertaken by multinationals in search of higher returns for their capital. National tax authorities engage in fiscal competition and tax concessions to attract foreign investment to advance national economic progress. The Asian meltdown in 1997 severely damaged the tempo of this global economy; yet a quick recovery of some of these economies pointed out the importance and resilience of market forces in the achieving economic prosperity for nations. The first year of the new millennium also witnessed a slow-down of the global economy as the US, Australia and some of the economic powerhouses in Europe seem to enter a gloomy recession. This will raise many questions about the robustness of the global economy and also about the tenability and the desirability of market principles. Issues and questions concerning the role of State in national economic prosperity will be re-visited in future years.

The main focus of our exercise in this volume is to understand the inner dynamics of the Asian region, though we have adduced case studies from Europe mainly for the sake of comparison and contrast. This volume is based on four major *themes*:

- First and foremost, we believe that international business is the harbinger of forces of internationalization and globalization and will drive the progress of the global economy in the new millennium. It is generally asserted that international business and multinational firms can bring opulence to the global economy beyond the dream of Croesus.
- Secondly, we harbor the view that globalization is a complex process entailing social, economic and cultural vicissitudes. It is a journey and not a

destination. There are a number of chapters that view globalization as a process of change and thereby provide an important perspective that has been typically missing in the existing literature on globalization. Both theoretical and empirical arguments are developed to understand this complex process in the light of the Asian crisis of 1997.

- Thirdly, we entertain the idea that forces of globalization have seriously emasculated the power of policy making by nation states. It is also widely held that globalization is accompanied by significant changes in microeconomic policies, such as national competition policy. Various chapters offer original insights and look into changing roles of nation states in the sphere of national policy making.

- Finally, we turn to the uneasy idea that globalization has resulted in serious imbalances in the global economy. Original research papers of accomplished economists look into these imbalances and potential problems of the global economy. In what follows we provide a glimpse of the major contribution of each paper from each of these four dominant themes.

The major concern of international business is to find a safe and prosperous haven for its foreign direct and portfolio investment. Returns and risks dominate their decision to invest in a country. The chapter of David Reid and John Walsh explores the implication of such risks. David Reid and John Walsh examine international business development in the context of East Asian and Southeast Asian markets. They question the established doctrine that international firms are able to determine their own policies and organizational structures from a position of sovereignty. The established doctrine simply assumes that international firms can decide what they wish to do and then they go and do it. In reality, experiences from East and Southeast Asia point out the contrary since internationalization of a firm in these regions is required to confront complexity and apparent chaos in the market place. Examples abound with the necessity to collaborate with the State and military officials in Southeast and South Asia. They stress that the main problem for international business is how to work around local complexities and sudden changes in environmental conditions. They also suggest an optimal management strategy for an international business firm in this context.

Tsuyoshi Koizumi makes an attempt to understand the dynamics of international business in Korea by focusing on the multinational investment behavior in the region. Koizumi's objective is to critically examine the hypothesis advanced by Professor Kiyoshi Kojima about the pattern of Japanese direct foreign investment (FDI) and additionally to present a more *general* hypothesis capable of explaining the dynamic pattern in industrial composition and other characteristics of Japan's FDI in South Korea. Recently Japan's FDI has become a significant player in international business. The relative decline in the US's position as an international direct investor was inevitable. It primarily reflects the reinstatement of Continental European countries as leading outward investors and the emergence of Japan as a major global player. In 1988, the four main European investors (the UK, Western Germany, the Netherlands and France) and Japan accounted for

46.9% of the accumulated stock of FDI compared with only 26.3% in 1960. More particularly, between 1980 and 1988, the net increase in the FDI of the UK, West Germany, and Japan rose by $237 billion – nearly twice that of the US of $125 billion.

Bartels and Mirza, in exploring managerial predictors of the Asian crisis from the perspective of multinationals (MNEs), offer three observations. The first is that at the time of formulating the research instrumentation and data acquisition, Asia's economic growth was 'assured'. Hence the presence, at the frequency level of analysis, of 'obstacles' was given insufficient critical attention. Second, the extracted factors point to the contradictory behavior of MNEs. It is apparent that while MNEs indicate their misapprehensions, they were up to and beyond mid-1997 pouring investment capital into the region. This mentality is understandable but does not invalidate the revealed signals to the Asian crisis. Third, it may be arguable that, without a formal predictive model, the extracted factors do not have a rigorous context. They would counter with two arguments. The first refers to the problematic of confirmatory factor analysis and its requirements for correct model specification and the danger of modeling being either specification or data bound. The second refers to the fact that at the time of survey, the economic performance of Asia (even with anecdotal evidence and experiences of obstacles and impediments to FDI) was astonishing. Consequently, priorities of looking for patterns of success, and continued success, far outweighed the search for clues as to why the 'Asian miracle' should not continue.

Lawrence Summers, Clive Hamilton, Chander Kant, Chang Woon Nam, Partha Gangopadhyay and Zelko Livaic; and Leong Liew examine the second theme. Larry Summers argues sound financial systems can contribute enormously to economic development around the world, and the flow of capital across international borders can confer enormous benefits. And yet there is the potential for massive accidents. Some may conclude that the game is not worth the candle and so the flow of capital should systematically be discouraged. Summers thinks the right lesson is the more optimistic one, that with good sense and hard work, and a great deal of creative thought, the Okun gaps can be avoided, and the gains from capital flows can translate into what is most important for any economy: namely, changes in its long-term growth rate. He described here some of the thinking that has guided the international community in responding to the dramatic developments of recent years.

Clive Hamilton raises thorny questions about the Asian crisis and the desirability of getting these Asian economies back to their growth path. Hamilton challenges the commodity-centered approach to human welfare and argues that economic growth beyond a critical point may not contribute to individual well-being. Clive Hamilton poses a seemingly trivial question for a simple-minded economist: is the Asian crisis an undesirable event? The answer to this question is in the affirmative since the crisis ruptured the growth process that caused a loss of incomes and, hence, a loss of 'social welfare'. The obvious answer from simple-minded economists turns on a profound philosophy that in turn pivots on a commodity-centric notion of 'social welfare'. Hamilton argues that the well-being of people cannot be expressed in such narrow materialistic terms since well-being is a 'many-splendoured thing'. The power of this simple argument is that economic growth does not necessarily result in reduction in poverty and increase in well-being. Social, political, cultural conditions and psychological health have a profound influence on a nation's welfare. Growth GDP per capita can therefore convey seriously wrong message about social welfare.

Both Chander Kant and Chang Woon Nam explore in detail the Asian crisis of 1997. Kant argues the immediate cause of the Asian crisis was a severe reversal of commercial bank and other private lending. He recommends that countries should liberalize their financial sectors and capital accounts only at the same pace as they strengthen their institutions and supervision in these areas. Kant propounds that financial and capital account liberalization leads to financial fragility and an increase in the probability of crises. Kant stresses that the affected Asian nations lacked an awareness, or appropriate expertise, necessary for supervision and regulation of their financial sector He notes two important financial events: first, significant progress was made in the liberalization of financial sectors in these countries. Secondly, the Asian crisis was precipitated by severe reversal of commercial bank and other private lending. This reversal proved extremely virulent because of a strong regional linkage among these economies. He also sheds light on the optimal sequencing of liberalization.

Chang Woon Nam examines the major causes of the Asian crisis and argues that the profession is too obsessed with problems of the financial sector. The crux of his argument is that these arguments typically turn on the 'Western' generalization of the origin of the crisis that fails to incorporate nation-specific differences in the crisis. He offers a number of financial and real sector specificities that can help us understand the origin of the Asian crisis. Nam further examines the controversies about Krugman's 1994 hypothesis and its relevance to the Asian crisis. Nam then highlights some Korea-specific weaknesses that made Korea vulnerable to external shocks and analyzes the possibility of an Asian monetary mechanism to prevent crises.

Gangopadhyay and Livaic make a simple observation about the explanation of the Asian crisis: the major thrust of papers explaining the Asian crisis has been couched in terms of poor governance by relevant national governments. The irony is that some of these nations used to enjoy enviably high reputation for their quality of governance till the onset of this crisis. They seek to explain possible transitions in the quality of governance by modeling the long-run dynamics of a stylized economy. From simple formulations they show that the stylized economy is characterized by stable multiple equilibria involving both low and high qualities of governance. The key point is that these equilibria can easily get unstable with a perturbation of resources under the control of a national state. It is further established that limit cycles may therefore characterize the quality of governance and, hence, economic fortunes of a nation.

Leong Liew proposes a novel ideal that the Asian crisis has reinforced the reform program in China. The crisis has had a dampening effect on the immediate economy since exports from China and foreign direct investment to China were adversely affected. Despite that the Chinese economy registered impressive growth records in 1998 (7.8 percent) and 1999 (7 percent). But this is a short-run phenomenon; the long-term effect of the crisis is on the reform process. Involved parties in the reform program were accorded a new insight concerning the appropriate paradigm for economic reform. It has caused the bureaucracy to rethink and reshape their approach to reform and secured vital support for the implementation of radical reform. The main argument is that the Asian crisis has provided an exogenous shock that altered the payoff matrix of the game played out between Chinese political leaders and state and party bureaucrats that will eventuate institutional changes and take reform to a new path. Liew develops a game to explain the evolution of Chinese economic reform and establishes that the moderate reform was an equilibrium outcome that fails to receive the support of bureaucrats. The sustainability of radical reform was not ensured and the Asian crisis altered the payoff structure to engender a new equilibrium that entails radical reform.

A string of chapters have analyzed four major themes in the context of national policy making in various Asian nations:

- Issues concerning deregulation and liberalization and development are analyzed by Alok Ray, Lilai Xu and J. C. Liu.
- New roles of fiscal policy is examined by Jocelyn Horne.
- Binh Tran Nam looks at the central issues of trade liberalization.
- Issues concerning development of human capital are examined by Koichi Mera.

Alok Ray studies the liberalization of the Indian economy that is a major player in the global economy. In the liberalization package, issues of timing, phasing, sequencing and exact mechanics have assumed critical importance. What is the lesson that we have learned from India's bit to globalize its mammoth economy? Ray outlines the conditions for successful liberalization that may convey important message for others. A series of important issues are also examined concerning the external sector liberalization.

Lilai Xu and J. C. Liu argue that the concept and strategy of economic development typically applied to the recent Chinese experience might have been erroneous. Since its adoption of economic reform and 'open-door' policy, China has achieved a high economic growth rate acknowledged by the whole world. However, such an achievement has been accompanied with a very high social cost. Facing the 21st century, China must forsake the lopsided approach of 'productivity alone' which pursues solely economic growth rate, and replace it with a comprehensive development model centering on 'people/human being'. Such a strategic shift will enable China, while maintaining a reasonable growth rate, to alleviate rather than aggravating poverty, unemployment and injustice in the society, to guarantee rather than hindering education for its nationals and equality between genders, to protect rather than destroying ecological balance and environment for human living, and to promote rather than restricting freedom of speech and political democracy.

Jocelyn Horne argues that fiscal policy was viewed as playing a benign role in stimulating economic growth prior to the Asian crisis. Increasing attention is being paid to fiscal policy in providing a stimulus to the growth process in East Asia. Horne studies the lessons for growth-promoting fiscal policy for East Asia. It is argued that intertemporal effects of fiscal policy must be taken into consideration. It is also argued that growth-promoting fiscal policy must center on the composition of the fiscal package rather than the budget thrust. Yet she admits the quantitative contribution of fiscal policy is relatively small in comparison with the effect of capital accumulation and productivity.

Binh Tran-Nam tries to understand the relationship between globalization and economic growth in Vietnam. Vietnam is a low income, agrarian, transitional economy with strongly entrenched socialist principles. Like China Vietnam has adopted an incremental and piecemeal approach to economic reform since 1986. It has achieved significant economic progress though the growth slowed down in 1998 and 1999. The year 2000 witnessed improvement in its growth, but it is unlikely that it will return to the old growth path. The Asian crisis has dampened its growth and so had the inability to implement reforms. However, Vietnam is a classic case as we expect Vietnam to get more and more integrated with the global economy. Nam examines the impact of this important process of internationalization of the Vietnamese economy on Vietnam's performance. He also sheds crucial lights on optimal economic strategies of Vietnam in extracting the maximum benefit from this process.

Koichi Mera argues that many developing countries are moving from a centralized system of governance to a decentralized one – with the onslaught of globalization. The need for capacity building in developing countries has long been seriously advocated. International organizations such as the United Nations, the World Bank, and the Asian Development Bank have been working on this issue. Many young people from developing countries are being trained in universities in advanced countries under the auspices of their own national governments, donors, and other international organizations. Many have gone back to their own country and, if they joined the public sector, are working for the central government rather than local governments. Behind successful national economic management of some developing countries, one can find highly trained bureaucrats, in some cases, they are called the Berkeley mafia or the Cornell mafia, depending on the university where many of these bureaucrats were trained. Capacity building of a select few might have been completed successfully for many countries. However, the developing countries are now demanding much more capacity building as they decentralize. Mera offers an insightful story of the Indonesian experience with capacity building and decentralization that will form the core of future strategy in spreading the fruits of economic development in South and Southeast Asia in the future.

The global economy has several areas of serious concerns: the slowdown of the Japanese economy is believed to affect the performance of the global economy. As a consequence it is important to raise a thorny question of whether the process of globalization has reached its limit. Economics globalization in the Asian region has also serious lessons to learn from Europe where the process started centuries ago. It is widely recognized that both economic growth and living standards of millions in Asia rely heavily on the small-scale sector. Despite an increased integration of the Asian economies, one notes a strong performance by small businesses in the region. It is therefore important to learn the dynamics of small businesses in the region. Globalization and consequent weakening of the public sector has caused serious problems for merit goods such as education and health services. These important issues are addressed in the following six chapters.

Bill Lucarelli and Joseph Halevi look at the causal factors for economic stagnation and recession in Japan. Is it merely the natural consequence of financial retrenchment after the collapse of the bubble economy in the late 1980s, or does this present slump signify a more profound historical phase of industrial maturity and decline? They provide several possible answers in terms of a Kaldorian theory of export-led growth. They also highlight the structural and strategic role of the state in the process of capital accumulation. A detailed analysis of the onset of crisis and stagnation in Japan is provided.

Menshikov raises important questions: has globalization reached its limit? How much scope is there for further economic integration? Are national economies bound to disappear giving way to one integrated economy? His answers follow: we should not expect foreign trade dependency to rise very much in the coming decades. However, capital movements initiate further economic interdependence. One can hardly expect globalization to lead to the demise of national economies.

A. Nekipelov argues that any transition in Russia will inevitably evoke serious problems regarding short-term shocks. Mitigation of these shocks has been typically accorded primacy. That is why the best method to adjust Russian economy to the requirements of the market consists, in his opinion, in combining the tools of (passive) industrial, and social policies. It is important to realize that the process of transition creates distortions within the economic system. Successful reforms must adequately address these distortions. Errors made by Russian reformers in the transformation of property rights resulted in the emergence of an extremely distorted system of corporate governance in a majority of big and middle-sized enterprises. The main issue here is to undertake measures, which would place the management of enterprises under a control of owners of capital and would thus reorient joint-stock companies towards profit maximization in the short-run and net-worth maximization of the firm in the long-run. An eradication of anti-market instruments of control – frequently used by Russian authorities at all levels – is of extreme importance for normalizing economic activity. To a significant degree an achievement of this goal is enmeshed with a consolidation of the rule of laws in the Russian society.

Jonathan Batten and Samanathala Hettihewa provide a detailed analysis of small businesses in Sri Lanka where these firms have performed remarkably well and played an important role in raising the standard of millions. The precise objective of this study is to investigate and explain, using the principal-agent framework, cross-sectional variation in the managers of small firms in Sri Lanka, by determining the relationship between key firm-specific variables and the characteristics of small firm managers. A countrywide, random survey is used as the basis for identifying cross-sectional variation due to differences in industry, size, ownership, and the relationship of the manager of the firm to the owners of the firm. The characteristics of firm managers include the age, education, management experience and employment background of the managers.

Amit S. Ray and Saradindu Bhaduri consider the political economy of rural health care in India. They argue public investment in health in India has been small compared with the demand for health care. The rural sector has suffered particularly. The proportion of private expenditure on health is alarmingly high in developing countries. Globalization has been accompanied with a retreat of the state in most developing nations leading to a reduction of public expenditure in merit goods such as education and health. But this is the reality in developing countries and backwardness in health and education can significantly affect the process of integration of developing nations with the global economy. It is sometimes viewed that the withdrawal of public money from health and education will be compensated by an increase in private funds. This is at best a moot point. Ray and Bhaduri develop a theoretical model to address this issue and also marshal evidence from India to shed light on the tenability of their theoretical model. They also provide crucial policy implications.

Chapter 1

The Role of Complexity Theory in International Business Strategy Development: Evidence from East and Southeast Asia

David McHardy Reid and John Walsh

Introduction

Much of the literature on international business development is written from the position that firms are able to determine their policies and organization from a position of sovereignty: they might decide what they wish to do and then go and do it. Although interaction with the environment might have an impact upon their activities, this possibility is often underplayed. However, we have witnessed, especially in the light of the recent Asian economic melt-down is that chaos and complexity can rapidly be introduced into the system or world of any corporate player. This necessitates that new paradigms and structures should emerge from the chaos and, in some cases, crystallize. Catastrophe and chaos theories are sometimes confused. Chaos theory tells us that simple laws can have complicated, even unpredictable consequences, whereas simple causes can produce complex effects. Complexity theory tells us the opposite: that complex causes can bring about simple effects (Cohen and Stewart 1994, p.2). This raises some key questions. For example, can the study of the East and Southeast Asian business environments both before and after the crisis be further illuminated by considering them against a framework that embodies some principles derived from chaos and complexity theory?

Method

The fieldwork carried out in Asia, including Japan, South Korea, Thailand, Indonesia and Malaysia, involved over 300 personal interviews with senior executives of successful multinational enterprises (MNEs) and other foreign affiliated companies (FACs). These firms were primarily consumer-products oriented mainly recognized household brand names. The research, using Grounded Theory (GT), studied a representative sample of enterprises in each market. These companies had successfully developed market positions in their respective markets. GT is inductively derived from the study it represents; that is it is discovered, developed and provisionally verified through systematic data collection and analysis pertaining to a phenomenon. Thus, data collection, analysis and theory stand in reciprocal relationship with each other. One does not begin with a theory, then prove it; rather one begins with an area of study and allows what is relevant to that area to emerge (Strauss and Corbin 1990, p.24). So far, the GT approach is underutilized in the management literature. For example, a search of ABI databases over the last decade uncovered a mere 34 articles dealing with or employing the approach. Nevertheless, the GT methodology has been employed in organizational research by some notable authors (Martin and Turner, 1986; Segev, 1988; Sarros, 1992; Simon, 1993; Linstead, 1997). Adler, Campbell and Laurent (1989) concluded that their Western-biased approach to research in China might have yielded more fruit had they adopted a GT methodology. Using snowball sampling, samples for the study were generated. This involved gathering a sample through chain referral (Burt and Ronchi, 1994). First using the principle of open sampling to uncover as many potentially relevant categories as possible (Strauss and Corbin, 1990, p.181), the process of selection began with a list of foreign consumer goods companies, industrial companies and financial services providers that had established a presence in each market. The list was developed with the help of major consulting firms like McKinsey and the Boston Consulting Group; major advertising agencies with offices in Tokyo, such as BBDO and McCann Erickson, were also asked to name the most successful foreign players. Major multinational enterprises with long-established positions in Asia, for example Unilever and Johnson & Johnson (J&J), were also consulted. The identified companies were then contacted by telephone and letter, invited to participate in the study and, over the course of a decade some 300 interviews were conducted. They have been supplemented by an extensive consultation of secondary sources and other contextual material.

The individual interviews, on average lasting around two hours, were conducted across a range of executive groups: CEOs (70 percent), vice-presidents (25 percent) and other senior representatives (5 percent). At the end of each interview, respondents were asked to suggest other organizations that, to their knowledge, had developed a presence in the respective markets. As the interviewing program proceeded, it became clear from the extent of duplication of the suggestions received, which of the foreign players were viewed major success stories.

Data was collected in Japan in two phases: initially, during the latter part of 1990, with follow-up by telephone and fax continuing through 1991-1992. A second phase of 24 interviews was conducted in 1995 to examine longitudinal issues. These second-phase interviewees were selected according to the principles of theoretical sampling, 'sampling on the basis of concepts that have relevance to the evolving theory' (Strauss and Corbin 1990, p.176). A telephone follow-up was made in 1996 to keep the research up-to-date. During this second (1995-1996) phase, some of the original companies (1990 fieldwork) were re-interviewed, and some technologically intensive companies were added. In some instances, the same individuals were still occupying the same positions, whereas in others, their replacements were interviewed. The emerging constructs were found to be stable from 1995 to 1996. The Thai data was collected in 1994 and 1998. The South Korean data was collected in 1997 and 1998. The Indonesian and Malaysian data was collected in 1998. The fieldwork followed a list of topics and themes derived from Figure 1.1 but was not confined to them so that 'grounded theory wisdom' (Bailey 1987; Glaser and Strauss 1967) could surface. The study was not limited by *a priori* hypotheses; rather the data was allowed to emerge according to the perceived importance of the interviewees.

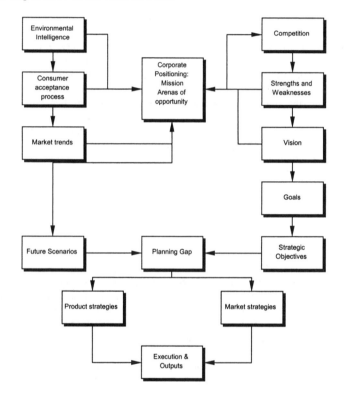

Figure 1.1 The Collection of Topics and Themes

The list of topics was committed to memory and each individual was asked the same questions in an identical fashion. However, the sequence was allowed to vary in order to facilitate what was constructed to be a conversational interaction. The interviewees were probed on the difficulties involved in developing their market positions in contrast to other markets. Although respondents were allowed to range broadly, coverage of key topics was ensured. All interviews were taped; in some cases company documents were provided for subsequent analysis. Some interviewees consented to being quoted, others did not. The tape recordings were transcribed and, in so doing, the contents of the interviews were reviewed several times. In this way, not only were the authors' memories refreshed but also an in-depth contextual understanding of the issues was achieved. The data was then analyzed qualitatively with NUD*IST (Non Numerical Data Indexing Search and Theorizing).

The Nomenclature of Chaos and Complexity

Fractals
In 1963, Mandelbrot introduced the concept of the 'fractal,' a geometric form with fine structures on all levels of magnification (Mandelbrot, 1977; Mandelbrot, 1982). The attraction of this concept is that it facilitates unification of hitherto unrelated occurrences. Mandelbrot (1997) broadened his interest to encompass the field of finance.

Attractors
Are there hidden forces that influence the development of broad response patterns? According to chaos theory there is a construct known as attractors. Cohen and Stewart (1994, p.204) depict attractors as a region of phased space that attracts all nearby points as time passes and a repeller as an unstable steady state. In other words, attractors have certain properties that draw other phenomena or behaviors towards them.

Edge of chaos
Eisenhardt and Brown (1998) maintain that while chaos theory helps businesses understand how markets change, they must look to 'complexity theory' to manage effectively in a tumultuous environment. 'Complexity theory says if a company is too tightly structured, it can't move; and if it's too chaotic, it can't move,' They aver: 'There is a point called the 'edge of chaos' where companies can move.' At that point, a company has enough structure to hold people and processes together, yet enough flexibility to allow innovation and adaptation. However, the mechanisms by which this state of dynamism may be maintained are not made fully clear.

Complex adaptive systems (CASs)
At the edge of chaos, the military, according to Conner (1998), best exemplifies this model of nimbleness. Military colleges teach principles instead of rules. However, in times of combat, what determines success is an application of those principles which recognize what is occurring in a chaotic environment. It is a balance between the adherence to policy to remain consistent and modifying it to keep it from becoming overly rigid. A classic example of a CAS is the flocking behavior of geese. They appear to follow a few simple rules, such as 'don't bump into each other, 'match up with the speed of other geese flying nearby,' 'replace the lead goose when it gets tired' and 'always stick with the group.' The group relies on constant feedback and adaptation to achieve its goal of remaining resilient in the face of changing circumstances. Stacey (1995) enhanced this concept and proposed a framework based on complexity: the study of nonlinear and network feedback systems incorporating theories of chaos, artificial life, self-organization and emergent order. Positive and negative feedback characterize system dynamics as systems co-evolve far from equilibrium, in a self-organizing manner, toward unpredictable long-term outcomes.

The Framework

In the pursuit of theory, it is important to note that when scientists select theories, they do not merely use the criterion of agreement or disagreement with observations, they also have aesthetic principles in mind. These principles help to remove the cloud of trivially competing theories that necessarily surround any theory. Moreover, they want the theory to be universal, not particular to some place or time. The overarching theme in the literature is that through a process of reductionism, complexity on one level is reduced to simplicity on another level. Complexity concerns the amount of information that it is necessary to describe.

Cohen and Stewart (1994, pp.220-225) maintain that scientists have been asking the wrong question, they have focused upon complexity as that which requires explanation. The result has been uninspiring as the interaction between several simple phenomena can indeed produce complexity. The question they failed to consider is what is the source of simplicity? Although chaos theory was discovered decades ago, only in recent years has it emerged as a model for explaining the chaotic business environment. The chaos model introduces the idea that chance, changing conditions and creativity can enter a complex system at any point and alter its course (Wah 1998). Although chaos theory helps businesses to understand how markets change, Eisenhardt and Brown (1998) maintain that they must look to 'complexity theory' to manage effectively in a tumultuous environment. Today, most people try to explain a messy, opportunistic global competitive game using mental models that focus on order, stability, cohesion, consistency, and equilibrium. Stacey (1992, p.21) maintains 'We are not paying enough attention to the irregular, disorderly, chance nature of the game. We do this because it is easier and more comfortable than feeling about the desk for explanations that describe the world in terms of disorder, irregularity, unpredictability, and chance.'

This slant is not too dissimilar to the approach taken by Mintzberg (1972) who argued that one must look at the actual emerging pattern of the enterprise's goals, policies and major programs to see its true strategy. In other words, one would find it difficult to find an *a priori* statement of strategy that the passage of time shows is actually followed. Mintzberg (1990) called into question some of the most fundamental beliefs of strategic management by questioning what he refers to as the *design school*—the approach which advocates a simple model that views the process as one of design to achieve an essential fit between external threats and opportunities and internal distinctive competence. He systematically attempts to demolish the essential premises upon which this mode of thinking was built.

In particular he focuses on one central theme, the idea that thought exists independently of action. Strategy formulation, he argues, is a process of conception rather than one of learning. Eisenhardt and Brown (1998) inform us that 'Complexity theory says if a company is too tightly structured, it can't move; and if it's too chaotic, it can't move. There is a point called the "edge of chaos" where companies can move.' At this point, a company has enough structure to hold people and processes together, yet enough flexibility to allow innovation and adaptation. In the temporal nature of the Asian business environment we will see how many companies have experienced the edge of chaos. In their book *Competing on the Edge*, Eisenhardt and Brown (1998) develop a framework that they argue qualifies a company to compete on the edge. This framework has been adapted here to interrogate our data. It comprises:

- Rule 1:   Advantage is temporary
- Rule 2:   Strategy is diverse, emergent and complicated
- Rule 3:   Reinvention is the goal
- Rule 4:   Live in the present
- Rule 5:   Stretch out the past
- Rule 6:   Reach into the future
- Rule 7:   Time pace change
- Rule 8:   Grow the strategy
- Rule 9:   Drive strategy from the business level
- Rule 10:   Repatch businesses to markets and articulate the whole.

Findings

We will now harness the framework established above to examine the business environment in Asia Pacific and the responses of foreign players to these developments.

Rule 1: Advantage is Temporary

Executives at several of the interviewed firms, across most markets studied, highlighted the transient nature of competitive advantage. This was true in Japan where firms were subject to astonishingly rapid paces of product and technological innovation and in Korea where Joint Venture partners have typically replicated the manufacturing facility of the JV companies only to set up in competition. This is also the case in China where counterfeiting is a serious problem and proves to be a major management distraction. Moreover the re-invention of many local PRC-based companies, which are harnessing the infrastructure that has followed the international foreign direct invested enterprises is proving to be a serious competitive obstacle. The advantage of being foreign may provide a rationale to enter these markets but it is certainly no long-term formula for success. The continuance of brand strategies that build and support a long-term relevant position in these markets is an effective long-term success formula.

Rule 2: Strategy is Diverse, Emergent and Complicated

Successful strategies in these times of change appear to be those that emerge as relevant in those markets whether they are radically different from those that have reaped success elsewhere or have been quietly adapted. Amway, for example, has been hugely successful in Japan, Hong Kong and China as well as Thailand. A raw American concept resonates with Japanese and Thais alike in this sector. Where there are independently minded people keen for success who are also prepared to believe in the advantage of the products, and willing to use the leverage of their social networks there are opportunities for Amway and other network marketing companies to follow this model.

In many Asian markets radical paradigms are required. For example, in Indonesia managers of foreign companies observe the business scenario to be very complex: As one consumer products CEO put it:

> Just take a look at the politics here. You only have to look at East Java. Don't take anything at face value. Ask simple and naïve questions. If you take it too seriously you are dead.

Contrary to popular opinion, there is a great deal of foreign money ready to be invested in Indonesia. For many it is a question of timing and price. Timing is connected with elections, price meaning a fair offer on the table. But they would all be wise, if they are not already based in Indonesia, before doing so, to consider placing a full-time executive from head office. We are not advocating a recruited person but someone from out of the corporate womb, someone who is totally imbued with the corporate culture and control mechanism so as to be able to assess events accurately and react accordingly. Indonesia, like other current Asian opportunities is a high-risk market. A CEO of an international bank expressed it this way:

> To come into it based on a classic investment analysis you will fail or at best you will lose a lot of money. It never works. Unless you know the ground rules, unless you where this market has a propensity to trip you up you do bear significant risk. There is a lot of smoke, a lot of mirrors, a lot of one-way glass. There is a lot of disinformation and a lot of rumor and I think it has been said that Javanese love a Machiavellian plot.

Rule 3: Reinvention is the Goal

Those that successfully compete on the edge, Eisenhardt and Brown (1998) maintain, strive to find new ways of creating value. The impact of the crisis in Indonesia varies according to geography. Java and Jakarta, for example, have been affected more than some of the outlying islands. This is highlighted by the decline of consumption of many consumer product categories. As of November 1998: sweetened condensed milk declined 60 percent, instant noodles by 11 percent and cigarettes by 21 percent. Research conducted in Indonesia during March 1998 by AC Nielsen asked consumer housewives for information on specific items they were still using post and prior to the Crisis, consuming less, or stopped entirely. Vegetables remain 92 percent unchanged, fresh meat, fish meat and chicken remain at 30 percent unchanged, sweetened condensed milk shows an unchanged value of only 16 percent of consumers. Many people have apparently dropped out of consumption altogether, they no longer seem to belong to the formal sectors of the economy. A similar situation exists in Thailand's labor market in which, in many cases, it was found that when a major breadwinner lost employment, many other members of the family will take up various informal tasks to contribute some money. Hence, total employment increases while income decreases. Against this backdrop, how can manufacturers of consumer products add value? Prices increased extensively: household products showed a 143 percent increase in value despite the decline in consumption. This was the quintessential response by foreign manufacturers. Given that many consumers no longer constituted a viable target market MNEs re-priced their products at more viable levels, recognizing that the basis to their market segmentation had changed. They targeted those remaining consumers who could still afford to buy.

Rule 4: Live in the Present

Eisenhardt and Brown (1998) aver the present to be the most important time frame. In some circumstances this was found to be true. For example, investors were sometimes pleased that they had made investments in a rising market knowing they would not have done so if prescient about the upcoming crash. According to a restaurateur in Bangkok:

> We have invested a lot of money on this and done very well. With hindsight we should not have changed anything. We were very glad that we did not know that the country was going to do down, because I am sure it would have deterred our decision.

In Indonesia, where the short-term interest rates reached a stable level of 60 percent many retail and other distribution businesses ceased to operate, their proprietors seeing the wisdom of investing their funds rather than trading. This required appropriate responses from those players dependent upon rapidly disappearing distribution channels. Adidas, for example, imports most of its products and raw materials so it was forced to increase its prices 4 to 5 times in line with the devaluation of the rupiah. Fortunately it had set up a chain of 25 flagship stores to compensate for the lack of quality retailers. Without these stores it would have gone out of business due to the migration from the retailing business precipitated by high interest rates.

By way of an additional example, British American Tobacco, based on its previous experience in South America, has learned the importance of managing cash in such times of high inflation and currency devaluation. Its emphasis is not merely on managing its own cash but offers extended help to its wholesalers and distributors to coach them in better cash management practice. It has speedily introduced replacement-costing principles. The President remarked:

> I am not sure that everybody has understood the importance of replacement costing and they are still costing on an historical basis so they have bought in product at 2000 rupiah to the dollar and to replace it is going to cost you 15000 rupiah. So where are you going to get the money to replace it.

Rule 5: Stretch out the Past

Eisenhardt and Brown (1998) argue, when chasing new business opportunities, that best practice managers realize that the past is often their competitive advantage. Wise use of the past diminishes risk and frees resources to focus on new ideas. This is clearly a property that MNEs operating in Asia exhibit. One of their clear advantages is that they accrue experience from market to market and accumulate wisdom in the center of the organization for use as necessary. Just as BAT was able to roll its experience, of managing in times of inflation, into the Indonesian arena many other companies cited similar examples. Unilever has deep pockets and sees opportunities to increase its market share by taking advantage of the demise of local competitors. Meanwhile it must handle the chaos introduced into the system as its Malaysian operations complain about dumping into Malaysia by the Indonesian company. Nestlé introduced a packaging format for its powdered milk product in Indonesia. Previously it used cartons that were only partially filled with the product; much of the volume was space. Its justification was that it presented with impact at the point of sales. Nestlé abandoned that kind of thinking and introduced a very cheap pack which looks inferior on the shelf but it cuts the packaging material element significantly. In this way it can pack more products on the shelves. Its advertising makes the point that the consumer gets the same amount of powder as before. It is called an Econopak, in this way it reflects the concerns of the moment. When the crisis hit, MNEs knew how to respond. There was a marked similarity between them in this regard. Typically cost committees were formed. All activities were scrutinized and those not adding value were discontinued. All items that incurred foreign currency expenditures were either eliminated or postponed indefinitely. During this sort of exercise one major MNE found that its rent, which was dollar denominated, exceeded its total salary cost. Distributors terms were reduced, cash was to be collected faster; profitability being quite sensitive to fast collection, with interest rates at 60 percent.

For other companies such as Boots and Tesco, the Asian Crisis was a signal of an opportunity to invest. With the advantageous relationship of the pound sterling to the Thai baht these companies entered the Thai market. The former is developing a chain of stores and had established 14 at the end of 1998 whereas Tesco took the opportunity to purchase the Lotus chain of supermarkets from CP. Where past experience was demonstrably diminishing risk was on the matter of security. Many companies were armed with crisis procedures in the event of social unrest, satellite phone back up, emergency back up offices and computer systems, even contracts with the military for protection and emergency evacuation to the nearest airport.

Rule 6: Reach into the Future

Those who compete on the edge, Eisenhardt and Brown (1998) aver, reach further into the future. Should the present be handled badly, however, there can be no future. Whatever future eventuates will be one that is forged with fewer expatriates. One thorny issue that had to be grasped by every foreign company was their cost. Often paid in dollars expatriate costs soared in relation to local employees. Companies had to adjust to that very rapidly and many repatriated their foreign employees or moved their remuneration from dollars to the local currency, set at an agreed rate. This, in turn, accelerated the drift away because many expatriates left since they were effectively being paid less. This is particularly true of Shanghai, where a number of leading MNEs, realizing at last that the market they had predicted was not currently available, have had rapidly to downscale the number of expatriate employees maintained in country. Amid the turmoil and the chaos many executives reported that consumers were switching away from their brands to cheaper and, sometimes, traditional alternatives. Colgate Palmolive in Malaysia, for example, highlighted how some consumers had resumed the use of tree bark instead of toothpaste. In the main, however, these companies were confident that their business would pick up with economic recovery because of the brand franchises they had established. As far as the companies, competing in markets hit by the Asian chaos and turmoil were concerned, their interest with the future is focused on surviving the present, by which they mean a two year time horizon, and in some cases searching for opportunistic acquisitions.

Rule 7: Time Pace Change

Those who compete on the edge impose a rhythm and tempo to initiatives such as new product launches or services launched. Like a tennis player making an approach shot, these managers manage the transitions that rhythm allows. Companies that were planning to survive gallantly in these markets were still intending to launch new products despite the recession. Pharmaceuticals and other companies interviewed, for example, were maintaining their training and education investment, funding local medical practitioners to attend international conferences, and such like. As the President of one such company in Thailand indicated:

> We are still considering launching new products here even in this recession. This market moves along so quickly that if you don't get on the boat at the beginning you will miss it altogether. You have to look at these situations and say times are tough we are short of resources but maybe that this is the time to invest.

Similarly another pharmaceuticals MNE CEO in Indonesia put:

> Even though we face difficulties like today we maintain training and developing programs.

Not all companies kept these activities running, but those that are competently competing on the edge are selective about what they do and remain opportunistic. A consumer products MNE president:

> We cut down dramatically on overseas training. These things I did not want to do but there was no choice. We have frozen recruiting. But at the same time if there is something you have to do you do it. Where cash is King you have to make sure that you have a good finance and a good marketing team to keep things going.

And this type of strategy appears to pay dividends. The same company president remarked:

> We said we would not lay off people we would keep them in the organization, keep training them, in case the volume comes through. The alternative argument was to

lay off people. The disruption of doing that would be enormous. Now the volume has come back to us. We are now gaining market share.

Other examples of time paced change are the constant review of marketing mix variables. Often this has constituted packaging format and size changes. When the product becomes expensive because of its sudden relative unaffordability the obvious option is to reduce the cost and price. Executives at several of the interviewed firms provided examples of how package sizes had been reduced or other changes in format had been initiated, for example detergents in polyethylene bags, in order to retain their product in the consumers' consumption repertoire. Some manufacturers have gone as far as introducing secondary low-cost brands. In many cases it is the more expensive premium products that are being re-positioned to meet lower priced competition. Canned drink sales collapsed. Coca-Cola responded by introducing seven ounce reusable bottles. As the Country Manager for McKinsey indicated, there are those that can work on the edge and those that cannot:

> The way I think of foreign companies, I see two groups. Those that have been doing it for a long time, very global, but thoughtful companies, they think long-term, companies like P&G. They build their positions through blood, sweat and tears. Then there are those who fly in and fly out again. They come and go and don't have the sense of rhythm for these countries. They reduce costs, sack people, say I can't make it work and close down. Their strategy is deficient. What has happened in Indonesia is bad for everyone but the situations which companies find themselves in are quite singular.

Other examples stem from those kinds of companies that are committed to a particular ethos. Janssen, for example, is committed to the credo of its parent company, Johnson and Johnson. As part of its commitment to its operating environment and its community it maintains benevolent support programs such as its de-worming initiative. Apparently 80 percent of the Indonesian population is affected by this parasitic invasion so it is an initiative that fits well with its mission while demonstrating an ongoing commitment no matter how negative the operating environment may appear to be.

Rule 8: Grow the Strategy

Eisenhardt and Brown (1998) maintain that those who compete on the edge grow their businesses like fields, rather than assembling them. They do not build the pieces at once and to rejuvenate them they begin by pruning back. This metaphor can best be related to the obsession that some people have with holding onto land. They don't necessarily tend and care for it beyond preservation. That is true for many companies that are operating in these troubled markets: they are holding onto their positions as best they can by cutting costs and by the application often of band aid policies. Simply holding on in the overseas market and hoping for better times in the future is a negative approach to strategy. Effectively, it represents a surrender of power to external forces and this must, surely, lead to greater instance of failure.

Rule 9: Drive Strategy from the Business Level

Effective managers control both parts of strategy: the what and the how. Strategy cannot be too top down, speed is a prerequisite. This assertion by Eisenhardt and Brown (1998) appears to hold. Even in the case of the big name MNEs the country management has much control over both parts of strategy. After all that is what they are paid for and is why they are there. MNEs are generally wise enough to know that everything cannot be driven by head office, whether that is in Cincinnati, London or Paris. For example, interviewees revealed that their views were sought and they were regarded as the founts of wisdom on matters relating to the crisis and the responses to it. Several companies had been given carte blanche to expand during the recession in the light of the knowledge that expansion now will be undoubtedly cheaper than later. Many of the foreign executives possessed an advantage denied to their local competitors, that is, many of them, whether American or European, had weathered several recessions before. Few Asian managers had this opportunity.

Rule 10: Repatch Businesses to Markets and Articulate the Whole

In a slowly changing world, opportunities can be permanently mapped by businesses once and for all. In a more chaotic situation things change continuously. This presents an ongoing challenge to re-define the nature of the concern. While many companies were attempting to hold onto their original business portfolios albeit taking cost cutting measures to weather the economic storm, in some cases it was admitted that the strategy was simply to maintain position, hold market share in the hope that competitors would drop out of the fray. Executives at several of the interviewed firms provided examples of how they were attempting to redefine their business portfolios in the way of lower priced brands, smaller package sizes. As consumers continue to trade down, this has often required new sourcing arrangements to be established, outsourcing and re-engineering of organizations are common responses. Interviewees often revealed concern that cost cutting measure had gone too far and that it had become a preoccupation to the detriment of opportunity identification. There were also complaints that they were failing to act quickly enough to adjust portfolios to map onto the new situation. This was true for companies in Indonesia and Malaysia, as well as Thailand. Some executives reported that the experience of the chaos and discontinuities, they had experienced, had enriched them as managers. A country manager of a major American company:

> Quality managers and quality thinkers really keep their cool during these kinds of situation. In this sort of climate, the good companies become totally obvious. I have

learnt a lot more and I have a lot more respect for people that have worked through these changes in the environment. It is easy for anyone to live through a rising tide.

Conclusion

GT derived data on the responses of foreign players to the turmoil in Asia was analyzed according to the precepts of Eisenhardt and Brown's (1998) framework. Some success was reaped in finding support for it. Having said this, their framework appears very general and in the light of the concepts of complexity theory (CT) such as fractals, complex adaptive systems, which go hand in hand with it, the framework is disappointing. This does not mean that complexity theory and its application to this type of scenario is disappointing. Rather, it means that our search continues for a framework that is more closely embedded with CT and offers the potential for greater discrimination to examine the behavior of companies competing on the edge of chaos.

References

Adler, Nancy J., Nigel Campbell and Andre Laurent. (1989), 'In Search of Appropriate Methodology: From Outside the People's Republic of China Looking', in *Journal of International Business Studies*, vol. 20(1), pp.61-74.
Bailey, Kenneth D. (1987), *Methods of Social Research*, 3rd Edition, The Free Press, New York. Burt, R. S and D. Ronchi. (1994). 'Measuring a Large Network Quickly', *Social Networks*, vol. 16(1), pp.91-135.
Cohen, Jack and Ian Stewart. (1994), *The Collapse of Chaos*, Penguin, New York.
Conner, Daryl. (1998), *Leading at the Edge of Chaos*, Wiley, London.
Eisenhardt, Kathleen and Shona Brown. (1998), *Competing on the Edge: Strategy as Structured Chaos*, Harvard Business School Press, Boston.
Glaser, Barney G. and Anselm L. Strauss. (1967), *The Discovery of Grounded Theory: Strategies for Qualitative Research*, Aldine, Chicago.
Linstead, Stephen. (1997), 'The social Anthropology of Management', *British Journal of Management*, vol. 8(1), pp.85-98.
Mandelbrot, Benoit B. (1977), *Fractals: Form, Chance and Dimension*, W. H. Freeman, San Francisco.
Mandelbrot, Benoit B. (1982), *The Fractal Geometry of Nature*, W. H. Freeman, San Francisco.
Mandelbrot, Benoit B. (1997), *Fractals and Scaling in Finance: Discontinuity, Concentration, Risk, Selecta volume E*, Springer, New York.
Martin, Patricia Yancey and Barry A. Turner. (1986), 'Grounded Theory and Organizational Research', *Journal of Applied Behavioral Science*, vol. 22(2), pp.141-157.
Mintzberg, Henry. (1972), 'Research on Strategy-making', *Academy of Management Proceeding: Thirty Second Annual Meeting*, August 13-16, pp.90-94.
Mintzberg, Henry. (1990), 'The Design School: Reconsidering the Basic Premises of Strategic Management', *Strategic Management Journal*, vol. 11, pp.171-195.
Sarros, James C. (1992), 'What Leaders Say They Do: An Australian Example', *Leadership and Organization Development Journal*, vol. 13(5), pp.21-27.

Segev, Eli. (1988). 'A Framework for a Grounded Theory of Corporate Policy', *Interfaces*, vol. 18(5), pp.42-54.

Simon, Herbert A. (1993), 'Altruism and Economics', *American Economic Review*, vol. 83(2), pp.156-161.

Stacey, Ralph D. (1992), *Managing the Unknowable: Strategic Boundaries between Order and Chaos in Organizations*, Jossey Bass, San Francisco.

Stacey, Ralph D. (1995), 'The Science of Complexity: An alternative Perspective for Strategic Change Processes', *Strategic Management Journal*, vol. 16(6), pp.477-495.

Strauss, Anselm L. and Juliet Corbin. (1990), *Basics of Qualitative Research*, Sage Publications, Newbury Park, California.

Wah, Louisa. (1998), 'Welcome to the Edge', *Management Review*, vol. 87(10), pp.24-29.

Chapter 2

Dynamic Changes of Japan's FDI in South Korea From 1985 to 1997

Tsuyoshi Koizumi

Introduction

The objective of the study is to critically examine the hypothesis advanced by Professor Kiyoshi Kojima about the pattern of Japanese foreign direct investment (FDI) and additionally to present a more general hypothesis capable of explaining the dynamic pattern in industrial composition and other characteristics of Japan's FDI in South Korea. Recently, Japan's FDI has become a significant player in international business. The relative decline in the US's position as an international direct investor was inevitable. It primarily reflects the reinstatement of Continental European countries as leading outward investors and the emergence of Japan as a major global player. In 1988, the four main European investors (the UK, Western Germany, the Netherlands and France) and Japan accounted for 46.9 percent of the accumulated stock of FDI compared with only 26.3 percent in 1960. More particularly, between 1980 and 1988, the net increase in the four capital stake of the UK, West Germany, and Japan rose by $237 billion – nearly twice that of the US of $125 billion (Dunning 1993).

Though the Continental European countries and Japan have become major outward investors in international business, recently most FDI theories are still based on US FDI and multinational corporations (Macs). Here we need FDI theories based on Japanese FDI and Macs. Professor Kiyoshi Kojima did this great job as the first scholar. His hypothesis is called 'Kiyoshi Kojima's macro economic theory of FDI' by Dunning (Dunning 1993). Thus Kojima's work is a much-cited reference for understanding Japanese FDI. Kojima's theory is essentially an extension of the neoclassical theory of factor endowments to explain trade in intermediate products, notably technology and management skills. But Kojima is as much interested in normative as in positive issues. A major part of his thesis, set out in Kojima (1973; 1978; 1982; 1990) and in Kojima and Ozawa (1984), is that whereas Japanese FDI is primarily trade-oriented and responds to the dictates of the principle of comparative advantage, US FDI is mainly conducted within an oligopoly market structure, is anti-trade oriented and operates to the long-term disadvantage of both the donor and recipient countries.

Dunning (1993) summarizes Kojima's theory's main points as follows: Kojima essentially believes that FDI should act as an efficient conduit for trading intermediate products, but that the timing and direction of such investment should be determined by market forces rather than by hierarchical control. His prescription is that the outbound direct investment should be undertaken by firms that produce intermediate products that require resources and capabilities in which the home country has a comparative advantage, but that generate value-added activities that require resources and capabilities in which that country is comparatively disadvantaged. By contrast, inbound direct investment should import intermediate products that require resources and capabilities in which the recipient country is disadvantaged, but the use of which requires resources and capabilities in which it has a comparative advantage. To this extent, the Kojima thesis is quite consistent with any macroeconomic inferences that might be drawn from the eclectic paradigm at least in respect of some kinds of FDI. The main criticism against Kojima's hypothesis is that it is static, as pointed out by many scholars.[1] According to one writer,[2] for example, the Japanese economy is growing and changing so rapidly that her own FDI is already in part of the product life-cycle type originated within Japan and likely to increasingly resemble the US type in years to come. Another writer[3] states that Kojima ignores the historical differences in the development pattern and relative levels of development today between the US and Japan. It was also suggested that Kojima's dichotomy between US and the Japanese FDI might only reflect a difference in the stage of economic development between the two countries. As the structure of Japanese manufacturing industries tends to resemble more and more that of US counterparts, they point out, too, that the difference in industrial composition of overseas manufacturing investment between the US and Japan will disappear.

Dunning (1993) criticized Kojima's hypothesis from another viewpoint. The point at which Kojima's theory ceases to be satisfactory as a general explanation of MNCs activity is precisely that at which neoclassical theories fail to explain much of modern trade. That is because they countenance neither the possibility of market failure nor the fact that firms are both producing and transacting economic agents. This means that they cannot explain the kind of trade flows (including trade in intermediate products) that are based less on the distribution of factor endowments and more on the need to exploit the economies of scale, product differentiation and other manifestations of market failure. Neither can they explain trade in intermediate products based upon the advantages of common governance, which itself reflects the inability of the market mechanism to ensure the first-best international allocation of economic activity in which the costs and benefits of transactions extend beyond those who are parties to the exchange; where there is uncertainty of the outcome of such exchanges; and where there is an asymmetry of knowledge between buyers and sellers.

To the extent that Kojima uses trade model to explain patterns of FDI, he follows in the Vernon tradition. To the extent that he regards MNCs as creators or sustainers of market imperfections whose impact on resource allocation must be less beneficial than that predicated by perfect competition, the genealogy of this thought can be traced back to Hymer. The result is that whereas he formulates a useful analysis of the cross-border transactions in intermediate products and correctly identifies some activities of MNCs as being the result of structural market distortions, he pays little attention to the impact of transaction costs on international resource allocation, and hence fails to appreciate that, in conditions of market failure, multinational hierarchies may improve rather than worsen such an allocation. This means by which this is accomplished, which include geographical diversification, exploitation of the economies of joint supply, better commercial intelligence and the avoidance of costs of enforcing property rights, have been spelled out by Gray (1982). Thus Kojima's theory is a less than satisfactory framework for explaining the changing pattern of Japanese FDI in Asian countries. Then the following questions automatically arise. Can Kojima's hypothesis explain the dynamic pattern in industrial composition of Japanese FDI? If not, why? What hypothesis explains it in a more generalized way?

We wrote a review article on Japanese FDI[4] before. From this review, we got our hypothesis: As recent changes in Japan's country-specific economic and technical characteristics (factor endowment) tend to make the Japanese industries more and more capital- and technology-intensive, and as changing demand for FDI in Asian LDCs tends to favor relatively large scale and capital-intensive industries in the dynamic process of rapid and diversified industrialization, the difference in industrial composition of the US and Japanese manufacturing investment in the host LDCs tends to be less and less discernible. The methodology was also derived from the review: the methodology will be made to synthesize Dunning's approach in explaining how Japan's factor endowments have changed, namely, change in supply-side, and Ranis's approach in explaining how the LDCs' demand for FDI has been related to the different phase for its growth process, namely, change in demand-side.' We will introduce Dunning's and Ranis's approaches now. Dunning proposed the eclectic theory of international production[5] in 1977 and has refined his theory until now. Then he proposed his approach as the eclectic paradigm of international production in Dunning (1993). According to Dunning (1993), the principal hypothesis on which the eclectic paradigm of international production is based is that the level and structure of a firm's foreign value-adding activities will depend on four conditions being satisfied. These are: the extent to which it possesses sustainable ownership-specific (O) advantages vis-à-vis firms of other nationalities in the particular markets it serves or is contemplating serving. These O advantages largely take the form of the privileged possession of intangible assets as well as those which arise as a result of the common governance of cross-border value-added activities. These advantages and the use made of them are assumed to increase the wealth creating capacity of a firm, and hence the value of its assets.

1.   Assuming condition (1) is satisfied, the extent to which the enterprise perceives it to be in its best interest to add value to its O advantages rather than to sell them, or their right of use to foreign firms. These advantages are called market internalization (I) advantages. They may reflect either the greater organizational efficiency of hierarchies or their ability to exercise monopoly power over the assets under their governance.

2. Assuming condition (1) and (2) are satisfied, the extent to which the global interests of the enterprise are served by creating, or utilizing, its O advantages in a foreign location. The distribution of these resources and capabilities is assumed to be uneven and, hence, depending on their distribution, will confer an (L) advantage on the countries possessing them over these who do not.

3. Given the configuration of the ownership, location and internalization (OLI) advantages facing a particular firm, the extent to which a firm believes that foreign production is consistent with its long-term management strategy.

The generalized predictions of the eclectic paradigm are straightforward. At any given moment of time, the more a country's enterprises – relative to those of another – possess O advantages, the greater the incentive they have to internalize rather than externalize their use, the more they find it in their interest to exploit them from a foreign location, then the more they are likely to engage in outbound production. By the same token, a country is likely to attract investment by foreign MNCs when the reverse conditions apply. Similarly, the paradigm can be expressed in a dynamic form. Changes in the outward or inward direct investment position of a particular country can be explained in term of changes in the O advantages of its enterprises relative to those of other nations, changes in its L assets relative to those of other countries, changes in the extent to which firms perceive that these assets (and any others it may acquire) are best organized internally rather than by the market, and changes in the strategy of firms which may affect their reaction to any given OLI configuration. Ranis introduced an interesting approach, 'the development approach of MNCs'. According to Ranis (1976), the role of the MNCs in development cannot be assessed independently of time and place, but such assessment must ·be related to the particular phase of a developing country's life cycle, as well as the type (for example, size and resources endowment) of the LDC in question. Thus the above methodology was derived from Dunning's approach built on Ranis's one. We think this synthesized methodology is better than Kojima's hypothesis for explaining the dynamic pattern of Japan's FDI. Then an empirical study remains. Asian LDCs have been the main targets for Japan's FDI. Thus it is appropriate to use them as cases to compare our proposed framework and Kojima's one. We presented a paper on Indonesia[6] at the Fourth Convention of the East Asian Economic Association in Taipei, Taiwan in 1994. At this Conference we use South Korea and compared these two approaches.

Our presentation is as follows:

1. We 'observe facts' of Japan's FDI in South Korea.

2. We 'explain observed facts' of Japan's FDI in South Korea. 'Observed facts' will be explained by the above methodology.

3. We show conclusion and policy implications.

Observed Facts of Japan's FDI in South Korea

Japan is the largest source of FDI in South Korea. In terms of trend, Japan's FDI in South Korea sharply increased in 1987, then decreased in 1988 and increased again in 1989. Then it continued to decrease until 1993 and increased from 1994 to 1996. The number of cases continued to keep over 100 from 1986 to 1988 and then decreased until 1992. Then it kept around 30 cases until 1996. Thus we observed Japan's FDI in South Korea concentrated from 1986 to 1989. In terms of sectors, Japan's FDI in South Korea concentrated in both sectors, the manufacturing and the non-manufacturing with almost same amount at the cumulative base from 1951 to 1996. In the non-manufacturing sector, Japan's FDI in South Korea concentrated in the service industry in 1987 because we guess Japan's FDI went to building hotels to prepare for the Seoul Olympic in 1988. Most Japan's FDI went to the manufacturing sector; however, Japan's FDI has been dominant in the non-manufacturing sector since 1993. We guess this shows Japan's FDI has been shifting to the service industry. In the manufacturing sector, Japan's FDI in South Korea has been dominant in the capital-and technology-intensive industries such as electric machinery, transportation, machinery and chemicals since 1987. On the other hand, Japan's FDI in South Korea has decreased in the labor-intensive industries such as textiles.

Explaining Observed Facts of Japan's FDI in South Korea

We try to explain observed facts in (1) by the above methodology: synthesis of supply-side (Japan) and demand-side (South Korea). On supply-side (Japan), there was a big change: the rapid appreciation of Japanese yen since the G-5 meeting in September 1985. This has been said as one of the main reason for Japanese FDI widely. However, Phongpaichit (1988) raised a following question: Is this the real explanations behind the drive to expand Japan's FDI in the late 1980s? Then he answered the following. There is no doubt that the rapid appreciation of the yen after September 1985 has accelerated the need for Japanese firms overseas. But the real forces behind this move are much more fundamental, and have been operating in the Japanese economy for some time. Thus he explained his reason as follows: Japanese manufacturing production has been and will continue to be dependent on imported oil, materials, and other natural resources. The oil price hike of the early 1970s showed Japan the importance of a secure access to oil, and also other natural resources. It was able to cope with the oil crisis very well through the success in energy saving devices and various ways to increase productivity (such as the use of robots) without raising the labor cost substantially. But it will become increasingly difficult to repeat the earlier success. The pressure for the cost of production to rise has remained. In the future it may also be expected that the labor cost will rise more, and there will be a limit to substitution of labor through the use of robots. The Japanese tradition of restricted immigration will over-rule the option of liberal immigration policy for solving the labor problems. Thus Japan needs to save on the cost of production by all means, and one of these is securing access to cheap natural resources and energy; and shifting production processes which are relatively more labor-intensive to other countries, which still have a large supply of labor. Thus there is a need for exporting capital in a big way (Phongpaichit 1988). We think Japanese firms' global strategy is also an important factor. According to the survey (Japan's Economic Planning Board 1990), Japanese firms consider FDI as a long-run management strategy.

On demand-side (South Korea), the South Korean government has newly introduced an automatic approval system and moved to a negative list system through revision of the Foreign Capital Inducement Act and other related regulations, effectively from July 1, 1984. With the implementation of such a system, the range of projects eligible for FDI has become substantially widened and the authorization procedure for some projects has become further simplified. In October 1985, the government again revised the Negative List and liberalized 102 more industrial sectors for foreign investors. At the same time the government simplified the approval procedures for foreign investors by amending Presidential Decree and the Working Rules of the Foreign Capital Inducement Act (Koizumi, 1989). In the mid-1980s, wage rose rapidly in South Korea and its major trading partners imposed trade restrictions on South Korean exports. And, to make matters worse, the South Korean won appreciated from 861 won to the US dollar to 680 between 1986 and 1989 (Lee, 1994). Between 1985 and 1990, wage increases in South Korea were dramatic with the hourly industrial wage doubling from US\$ 1.62 to US\$ 3.46. The manufacturing wage rate has also increased dramatically – more rapidly than industrial wage rate – since 1985. Increases in labor productivity did not, however, keep pace with increases in wage rates. Labor productivity in manufacturing doubled between 1985 and 1990 but wages increased by 220 percent in the same period. The excessive wage increases occurred throughout most of the manufacturing industries with the exceptions in the footwear, other chemical products, electrical and electronic machinery, and medical and optical equipment industries.

Wage increases that outpaced productivity gains were a consequence of the increasing power of labor unions in South Korea since the middle of the 1980s. Until that time, there had been virtually no strikes in South Korea. In 1985, however, there were 265 incidences of labor disputes, and in 1987 the number of cases shot up to 3,749 with a resulting loss of 7 million working days. Union membership also doubled to 1.9 million between 1985 and 1990 (Lee, 1994). South Korean industries have been confronted with import restrictions in their major export markets. In 1989, there were 96 cases of import restrictions on South Korean exports – 55 cases were volume restrictions on exports and 29 cases were restrictions on price. As of 1991, 15 cases were pending further investigation including 11 anti-dumping cases. Such restrictive measures on South Korean exports have induced South Korean firms to move their manufacturing facilities to offshore sites (Lee, 1994). South Korea's average annual growth rate was 9.3 percent in the 1970s, 8.0 percent in the 1980s, and 7.8 percent in the 1990s (1990-1995). Government industrial policy has played a key role in this remarkable record of economic development. However, it has become necessary to change that industrial policy for the years ahead. The conventional interventionist industrial policy has already become ineffective for dealing with the rapid changes that are occurring in companies and in the trade situation. The South Korean economy of today is already at an advanced stage of development. At this stage, such steps as selecting promising industries and setting special guidelines exceed the appropriate boundaries of government policy. OECD membership in 1996 has brought with it even stronger calls for loosening regulations and liberalizing capital transactions (Kitamura and Tanaka, 1997). Thus we could explain the observed facts of Japanese FDI in South Korea by synthesis between supply-side (Japan) and demand-side (South Korea).

Concluding Comments

Our empirical test in South Korea supports our hypothesis. This study shows the dynamic pattern of Japanese FDI and importance of its demand side, which Professor Kojima neglected. This approach is based on Professor Gustav Ranis's development approach to the role of MNCs. His basic position once again is that the role of MNC must be assessed in relation to the particular phase of a developing country's growth process, as well as to the type (for example, size and resource endowment) of the LDC in question.

Notes

1. They are Arndt (1974), Roemer (1975, 1976), Mason (1980), Lee (1980), Sekiguchi and Krause (1980), Sato (1979), Dunning (1977), Smith (1980) and Findlay (1980). According to Smith (1980), there is no obvious reason to believe that any different results of Japanese and US investment will continue to be observed as Japan passes into more capital/technology-abundant phase of development. According to Lee (1980), one would expect FDI to change the growth rate of the host country's economy and to have a long-run dynamic effect on its trade pattern. If US FDI with an anti-trade-oriented impact effect is more growth-promoting than Japanese FDI with a trade-oriented impact effect and if trade is positively associated with growth, it is conceived that the net effect of US FDI is more trade-oriented that that of Japanese FDI. Without specifying the long-run dynamic effect, one cannot, therefore, designate any given FDI as either trade-oriented or anti-trade-oriented.
2. Findlay (1980).
3. Sekiguchi and Krause (1980).
4. Koizumi (1987).
5. Dunning (1977).
6. Koizumi (1994).

References

Arndt, H. W. (1974), 'Professor Kojima on the Macroeconomics of Foreign Direct Investment', *Hitotsubashi Journal of Economics*, June 1974, pp.26-35.

Ditamura, Kayoko and Tanaka, Tsuneo. (1997), *Examining Asia's Tigers*, Tokyo, Institute of Developing Economies.

Dunning, J. H. (1993), *Multinational Enterprises and the Global Economy*, Addison-Wesley Publishing Company, Wokingham.

Dunning, J. H. (1977), 'Trade, Location of Economic Activity and the MNE: A Search for an Eclectic Approach', in Ohlin, B. (ed.), *The International Allocation of Economic activity*, Meier Publisher Inc., New York.

Findlay, R. (1980), Discussion on Sekiguchi and Krause.

Gray, H. P. (1982), 'Towards a Unified Theory of International Trade, International Production and Direct Foreign Investment', In *International Capital Movements*, pp.58-83, Macmillan, London.

Koizumi, Tsuyoshi. (1989), 'Trend of Japan's DFI in South Korea', Paper presented at Annual Meeting of Academy of International Business, Singapore.

Koizumi, Tsuyoshi. (1994), 'Drastic Change of Japan's DFI in Indonesia after 1985', Paper presented at the Fourth Convention of the East Asian Economic Association, Taipei, Taiwan.

Koizumi, Tsuyoshi. (1987), 'Review of the Literature on Japanese DFI in Asian LDCs', Paper presented at Academy of International Business South East Asia Regional Conference, Kuala Lumpur, Malaysia.

Kojima, Kiyoshi. (1990), *Japanese Direct Investment Abroad*, Mitaka, Tokyo: International Christian University, Social Science Research Institute Monograph Series 1.

Kojima, Kiyoshi. (1982), 'Macroeconomic Versus International Business Approach to Foreign Direct Investment', *Hitotsubashi Journal of Economics*, vol. 23, pp.630-640.

Kojima, Kiyoshi. (1978), *Direct foreign Investment: a Japanese Model of Multinational Business Operations*, Croom Helm, London.

Kojima, Kiyoshi. (1973), 'Reorganization of North-South trade: Japan's Foreign economic policy for the 1970s', *Hitotsubashi Journal of Economics*, vol. 13, pp.1-28.

Kojima, Kiyoshi and Ozawa, Terutomo. (1984), 'Micro and Macro Economic Models of Foreign Direct Investment: Towards a Synthesis', *Hitotsubashi Journal of Economics*, vol. 25, pp.1-20.

Lee, Chung H. (1980), 'United States and Japanese Direct Investment in Korea: A Comparative Study', *Hitotsubashi Journal of Economics*, vol. 21, pp.26-41.

Lee, Chung H. (1994), *Changing Comparative Advantage and Outward DFI*, First Economic Research Institute, Han Wha Group, Seoul Korea.

Mason, R. H. (1980), 'A comment on Professor Kojima's Japanese Type Versus American Type Technology Transfer', *Hitotsubashi Journal Of Economics*, vol. 21, pp.42-52.

Phongpaichit, Pasuk. (1988), 'Decision Making on Overseas Direct Investment by Japanese Small and Medium Industries in ASEAN and the Asian NICs', *ASEAN Economic Bulletin*, pp.302-315.

Ranis, Gustuv. (1976), 'The Multinational Corporation as an Instrument of Development', in D. E. Apter and L. W. Goodman (eds), *the Multinational Corporation and Social Change*, Praeger, New York.

Roemer, J. E. (1976), 'Japanese DFI in Manufactures', *The Quarterly Review of Economics and Business*, Summer, pp.91-111.

Roemer, J. E. (1975), 'US-Japanese Competition in International Market', University of California, Berkeley.

Sato, S. (1979), 'Possibility and Limitation of Multinationalization of Japanese Enterprises', In *Evolution of JapaneseStyle-MNC*. Edited by MNC study group. Tokyo: Horitsu Bunkasha (in Japanese).

Sekiguchi, S. and Krause, L. B. (1980), 'Direct foreign investment in ASEAN by Japan and the United States', in R. Garnuat. (ed.), *ASEAN in a Changing Pacific and World Economy*, Australian National University Press, Canberra.

World Bank (1989), Indonesia-Policies for Sustained Growth, Jakarta.

Chapter 3

The Asian Crisis – Signals from Multinational Enterprises: Obstacles and Managerial Impediments to Foreign Direct Investment

Frank L. Bartels and Hafiz Mirza

Introduction

The perturbation that began as 'a little local difficulty' in Thailand, with the failure of Finance One (a non-bank financial intermediator) on 23 May 1997[1] turned into the Asian Economic Crisis (AEC)[2] – an 'event horizon' of globalization. The contagion became amplified globally and made red raw the nerves of the world banking system and weakened its financial architecture. In retrospect, the AEC had signals (Krugman, 1994; UNCTAD, 1996).[3] There were also managerial signals indicated by multinational enterprises (MNEs) in the region that hitherto have received insufficient attention.

Plaudits (World Bank, 1993), pre-crisis capital movements (Mathieson, Richards and Sharma, 1998) and information asymmetries distorted risk appraisal of Asia's investment climate and prospects. Retrospection provokes the thought of features distinguishing the region's Host locations as pervasive and uniformly attractive. This was (is) not so, nevertheless, the region has attracted international business (Mirza, Kee and Bartels, 1998). The region is Host to US$493.1b of FDI stock in 1993 owned 13.2 percent, 16.5 percent and 23.4 percent by NAMNEs, EUMNEs and JPMNEs respectively (Bartels, Mirza and Kee, 1997). ASEAN's capture of in-FDI stock grew spectacularly in absolute terms from US$35.5b in 1980 to US$ 493.1b in 1996. Although ASEAN's share of Developing Country FDI stock declined from 71 percent of total in 1980 to 42 percent of total in 1996, its FDI in-flows as a share of in-FDI to Developing Countries nearly doubled from 29.8 percent of total in 1980 to 51.9 percent of total in 1996.[4] Furthermore, of the US$256b FDI in-flows to Developing Countries US$90b went to S. E. Asia (UNCTAD, 1997). FDI in Asia has provided MNEs with low factor cost manufacturing platforms. It is viewed best in the context of rising global FDI and its asymmetric distribution.[5] The view benefits also from the intra-regional trade perspective.[6] Between 1980 and 1996, the stock of world FDI increased from about US$514b to around US$3,233b. In this, South and East Asia's share rose from 6.7

percent of the total to 14.7 percent. This was partly at the expense of other developing countries since the Asian share of FDI into developing countries increased. MNEs from the Triad, remain the largest investors on a global basis and the *absolute* stock of FDI in ASEAN has risen over six-fold since 1980 and by two-thirds since 1990. This represents a significant achievement.[7]

However, Asia's impressive inward FDI record conceals obstacles (physical and procedural) and managerial impediments that signaled its coming economic crisis. Although intensities of these encumbrances vary, as a function of individual country political economy development across ASEAN, their dimensions are general. Our analysis records that, despite MNEs pragmatism, a discernible pattern in incentives; relative ease or difficulty in transferring technology and business culture; and barriers *inter alia*, emerges from MNEs misgivings about the impediments to FDI at both the level of specific Hosts and ASEAN. In comparison to some arguments on Asia,[8] this paper delineates Factors representing clear signals of the AEC that are significant in the ex-post rationalization of negative sentiment. It suggests that the location-bound inertia of MNEs and persistence of FDI (UNCTAD-ICC, 1998; Mudambi, 1998) ex post do not compromise the strength of the signals. Arguably, as post-AEC explanations suffer from lack of corroborative evidence, our analysis partly addresses this lacuna.

Dimensions of the Asian Economic Crisis

Two years after the Mexican Crisis, the search for higher yields made investment obsession with Emerging Markets (EMs) in Asia respectable.[9] The debacle in Asia is prima facie evidence of market failure arising out of the dilemma of attempting to maintain simultaneously capital account liberalization, fixed exchange rates and independent domestic monetary policy.[10] The AEC, arguably a Kuznets cycle phenomenon (Berry, 1991), was neither a local difficulty nor purely economic (Fischer, 1998). It became a 'total crisis' and potentially geo-politically destabilizing.

Financial crises are normal, but global recessions leading to depressions are exceptional (Wyplosz, 1998). In the wake of financial crises comes a policy battle between orthodoxy espoused by the 'Washington Consensus' and countervailing nationalistic policies.[11] Evidence[12] points to converging interests of European and North American regional trade blocs, and European and North American MNEs in rescuing assets from EMs.[13] The debate on liberties for finance capital and state interventionist roles contrasts with arguments of economists of differing perspectives.[14] The AEC is distinguishable from other crises by its implications for globalization[15] and the contention in political and economic ideology unleashed.[16] The competition dimension of this (Brzezinski, 1998) is likely to be executed by Nation-States, one against another, with the interests of their MNEs uppermost and exemplified forcefully by the homily 'what's good for General Motors is good for America'.[17] Arguments dismissive of the Huntington thesis are no longer as assured[18] and parallels in history and grim prospects for a 1930s-style depression and conflagration have been drawn.[19] Clearly, these call for a more sober reassessment of globalization.[20]

Reflections on the Literature

While the focus of IB is overwhelmingly FDI, the manifestations of two set of actors – governments, and the controversial behavior of MNEs (Inkpen and Beamish, 1994), the literature has yet to substantiate fully its links with managerial economics. Nevertheless, it is undeniable that MNEs are the most significant forces in socio-economic development and thereby integrate (Vernon 1992; Fortin, 1994) Triad geo-economic hegemony (Thurow, 1996). The central feature of this dynamic, especially that associated with emerging new forms of internationalization (Oman, 1984,1994) between the Triad and 'clusters' of client states (UNCTAD, 1993, p.167), reflects neo-mercantilistic goals in the competition for wealth and distribution of power (Grosse and Behrman, 1992).

Within IB, controversy is sustained firstly by the view, ascendant in the 1960s and 1970s, of MNEs as 'agents provocateurs' and then (because of 'Tiger' economics in the 1980s and 1990s) as 'agents producteurs' (Vernon, 1966, 1971, 1977; UNCTC, 1992; UNCTAD, 1994). Secondly, controversy ranges over whether by adopting the Ghoshal and Bartlett (1990) perspective the analysis of MNEs as stateless global corporations is conceptually desirable or practically possible. According to Fleenor (1993), the global corporation is a figment of academic imagination and disparate views on 'globalization' among experts renders the idea superfluous.[21] However, Moran and Reisenberger (1994) indicate that of 2400 IB articles on 'globalization' between 1987 and 1992, 42 percent focused on 'multinational and global' issues of intra- and inter-organizational network processes and organization. Defining and understanding globalization remains elusive and even precarious and so the temptation to ascribe to the permutations of these networks, the term 'multi-transnational enterprises' to capture better the commercial and industrial expressions of the versatility in spatial integration (Kanter, 1989) is strong but not yet fully accepted. A third area of the controversy concerns political behavior. Boddewyn and Brewer (1994) propose that IB behavior *has to be political*. In this scheme the existence of political and economic, markets is accepted and governments (i.e. obstacles) are seen by MNEs either as additional factors of production to be managed (Kindleberger, 1970; Mitnick, 1993) or external factor markets to be co-opted and internalized (Buckley, 1988). In this schema of intermediation, signaling deficiencies in Asia's investment environment by MNEs suggests a potential for MNEs-State conflict.[22]

IB literature may be read in terms of gubernatorial structural barriers, generated with regard to the distribution of value, and the protagonistic and antagonistic postures of actors that are tectonic in effect.[23] Smooth and uneventful relations are subject to unpredictable dislocations or 'punctuated equilibria' (Chomsky and Herman, 1973; Sampson, 1975; Vernon, 1977; Servant-Schreiber, 1980; Korten, 1995). Given that governments in Asia have been interventionist, an examination of signals from MNEs is cogent to the debate on economic development, reform and globalization, as well as opportunities and challenges for IB.

Methodology and Research Design

The Surveys for Analyzing MNEs' FDI in Asia

Our Survey captures manufacturing MNEs' data for two reasons. Firstly, they face contingencies different from portfolio and services investment. Secondly, manufacturing investments have heavily influenced Asian economic performance. Survey questions are multi-level (Host, ASEAN and general) and capture a wide variable array.[24] Responses returned by MNEs (36 NAMNEs, 19 EUMNEs, 149 JPMNEs, 37 TAMNEs and 13 AUMNEs), indicating a representativeness of 21.5 percent, are analyzed. This is consistent with similar field research (Erramilli, 1991; Kim and Hwang, 1992; Bartels and Freeman, 1995a). Measuring properties of, and obtaining data on, MNEs and FDI with mail survey instrumentation possesses strong validity (Cronbach and Meehl, 1955; Campbell and Fiske, 1959; Bryman and Cramer, 1990).

Factor Analysis of MNEs' FDI in Asia

The independent variable (V_I) (Table 2) constructs encapsulate signals of Asia's demise. Factor analysis of Likert scale variables was performed with the following criteria:

(a) Oblique rotation – firstly, because the variable set is assumed to relate to the constructs. Secondly, to avoid forcing the variables to be unrelated through orthogonal rotation (Bryman and Cramer, 1990) as the orthogonal restriction ensures 'that factors will delineate statistically independent variation.' (Rummel, 1970, p.385).

(b) To interpret and delineate factors with reference to oblique rotation, the correlation of variables with factors is provided by the Structure Matrix. Comrey (1973, p 225) refers to the 'crude index of usability of a given data variable for interpretative purposes is the square of the correlation between the factor and the data variable' and suggests a number of criteria for including variables. Assuming the Standard Error to be approximately 0.06 [observed correlation standard error is $1/(n)^{0.5}$ where n = sample size 254] a factor loading of 0.5 (variables not accounting for 25 percent or more of variance in common with factors are not included in the data set) was chosen.

(c) The factor technique selected was Principal Components because Total Variance = Common Variance + Specific Variance + Error Variance where Specific Variance + Error Variance is the Unique Variance, on the basis that the test used 'to assess the variable is perfectly reliable and without error' (Bryman and Cramer, 1990, p.258). The chosen factor technique was based as much on considerations for parsimony as on a reluctance to impose a strictly hypothetical causal model, and for simplicity in comparing the linear combination(s) of observed data (Kim and Meuller, 1978, p.19-20).

(d)   The extraction of factors was based on statistical inferences and 'rules of thumb':

    (i)   The first criterion was 'meaningfulness' of the factor in terms of its constituent variable set Rummel, 1970, p.356-357) and the need to avoid eliminating variable sets resonating with theory.

    (ii)   The second criterion was based on a certain level of variance among the variables, that of Eigenvalue ≥ 1.0. According to Rummel (1970, p.356) Since the eigenvalue measures the variance accounted for by a factor. The eigenvalue-greater-than-one criterion assumes that the common factors extracted define a certain level of variance among the variables. Hence, since the variance of a variable is unity, the cut-off rejects factors that do not account for at least the variance of one variable.

    (iii)   The third criterion was the plot of proportion of total variance against number of factors (Cattell, 1952; 1966) delineating the factor cut-off or discontinuity after which the percentage of variance accounted for is marginal.

    (iv)   The last criterion was based on the requirement to have an appropriate number of factors to rotate. That is a number that, given the relation between sample size and number of variables (254/240), avoids auto-correlation. Given the non-random characteristics of the sample, it is crucial, therefore, that a sufficient number of variables and cases be included in an analysis to enable the major factors in a domain to emerge (Rummel, 1970, p.220). The analysis heeded Comrey (1973, p.202) 'for exploratory work, it is much more important to ensure that there is plenty of variance in the sample than it is to have a representative sample from the population at large.'

(e)   The fundamental characteristics of Principal Component Factor Analysis (Harman, 1967) on the SPSS Windows Version 6 occupy the vector space defining the total variance with no assumption being made about the common and unique variance. This convention solves the problem of communality and reduces parsimoniously the number of variables. The final data variable set used was inclusive of interval variables relating to constructs (Labovitz, 1970; 1971).

Measurement Characteristics

Variables relate to theoretical foundations of international business, FDI and MNEs. In applying the criteria of Catholicity, one may wish to divide the area into substantive domains and then to select phenomena out of each domain without allowing one domain to be overly represented in the final sample (Rummel, 1970, p.210). Therefore, all the major dimensions are delineated in the factor analysis. Reliability, in which Nunnally (1967, p.226) indicates that 'reliabilities of 0.60 or 0.50 will suffice', was confirmed by running Cronbach Alpha tests on the variable constituents of factors. Computational analysis was performed with the missing values substituted for by the mean.

Empirical Results of Survey Analysis

The Characteristics of MNEs

Table 3.1 presents the characteristics of the firms analyzed.

Table 3.1 The Characteristics of MNEs in ASEAN

MNEs Feature	Namnes	Eumnes	Jpmnes	Aumnes	Tamnes
Number of MNEs[1]	36	19	149	13	37
Mean Employment	52,300	46,500	7,200	19,900	2,150
Median Employment	50,000	16,000	3,000	2,400	350
Three most common industries of MNEs from each source	Telecoms, Petro-chemicals, Speciality Chemicals	Telecoms, Petro-chemicals, Speciality Chemicals	Automobiles, Electronics, Metal Products	Automobile Components, Industry Machinery, Food Products	Building Materials, Rubbers & Plastics, Metal Products

Source: ASEAN Foreign Direct Investment Database
Note: 1 – The number of firms analyzed for this Paper. The actual number in the Survey is greater.

Japanese firms predominate reflecting 'psychic' proximity pressures for regional FDI (Johanson and Vahlne, 1977; Johanson and Wiedersheim-Paul, 1975). Several points are noteworthy. Firstly, there is asymmetry. Secondly, there is a big size gap between firms: the average size of Japanese firms is one-seventh of North American firms. The low median implies a greater proportion of smaller MNEs [or International Small to Medium Sized Enterprises (ISMEs)] among the Japanese. Thirdly, there is the difference in the most common industries for investment. Atlantic firms are 'supply-siders' where economies of scale considerations influence FDI decisions. Japanese firms are 'demand-siders' where economies of scope influence decisions. MNEs from Australia and Taiwan, fewer as might be expected, contrast sharply. The size of Australian firms is on average nine times that of Taiwanese counterparts. However, their predominant industries, while not being the same, are spread across a variety of industries some supply side and some demand side.

Results of Factor Analysis

The following constructs and related independent variables (Table 3.2), encapsulate signals of the AEC in managerial terms. Results of factor analysis of 254 cases are tabulated in the Appendix.

Table 3.2 Constructs, Independent Variables and Number of Factors Extracted

Constructs	Independent Variables (V_I)	No. Factors Extracted
C1 – Host Location Barriers (physical and procedural) and Managerial Impediments to FDI	40	4
C2 – ASEAN Regional Barriers (physical and procedural) and Managerial Impediments to FDI	40	4
C3 – Policy framework for increasing the attractiveness of Host Location for FDI	22	6
C4 – Policy framework for increasing the attractiveness for Intra-ASEAN FDI	22	6
C5 – Policy framework for increasing the attractiveness for ASEAN as a Region for FDI	22	6

The factor analysis for C1 to C5 yielded acceptable Kaiser-Meyer-Olkin (KMO) measures of sampling adequacy of 0.76749 to 0.96435 that compare favorably with exemplary measures indicated by Kaiser (1974) and cited by Kim and Meuller (1978, p.54) as 'meritorious' and 'marvelous'. There were no off-diagonal elements of the Anti-Image Correlation Matrix (AIC) > 0.09 i.e. those correlation coefficients accounting for trivia. Concerning residuals (above diagonal) on the Reproduced Correlation Matrix that are >0.05 – the amount of variation accounted for by variables other than those in extracted factors – the residual profile for constructs C1 to C5 ranged from 12.0 percent to 46.0 percent. This range represents robust analysis and indicates that extraneous explanations are limited rather than general.

In applying the Principal Components Structure Matrix cut-off factor loadings of ≤0.5, Reliability tests on the refined non-overlapping variable sets of factors were performed. Cronbach's Alpha values – the 'average of all possible split-half reliability coefficients' (Bryman and Cramer, 1990, p.71) where 'a coefficient of 0.8 or above is usually taken as indicating a reliable measure' (Bryman and Cramer, 1990, p.204) – were determined. The meaning of the value is that its measure represents the correlation between the items of the variable set and all other possible tests containing the same number of items (Norusis, 1990). The Reliability of each factor was measured to: (a) indicate the variable set by labeling;

and (b) check individual reliabilities for each of the extracted factors. The Cronbach's Alpha for all factor variables vary between 0.4123 to 0.9924. Thus, the internal consistency of the factor variables and the factorial validity is robust and Extracted Factors constitute reliable measures as markers in the signals of the AEC.

Extracted Factors as Signals of Asia's Crisis

Holistically, Extracted Factors – generally reliable and statistically significant in particular – contribute to an understanding of IB relations by encapsulating how MNEs view Asia and ASEAN. They represent what MNEs expect from an Asia committed to further global integration and are precursors for managerial reasons advanced for the AEC.

Barriers to FDI in Host Locations

At the level of specific locations, the four Factors that constitute Host Location Barriers and Managerial Impediments to FDI are highly significant and very reliable (Table C1). Comprising – Political Instability and Restrictive Regulations, Poor Infrastructure and Non-Transparency, Lack of Quality Management and Skills, and High labor Costs – they are conspicuously predictive and have become ex post rationale for the AEC. In particular, the first two Factors are prominent in this reasoning whereas the second two have received little attention in IB excepting from economists more concerned with total factor productivity growth. The first – Political Instability and Restrictive Regulations – as a central feature in the face of political regimes of established longevity (pre-AEC), is highly significant as the Political Instability variable accounts for almost three-quarters of all the variation in the Factor. One way of viewing this first Factor is in terms of MNEs as information accumulation and processing networks (Egelhoff, 1991) with purposeful intelligence. What is beyond doubt is how the AEC has exposed the underlying fragility of national political institutions in Asia in general and ASEAN in particular (Godement, 1999).

The second Factor, again highly significant and reliable, resonates with the analysis of the AEC. The World Bank and IMF, and other commentators have pointed to the lack of transparency in the structures and governance of Asia's business. A measure of the opaqueness is obviously due to international business across cultural barriers. In conjunction with other impediments this Factor is a significant pointer to the AEC. The third and fourth Factors – Lack of Quality Management and Skills, and High labor Costs – together point to contradictions in Asia's growth trajectory – one that was bound to come to maturity and face diminishing returns. The imbalance therein implied (low productivity at high cost) is partly responsible for the sequence of development referred to as the 'flying geese paradigm' (Ozawa, 1990). However, the Factors point to limits of revealed comparative advantage unless upgrading of human and social capital occurs. It is impossible, without increasing revealed comparative advantage in capital intense operations, to continuously shed high labor intense production to less developed locations (Ozawa, 1992). Even with China as a vast pool of labor, the region as a whole was bound to suffer as MNEs began to look to other regions for labor-intensive production. These Factors together are strongly suggestive of managerial dimensions of AEC at the individual country level.

Barriers to FDI in ASEAN

With respect to the enveloping region, the four reliable Factors that constitute ASEAN Regional Barriers and Managerial Impediments to FDI (Table C2) – Lack of Potential Partners/Targets & State Intervention, Non-Predictable Regulations and Poor Physical & Commercial Infrastructure, Lack of Quality Management and Skills, and Intra-ASEAN Non-Tariff Barriers – signal strongly and clearly managerial fault-lines underlying the Asian 'miracle' and point to the crisis.

It is noteworthy that Factor 1 – Lack of Potential Partners/Targets & State Intervention – comprises two sub-Factors. These are – Lack of Potential Partners and Economic Instability. Although this Factor 1 is not significant, it is reliable and indicative of potential failure. Dirigiste control from, and interventionism by, the state has characterized the Asian development model. In this model resource allocations have been directed by the principle that 'government knows best' in opposition to the private actions of independent economic agents in the free-market. In an era of alliance capitalism, Asian governments, in resisting 'modal neutrality', have been known to force their own preferred partners onto MNEs willing to enter their domestic markets rather than permitting investors to select their own partners. It is evident that Asian governments display an attitude towards the purpose of an economy that is different to that of Western governments in general. This is reflected in the policy arena and the dynamic contention – regulation (the interests of development) versus globalization (the interests of finance capital) (Fallows, 1993; 1994). The abnormally high growth rates of 'Tiger' economies can be seen as unmanageable economic performance and is not the only evidence of economic instability. The self-evident variety of the economic philosophies in, and performance of, ASEAN points to centrifugal forces being greater than integrative pressures and is cause for continued alarm.[25]

The AEC has been explained partly by reference to the wrong investment decisions of Asian governments (input driven development instead of total factor productivity growth). These decisions have allowed parastatals, government-related firms and *Chaebols* to expand and gain market-shares,[26] either in areas of limited competence (Indonesia's once aerospace ambitions is a vivid example), or on the back of cheap capital cost and uncompetitive loan financing. Furthermore, this occurred without the disciplining forces of shareholders and shareholder value (the docility of Japanese and South Korean shareholders is legendary). Interestingly, the presence of the Variable – Non-Market Pricing/Price Controls – in the Factor points to adequate risk assessments being compromised by cronyism.

Factor 2 – Non-Predictable Regulations and Poor Physical & Commercial Infrastructure – is significant and extremely reliable. Par excellence, post-AEC rationalizations have focused on the volatility of regulations, non-transparency, red-tape, obfuscation and obscurantism and attendant policy instabilities that have been telling features, at a regional level, of the Asian business and commercial landscape with few notable exceptions (Singapore and Hong Kong).[27] The Variable – Rules Volatility – accounts for over 60 percent of the variation in this important Factor. It is posited that the widespread inability of Asian authorities since mid-1997 to manage legislation, and establish appropriate legal structures for dealing with bankruptcies and permitting necessary industrial restructuring and economic reform, is evidence of this signal.

Factor 3 – Lack of Quality Management and Skills – reflects Asia's eroding competitive advantage i.e. low cost labor. Moreover, the asymmetric distribution of managerial capabilities in Asia, in retrospect, has exacerbated the problems of the AEC. It is not unreasonable to suggest that this Factor points to frictions apparent in the reorganizing of operations and assets of ASEAN government-related firms, Japanese *Keiretsu* and South Korean *Chaebols* due not only to their unchanging predilection for revenue over profitability but also to their addiction to debt in preference to equity.[28]

Factor 4 – Intra-ASEAN Non-Tariff Barriers – would need to be viewed in the light of Factors of historic and future motives for FDI which emphasize ASEAN market access arrangements and the ex-ante conducive environment. The past is little guide for the future as MNEs (usually those with 'outsider' status) perceive non-tariff barriers as impediments to their FDI. It is evident that ASEAN's progress towards the ASEAN Free Trade Area (AFTA) and ASEAN Investment Area (AIA) is hampered by the diversity in its members' economic performance and inability to remove tariffs.

Tables C1 and C2 point to the discernible consistency of country and region level signals in terms of non-conducive regulation and restrictive practices,[29] as well as lack of higher levels of locally available managerial skills.

Policy Framework for Increasing Attractiveness of Host Country

The six Factors (Table C3) that constitute this construct – Market and Policy Information Provision especially for SMEs, Completion of AFTA, Specific ASEAN-wide Assistance and Schemes, ASEAN-wide Risk Reduction Schemes especially for SMEs, ASEAN-wide FDI Policies, and Regional Economic and Political Stability – some of which are highly significant and very reliable measures, point to the persistent problems of doing business in Asia. Factor 1 – Market and Policy Information Provision especially for SMEs – though not reliable is highly significant and reflects the presence of debilitating information asymmetries and absence of transparency as a barrier to FDI in Asia. Not only are search costs of information high but also the results are often contradictory. Information asymmetries have been proposed as contributing to the AEC.

Concerning Factors 2 and 4, although individual Factors – Completion of AFTA, and ASEAN-wide Risk Reduction Schemes especially for SMEs – are not significant, each is reliable. However, Factors 3 and 5 – Specific ASEAN-wide Assistance and Schemes, and ASEAN-wide FDI Policies – are very reliable and highly significant. Together these four Factors are powerfully suggestive of signals. Although intra-ASEAN trade is extensive[30] the nature of the archipelago's fragmented markets points to difficulties for integrated international sourcing, production and marketing and the need to cohere individual Hosts into a regional economic bloc with 'single market' dimensions. The idea of a 'single currency' for Asia has been raised seriously. However, the AEC, although producing worthy reactions about the urgency for regionalism and acceleration of the AFTA process, also has exposed ASEAN's relatively weak institutional intentions. Factor 4 with its emphasis on SMEs is germane. The industrial dynamics of SMEs, in terms of innovation and its employment effects in the presence of severe resource constraints, are well documented.

Factor 6 – Regional Economic and Political Stability – is highly significant and reliable and reinforces the other Factors that are barriers to FDI. MNEs perceive that at the Host country level, insufficient is being done to improve policies for stability of the regional political economy. This is a clear signal reflecting Asia's crisis points.[31]

Policy Framework for Increasing Attractiveness for Intra-ASEAN FDI

Six Factors constitute this construct (Table C4) – ASEAN-wide Information and Market Services especially for SMEs, ASEAN-wide Trade Policy Harmonization, Increased Regional Political and Economic Stability, ASEAN-wide FDI Policies, Specific ASEAN-wide Assistance Schemes, and ASEAN-wide Risk Reduction Schemes for SMEs – but are not statistically significant or reliable except Factor 1 – ASEAN-wide Information and Market Services especially for SME, and Factor 5 – Specific ASEAN-wide Assistance Scheme. Again MNEs are signaling that, despite the nature of intra-Asian exports, lack of 'info-structure' and assistance to firms to overcome difficulties require addressing. The consistency of responses at the country and regional level deserves mention. Clearly, the absence of frameworks for creating, and benefiting from, 'single market' co-ordination dynamics is a major concern for MNEs and, in the event of the AEC, has resulted in unilateral policy decisions that have produced adverse and detrimental effects. In this regard, the capital controls imposed by Malaysia, and its neighborly effects on Singapore in particular, is a case in point.

Policy Framework for Increasing Attractiveness for ASEAN as a Region

There are six Factors (Table C5) that point to making the region more attractive – Enhanced Specific ASEAN-wide Assistance and Schemes, Regional Political and Economic Stability, ASEAN-wide FDI Policies, Completion of AFTA, ASEAN-wide Risk Reduction Schemes especially for SMEs, and ASEAN-wide Information and Market Service especially for SMEs – that are all significant and reliable except – *Completion of AFTA*. The implication is that these policies are established insufficiently and reflect the fragmented nature of the region.

When viewed in concert, Tables C3, C4, C5 show remarkable coherence. Clearly, the operations of MNEs provide a robust mechanism for signaling difficulties. The question is, given the behavioral theories of FDI (Aharoni, 1966; Knickerbocker, 1973) and evidence of the 'herd behavior' (World Bank, 1998/99, p.48), how MNEs react to their own signaling is of immense interest for further research. It is particularly relevant in the area of incumbency and strategy. Here the political dimension of IB comes clearly into focus and the pre-AEC persistence of certain political regimes, or rather the persistence of 'Asian values' translated as ways of economic performance, deserves further attention.[32]

Concluding Comments

In exploring managerial predictors of the AEC from the perspective of MNEs, three observations are cogent. The first is that at the time of formulating the research instrumentation and data acquisition, Asia's economic growth was 'assured'. Hence the presence, at the frequency level of analysis, of 'obstacles' was given insufficient critical attention. Second, Extracted Factors point to the contradictory behavior of MNEs. It is apparent that while MNEs indicate their misapprehensions, they were up to and beyond mid-1997 pouring investment capital into the region. This mentality is understandable but does not invalidate the revealed signals to the AEC. Third, it may be arguable that, without a formal predictive model, Extracted Factors do not have a rigorous context. We would counter with two arguments. The first refers to the problematic of confirmatory factor analysis and its requirements for correct model specification and the danger of modeling being either specification or data bound. The second refers to the fact that at the time of survey, the economic performance of Asia (even with anecdotal evidence and experiences of obstacles and impediments to FDI) was astonishing. Consequently, priorities of looking for patterns of success, and continued success, far outweighed the search for clues as to why the 'Asian miracle' should not continue.

The Extracted Factors are statistically robust and powerful signals of the shortcomings in the managerial dimension of Asia's economic 'miracle'. Subsequent explanations of the unprecedented regional collapse are laden with the above Factors. There is usually a lag between macro-economic phenomena like the AEC and its general equilibrium effects. The analysis herein not only points to the value of perceptions and their concrete indices that have as their source micro-level operations; also, it enables a more coherent integration of macro-economic and micro-economic factors in IB.

The data, in the light of this exploration, is capable of yielding further exciting insights and invites analysis along at least two dimensions. Firstly, a cross-sectional analysis of different source MNEs. It may well be that MNEs, irrespective of source, share the same view as to the obstacles and managerial impediments to FDI. The recent report by UNCTAD-ICC (1998) suggests that MNEs from Europe, North America, and Japan behave similarly with respect to the aftermath of the AEC. Secondly, an analysis of different sectors within and across source MNEs. It may well be that different industrial sectors perceive the obstacles to FDI in different ways and at different levels of intensity. This is not unreasonable given the ambitions of Hosts in creating certain strategic industries. Lastly, now that the AEC is some four years in evolution, a reapplication of the survey may yield a data set useful in modeling firm predictors in confirmatory factor analysis.

Notes

1.   Rescuing the firm would have consumed US$ 6.7 Billion or 3.5 percent of Thailand's GDP!
2.   See Reuters, OECD paints grim outlook for Asia, The Straits Times, 18th November 1998, p.59 and Christopher Wood, Asia's Still Fragile Recovery, The Asian Wall Street Journal, 6th January 1999, p.8 for the extent of the regional economic contraction.
3.   Jim Walker, Chief Economist of Credit Lyonnais Securities reported in January 1995 on the potential of Thailand to emulate Mexico in a currency crisis [The Straits Times, 23rd March 1998, p.34-35].
4.   These figures are extracted from the UNCTAD-DTCI Database; the European Commission UNCTAD-DTCI Report, Investing in Asia's Dynamism, July 1996, and UNCTAD World Investment Report 1996.
5.   The World Bank estimates that private capital flows to Developing Countries increased to US$244 Billion in 1996 [Global Development Finance Report] cited in The Economist, 29th March 1997, p.128.
6.   Pressures that have coerced 18 Asian-Pacific countries to initiate the Asia-Pacific Economic Co-operation Forum (APEC) may be encapsulated by needing 'a tool for prising open fast-growing Asian markets' [Guy de Jonquieres, 1994, Different aims, common causes, Financial Times, 18th November, p.16] due to the expansion of intra-regional trade.

Intra-regional Trade – Percentage of Total World Trade

Region	1938	1955	1969	1979	1985	1990
East Asia	10.0	2.2	2.9	4.2	6.4	7.9
North America	3.0	6.7	6.9	4.2	6.4	5.3
Pacific Region	18.0	13.5	16.9	15.6	24.8	24.6
Western Europe	18.2	19.6	28.7	29.3	27.1	33.8

Source: Financial Times, 10th November 1994, p.4

7.   This performance is no less due to the formidable World competitiveness of ASEAN notably Singapore which has been ranked the World's second most competitive economy (behind that of USA) for the fourth consecutive year since 1993 by the Swiss-based Institute for Management Development (IMD) World Competitiveness Project. On a wider regional level, it is noteworthy that Hong Kong ranks at number three in the World's ten leading competitive economies [The Straits Times, 26th March 1997, p.40].
8.   See Mike Loh, US pillar of growth stands on shaky ground, The Business Times, 22nd January 1999, p.10 for the post hoc ergo propter hoc perspective that 'any problem that existed before the onset of the crisis is automatically a cause of the crisis itself.' Attributed to James D. Wolfhensohn – President of the World Bank.
9.   See Financial Times Survey, 1996, International Capital Markets, Financial Times, London.
10.   See Milton Freidman, Markets To The Rescue, The Asian Wall Street Journal, 14th October 1998, p.10.
11.   See The Straits Times, 3rd September 1998, p.49-50 for a vivid illustration of this tension in Malaysia's response to the Asian Crisis and its own recession.
12.   See M. Clifford, M. Ihlwan, J. Rossant, K. Naughton, P. Engardio, 'The Age of The Deal', Business Week, 2nd March 1998, p.16-20; and K. Y. Lee, 'East Asian govts have

to take painful reforms, says S. M. Lee', The Straits Times, 21st February 1998, p.48.

13.   The IMF-IBRD led resolution of the 1982 international debt crisis involving Latin America and Sub-Saharan Africa was arguably in this vein; and see Avoiding a world slump, The Straits Times, 2nd September 1998, p.34 for a measure of the equity asset values lost by investors.

14.   See Jeffrey D. Sachs, The Wrong Medicine for Asia, 3rd November 1997, New York Times, Internet Version accessed 30th March 1998 for this viewpoint; Linda Lim, 'Asian values' idea: Is it out?, The Sunday Times, 29th March 1998, p.36-37; The Sunday Times, US expert slams 'snake-oil' cures, 29th March 1998, p.4 for an appreciation of the vituperative nature of the arguments; See The Straits Times, Coping with a crisis of legitimacy, 26th March 1998, p.24-25; and Mahathir Mohamad, Call Me A Heretic, Time, 14th September 1998, p.21.

15.   See Asad Latif, Radical times require radical thinkers, The Straits Times, 17th October 198, p.66.

16.   See Europe Asia Forum, Next Century will still belong to the US says Hurd, The Sunday Times, 22nd February 1998, p.25 for an informed view on the geo-strategic capability of the remaining superpower.

17.   See Let's not rip Central Asia apart for its oil: US policy-maker, Reuter, The Straits Times 23rd July 1997, p.4; Ahmed Rashid, Power Play, Far Eastern Economic Review, 10th April 1997, vol. 160, No. 15, pp.22-33 for an analysis of how the interests of state and MNEs are affecting the political economy of Central Asia; and Sunanda K. Datta, Will History repeat itself in Russia?, The Straits Times 12th September 1998, p.45 for an analysis of the fusion of State-MNEs interests.

18.   See W. R. Mead, Markets are biggest threat to peace, The Straits Times, 29th August 1998, p.46.

19.   See The Economist, The World Economy, 5th September 1998, p.17-19; David Smith and Norman Stone, Will The west get Vertigo, The Sunday Times, 6th September 1998, Internet Version, http://www.Sunday-times.co.uk, accessed 6th September 1998 and G. Pierre Goad, Great Depression Redux?, The Asian Wall Street Journal, Survival Guide: Where to Invest in 1999, 11th January 1999, p.5.

20.   See The Economist, Second thoughts about globalization, 21st June 1997, p.90.

21.   Globalization has its fair share of adherents, however, is called into question by others notably; Korten (1995). There is wide consensus accepting the profoundness of changes being wrought by long-term reduction of barriers to investment and trade in technological, informatics and policy areas.

22.   See Bartels F. L., Pavier B. H., 1997, ENRON in India: Developing Political Capability: An Imperative for Multinational Enterprise in an Era of Globalization, Economic and Political Weekly, vol. XXXII, No. 8, February 22-28, p.M11-M20 for an in-depth analysis and discussion of the real-politik of FDI in an economic environment characterized by fusion of markets (deepening access and efficiency gains) and fission of nation-states (thinning of central political authority).

23.   See Lester Thurow, 1996, The Future of Capitalism, Nicholas Brealey, London, p.8-19 for a conceptualization of economic forces in terms of plate tectonics.

24.   There are effectively well over 600 variables (actually 639) in the questionnaire and given 394 cases in total (interviews and postal responses) the total number of observations in the Bradford ASEAN FD1 Database contains in the region of a quarter of a million observations.

25.   The political economic structure of pre-AEC ASEAN may be conveniently, though not without contention, configured in terms of low population – high income, middle population – middle income, and high population – low income and low population – low income as shown below:

Members Configuration	Population (Millions)	GDP/Capita (US$)
Low Population – High Income		
Singapore	3.1	22,520
Brunei	0.3	20,000
Middle Population – Middle Income		
Malaysia	20.1	3,530
Thailand	60.6	2,315
High Population – Low Income		
Indonesia	196.5	780
Philippines	67.7	1,010
Vietnam	74.6	220
Myanmar	47	250
Low Population – Low Income		
Cambodia	10.5	270
Laos	4	350

Source: 1995 ASEAN Secretariat

26.   See Douglas Wong, The Straits Times, 7th February 1997, p.30 and 27th February 1997, p.48; Ho Wah Foon, The Straits Times, 24th January 1997, p.80; Quak Hlang Whai, The Straits Times, 25th February 1997, p.40 for contemporary analysis of the 'push' factor – essentially the Government – driving Singapore's outward FDI strategy that has been emulated by other Asian countries – Malaysia for instance.

27.   See Corruption In Asia In 1998, excerpted from Asian Intelligence Issue #507, 1 April 1998; and Transparency Problems in Asia, excerpted from Asian Intelligence Issue #523, 25th November 1998.

28.   See Report by the Institute of International Finance, Capital Flows to Emerging Market Economies, 29th January 1998, p.12 indicating that the average debt-equity ratio of South Korea's top 30 Chaebols stood at approximately 400 percent in 1996.

29.   See for example Clarissa Tan, High-level panel urges full foreign participation in S'pore banking, The Business Times, 27th January 1999, p.1 for an appreciation of the issues.

30.   The following provides ample evidence of this trends for Asia:

Intra-regional Trade

Intra-regional exports as percentage of total exports

Region	1989	1996
Within Asia	31.4	40.4
Within Latin America	15.3	20.3
Within Europe	31.2	36.3

Source: Finance & Development, June 1998, p.12

31.   See Asia's political faultlines, The Economist, 14-20 March 1998; and Asia's delicate balance, The Economist, 25-31 July 1998.

32.   See Kwok Kian-Woon, Asian Crisis as A Moral Crisis, The Sunday Times, 24th January 1999, p.45.

References

Aharoni, Y. (1966), *The Foreign Investment Decision Process*. Boston, Mass: Graduate School of Business Administration, Harvard University.

Bartels, F. L. and N. J. Freeman. (1995), '*Multinational Enterprises in Emerging Markets: International Joint Ventures in Cote D'Ivoire and Vietnam*', University of Bradford Management Centre, Working Paper Series, No. 6405, December, Bradford.

Bartels, F. L. and N. J. Freeman. (1995), 'European Multinational Enterprises in two Francophone Emerging Markets: Evidence from International Joint Ventures in Cote D'Ivoire and Vietnam', *Proceedings of the 21st Annual Conference of the European International Business Academy*, Urbino, Italy, December, pp.87-107.

Bartels, F. L., Hafiz Mirza and Kee Hwee. (1997), 'Locational Strategy and Foreign Direct Investment of Operations in Asia-Pacific: An Empirical Study of Multinational Enterprise Business Development', *Proceedings of An International Conference on Business Development Strategies in Asia-Pacific*, University of Brunei, 21-22 November, pp.53-77.

Berry, B. J. L. (1991), *Long-wave Rhythms in Economic Development and Political Behaviour*, John Hopkins Univ. Press, Baltimore.

Boddewyn, J., T. L. Brewer. (1994), 'International Business-Political Behavior: New Theoretical Directions', *Academy of Management Review*, vol. 19(1), pp.119-143.

Bryman, A., D. Cramer. (1990), *Quantitative Data Analysis for Social Scientists*, Routlegde, London.

Brzezinski, Z. (1998), *The Grand Chess Board: American Primacy and its Geostrategic Imperative*, Basic Books, New York.

Buckley, P. J. (1988), 'The Limits of Explanation: Testing the Internalization Theory of Multinational Enterprise', *Journal of International Business Studies*, vol. 19(2), pp.181-193.

Cattell, R. B. (1952), *Factor Analysis: An Introduction and Manual for the Psychologist and Social Scientist*, Harper and Row, New York.

Cattell, R. B. (1966), 'The Screen Test for the Number of Factors', *Multivariate Behavioural Research*, vol. 1, pp.245-276.

Campbell, D. T., D. W. Fiske. (1959), 'Convergent and Discriminant Validation by the Multitrait-Multimethod index', *Psychological Bulletin*, vol. 56: pp.81-105.

Chomsky, N., E. S. Herman. (1973), *The United States versus Human Rights in The Third World: The Pentagon-CIA Archipelago*, Basic Books, New York.

Comrey, A. L. (1973), *A First Course in Factor Analysis*, New York: Academic Press.

Cronbach, L. J. and P. E. Meehl. (1955), 'Construct Validity in Psychological Testing', *Psychological Bulletin*, vol. 52, pp.282-302.

Egelhoff, W. G. (1991), 'Information-Processing Theory and The Multinational Enterprise' *Journal of International Business Studies*, vol. 22(3), pp.341-368.

Erramilli, M. K. (1991), 'The Experience Factor in Foreign Market Entry Behaviour of Service Firms', *Journal of International Business Studies*, 22(3): 479-501.

Fallows, J. (1993), 'How the World Works', *The Atlantic Monthly*, December, Internet Version, http://www.theatlantic.com, accessed 7th September 1998.

Fallows, J. (1994), 'What is an Economy for?' *The Atlantic Monthly*, January, Internet Version, http://www.theatlantic.com, accessed 7th September 1998.

Fischer, S. (1998), 'Economic Crises and The Financial Sector, Paper presented at Federal Deposit Insurance Corporation Conference on Deposit Insurance', 10 September, Washington DC, Internet Source, http://www.imf.org, accessed 13th September 1998.

Fleenor, D. (1993), 'The Coming and Going of the Global Corporation', *Columbia Journal of World Business*, vol. 28(4), pp.7-16.

Fortin, C. (1994), 'The Drivers of World Prosperity', *Business Strategy Review*, vol. 5(3), pp.69-83.

Ghoshal, S., Bartlett, C. A. (1990), 'The Multinational Enterprise as an Interorganizational Network', *Academy of Management Review*, 15(4), pp.603-626.

Godement, F. (1999), *The Downsizing of Asia*, Routledge, London.

Grosse, R. E., Behrman, J. N. (1992), 'Theory in International Business', *Transnational Corporations*, vol. 1(1), pp.93-126.

Harman, H. H. (1967), *Modern Factor Analysis*, Univ. Chicago Press, Chicago.

Inkpen, A. C., Beamish, P. W. (1994), 'An Analysis of Twenty-five Years of Research in The Journal of International Business Studies', *Journal of International Business Studies*, vol. 25(4), pp.703-713.

Johanson, J., Vahlne, J. E. (1977), 'The Internationalization Process of the Firm – a model of knowledge development and increasing foreign market commitments', *Journal of Interntional Business Studies*, vol. 8(1), pp.23-32.

Johanson, J., Wiedersheim-Paul, P. (1975), 'The Internationalization of the Firm – four Swedish Cases', *Journal of Management Studies*, October, pp.305-322.

Kanter, B. M. (1989), *When Giants Learn to Dance*, Unwin, London.

Kaiser, H. F. (1974), 'An Index of Factorial Simplicity', *Psychometrika*, 39: 31-36.

Kim, W. C., Hwang, P. (1992), 'Global Strategy and Multinationals' Entry Mode Choice', *Journal of International Business Studies*, vol. 23, No. 1, 1st Qtr, pp.29-53.

Kim, Jae-On and Meuller, C. W. (1978), *Factor Analysis: Statistical Methods and Practical Issues*, Sage, London.

Kindleberger, C. P. (1970), *Power and Money*, Basic Books, New York.

Knickerbocker, F. T. (1973), *Oligopolistic Reaction and Multinational Enterprise*, Boston: Harvard Business School.

Korten, D. C. (1995), *When Corporations Rule the World*, Earthscan, London.

Krugman, P. (1994), 'The Myth of Asia's Miracle', *Foreign Affairs*, vol. 73(6), pp.62-78.

Labovitz, S. (1970), 'The Assignment of Numbers to Rank Order Categories', *American Sociological Review*, vol. 35, pp.515-525.

Labovitz, S. (1971), 'In Defense of Assigning Numbers to Ranks', *American Sociological Review*, vol. 36, pp.521-522.

Mathieson, D. J., Richards, A. and Sharma, S. (1999), 'Financial Crises in Emerging Markets', *Finance & Development*, vol. 35(4), pp.28-31.

Mirza, H., Hwee W. K. and Bartels, F. A. (1998), 'Towards a Strategy for Enhancing ASEAN's Locational Advantages for Attracting Greater Foreign Direct Investment', in K. W. Radtke (ed.), *Dynamics in Pacific Asia*, Kegan Paul International, London.

Mitnick, B. M. (1993), *Corporate Political Agency: The Construction of Competition in Public Affairs*, Sage, Newbury Park.

Moran, R. T. and Reisenberger, J. R. (1994), *The Global Challenge: Building the New Worldwide Enterprise*, McGraw Hill, London.

Mudambi, R. (1998), 'The Role of Duration in Multinational Investment Strategies', *Journal of International Business Studies*, vol. 29(2), pp.239-261.

Norusis, M. J. (1990), *SPSS: Base System User's Guide*, SPSS Inc, Chicago.

Nunnally, J. C. (1967), *Psychometric Theory*, McGraw-Hill, London.

Oman, C. (1984), *New Forms of Investment Flows to Developing Countries*, OECD, Paris.

Oman, C. (1994), *Globalization and Regionalization: The Challenge for Developing Countries*, OECD, Paris.

Ozawa, T. (1990), 'Multinational Corporations and the 'flying geese' paradigm of economic development in the Asian Pacific Region', Paper presented at 20th Anniversary World Conference on Multinational Enterprises and 21st Century Scenarios, Tokyo.

Ozawa, T. (1992), 'Foreign Direct Investment and Economic Development', *Transnational Corporations*, vol. 1(1), pp.27-54.

Rummel, R. J. (1970), *Applied Factor Analysis*, Northwestern University Press, Evanston.

Sampson, A. (1975), *The Seven Sisters: The Great Oil Companies and the World they Made*, Hodder and Stoughton, London.

Sevant-Schreiber, J. J. (1980), *The American Challenge*, Atheneum, New York.

Thurow, L. (1996), *The Future of Capitalism*, Nicholas Brealey, London.

UNCTC (1992), *World Investment Report 1992 Transnational Corporations as Engines of Growth*, United Nations, New York.

UNCTAD (1993), *World Investment Report: Transnational Corporations and Integrated International Production*, United Nations, New York.

UNCTAD (1994), *World Investment Report: Transnational Corporations, Employment and The Workplace*, United Nations, New York.

UNCTAD (1996), *Trade and Development Report 1996*, United Nations, Geneva.

UNCTAD (1997), *World Investment Report 1997, Transnational Corporations, Market Structure and Competition Policy*, United Nations, New York.

UNCTAD-ICC (1998), 'The Financial Crisis in Asia and Foreign Direct Investment', Internet Version, http://www.unctad.org/en/pressref/bg9802en.htm, accessed 27th March 1998.

Vernon, R. (1966), 'International Investment and International Trade in the Product Cycle', *Journal of Economics*, vol. 80, pp.190-207.

Vernon, R. (1971), *Sovereignty at Bay*, Basic Books, New York.

Vernon, R. (1977), *Storm over the Multinationals*, Harvard University Press, Cambridge.

Vernon, R. (1992), 'Transnational Corporations: Where are they coming from, where are they headed?', *Transnational Corporations*, vol. 1(2), pp.7-35.

Wyplosz, C. (1998), 'Globalized Financial markets and Financial Crises', Paper presented at Conference on Coping with Financial Crises in Developing and Transition Countries: Regulatory and Supervisory Challenges in a New Era of Global Finance, Forum on Debt and Development, Amsterdam.

World Bank (1993), *The East Asia Miracle*, World Bank, Washington DC.

World Bank (1998/99), Global Economic Prospects and the Developing Countries: Beyond Financial Crisis, World Bank, Washington DC.

Appendix

Table C1 Host Location Barriers and Managerial Impediments to Foreign Direct Investment

KMO: 0.96435[a]   No of Factors Extracted: 4

RESIDUALS: 12.0 percent (Variation not accounted for by extracted factors)

Factor/Variables/ Other Items	Variable Names/Variation Explained by Factor/Reportage of Significance and Reliability	Factor Names/Variation Explained by Variables/Comments
Factor 1	64.5 percent	Political Instability and
(31 Variables)		Restrictive Regulations
• No of cases	65	**Low Reportage**
• Significance	0.0764	Highly Significant
• Alpha	0.9924	Extremely Reliable
• Variable 1	Political Instability	73.2 percent
• Variable 2	Lack of Privatization Programme	2.9 percent
• Variable 3	Foreign Exchange Controls	2.6 percent
• Variable 4	Inappropriate Tax Regime	1.9 percent
• Variable 5	Limits on Inward Investment	1.7 percent
• Variable 6	Legal & Regulatory Restrictrictions	1.7 percent
• Variable 7	Tariff Barriers	1.5 percent
• Variable 8	Non Tariff Barriers	1.4 percent
• Variable 9	Testing Requirements	1.4 percent
• Variable 10	Regional Instability	1.2 percent
• Variable 11	Pressure against Profit Repatriation	1.0 percent
	Pressure against Royalties Repat.	1.0 percent (Cum 91.4 percent)
Factor 2	3.5 percent	Poor Infrastructure and Non-
(5 Variables)		Transparency

- No of cases — 61 — **Low Reportage**
- Significance — 0.0000 — **Highly Significant**
- Alpha — 0.8379 — Reliable
- Variable 1 — Poor Physical Infrastructure — 57.2 percent
- Variable 2 — Language/Cultural Barriers — 13.6 percent
- Variable 3 — Bureaucracy — 12.5 percent
- Variable 4 — Rules Volatility — 9.7 percent
- Variable 5 — Other Specific Barriers — 7.0 percent (Cum 100 percent)

Factor 3 — 2.7 percent — Lack of Quality Management and
(3 Variables) — Skills
- No of cases — 78 — **Low Reportage**
- Significance — 0.3041 — Not Significant
- Alpha — 0.8251 — Reliable
- Variable 1 — Lack of Quality Managers — 69.9 percent
- Variable 2 — Low Quality Inputs — 17.4 percent
- Variable 3 — Lack of Suitable Skilled Manpower — 12.7 percent (Cum 100 percent)

Factor 4 — 2.5 percent — High labor Costs
(1 Variable)
- No of cases etc — Na
- Variable 1 — High labor Costs — 100 percent

a – Marvellous KMO

Table C2 ASEAN Regional Barriers and Managerial Impediments to Foreign Direct Investment

KMO: 0.95245[a]   No of Factors Extracted: 4

RESIDUALS: 16.0 percent (Variation not accounted for by extracted factors)

Factor/Variables/ Other Items	Variable Names/Variation Explained by Factor/Reportage of Significance and Reliability	Factor Names/Variation Explained by Variables/Comments
Factor 1 (25 Variables)	59.9 percent	Lack of Potential Partners/Targets and State Intervention
• No of cases	63	**Low Reportage**
• Significance	0.2237	**Not Significant** (but factors 1A and
• Alpha	0.9856	1B are significant; see note below) Extremely Reliable
• Variable 1	Lack of Potential Partners	70.7 percent
• Variable 2	Socio-economic Intervention	4.3 percent
• Variable 3	Exclusionary Business Practices	3.0 percent
• Variable 4	No Privatisation Programme	2.5 percent
• Variable 5	Lack of Firms to Acquire	2.1 percent
• Variable 6	Testing Requirements	1.9 percent
• Variable 7	Attitude to Private Sector	1.7 percent
• Variable 8	High labor Costs	1.6 percent
• Variable 9	Political Intervention	1.4 percent
• Variable 10	Pressure against Royalty Payments	1.2 percent
	Non-Market Pricing/Price Controls	1.2 percent (Cum 91.8 percent)

NOTE ON FACTOR 1

Refining the factor analysis results in two sub-factors. A lack of **potential partners** accounts for 75 percent of the variation in factor 1A. **Economic Instability accounts** for 71.2 percent of variation in factor 1B. However, factor 1A accounts for 70.7 percent of all variation in factor 1, whereas factor 1B accounts for only 4.3 percent.

Factor 2 (9 Variables)	5.5 percent	Non-Predictable Regulations & Poor Physical & Commercial Infrastructure
• No of cases	71	**Low Reportage**
• Significance	0.1273	Significant
• Alpha	0.9377	Extremely Reliable
• Variable 1	Rules Volatility	61.3 percent

•	Variable 2	Poor Physical Infrastructure	7.9 percent
•	Variable 3	Bureaucracy	6.7 percent
•	Variable 4	Legal & Regulatory Restrictions	5.6 percent
•	Variable 5	Language/Cultural Barriers	5.0 percent
•	Variable 6	Inadequate Legal Infrastructure.	4.6 percent
•	Variable 7	Financial Risk	3.4 percent
•	Variable 8	Inadequate Commercial Infrastructure	2.8 percent
		Political Instability	2.6 percent (Cum 100 percent)
Factor 3		3.6 percent	Lack of Quality Management and
(4 Variables)			Skills
•	No of cases	74	**Low Reportage**
•	Significance	0.0007	Highly Significant
•	Alpha	0.8184	Reliable
•	Variable 1	Lack of Quality Managers	62.5 percent
•	Variable 2	Lack of Suitable Skilled Manpower	18.0 percent
•	Variable 3	Low Quality Inputs	12.6 percent
•	Variable 4	Low Educational Levels	7.0 percent (Cum 100 percent)
Factor 4		3.2 percent	Intra-ASEAN Non-Tariff Barriers
(1 Variable)			
•	No of cases	Na	
•	Significance	na	
•	Alpha	na	
•	Variable 1	Other Specific Barriers (NTBs)	

a – Marvellous KMO

Table C3 Policy Framework for Increasing Attractiveness of Host Location for Foreign Direct Investment

KMO: 0.79712[a]   No of Factors Extracted: 6
RESIDUALS: 41 percent (Variation not accounted for by extracted factors)

Factor/Variables/ Other Items	Variable Names/Variation Explained by Factor/Reportage of Significance and Reliability	Factor Names/Variation Explained by Variables/Comments
Factor 1 (3 Variables)	32.0 percent	Market & Policy Information Provision specially for SMEs.
• No of cases	131	High Reportage
• Significance	0.0000	Highly Significant
• Alpha	0.4123	Not Reliable
• Variable 1	Prov. of ASEAN-wide Mkt Info (SMEs)	53.0 percent
• Variable 2	ASEAN-wide Data/Info Banks (SMEs)	33.2 percent
• Variable 3	ASEAN Trade Policy Harmonisation	13.9 percent (Cum 100 percent) *Variable 3 Negatively Correlated with Factor: harmonisation means less searching is needed*
Factor 2 (2 Variables)	9.7 percent	Completion of AFTA
• No of cases	154	High Reportage
• Significance	0.8664	**Not Significant**
• Alpha	0.6585	Reasonably Reliable
• Variable 1	Completion of AFTA	74.1 percent
• Variable 2	Tackle Non Tariff Barriers	25.95 (Cum 100 percent)
Factor 3 (6 Variables)	7.6 percent	Specific ASEAN-wide Assistance and Schemes
• No of cases	117	Medium Reportage
• Significance	0.0000	Highly Significant
• Alpha	0.8793	Very Reliable

•	Variable 1	Enhance BBC Scheme	57.1 percent
•	Variable 2	ASEAN-wide Proj.Man. Ass. (SMEs)	15.2 percent
•	Variable 3	ASEAN-wide Contact Brokers (SMEs)	8.7 percent
•	Variable 4	Enhance AIJV Scheme	7.2 percent
•	Variable 5	Launch Further ASEAN Schemes	6.6 percent
•	Variable 6	ASEAN-wide Awareness Serv.(SMEs)	5.2 percent (Cum 100 percent)
Factor 4		5.9 percent	ASEAN Wide Risk Reduction
(4 Variables)			Schemes, especially for SMEs
•	No of cases	4	**Low Reportage**
•	Significance	0.4363	**Not Significant**
•	Alpha	0.9868	Extremely Reliable
•	Variable 1	ASEAN-wide Arbitration Serv. (SMEs)	55.0 percent
•	Variable 2	Other ASEAN-Wide Schemes	22.0 percent
•	Variable 3	ASEAN-wide Financial Ass.(SMEs)	13.3 percent
•	Variable 4	ASEAN-wide FDI Guarantees (SMEs)	9.7 percent (Cum 100 percent)
Factor 5		5.5 percent	ASEAN-Wide FDI Policies
(4 Variables)			*Variables Negatively Correlated with Factor: Such policies further intra-ASEAN FDI.*
•	No of cases	135	High Reportage
•	Significance	0.0000	Highly Significant
•	Alpha	0.7614	Reliable
•	Variable 1	Establish Complementary FDI Policies	55.7 percent
•	Variable 2	ASEAN FDI Policy Harmonisation	19.0 percent
•	Variable 3	Enhanced Investment Guarantees	16.3 percent
•	Variable 4	Joint FDI Promotion By AS. Govts.	9.0 percent (Cum 100 percent)
Factor 6		4.7 percent	Regional Economic and Political
(3 Variables)			Stability
•	No of cases	151	High Reportage
•	Significance	0.0001	Highly Significant
•	Alpha	0.7437	Reliable
•	Variable 1	Regional Pol. to Improve Ec. Stability	65.7 percent
•	Variable 2	Regional Pol. to Improve Pol. Stability	25.2 percent
•	Variable 3	Measures to Fascilitate Flow of Goods	9.1 percent (Cum 100 percent)

a – Meritorious KMO

Table C4 Policy Framework for Increasing Attractiveness for Intra-ASEAN Foreign Direct Investment

KMO: 0.79933[a]   No of Factors Extracted: 6

RESIDUALS: 35.0 percent (Variation not accounted for by extracted factors)

Factor/Variables/ Other Items	Variable Names/Variation Explained by Factor/Reportage of Significance and Reliability	Factor Names/Variation Explained by Variables/Comments
Factor 1 (5 Variables)	29.3 percent	ASEAN-wide Information and Market Services, especially for SMEs
• No of cases	119	Medium Reportage
• Significance	0.0000	Highly Significant
• Alpha	0.8337	Reliable
• Variable 1	ASEAN-wide Info Banks (SMEs)	59.9
• Variable 2	ASEAN-wide Awareness Serv. (SMEs)	15.7
• Variable 3	ASEAN-wide Contact Brokers (SMEs)	11.2
• Variable 4	ASEAN-wide Prov. of Mkt Info (SMEs)	7.7
• Variable 5	ASEAN-wide Project Man. Ass. (SMEs)	5.5 (Cum. 100 percent)

Factor/Variables /Other Items	Variable Names/Variation Explained by Factor/Reportage of Significance and Reliability	Factor Names/Variation Explained by Variables/Comments
Factor 2 (4 Variables)	11.9 percent	ASEAN-Wide Trade Policy Harmonisation
• No of cases	133	High Reportage
• Significance	0.1679	Low Significance
• Alpha	0.7576	Reasonable Reliability
• Variable 1	Asean Trade Policy Harmonisation	56.3
• Variable 2	Completion of AFTA	17.5
• Variable 3	Measures to Tackle NTBs	15.5
• Variable 4	Measures to Facilitate Flow of Goods	10.8 (Cum. 100 percent)
Factor 3 (2 Variables)	7.3 percent	Increased Regional Political and Economic Stability
• No of cases	138	High Reportage
• Significance	0.6846	**Not Significant**
• Alpha	0.7440	Reasonable Reliability
• Variable 1	Regional Pol. to Improve Pol. Stability	79.4
• Variable 2	Regional Pol. to Improve Ec. Stability	20.6 (Cum. 100 percent)
Factor 4 (3 Variables)	6.4 percent	ASEAN-Wide FDI Policies
• No of cases	129	High Reportage
• Significance	0.2580	**Not Significant**
• Alpha	0.6317	Reasonable Reliability
• Variable 1	ASEAN FDI Policy Harmonisation	57.4
• Variable 2	Establish Complementary FDI Policies	23.8
• Variable 3	Enhanced Investment Guarantees	18.8 (Cum. 100 percent)
Factor 5 (4 Variables)	5.4 percent	Specific ASEAN-wide Assistance and Schemes
• No of cases	115	Medium Reportage
• Significance	0.0027	Highly Significant
• Alpha	0.7636	Reasonable Reliability
• Variable 1	Enhanced BBC Scheme	56.2
• Variable 2	Enhanced AIJV Scheme	18.0
• Variable 3	New ASEAN-wide Schemes	15.8
• Variable 4	Joint FDI Promotion By AS. Govts.	10.1 (Cum. 100 percent)
Factor 6 (4 Variables)	4.6 percent	ASEAN Wide Risk Reduction Schemes, especially for SMEs
• No of cases	4	**Low Reportage**
• Significance	0.4363	**Not Significant**
• Alpha	0.9915	Extremely Reliable
• Variable 1	ASEAN-wide Arbitration Serv. (SMEs)	59.0
• Variable 2	Other ASEAN-wide Serv. (SMEs)	18.8
• Variable 3	ASEAN-wide Fin. Ass. Serv. (SMEs)	12.7
• Variable 4	ASEAN-wide FDI Guarantees (SMEs)	9.5 (Cum. 100 percent)

a – Meritorious KMO

Table C5 Policy Framewirk for Increasing Attractiveness of ASEAN as a Region for Foreign Direct Investment

KMO: 0.76749[a]   No of Factors Extracted: 6

RESIDUALS: 46.0 percent (Variation not accounted for by extracted factors)

Factor/Variables /Other Items	Variable Names/Variation Explained by Factor/Reportage of Significance and Reliability	Factor Names/Variation Explained by Variables/Comments
Factor 1 (6 Variables)	24.9 percent	Enhanced Specific ASEAN-wide Assistance and Schemes
• No of cases	114	Medium Reportage
• Significance	0.0952	Significant

•	Alpha	0.8236	Reliable
•	Variable 1	Enhanced BBC Scheme	48.9 percent
•	Variable 2	Enhanced AIJV Scheme	14.5 percent
•	Variable 3	Launch New Schemes	11.8 percent
•	Variable 4	ASEAN-wide Contact Brokers (SMEs)	9.3 percent
•	Variable 5	ASEAN-wide Proj. Man. Ass. (SMEs)	8.3 percent
•	Variable 6	Joint FDI Promotion By AS. Govts.	7.2 percent (Cum 100 percent)
Factor 2 (3 Variables)		11.0 percent	Regional Political and Economic Stability
•	No of cases	151	High Reportage
•	Significance	0.0000	Highly Significant
•	Alpha	0.6776	Reasonable Reliability
•	Variable 1	Regional Pol. to Improve Pol. Stability	60.8 percent
•	Variable 2	Regional Pol. to Improve Ec. Stability	25.3 percent
•	Variable 3	Measures to Fascilitate Flow of Goods	13.9 percent (Cum. 100 percent)
Factor 3 (3 Variables)		6.9 percent	ASEAN-Wide FDI Policies Variables Negatively Correlated with Factor: Such policies tend to further intra-ASEAN FDI in other host countries. See the result for policies to further intra-ASEAN investment.
•	No of cases	138	High Reportage
•	Significance	0.0608	Significant
•	Alpha	0.6322	Reasonable Reliability
•	Variable 1	Enhanced Investment Guarantees	56.0 percent
•	Variable 2	ASEAN FDI Policy Harmonisation	22.9 percent
•	Variable 3	Establish Complementary FDI Policies	21.2 percent
Factor 4 (3 Variables)		6.6 percent	Completion of AFTA
•	No of cases	149	High Reportage
•	Significance	0.3295	**Not Significant**
•	Alpha	0.6337	Reasonable Reliability
•	Variable 1	Completion of AFTA	56.9 percent
•	Variable 2	ASEAN Trade Policy Harmonisation	27.0 percent
•	Variable 3	Tackle NTBS	16.1 percent (Cum 100 percent)
Factor 5 (4 Variables)		5.5 percent	ASEAN Wide Risk Reduction Schemes, especially for SMEs
•	No of cases	7	**Low Reportage**
•	Significance	0.0159	Significant
•	Alpha	0.9610	Extremely Reliable
•	Variable 1	ASEAN-wide Arbitration Serv. (SMEs)	48.8 percent
•	Variable 2	ASEAN-wide Fin. Ass. (SMEs)	22.9 percent
•	Variable 3	Other ASEAN-wide Services	16.8 percent
•	Variable 4	ASEAN-wide FDI Guarantees (SMEs)	11.5 percent (Cum 100 percent)
Factor 6 (3 Variables)		4.9 percent	ASEAN Wide Information and Market Services, especially for SMEs
•	No of cases	129	High Reportage
•	Significance	0.0000	Highly Significant
•	Alpha	0.7378	Reasonable Reliability
•	Variable 1	ASEAN-wide Info Banks (SMEs)	65.6 percent
•	Variable 2	ASEAN-wide Aware. Serv (SMEs)	23.6 percent
•	Variable 3	ASEAN-wide Mkt. Info (SMEs)	10.8 percent (Cum 100 percent)

Chapter 4

International Financial Crises: Causes, Prevention and Cures

Lawrence H. Summers

Introduction

I am sometimes asked by friends about the difference between academic life and life as a public official. There are many. But two stand out. First, as an academic, the gravest sin one can commit is to sign one's name to something one did not write. As a public official it is a mark of effectiveness to do so as often as possible. Second as an academic, if a problem is too hard and does not admit of a satisfactory solution, there is an obvious response: work on a different problem. I have been reminded of this often in recent years as we grappled with financial crisis in a number of what had been considered emerging markets with unrestrained futures. Anyone who doubts the social importance of what. economists do should consider debates surrounding these crises. Hundreds of millions of people who expected rapidly rising standards of living have seen their living standards fall; hundreds and thousands if not millions of children have been forced to drop out of school and go to work; hundreds of billions of dollars of apparent wealth has been lost; the stability of large nations as nations has been called into question; and the United States has made its largest nonmilitary foreign-policy related financial commitments since the Marshall Plan, Almost all of the issues involved in understanding, preventing, mitigating these crises are the stuff of economic courses and research: fixed versus flexible exchange rates, moral hazard and multiple equilibria, speculation and liquidity, fiscal and monetary policies, regulation and competition. What economists think, say, and do has profound implications for the lives of literally billions of other fellow citizens. Whether it is discussing the role of derivatives in signaling exchange-rate commitments with Chinese Premier Zhu Rongji, or discussing the an NBER working paper on inflation targeting with the Brazilian central bank governor Arminio Fraga, or discussing alternative approaches to bankruptcy law with Indonesia's economic team, or optimal debt durations with the Mexican authorities, I am consistently struck by the impact of the kind of research discussed at the ABA meetings. The future well-being of the world's people in larger part will depend on how the ongoing process of global integration works out. This is a strong statement, but one that is supported by the global economy's post-World War I failure and its post-World War II success. Central to global integration is financial integration: the flow of funds and of capital across international borders. And as the events of the late 1920s and early 1930s reminds us, central to global disintegration can be international financial breakdowns. I want to reflect on the issue of global financial integration in the light of the dramatic and largely unpredicted events of recent years. It is perhaps a good time for reflection. There has been enough repair that priority can shift from immediate crisis management, but the crises are sufficiently recent that the sense of urgency that they create to improve the system has not been lost. I shall address four issues: what it means to have an efficient financial system, highlighting the important fact that accident prevention is only one aspect of how that system performs.

(i)   the alternate sources of financial crises in general, and roots of the recent crises in particular;

(ii)   the best ways to design a system, both at national and international level, that will work well and more effectively prevent crisis;

(iii)   the question of effective crisis response, again, both at the level of national policies and the response of the international community.

The Goal of an Efficient Global Financial System

Recent years have witnessed a sea change in the global financial system, as the flow of private capital from industrial to developing countries has mushroomed from $174 billion in the 1980s to $1.3 trillion during the 1990s. In 1990, one emerging-market economy issued sovereign Eurobonds. By 1998, 40 or so emerging-market economies had issued them over the course of the 1990s. And the incidence of major financial accidents has risen sharply, to the point where in the fall of 1998 we experienced what many regarded as the worst financial crisis of the last 50 years following Russia's default, leading many to question the premise that an integrated global financial system is desirable. The question is an important and fair one. But it can be answered. There is much about a market economy that we take for granted. One of the more remarkable aspects is the work of a well-functioning financial system. On the one side there are consumers who want to set aside resources to prepare for their retirement, or to prepare for a rainy day, or to accumulate resources to purchase a car but who have essentially no productive opportunities for investment. On the other side there are those with opportunities to use resources today to produce more resources tomorrow by investing in equipment, structures, or schooling, or to permit consumers to smooth their consumption streams. It is the task of the financial system to bring the wants and the opportunities together. When this is done better, a number of benefits result. An economy grows because investments earn higher returns. Scarce capital is put to its best use. Consumers benefit from more future consumption in return for consumption opportunities foregone. Risks are better shared, and individuals face less volatility in the amounts they are able to consume. These are real and tangible benefits, and so it is appropriate that financial systems absorb real resources. As is now widely understood, the abstract argument for a competitive financial system parallels the argument for competitive markets in general.

As the textbooks teach, the appropriate rates of substitution and transformation are equated. Intermediation activity will be profitable when it is efficient; that is, when the gains generated outweigh the costs of the activity. Thus, for example, specialists who provide liquidity to a market will earn profits that reflect the benefit they are bringing buyers and sellers, just as those who transport goods between high-and low-price regions can earn revenues that reflect the benefits they are providing.

In the United States economy today, 7 percent of GNP is devoted to financial intermediation, more than double the share 40 years ago. And this takes no account of the large effort within nonfinancial corporations that is devoted to raising and allocating capital. It is tempting but. I have become convinced. wrong to think of all this intermediation activity as deadweight loss efforts to win zero-sum gains. While there may be some elements of this kind of thing, the larger point is this: even small increases in the efficiency with which capital is allocated have enormous social benefits. If a typical economy has a capital output ratio of 3:1, it follows that an increase in the efficiency with which capital is allocated of 2 percent or roughly 20 basis points has a social benefit equivalent to that of 6 percent of GNP in forgone consumption. What does all this have to do with the international financial system or with international financial crisis? The implication is that, insofar as international financial integration represents an improvement in financial intermediation (whether because of the transfer of saving from low-to high-return jurisdictions, because of better risk-sharing, or because institutions involved in the transfer of capital across jurisdictions improve the efficiency with which capital is allocated), it offers a potentially significant increase in economic efficiency with benefits both for consumers and for investors around the world. Just as trade in goods across jurisdictions has benefits, so too will intertemporal trade and trade that shares risks across jurisdictions have benefits.

These are not just abstractions. There are *a priori* reasons to suppose that the gains from intertemporal trade and from trade in financial services have the potential to be very large. Essentially all of the growth in the world's labor force over the next few decades will take place in the developing world, as the industrialized world ages. Yet most of the world's saving will take place in industrialized countries. And the abundant evidence of unutilized steel mills and what Federal Reserve Chairperson Alan Greenspan has called 'conspicuous construction' speaks to the potential for improved systems of intermediation to allocate capital more efficiently within developing countries, as well as between the developed and the developing world.

Some, notably Jagdish Bhagwati (1998), have taken the position that these benefits apply only to long-term direct investment. But while, as I will discuss, there are certainly dangers from creating excessive biases in favor of financial flows, one should remember that in the right kind of environment financial flows can also provide important benefits. First, they are the outcome of transactions that finance real trade and related financial transactions and provide cross-border liquidity to the interbank market.

Second, they provide capital to local businesses on what are often the best available terms. Third, they are closely associated with the presence of foreign businesses and foreign financial institutions, which themselves bring significant benefits. More generally, generic attempts to distinguish between good (direct) and bad (financial) capital flows remind me of attempts to distinguish between good and bad imports of goods and services in international trade-and may prove equally counterproductive. While all that potential is certainly there, words like 'moral hazard,' 'adverse selection,' 'noise trading,' and 'herding' remind us that economic theory has identified many reasons why financial markets do not always perform perfectly. And the centuries, long history of financial crisis teaches us no less clearly that the flows of capital teaches us no less clearly that the flows of capital driven by financial markets can be, very different from an efficient and optimal allocation of savings to the right investment projects.

How best to think about financial innovation? An analogy may be helpful. The jet airplane made air travel more comfortable, more efficient, and more safe, thought the accidents were more spectacular (and for a time) more numerous after the jet was first invented. In the same way, modem global financial markets carry with them enormous potential for benefit, even if some of the accidents are that much more spectacular. As the right public policy response to the jet was longer runways, better air-traffic control, and better training for pilots, and not the discouragement of rapid travel, so the right public policy response to financial innovation is to assure a safe framework so that the benefits can be realized, not stifled the change.

That said, the development of a proper air transport system also depended on understanding and addressing the reasons for crashes. In the same way, the development of the right kind of international financial system will depend on understanding the causes of crisis, a topic to which I now turn.

Understanding International Financial Crises

Leo Tolstoy famously observed that 'every happy family is the same. Every unhappy family is miserable in its own way.' Every financial crisis is different and involves its own distinctive elements. There are, however, some elements that are common to many of the emerging-market financial crises we have seen in recent years. International financial crises can be defined in many ways and can take many forms. What I mean by an international financial crisis is a situation where the international dimension substantially worsens a crisis in ways that would not occur in a closed economy. By this definition, I do not mean to understate the major role that domestic fundamental weaknesses can play in bringing on a crisis. I do mean to exclude situations where it is primarily poor domestic economic performance that leads to debt-servicing problems? I also mean to exclude currency crisis in which countries are forced to adjust exchange rates although, as we shall see, devalutions can frequently presage international financial crisis. If we are to prevent accidents as effectively as possible, and mitigate them where we cannot prevent them, it is important to understand how they happen and the nature of their antecedents. There have been six major international financial crises during the 1990s: Mexico in 1995; Thailand, Indonesia, and South Korea in 1997-1998; Russia in 1998, and Brazil in 1998-1999. Table provides some information on these crises.

Elements in common include a dramatic swing in the current account, a large real depreciation, and a significant decline in real output. With some differences between cases, the pattern in all these crises, and indeed, a number of crises historically, appears to involve three broad elements. First, after a period of substantial capital inflows, investors (both domestic and foreign) decided to reduce the stock of their assets in the affected country in response to a change in its fundamentals. This can have many sources: concern about the viability of the exchange-rate regime, as in most of these cases; concern about large fiscal deficits, as in Russia and Brazil; concern about large current-account deficits, as in Thailand and Brazil; and the increasing salience of long-standing financial-sector weaknesses, arising from some combination of insufficient capitalization and supervision of banks and excessive leverage and guarantee-the combination that, along with directed, lending, has been captured in the term crony capitalism.

Second, after this process went on for some time in these emerging-market countries, investors shifted their focus from evaluating the situation in the country to evaluating the behavior of other investors. The rate of withdrawal increased as a bank-run psychology took hold, and investors sought to avoid being the last ones in as they saw the country's reserves being depleted. This was manifested in the shift of the mode of investment analysis from economics to hydraulics, with an accounting-spreadsheet exercise that made no reference to prices on the sources and uses of funds. Rumors of drastic action (a moratorium, capital controls, or some such) began to circulate, and a panic mentally developed. This phenomenon was particularly evident in Mexico in early 1995 and in South Korea between Thanksgiving and Christmas in 1997, and it seems a particularly pervasive feature of recent emerging-market crisis. No one, after all, raised questions about debt rollover in the United Kingdom following sterling's exit from the European Exchange Rate Mechanism (ERM) in 1992, or in continental Europe after the breakdown of the ERM in 1993.

Third, the withdrawal of capital and the associated sharp swing in the exchange rate and reduced access to capital exacerbated fundamental weakness, in turn exacerbating the financial-market response. The real depreciation of the exchange rate reduced real incomes and spending. Extrapolative expectations regarding a falling exchange rate increased pressure for capital flight. And, most importantly, the increased domestic value of foreign-currency liabilities and reduced creditworthiness of domestic borrowers further degraded an already ailing financial system, in turn causing further reductions in lending and worsening of the fundamentals.

In order to understand the economics of the crises we have seen, each of these three critical elements is essential. Without a change in sentiment, driven by a weakening in the economic fundamentals, it is not possible to account for decisions to withdraw capital. Without the bank-run psychology, it is not possible to account for the scale of the change in investors' allocation decisions, which seem so discontinuous with respect to any easily observable aspects of fundamentals. Without reference of the strains on domestic financial systems and corporate firms, it is hard to account for the magnitude of the observed declines in economic performance and the failure of real exchange-rate depreciations to trigger large immediate increases in exports in a number of cases.

Another feature of the 1990s episodes of turmoil is the presence of international 'contagion,' seen in the ERM crisis of 1992-1993, the 'tequila' effects of the Mexican peso crisis of 1994-1995, the 'yellow fever' effects of the Asian crisis of 1997-1998, and the asset-market contagion following the Russian evaluation and default in August 1998 and the Brazilian devaluation in January 1999. There are many explanations and models of contagion:

(i) It can be due to common shocks (like terms of primary commodity price shocks) that simultaneously hurt the commodity-exploring countries. Trade linkages transfer relative price and income (demand) shocks from one country to the other.

(ii) Competitive devaluations among countries competing among themselves or in the third markets may explain excessive currency depreciation of many currencies.

(iii) Financial linkages lead to asset-market correlations: if one country invests in and lends to another one, poor economic news in the latter will also affect asset markets in the former.

(iv) Market illiquidity may have exacerbated contagion. For example, when some highly leveraged institutions experienced significant loses following the Russian crisis, margin calls and lack of liquidity may have led them or forced them to reduce their positions in other markets, thus feeding contagion.

(v) Some elements of investors' irrationality may have been at work; panic, herding, and positive feedback trading may partly explain why investors withdrew indiscriminately from many markets without careful distinction among different emerging markets based on their fundamentals.

(vi) Finally, and in my view, more importantly, 'reputational externalities were almost certainly at work. A crisis in one country can affect investors' expectations and perceptions about common structural conditions and vulnerabilities in other countries and the likely policy response to such vulnerabilities.

From the perspective of actual experience, analytical distinctions between 'multiple-equilibrium crisis' and 'fundamentals-driven crises' seem less sharp than they sometimes do in the academic literature. It seems difficult to point to any emerging-market economy that experienced a financial crisis but did not have significant fundamental weaknesses that called into question the sustainability of its policies. Yet it seems equally difficult to avoid the judgment that, in many of these recent cases, the punishment was in a sense disproportionate to the crime with the process of capital withdrawal greatly exacerbating any underlying weakness. A crude but simple game, related to Douglas Diamond and Philip Dybvig's (1983) celebrated analysis of bank runs, illustrates some of the issues involved here.

Imagine that everyone who has invested $10 with me can expect to earn $1, assuming that I stay solvent. Suppose that if I go bankrupt, investors who remain lose their whole $10 investment, but that an investor who withdraws today neither gains nor loses. What would you do? Each individual judgment would presumably depend on one's assessment of my prospects, but this in turn depends on the collective judgment of all of the investors. Suppose, first, that my foreign reserves, ability to mobilize resources, and economic strength are so limited that if any investor withdraws I will go bankrupt. It would be a Nash equilibrium (indeed, a Pareto-dominant one) for everyone to remain, but (I expect) not an attainable one. Someone would reason that someone else would decide to be cautious and withdraw, and so forth. This phenomenon, which Douglas Hofstadter has labeled 'reverberant doubt,' would likely lead to large-scale withdrawals, and I would go bankrupt. It would not be a close-run thing. John Maynard Keynes' beauty contest captures a similar idea.

Now suppose that my fundamental situation were such that everyone would be paid off as long as no more than one-third of the investors chose to withdraw. What would you do then? Again, there are multiple equilibria; everyone should stay if everyone else does, and everyone should pullout if everyone else does, but the more favorable equilibria seems much more robust. I think that this conceptual experiment captures something real. On the one hand, bank runs or their international analogues do happen. On the other hand, they are not driven by sunspots: their likelihood is driven and determined by the extent of fundamental weaknesses. These questions of equilibrium selection can be and indeed have been more formally analyzed. For my purposes, the point is that preventing crisis is heavily an issue of avoiding situations where the bank-run psychology takes hold, and that will depend heavily on strengthening core institutions and other fundamentals.

Crisis Prevention at the National and International Level

National Crisis-Prevention Efforts

Many countries experience major shocks-to their terms of trade, to investor confidence, or within their domestic financial systems, or within their domestic financial systems. Relatively few of them have major financial crisis. Why? Four primary conclusions emerge:

(i)   In nearly all the cases, serious banking and financial-sector weaknesses played an important role.

(ii)   Fixed exchange rates without the concomitant monetary-policy commitments were present as antecedents to crisis in all the cases.

(iii)   Traditional macroeconomic fundamentals, in the form of overly inflationary monetary policies, large fiscal deficits, or even large current account deficits, were present in several cases but are not necessary antecedents to crisis in all episodes.

(iv)   National balance-sheet weaknesses, including large short-term liabilities either of government or the private sector, were important elements in each of the crisis.

A substantial literature has sought more systematically to analyze the antecedents and non-antecedents of financial crisis with broadly similar conclusions to my idea. These four observations, in turn, help identify the four elements of an effective national strategy for minimizing the risk of this kind of crisis.

First, and easier said than done, is maintaining a strong domestic financial system. While many authors emphasize vulnerability measures comparing the level of foreign reserves to measures of short-term liabilities, the work of Simon Johnson et al. (2000) is particularly persuasive in highlighting the strength of domestic financial systems and institutions. When well-capitalized and supervised banks, effective corporate governance and bankruptcy codes, and credible means of contract enforcement, along with other elements of a strong financial system, are present, significant amounts of debt will be sustainable. In their absence, even very small amounts of debt can be problematic. The second element is the choice of appropriate exchange-rate regime, which, for economies with access to international capital markets, increasingly means a move away from the middle ground of pegged but adjustable fixed exchange rate supported, if necessary, by a commitment to give up altogether an independent monetary policy. The practical choice between these two poles, for emerging-market economies today, probably has less to do with Robert Mundell's traditional optimal-currency-area considerations than with a country's capacity to operate a discretionary monetary policy in a way that will reduce rather than increase variance in economic output. Third, a sound and stable macroeconomic policy environment is needed where monetary-policy and fiscal-policy vulnerabilities are minimized, including especially the avoidance of fiscal deficits that are substantially beyond a country's sustainable domestic financing capacity. What this deficit level will be will depend on a country's savings behavior and the quality of its capital markets. Fourth, countries should reduce their vulnerabilities to liquidity/rollover risk and balance-sheet risk. Foreign reserves need to be compared to meaningful measures of liabilities that can become a claim against a country's reserves; traditional ratios of reserve to imports are thus of little use. Also, policy biases toward short-term capital need to be avoided. This last point deserves emphasis because we have seen this kind of bias time and time again in the recent crises:

(i)   We saw it in Mexico, with the increasing resort to issuing dollar-denominated Tesobonos in the lead-up to crisis.

(ii)   We saw it in Thailand, in the tax breaks on offshore foreign borrowing and the government's decision to mortgage all of its reserves on forward markets.

(iii)   We saw it in South Korea, where discriminatory controls kept long-term capital out and ushered short-term capital in.

(iv)   And we saw it in Russia, in the government's determined efforts to attract international investors to the market for ruble-denominated GKa's.

In this context the question naturally arises of controls on short-term capital inflows as a crisis-avoidance measure. But the first and usually neglected point is that, just as economists usually recommend that efforts to reduce energy consumption should start with the elimination of energy subsidies rather than the introduction of new energy taxes, so the first priority with regard to capital flows must be to do no harm: that is, to avoid policies that reach excessively for short-term capital, such as those we have seen in recent crisis economies.

A measure of sound management of short-term flows is implicit in any prudential regulation of banks. Where controls are in place it is a mistake to be theological about their removal; but experience suggests that such controls tend to become more ineffective over time, create their own costs and distortions, and discourage the integration of financial services that can be an important source of stability. They are no panacea and indeed can degrade the performance of the very functions of the financial system described before.

Still, policy biases that lead to an excessive accumulation of short term debt should be addressed via policy changes that eliminate such biases, including: the distortions that can result from restrictions on foreign direct investment, inward equity portfolio investment, or the access of nonresidents to long-term bond markets; or policy distortions and tax incentives that can lead to an excessive reliance on debt relative to equity finance. Of course, underdeveloped capital markets, where a lack of long-term bond markets; or policy distortions and tax incentives can lead to an excessive reliance on debt relative to equity finance. Of course, underdeveloped capital markets, where long-term forms of finance (i.e., equity, long-term bonds) are not widely available, will themselves create a bias in favor of short-term capital flows in the right environment. When we consider the recognized role that efficient capital markets can play in providing finance for long-term growth, it is clear that their development should be given high priority in the process of domestic and international capital-market liberalization. Just as better airplanes and airports are good in ways that go beyond accident-prevention, all of these steps are valuable not simply as crisis prevention measures, but in their own right, as proven strategies for promoting economic efficiency and growth.

International Crisis-Prevention Efforts

Ultimately, the likelihood of plane crashes depends on the training and judgment of pilots and sound manufacture of planes. But the system in which pilots operate will equally be important and demands careful consideration. The same applies to the international dimension of crisis prevention. The overwhelming contribution that the international community can make toward preventing crises is to succeed in encouraging sound national economic policies, and the most important thing that the international community can do in achieving this goal is to promote transparency.

If one were writing a history of the American capital market, I think one would conclude that the single most important innovation shaping that market was the idea of generally accepted accounting principles. The transparency implicit in the generally accepted accounting principles (GAAP) promotes efficient market responses to change, and it supports stability. Furthermore, if as Ken Galbraith has observed, conscience is the fear that someone may be watching, it may be the single most effective means of promoting self-regulation in emerging economies. Very much the same kind of transparency is needed in the There is also an important role for better international surveillance of the quality of national policies in the areas just described. This is a role that is increasingly being taken on by the IMF in a broader range of areas, as it moves away from the time when it could be said that IMF stood for 'It's Mostly Fiscal.' International forums such as the G-7, the new G-20, the APEC finance ministers, and so forth can also be helpful. Indeed, their major accomplishments is not the specific decisions that are taken when they meet--sometimes there are none. Rather, it is the gradual spread of common ways of thinking about and responding to economic developments. The value of the diffusion of best practice, or at least, better practice, is not to be discounted. Over time these forums provide important opportunities to use political pressure to nudge national policies in the right direction.

Beyond the approbation of their peers, the question does arise as to what will motivate countries to pursue stronger policies. The basic answer has to be self-interest. The ultimate reward for countries with improved policies will be better economic outcomes and a higher standard of living for their citizens. The proximate and more immediate indicator and incentive can be the lower borrowing costs that come from being well-regarded by the market.

There are some who suggest that systematic augmentation of countries' foreign reserves, through the availability of generalized, unconditional emergency finance, would make accidents less likely by reducing the risk of the kind of self-fulfilling expectations-driven crises that I have discussed. While conditioned, precautionary financial support is constructive in some cases, the risk inherent in systematic availability of unconditional credit to countries can be summarized in two words: moral hazard. Crises are typically preceded by significant depletion of reserves. There is the real prospect that automatic availability of reserves would simply delay necessary adjustments and thereby prove highly destructive. While the best preventive policies would minimize the chance that crisis would occur, they would never eliminate them entirely. When they do occur, it will be important to follow policies that minimize their virulence and consequences.

National and International Crisis Response

Crisis response, like crisis prevention, has two dimensions: national policies that can restore confidence and international efforts to finance a credible path out of crises. Of these, by the far the most important is the response of national authorities in the countries concerned. If there is one lesson that has been brought home most forcefully by the events of recent years, it is that countries shape their own destinies and the international community can never want sound policies or economic stability more than the government and people of the country itself.

Effective Crisis Response at the National Level

The best national response to crisis is not to have one. The next best is to have a sufficiently robust set of domestic institutions and national economic system that the crisis is contained and self-limiting and does not reach the stage where a country's capacity to meet its international obligations comes into question. This goes back to questions of crisis-prevention. Here I am talking about full-blown crisis of the kind suggested by the six examples we have seen in the 1990s.

In my experience, policymakers in a country facing such a crisis tend to go through stages reminiscent of the five stages of grief. First, there is the denial that a crisis could be taking place. Second, we see anger, with a wish to blame speculators and others outside sources, and often, domestically, a change in government. Third, there is the bargaining: The desperate search for magic bullets that we crave, for example, in the pressure for a currency board in the depth of the crisis in Indonesia. Fourth comes despair, leading eventually to the decision to call in the IMF. Finally, in the fifth stage, there is acceptance and the agreement of a credible plan.

As an academic I used to be impatient with the seemingly mundane advice of former officials and worldly sorts who counseled the victims of financial crisis to communicate with their creditors, get the bad news out early, take decisive steps early to resolve a crisis, and so forth. More recently, I have come to appreciate more keenly that propositions become cliches because they the capture truth. In situations where confidence is central, it is a mistake to think that it is only the substance of what national authorities do that matters.

Perhaps the best advice that I have heard about the right policy following a crisis is President Ernesto Zedillo's admonitions, based on his experience leading Mexico out of crisis in 1995, that markets overreact, so policy needs to overreact as well. All of this speaks to the force of an effective policy response to crises. What about its content? It will vary from case to case. But experience suggests some important lessons.

Providing confidence to markets and investors that a credible path out of crisis exists and will be followed is essential. That requires transparency (providing all relevant information to markets so that risk-averse investors are not uncertain about how deep and serious problems are), consistent and credible commitment to a coherent policy-adjustment package (so that political and policy uncertainty does not undermine investors' confidence), and close consultation with creditors (so that sudden negative policy and informational surprises are minimized, and so that creditors are reassured that cooperative approaches to debt servicing difficulties will be pursued).

If lax fiscal policy is a contributor to the crisis, then tightening will be a key part of restoring confidence, but in a situation in which large-scale outflows of capital are likely to have their own contractionary effect, it is neither necessary nor desirable to tighten fiscal policy solely in response to the crisis itself. Indeed, since devaluation may be deflationary in the short run (through its expenditure reduction effects) rather than expansionary (via the expenditure switching effect that kicks in the medium run), less stress may have to be put on other forms of expenditure-reduction in the adjustment process (i.e., fiscal contraction) when these are not warranted based on fundamentals. And, in fact, fiscal policy was allowed to loosen in several Asian crisis economies when the depth of the recession emerged in early 1998, Countries need to set the right monetary policy to establish confidence, and in a situation in which a currency is in free-fall it is difficult to believe that the way to restore stability is to produce more of that currency.

The right monetary policy at times of crises has to be one that will minimize the average interest rate over the medium term; and where confidence is at issue, that may imply a significant tightening in the short run, Given the free fall of currencies (and ensuing exacerbation of contractionary balance-sheet effects) in cases such as Indonesia, where monetary conditions were kept lax at the onset of the crisis, the argument that lower interest rates early on would have strengthened currencies seems neither convincing nor supported by the evidence. Indeed, currencies stabilized and recovered in Asian-crisis economies after a period of tight money restored confidence in early 1998, paving the way for a rapid and significant reduction in interest rates in the second part of the year.

Prompt action needs to be taken to maintain financial stability, by moving quickly to support healthy institutions and by intervening in unhealthy situations. The loss of confidence in the financial system and episodes of bank panics were not caused by early and necessary interventions in insolvent institutions. Rather, these problems were exacerbated by (a) a delay in intervening to address the problem of mounting non-performing loans; (b) implicit bailout guarantees that led to an attempt to 'gamble for redemption'; (c) a system of implicit, rather than explicit and inventive-compatible, deposit guarantees at a time when there was not a credible amount of fiscal resources available to back such guarantees; and (d) political distortions and interferences in the way interventions were carried out (as when an Indonesian bank owned by a son of President Soeharto was closed one day only to be reopened the next, under a different name in the same premises).

Strong and effective social safeguards need to be in place. Effective social policy and spending can ease the task of adjustment during times of crisis, help build support for necessary reforms, and ensure that the burden of adjustment does not fall disproportionately on the poorest and most vulnerable groups in society. This is a moral imperative. It can also be a political imperative if strong adjustment policies are to be sustained. Countries need to own the adjustment program, and governments have to be democratic and have popular support for policies that are painful in the short run but necessary to restore growth in a rapid manner. Indeed, in several Asian countries (Thailand, South Korea, and Indonesia), the process of confidence-restoration and asset-price recovery was associated with the rise to power of new governments that had greater political legitimacy and popular support. Clearly, in all of these judgments there will be difficult issues of balance, and we can never guarantee that they will be made correctly in every case. But there can be no question (and there has not been any question) that the goal is to restore confidence and stability as rapidly as possible and so to pave the way for renewed growth.

International Crisis Response

As I noted earlier, a hallmark of crisis in its most virulent phase is that a country's creditors come to focus on hydraulics, not economics, looking to see whether there are adequate resources to finance all obligations coming due. Without this assurance, the restoration of confidence will not be possible. The central task for the international response to a crisis is the establishment of a path that will see a country and its creditors out of the crisis through a series of mutually consistent and reinforcing actions. The goal must be the restoration of confidence and the normal flow of private capital. This goal can be addressed in two broad ways in the context of credible policy adjustment:

(i)   through the provision of official finance; or
(ii)   through some coordination of private creditors to reduce overflows or roll over obligations coming due.

Along with spurring sound policy in the affected country, the crucial objective of the international community in responding to crisis is using these two tools to promote the restoration of confidence. The provision of emergency finance can, in principle and in practice, be highly effective in restoring confidence. Unlike in the 1980s, when the international financial institutions and bilaterals provided only relatively minor sums to countries in crisis, large-scale provision of emergency finance has been a central part of the international financial community's response to the crisis of the 1990s. The approach followed, as embodied in the IMF's supplemental Resources Facility, has had something in common with Walter Bagehot's dictum of lending freely at penalty rates on collateral that is sound in normal times. While the counterfactual is not available, I believe that the availability of substantial resources has contributed to the relatively rapid recovery from deep crises in countries such as Mexico and South

Korea, which were successful in carrying out their policy commitments. Korea's economy, for example, is currently growing by around 9 percent.

The provision of conditioned finance at premium rates to respond to crises does raise certain difficulties. First, there is the real question of balancing the desire to apply conditionality to country policies with the desire to add confidence to the market. The former requires uncertainty as to whether resources will be forthcoming; the latter is best served by confidence, so the balance that must be struck in a transparent world where national authorities and the market hear the same message is a complicated one.

Second, there is the issue of moral hazard and the possible systemic implications of the expectations of bailouts. There is considerable debate about the importance of this issue. While many disagree, I think it is hard to make the case that investments in emerging markets have been heavily influenced by the expectation of the availability of official resources for bailouts. For example, there is no systematic evidence that flows to official creditors rose relative to flows to private creditors following, the official response to the Mexican financial crisis. Furthermore, there is the analytical point that, if official-sector lending into financial crisis is judged properly and is paid back at premium interest rates, it can benefit the lenders, creditors, and countries involved and does not impose a taxpayer cost in the same way that deposit insurance does. Indeed, a well-designed official lending facility that is profitable and makes all relevant agents better off is a clear Pareto-improvement. However, as in the case of an efficient and incentive-compatible deposit-insurance and safety-net scheme, possible moral-hazard distortions induced by automatic guarantees need to be avoided to ensure that the scheme does not lead to systemic losses and distortions. Thus, it is certain that a healthy financial system cannot be built on the expectation of bailouts.

The third question raised by large-scale official lending as a response to crisis is one of feasibility. As capital markets integrate and capital flows increase, in at least some cases it may well become impossible for official finance to fill gaps entirely or restore confidence. These considerations lead to private-sector coordination as an alternative response to crisis. Coordination of bank creditors played a crucial role in the resolution of the South Korean financial crisis and a significant role in Brazil. Private-sector involvement as an approach to crisis resolution has the virtues of avoiding the need for public-sector money and of reducing moral hazard. But it too raises difficulties.

There is the question of achieving coordination. Individual creditors have little incentive to cooperate in reschedulings or debt reductions, and ample opportunities to free ride if approaches based on voluntarism are pursued. At the same time, if approaches based on coercion are pursued, there are real questions of fairness: for example, how should a country's domestic debts be treated? And what about efforts on the part of local residents to convert domestic into foreign currency? There is also the real risk of the destruction of confidence undermining new flows, either to the country in question or to its neighbors. For these and other related reasons, the question of private-sector involvement in crisis resolution has rightly been treated with some delicacy.

What is the right mix of private-sector involvement and financing in response to crisis? While case-by-case judgmental approaches are rarely satisfying to analysts, they will, expect, be pursued by the international community for some time to come. Cases will differ in the nature of the debts coming due, the likelihood that they can ultimately be paid, the ease with which creditors can be organized, the magnitude of contagion risks, and the availability of financial resources, to mention just a few factors. For all these reasons, the G-7 has rightly laid out principles but not detailed procedures for handling issues of private-sector involvement.

Concluding Remarks

I will conclude where I began. Sound financial systems can contribute enormously to economic development around the world, and the flow of capital across international borders can confer enormous benefits. And yet as we have seen, there is the potential for massive accidents. Some, remembering Jim Tobin's admonition, that it takes a heap of Harberger triangles to fill an Okun gap, conclude that the game is not worth the candle and so the flow of capital should systematically be discouraged. I think the right lesson is the more optimistic one, that with good sense and hard work, and a great deal of creative thought, the Okun gaps can be avoided, and the gains from capital flows can translate into what is most important for any economy: namely, changes in its long-term growth rate. I have described here some of the thinking that has guided the international community in responding to the dramatic developments of recent years. Do so not in the conviction that we have all the answers, but in the certainty that the questions are profoundly important. If I have provoked further thought on a set of issues that economists are uniquely qualified to address, I will have succeeded in my purpose.

References

Aghion, Philippe; Banerjee, Abhijit and Bachetta, Philippe. (1999), 'A Simple Model of Monetary Policy and Currency Crisis.' Mimeo, University of Lausanne, Switzerland, September 1999.

Berg, Andrew and Pattillo, Catherine. (1998), 'Are Currency Crises Predictable? A Test.' International Monetary Fund (Washington, DC) Working Paper No. 98/154, December 1998.

Bhagwati, Jagdish. (1998), 'The Capital Myth,' Foreign Affairs, May/June.

Calvo, Guillermo. (1998), 'Capital Flows and Capital-Market Crises: The Simple Economics of Sudden Stops.' Memeo, University of Maryland, July.

Chang, Roberto and Valasco, Andres. (1998), 'The Asian Liquidity Crisis.' National Bureau of Economic Research (Cambridge, MA) Working Paper No. 6796, November (1999), 'Liquidity Crises in Emerging Markets: Theory and Policy.'

Corsetti, Giancarlo; Presenti, Paolo and Roubini, Nouriel. (1999a), 'What caused the Asian Currency and Financial Crisis?' Japan and the World Economy, September, pp.305-73.

Corsetti, Giancarlo; Presenti, Paolo and Roubini, Nouriel. (1999b), 'Paper Tigers? A Model of the Asian Crisis.' European Economic Review, 43(7), pp.1211-36.

Corsetti, Giancarlo, Presenti, Paolo and Roubini, Nouriel. (1999c), 'Fundamental Determinants of the Asian Crisis.' The Role of Financial Fragility and External Imbalances.' Unpublished manuscript. Yale University.

Council of Economic Advisers (1999), Economic report of the President. Washington, DC: U.S. Government Printing Office.

Council on Foreign Relations (1999), 'Safeguarding Prosperity in a Global Financial System: The Future International Financial Architecture.' Report of an Independent Task Force sponsored by the Council on Foreign Relations, Institute for International Economics, Washington, DC.

Diamond, Douglas and Dybvig, Philip. (1989), 'Bank Runs, Deposit Insurance, and Liquidity.' Journal o/Political Economy, vol. 91(3), pp.401-419.

Dornbusch, Rudiger, Park, Yung Chul and Claessens, Stijn. (2000), 'Contagion: How It Spreads and How It Can Be Stopped?' Unpublished manuscript, Massachusetts Institute of Technology, January.

Eichengreen, Barry. (1997), Toward a new international financial architecture: A practical post-Asia Aagenda. Washington, DC: Institute for International Economics.

Eichengreen, Barry and Rose, Andy. (1998), 'The Empirics of Currency and Banking Crises.' Mimeo, University of California-Berkeley, 1998.

Feldstein, Martin. (1999), 'Self-Protection for Emerging Market Economies.' National Bureau of Economic Research (Cambridge, MA) Working Paper No. 6907, January.

Frankel, Jeffrey and Rose, Andy. (1996), 'Currency Crashes in Emerging Markets: An Empirical Treatment.' Journal of International Economics, November, vol. 41(3-4), pp.351-66.

Goldfajin, Ilan and Valdes, Rodrigo O. (1998), 'The Twin Crisis and the Role of Liquidity.' Mimeo, International Monetary Fund, Washington, DC.

Goldfajin, Ilan and Valdes, Rodrigo O. (1999), 'Liquidity Crisis and International Architecture.' Unpublished manuscript, Central Bank of Chile, Santiago, July.

Goldstein, Morris. (1998), The Asian financial crisis: Causes, cures and systemic implications. Washington, DC: Institute for International Economics, 1998.

Goldstein, Morris; Kaminsky, Graciella and Reinhart, Cannen. (1999), 'Assessing Financial Vulnerability: An Early Warning System for Emerging Markets.' Mimeo, Institute for International Economics, Washington, DC.

Jeanne, Oliver. (1999), 'Sovereign Debt Crisis and the Global Financial Architecture.' Unpublished manuscript. International Monetary Fund, Washington, DC, November.

Jeanne, Olivier and Wyplosz, Charles. (1999), 'The International Lender of Last Resort: How Large is Large Enough?' Mimeo, International Monetary Fund, Washington, DC, September 1999.

Johnson, Simon, Boone, Peter; Breach, Alastar and Friedman, Eric. (2000) 'Corporate Governance in the Asian Financial Crisis.' Journal of Financial Economics, (forthcoming).

Kaminsky, Graciella and Reinhart, Cannen. (1999), 'The Twin Crisis: The Causes of Banking and Balance-of-Payments Problems.' American Economic Review, June, vol. 89(3), pp.473-500.

Krugman, Paul. (1998), 'What Happened to Asia?' Unpublished manuscript, Massachusetts Institute of Technology, January.

Krugman, Paul. (1999), 'Balance Sheets, the Transfer Problem, and Financial Crisis.' In Peter Isard, Assaf Razin, and Andrew K. Rose, eds., International finance and international crises: Essays in honor of Robert Flood, Jr. Washington, DC: International Monetary Fund.

McKinnon, Ronald and Pill, Huw. (1996), 'Credible Liberalization and International Capital Flows: The Overborrowing Syndrome', in T. Ito and A. O. Krueger, eds., Financial deregulation and integration in East Asia. Chicago: University of Chicago Press, pp.7-42.

Morris, Stephen and Shin, Hyun Song. (1998), 'Unique Equilibrium in a Model of Self-Fulfilling Currency Attacks.' American Economic Review, June 1998,88(3), pp.587-97.

Prisker, Matthew. (2000), 'The Channels for Financial Contagion.' Unpublished manuscript, Board of Governors of the Federal Reserve System, Washington, DC, January 2000.

Rodrik, Dani and Velasco, Andres. (1999), 'Short-Term Capital Flows.' National Bureau of Economic Research (Cambridge, MA) Working Paper No. 7364, September.

Rogoff, Kenneth. (1999), 'International Institute for Reducing Global Financial Instability.' Journal of Economic Perspectives, Fall 1999, vol. 13(4), pp.21-42.

Sachs, Jeffrey and Radelet, Steven. (1998), 'The Onset of the East Asian Financial Crisis,' National Bureau of Economic Research (Cambridge, MA) Working Paper No. 6680, August 1998.

Sachs, Jeffrey and Radelet, Steven. (1999), 'What Have We Learned, So Far, From the East Asian Financial Crisis?' Mimeo, Harvard University, January.

Sachs, Jeffrey; Tomell, Aaron and Velasco, Andres. (1996), 'Financial Crisis in Emerging Markets: The Lessons from 1995.' Brookings Papers on Economic Activity, 1996, (1), pp.147-98.

Summers, Lawrence H. (1999), 'The Right Kind of IMF for a Stable Global Financial System.' Speech presented at the London School of Business, London, U.K., 14 December.

Summers, Lawrence H. and Summers, Victoria P. (1989), 'When Financial Markets Work Too Well: A Cautious Case for a Securities Transaction Tax.' Journal of Financial Services Research. December 1989, 3(2-3), pp.261-86.

Wallace, Neil. (1998), 'Another Attempt to Explain and Illiquid Banking System: The Diamond at Dybvig Model with Sequential Services Taken Seriously.' Federal Reserve Bank Minneapolis Quarterly Review, Fall, 12(4), pp.3-16.

Zeckhauser, Richard. (1986), 'The Muddled Responsibilities of Public and Private America,' Winthrop Knowlton and Richard Zeckhause eds. American society: Public and private responsibilities. Cambridge, MA: Balling, pp.45-77.

Zettelmeyer, Jeronim. (1999), 'On the Short-Run Effectiveness of Official Crisis Lending.' Unpublished manuscript, International Monetary Fund, Washington, DC, December.

Chapter 5

Social Progress and the Asian Crisis

Clive Hamilton

Introduction

Why has the Asian economic crisis been a bad thing? This may seem like a trivial question because the answer appears to be so obvious. But in this chapter I would like to examine the assumptions that underlie the process of growth and development that appears to have been so cruelly interrupted by the crisis. By exploring the reasons for believing that the crisis has been undesirable we will raise the question of whether the objective now should simply be to get the affected economies back on to the paths they previously followed. First of all, while we are on issues of blinding obviousness, I will state at the outset that I am assuming that the purpose of economic activity, and the purpose of government, is to improve national well-being, or 'social welfare' as the economics books call it. These are both assumptions only. We know that Adam Smith is remembered above all for arguing that market activity will maximize social welfare, although it was not until this century that neoclassical economist set out to prove, on the basis of a number of axioms, the Fundamental Theorem of Economics, which says that under certain conditions, the activities in the market of private producers and consumers, in pursuit of their own interests, will result in the most efficient allocation of resources. As for the objective of government, a persuasive argument could be made that the objective of the Suharto Government in Indonesia was personal enrichment and that the apparently good growth rates were an incidental consequence. I think the true story would combine both national objectives and personal ones.

Aspects of Well-being in Developing Countries

At the most general level, it is believed that the Asian crisis is a bad thing because it has interrupted the growth process, and the growth process is a good thing because rising incomes make people better off. It is useful, therefore, to examine briefly the evidence on the relationship between income levels and well-being. There has been some interesting work around the world on measuring perceived well-being and relating well-being to various national characteristics. Measures of life satisfaction for a various countries are based on self-reported levels of happiness. Wearing and Headey (1998) report levels of happiness or life appreciation for a variety of nations. Table 5.1 shows reported 'average appreciation of life', on a scale of 0 to 1, for selected countries. The first column shows the ranking of each country out of a total of 48 available. The figures on average appreciation of life apply to the early 1990s. The last column shows real GDP per capita in 1995 at purchasing power parity.

Table 5.1 Reported levels of happiness and GDP per capita in selected nations, early 1990s

Rank out of 48	Country	Average appreciation of life	Real GDP per capita 1995 (US$ PPP)
1	Netherlands	0.797	19,900
7	Australia	0.767	19,600
11	USA	0.760	27,000
17	Philippines	0.693	2,800
23	Japan	0.666	21,900
31	China	0.640	2,900
33	South Korea	0.620	11,600
35	India	0.603	1,400
44	Russia	0.510	4,500
48	Bulgaria	0.433	4,600

Sources: Appreciation of life – Wearing and Headey 1998, Table 10.1; Real GDP – UNDP, Human Development Index (www.undp.org/hdro/98hdi.htm).

While the assumption that more economic growth will increase national welfare is accepted as an article of faith almost universally, in fact the evidence indicates that there is only a weak correlation between a country's income and perceived well-being. Moreover, the weak relationship may be due to factors other than income, such as the prevalence of political freedom and democracy, or tolerance of difference. Some evidence also suggest the opposite. For example, within Asia residents of wealthy countries such as Japan and Taiwan regularly report the highest proportion of unhappy people while the countries with the lowest incomes, such as the Philippines, report the highest number of happy people (Dodds 1997, p.115). Social researchers have attempted to relate levels of subjective well-being to various characteristics of a nation. Some of the aspects that are positively and negatively related to happiness are listed in Table 5.2.

Table 5.2 Factors correlated with happy life expectancy in 48 countries

Factors associated with more happiness	Factors associated with less happiness
Knowledge	Unsafe drinking water
Industrialisation	Murder rate
Civil rights	Corruption
Tolerance	Lethal accidents
Income	Gender inequality

Source: Wearing and Headey (1998).

Although this in not the place to go into detail, the evidence overall indicates that it is unlikely that additional income would make much difference to well-being in developed countries such as Australia. These results suggest that the assumption that the best way to improve national prosperity is to maximize the rate of economic growth is simplistic and perhaps misplaced. In fact, the limitations of placing too much emphasis on income growth have been prominent in the development literature for decades. In his classic text *Economics for a Developing World*, first published in 1977, Michael Todaro wrote of the three core values of development:

- Life-sustenance: the ability to provide basic necessities.
- Self-esteem: a sense of worth and self-respect, of not being used as a tool by others for their own ends.
- Freedom from servitude: to be able to choose.

Todaro observed that development is both a physical reality and a state of mind (Todaro 1977, p.96-98). The relative character of development was captured by Denis Goulet when he wrote in 1971:

> Once the prevailing image of the better life includes material welfare as one of its essential ingredients, it becomes difficult for the materially 'underdeveloped' to feel respected or esteemed ... nowadays the Third World seeks development in order to gain the esteem which is denied to societies living in a state of disgraceful 'underdevelopment' (quoted in Todaro 1977, p.97).

Over the last two decades the international debate has shifted away from the sorts of complexities reflected in Todaro's discussion of development. Now all of the emphasis is on maximizing the rate of economic growth. Instead of policies emphasizing literacy, public health and rural development, attention is now centered on trade liberalization, privatization and macroeconomic stability. The glitter of the economic miracle has replaced the hard slog of social development. It is now believed that growth itself, through the trickle down process, will solve the complex of problems that once were captured by the term 'underdeveloped', and that maximizing the growth rate should occupy our full attention. Let us examine some of the essential presumptions about the growth process, asking ourselves how and to what extent economic growth make people better off and how the Asian crisis has affected development. The benefits of growth for social welfare are often measured by changes in poverty, inequality, educational attainment and, more recently, environmental quality. The UNDP's Human Development Index (considered further below) includes measures of real GDP per capita, life expectancy, adult literacy and primary school enrolments. Let us examine the effect of growth in Asia on these variables and the effect of the crisis on them.

Growth and Poverty

Absolute poverty is defined as a state in which a person, household or section of the community is able to meet only its bare subsistence essentials of food, clothing and shelter from the elements (Todaro 1977, p.411). People above this level can exercise some choice over what they consume or their living conditions. In the South, poverty is usually thought of in absolute terms, although as soon as we begin to consider the effect of poverty on human well-being we cannot avoid the influence of relative factors on the state of mind of the poor. The role of custom must be acknowledged, even at the lowest levels of living. Observing the state of under-development in 18th century England, Adam Smith wrote:

> By necessities I understand not only the commodities which are indispensably necessary for the support of life, but whatever the custom of the country renders it indecent for creditable people, even of the lowest order, to be without (Smith nd p.693).

Smith illustrated his point by reference to leather shoes: 'The poorest creditable person of either sex would be ashamed to appear in public without them'. Leather shoes should thus properly be regarded as necessities. At the time of the French revolution, the term used to for poor of Paris was *sans culottes*, those who could not afford knee-breeches. In a modern parallel, a columnist in the *Australian Financial Review* recently noted that the lack of money can lead to feelings of deprivation and personal failure:

> I reached similar conclusions at hearings this year on the ACTU's 'living wage' claim, listening to a low-paid factory worker who struggled to afford necessities talk about his children's desire for Nike and Reebok. … in a culture where consumption means so much, not having much money becomes a profound social disability (Stephen Long, AFR, 29 June 1999).

Smith's leather shoes are today's Reeboks, even in the *kampongs* of Jakarta. It might seem perverse to consider being deprived of Reeboks as being in the same category as insufficient food, but in the end we are comparing factors that affect self-perceived well-being. Hunger and shame both cause distress. So do boredom and alienation from society, and this helps explain why we often see a forest of television aerials rising above the most decrepit slums. In the North, poverty is thought of a little differently; it is the state in which people are unable to afford what is considered to be the basic requirements of a decent life. Poverty rarely involves an insufficiency of food (although often it means poor nutrition), and most people living in poverty have adequate if not comfortable shelter. The relative notion of poverty is a more important concept. While poverty in this sense is related to inequality it is not the same thing.

It is almost an obvious fact that poverty prevents people from attaining some of the essential ingredients of a good or decent life. I say 'almost' because there are counter-examples. There are instances of voluntary poverty as in some religious orders. Some siddhis, for example, choose to live for years in caves or on rubbish heaps eating very little and wearing rags. Early Western travelers to the Pacific Islands found people with very little in the way of consumer goods but who appeared to have enough to eat and adequate living conditions. They seemed to live a rich social life and, though materially poor by any modern standard, did not seem to go without, and the apparent oxymoron 'subsistence affluence' was coined. Similarly, when Captain James Cook sailed to Australia in 1770 he wrote in his journal of the Indigenous people he encountered that, in contrast to William Dampier's description of 'the miserablest people in the world':

> They may appear to some to be the most wretched people upon the earth: but in reality they are far more happier than we Europeans; ... They live in a Tranquility which is not disturbed by the Inequality of Condition (Quoted in Clark 1963, p.19).

It is hard to avoid the conclusion that the growth process in Australia has led to enormous immiserization of Aboriginal people. This is why the Mirrar people in Kakadu reject the argument that higher incomes that would flow from the development of the Jabiluka uranium mine would compensate for any damage that the development would cause to their social and cultural structures. There is no guarantee that economic growth, even over a long period, will reduce the incidence of poverty. There is no question, however, that growth over the last three decades or so in East Asian countries has markedly reduced absolute poverty. Nor is there any doubt that the Asian crisis has seen a sudden and sharp increase in poverty levels, and this is the principal reason why such crises are so damaging. Table 5.3 shows recent changes in the incidence of poverty and in average standards of living in the three countries hardest hit by the crisis, Indonesia, Thailand and South Korea. Poverty has increased sharply and living standards generally have fallen precipitously because of the dual effects of rising unemployment and a collapse in the purchasing power of local currencies.

Table 5.3 Effect of the Asian crisis on poverty and living standards

Country	Incidence of poverty[a]		Change in average living standard 1997/98 (percent)
	1997[b]	1998	
Indonesia	11.0	19.9	− 24.4
Thailand	11.4	12.9	− 13.6
Korea[c]	8.6	19.2	− 21.6

a.   Using national poverty lines of around US$1/day in Indonesia, $2/day in Thailand and $4/day in Korea.
b.   For Thailand the figure is for 1996
c.   Urban Korea only

Source: World Bank 1999. Trends in Poverty Over Time: Income poverty – Recent regional trends (www.world.bank.org/poverty/data/trends/regional.htm).

This points to the importance of employment creation as the critical component of the growth process. Rapid economic growth in East Asia has generated a rapid job growth, although official figures showing close to full employment disguise extensive underemployment, especially in Indonesia where the informal sector and agriculture still take up well over half the economy. Lee and Rhee (1999) argue that the impact of the crisis on employment patterns varied between the worst affected countries. In Thailand and Indonesia, urban white-collar workers were most affected by lay-offs, although in general 'marginal workers' were hardest hit – women, young workers, and the poorly educated. Women, in particular, tend to be concentrated in the more precarious forms of wage employment and are more likely to be first on the list of workers to be laid off. Since their incomes are lower on average they are likely to bear the brunt of increases in poverty and the impacts will be particularly severe on households headed by women (ILO 1998). The ILO wrote of Korea, Thailand and Indonesia:

> … social expectations in these countries have been shaped by a long period of increasing employment opportunities and this makes the current shock in the labour market all the ruder. Indeed this combination of sharp and unexpected social pain on the one hand, and the lack of collectively provided relief on the other, is fertile ground for breeding social unrest (ILO 1998, p.2).

In some respects, redundant white-collar workers may have been the most severely affected by the crisis because the circumstances in which they found themselves deviated so drastically from their expectations and social position.

Growth and Inequality

As a generalization, it is probably true to say that economic growth is more likely to improve poverty levels than it is to reduce inequality. It is also probably true to say that growth leads to more inequality unless governments have long-term policies and institutions that avoid it. The issue of the relationship between inequality and improvements in well-being is less clear cut than the relationship between growth and poverty. In general, more equal societies are more happy societies, *ceteris paribus*. There are two sets of reasons for believing this. First, there is a body of evidence showing that, with respect to income, people judge their level of well-being not by the absolute level but by the level relative to others. Thus psychological well-being is shown to depend not on one's level of income, but on the perceived gap between one's level of income and what one wants, what one expected to have and what others have. Easterlin, who did much of the early work in this field, referred to a 'hedonic treadmill' in which people have to keep running in order to keep up with the others, but they never go forward (Easterlin 1973). Other studies suggest that as incomes rise, income and economic factors become less important in welfare. This has been described by the British economist Sir John Hicks as the 'law of diminishing marginal significance of economics'.[1] It is widely accepted that the growth processes in East Asian countries have been remarkable for combining high growth rates with relatively little decline in income inequality. Sometimes the relative equality of income at the start of the rapid growth process is adduced as a reason for economic success. South Korea, Taiwan and Indonesia are often mentioned. Malaysia and Hong Kong appear to be exceptions in that inequality has worsened. Table 5.4 shows Gini coefficients and income shares of the bottom quintile for East Asian countries. South Korea, Japan, Indonesia and China all have coefficients in the 30s, reflecting a relatively high degree of income equality, while Thailand, Malaysia and the Philippines are significantly more unequal. Overall, the data indicate that East Asian countries are more egalitarian than countries in Latin America where Gini coefficients are typically in the 50s. It is too early to have the data to measure changes in the distribution of income in countries hit by the crisis, but some increase in inequality is likely. As we have seen, poverty has risen sharply in the countries most affected by the crisis. The extent to which the resumption of growth reduces this poverty will depend on the distribution of the fruits of growth. The World Bank has made some estimates of the impact of the crisis on the incidence of poverty; the key factors are the decline in national income and the change in inequality. In terms of the incidence of poverty, a 10 percent decline in inequality can more than offset a 10 percent fall in national income. As an exercise, Table 5.5 shows expected poverty levels in the year 2000 after a 10 percent fall in national output between 1998 and 2000, combined with a 10 percent deterioration and a 10 percent improvement in inequality.

Table 5.4 Growth rates and inequality in Asian countries

Country	GDP growth rate 1990-95	GDP growth rate 1997	Latest Gini coefficient	Income share bottom 20%
South Korea	7.8	5.5	33.6	7.4
Thailand	9.0	−0.4	51.5	3.7
Malaysia	8.8	7.8	48.3	4.6
Japan	2.1	0.9	34.8	5.9
Indonesia	8.0	5.0	31.7	8.7
Philippines	2.3	5.1	45.7	5.2
China	10.6	8.8	37.8	6.0

Source: Lee and Rhee 1999, Table 2.1. Gini coefficients are for the following years:
South Korea – 1988; Thailand – 1992; Malaysia – 1989; Japan – 1982; Indonesia – 1993;
Philippines – 1988; China – 1992.

Table 5.5 Effect of economic contraction and change in inequality on the poverty rate

Country	Poverty rate in 2000	
	10 percent increase in inequality	10 percent decrease in inequality
Indonesia	19.6	6.0
Malaysia	31.4	18.3
Philippines	34.1	22.6
Thailand	27.5	10.5

Source: World Bank, Social Crisis in east Asia
(www.worldbank.org/poverty/eacrisis/sector/poverty/povcwp4.htm)

Growth and Education

It is widely accepted that increasing education levels are an essential component of national development and a major contributor to improved well-being of individuals. An educated society is a better society. The UNDP's Human Development Index includes two measures of education, literacy and primary school enrollments, among the four factors, the other two being real GDP per capita and life expectancy. Table 5.6 shows the latest HDI for selected countries.

Table 5.6　Human Development Index and GDP per capita in selected nations, 1995

Country	HDI 1995	HDI rank of 174	Real GDP per capita 1995 (US$ PPP)	Real GDP rank minus HDI rank
USA	0.943	4	27,000	−1
Japan	0.940	8	21,900	2
Australia	0.932	15	19,600	5
Hong Kong	0.909	25	22,900	−19
South Korea	0.972	30	11,600	6
Thailand	0.838	59	7,700	−10
Malaysia	0.834	60	9,600	−18
Indonesia	0.679	96	4,000	−9
Philippines	0.677	98	2,800	11
China	0.650	106	2,900	1

Source: UNDP, Human Development Index (www.undp.org/hdro/98hdi.htm)

Perhaps the most important reason for believing that education improves well-being is that it is believed to make workers more productive and, by implication, better off. But the story is not as clear-cut as it might seem.

In 1994 Paul Krugman wrote an article entitled 'The Myth of Asia's Miracle' which upset a lot of people. On the basis of a number of growth accounting studies, Krugman argued that the remarkable economic performance of Singapore, along with other East Asian countries, has a rather mundane rather than a miraculous explanation.

> ... the miracle turns out to have been based on perspiration rather than inspiration: Singapore grew through a mobilization of resources that would have done Stalin proud. The employed share of the population surged from 27 to 51 percent. The educational standards of that work force were dramatically upgraded ... Above all, the country had made an awesome investment in physical capital ... (Krugman 1997, p.175).

Thus, along with numbers of workers and physical capital, the improvement in the potential productivity of the workforce was a key factor in explaining high growth rates. The point about this is that this level of resource mobilization is a once-off event in the history of a country, and that growth will inevitably slow to rates more like the 3-4 percent that characterize industrialized countries, a club of moderate growth countries that Japan has now joined. As Krugman notes:

> A half-educated workforce has been replaced by one in which the bulk of workers has high school diplomas; it is unlikely that a generation from now most Singaporeans will have Ph.D.s. (Krugman 1997, p.175).

I would go further and say that even if half the workforce did have PhDs it would have nowhere near the impact on growth rates as achieving a rate of 90 percent high school graduation. We might characterize this as the diminishing returns from investment in education. The value of education is probably greatly overstated in industrialized countries. While there is no doubt that in the labor market of today someone with a higher level of education will be in a better position to secure employment than someone without, this does not mean that a country that invests more in education will grow more quickly as a result. According to one recent review: 'There is surprising little evidence to suggest that pouring public funding into higher education or vocational training has any direct effect on economic growth' (Wolf, 1999, p.34). The huge increases over the last three decades in upper secondary and university enrolments in countries like France, Germany, Britain and Australia reflect changes in the labor market and social conditions more generally rather than the demands of continued economic growth. The educational requirements of job entry increasingly surpass the educational requirements of the jobs themselves. In the rich countries at least, growth generates education rather than education generating growth (Wolf 1999, p.35). In other words, the assumption that what is good for an individual is good for a society is an example of the fallacy of composition. It would be wrong to conclude from this that countries should abandon investment in education once they reach rich country status. Education is intrinsically valuable. The richer a country becomes, the less increasing education levels contribute to economic growth, and the more one can afford to direct education to enriching the quality of life and culture.

This raises an age-old question. Putting aside the other effects, such as the ability to earn higher income, are more educated people better off as a result of their education? Or is ignorance bliss? I am inclined to believe that the development of intellectual capacity is a good thing both for the individual and for society. As a rule, intolerance, fear of the other, and insularity are more likely to flourish in conditions of ignorance, and education opens people to possibilities in life and makes them more interested in democracy. The implications of this is that we should maintain a balance in the type of education we promote and the modern preoccupation with job preparation and commercialization of universities, at the expense of intellectual development and cultural enrichment, is a grave mistake.

Growth and the Environment

It is frequently argued that poor people cannot afford to worry about the environment. But a deteriorating environment can be the reason for sharply lower quality of life. Air pollution, for example, is associated with a range of more or less serious diseases. Asia's cities are some of the dirtiest in the world measured by particle emissions and oxides of sulphur. Particle pollution is of special concern. Alone or combined with sulfur dioxide, is estimated to result in 500,000 deaths and 4-5 million new cases of chronic bronchitis each year (World Bank 1999, Table 3.12). To illustrate the general level of air quality, Table 5.7 shows particulate and sulfur dioxide levels for a number of Asian and other cities. Note that the World Health

Organization recommends annual mean standards for air quality of 90 micrograms per cubic meter for particulates and 50 micrograms per cubic meter for sulfur dioxide. These levels are not only bad but are deteriorating rapidly. One study of the effects of the growth process on the state of the environment in Indonesia concluded that over the period 1985-2020, even under optimistic assumptions about adoption of cleaner technologies and moderate rates of economic growth, air pollution levels will increase four-fold (Duchin, Hamilton and Lange 1993, Table 3.1). As a result, large numbers of people will fall ill and die.

The principal sources of air pollution are combustion of fossil fuels, notable coal for electricity and petrol and diesel for transportation. Fine particles from diesel exhausts are particularly dangerous. The World Bank (1992, p.53) reports that children in Bangkok lose an average of 4 or more IQ points by the age of 7 because of exposure to high levels of lead in the air It would be reasonable to suppose that the children of poor families are most affected since wealthier families can afford to protect themselves from some of the worst impacts. Air pollution can have a dramatic impact on quality of life. Perversely, for the countries worst affected, the Asian crisis has provided a temporary respite in worsening pollution levels, since growth in pollution is closely associated with economic growth. On the other hand, higher levels of income are often associated with greater public efforts to reduce pollution through standards and adoption of cleaner technologies, although the so-called environmental Kuznets curve is far from an iron law. While air pollution has a direct impact on people's health, and illness causes a serious decline in well-being, other environmental factors can affect well-being in an ambient way. The availability of space, for instance, is an important determinant of perceived well-being, albeit one that is highly culturally conditioned.

Table 5.7 Air pollution levels for selected cities 1995

City	Total suspended particulates μ/m^3	Sulfur dioxide μ/m^3
WHO standard	90	50
Sydney	54	28
Beijing	377	90
Taiyuan	568	211
Delhi	415	24
Jakarta	271	–
Tokyo	49	18
Seoul	84	44
Kuala Lumpur	85	24
Mexico City	279	74
Manila	200	33
Bangkok	223	11

Source: World Bank 1999, World Development Indicators, Table 3.13.

Ian Castles has compared the availability of space in Japan and Australia. The Japanese cities he studied (Tokyo, Kanagawa, Kyoto and Osaka) have population densities around 5 or 6 times higher than that of Sydney. Japanese people in these cities have much less private space and public space, as Table 5.8 shows.

Table 5.8 Private and public space in Sydney and four Japanese prefectures

	Sydney	Japan
Residential land allotment size 1988 (sq. m.)	591	157
Average floor area of new dwellings 1984-87 (sq. m.)[a]	139	75
Public open space per million of population 1982 (ha.)	4283	253
Playing fields per million of population 1982 (no.)	517	32

Source: Castles 1992, Tables 11, 12, 13 and 16.
'Japan' refers to a simple average of the four prefectures.

In ₋apanese cities dwellings are less spacious, closer together and on smaller allotments of land. Australian city dwellers have 3 or 4 times as much land to live on. The level of public amenities – parks, roads, school grounds, hospital grounds and sporting facilities – is much higher in Sydney than the Japanese cities.

These facts have a great bearing on living standards. Perhaps Australians have decided that there is a point at which higher money incomes come at too high a price. The decision to sacrifice more income for greater leisure shows up as a fall in GDP. If GDP is used as a measure of national prosperity, then well-being appears to fall when in fact it has risen.

Summing Up

The first conclusion to draw from this review is that human well-being is a many-splendoured thing, and that the use of GDP per capita as a proxy for changes in national welfare is profoundly misleading. Economic growth may or may not result in falling poverty levels, it may or may not lead to improvement of the environment in which people live, and, beyond a certain point, higher incomes contribute less to individual well-being. Comparison with others, and with social and cultural standards, is a critical determinant of perceptions of well-being, in both rich and poor countries alike, and the misery caused by the Asian crisis is all the sharper because it meant that hopes and expectations came crashing down for most of the affected populations. Even the notion of poverty must accommodate expectations if one is to go beyond sheer physical survival, a benchmark which few would agree is acceptable anywhere. If we agree with Todaro that self-esteem, and more generally psychological health, is a critical component of the development process, it could well be argued that some rich countries have become less developed over the last two to three decades. I would include Australia among those, even without taking account of factors such as the increase in homelessness.

In response to the recognition of the short-comings of GDP, a number of more comprehensive measures of social progress have been developed. I have already referred to the Human Development Index, and suggested that there are some significant problems with it. Another is the Index of Sustainable Economic Welfare (also known as the Genuine Progress Indicator) which incorporates 20 or so additional factors that can be measured in dollar terms, including the value of household work, income distribution, the costs of unemployment, the costs of crime and depletion of stocks of natural capital. The ISEW was developed for rich countries and tends to emphasize the costs of the growth process. It could, however, be adapted to developing countries. There is a strong need for indicators that broadly reflect the main influences on economic well-being, including changes over time in the value of marketed goods and services, the contribution of the informal and household economies, the distribution of market and non-market income, the incidence of poverty and unemployment, and the quality of the physical environment. Putting together in an illustrative way some of the data and analysis of this chapter we could represent the effect of the East Asian growth process and the crisis as in Figure 5.1. Some index that aggregates these, and a few other important influences on well-being, would perform a powerful educative function and help wean policy makers, if not the screen jockeys of the financial markets, off their obsession with GDP growth. This would help emphasize the need to make the growth and development process focus more on the factors that actually improve human well-being in the long term. The discussion so far relates to material living conditions. We know that social, political and cultural conditions can also have a vital influence on a nation's welfare. Until recently there was a convenient belief, fashionable among the global economic and political elites, that there are no more competing ideologies. Only market capitalism could survive, and we are witnessing a process of 'convergence' in which the globalizing forces of market capitalism and the inherent power of liberal democracy will ineluctably take over the world, brushing aside the last of the dictators. In one of the silliest statements of the century, Francis Fukuyama actually announced 'the end of history'. One of the more interesting aspects of the Asian meltdown was that, while there was enormous concern about contagion, the fact that many countries at risk from contagion were in fact quarantined tells us something important about the limits to globalization.[2]

In the case on Indonesia, it was not the growth process and the emergence of the middle classes that led to popular democracy, but the *breakdown* of the growth process. The crisis robbed the Suharto regime of the legitimacy conferred on it by a high rate of GDP growth, a legitimacy that Western governments were willing to cede it despite egregious abuses of human rights. It is more likely that the crisis of capitalism will lead to the emergence of democracy than continued growth. One of the minor benefits of the Asian crisis is that we no longer have to listen to pundits declaring that the 21st century will be the Asian century. This in fact is the implication of Krugman's argument that the Asian 'miracle' has been due to perspiration rather than inspiration and that growth rates will inevitable slow. My final hope is that in a decade or two the next crop of pundits will be talking of the 'African miracle'.

Notes

1.   Quoted by Dodds 1997.
2.   The problem of course is that these are at the mercy of the financial markets. The task for policy makers is to attempt to rebuild growth processes that are sustainable, robust and resilient. Sustainability refers to the ability to maintain growth rates of consumption without eroding the stock of natural and other capital on which growth and human well-being depend. Robustness refers to the ability of an economy to resist being decimated by external shocks and the mood swings of market sentiment. Resilience refers to the ability of the economic system to bounce back from sudden shocks.

References

Castles, I. (1992), 'Living Standards in Sydney and Japanese Cities – A Comparison' in Kyoko Sheridan (ed.), *The Australian Economy in the Japanese Mirror*, University of Queensland Press.

Clark, M. (1963), *A Short History of Australia*, Mentor Books, New York.

Dodds, S. (1997), 'Economic Growth and Human Well-being' in Mark Diesendorf and Clive Hamilton (2002), *Human Ecology, Human Economy*, Allen & Unwin, Sydney.

Duchin, F., Hamilton, C. and Lange, G. M. (1993), 'Environment and Development in Indonesia: An Input-Output Analysis of Natural Resource Issues' Natural Resource Management Project, Jakarta.

Easterlin, R. (1973), 'Does Money Buy Happiness?', *The Public Interest*, vol. 30, pp.3-10.

ILO (1998), 'The Social Impact of the Asian Crisis', technical report, Bangkok April (www.ilo.org/public/english/60empfor/cdart/bangkok/chapter2.htm).

Krugman, P. (1997), *Pop Internationalism*, MIT Press, Cambridge, Mass.

Lee, Jong-Wha and Rhee, Changyong. (1999), 'Social Impacts of the Asian Crisis: Policy Challenges and Lessons', United Nations Development Program, January, http://www.undp.org/hdro/oc33a.htm.

Sen, A. K. (1984), *Resources, Values and Development*, Harvard University Press, Cambridge, Mass.

Smith, Adam. (nd), *The Wealth of Nations*, Originally 1776, re-print 1964, Dent, London.

Todaro, Michael. (1977), *Economic Development*, First Edition, Longman, London.

Wearing, A. and Headey, B. (1998), 'Who Enjoys Life and Why? Measuring Subjective Well-being', in Richard Eckersley (ed.), *Measuring Progress: Is Life Getting Better?*, CSIRO Publishing, Collingwood.

Wolf, A. (1999), 'Education and economic growth', *New Economy*, vol. 6, No. 1 March, Institute for Public Policy Research, London.

World Bank (1992), *Indonesia: Growth, Infrastructure and Human Resources*, World Bank, Jakarta, September.

Chapter 6

The Asian Crisis and Financial and Capital Account Liberalization

Chander Kant

Introduction

One of the puzzling phenomena recently had been the sudden drop of external confidence in five Asian economies: South Korea, Indonesia, Malaysia, Thailand and the Philippines. This lack of faith spread in varying degrees to other 'miracle economies' like Singapore, Taiwan, and Hong Kong. The abrupt change in fortunes was shocking because even as late as June 1997, policy makers and economists were trying to imitate these miracle economies. Now, the attempt is to learn how to avoid such a pointed discontinuity in economic performance.

Given the relative novelty of this crisis, theoretical analysis of this crisis is relatively sparse. Some parallels to the Mexican crisis of 1994-95 and the Chilean crisis of 1982-84 can be found. All these crises were accentuated by sharp reversal in the non-traditional external financing sector, viz. external financing not mediated or guaranteed by governments. Yet, as we shall see below, the persistence, wide-impact, and underlying causes of the Asian crisis sets itself apart from the earlier Chilean and Mexican experiences.

Crises and the Asian Crisis

Surveying crises faced by developing countries since 1960, Bruno (1996) distinguishes between three kinds of economic crises: inflation, debt, and growth. Inflation crisis is defined as high inflation followed by stabilization. High inflation means 40 percent annual inflation for at least two years in a row. Stabilization implies returning below that threshold for at least two years in a row. On the other hand, countries rescheduling their private debt at least once since 1980 are said to be facing debt crisis. Lastly, at least three consecutive years of decline in economic activity (cumulating to a drop of at least 9 percent in GDP) is defined as growth crisis. We present data on the recent Asian crisis to see whether these countries faced any of these crisis.[1]

Asian crisis manifests itself first by a sharp decline in exchange rates and asset values. The IMF, the World Bank, Asian Development Bank, and individual countries like Japan had committed $117.7b to Indonesia, Korea, and Thailand by

August 31, 1997. Also, Hong Kong has a large stock of foreign reserves, and has one of the most liberal and open financial markets in the world with its currency's long-standing peg to the U.S. dollar. Yet, the financial markets in Korea and Hong Kong suffered great turbulence in October 1997 (following Taiwan's depreciation of its new dollar by 10 percent).

Tables 6.1 and 6.2 present information on the decline in exchange rates and stock indices, respectively, in East Asian countries since July 1, 1997. Five countries stand out has having extreme exchange rate and stock value depreciations. These are Indonesia, Korea, Malaysia, the Philippines, and Thailand.[2] Out of these five economies, Indonesia, Thailand, and Korea had to reschedule their private debt. Although inflation was expected to increase in these countries due to sharp exchange rate depreciation, it has remained moderate due to outflow of $17.2b), and a decline of $15.8b in non-bank private creditors, and a decrease of $15.4b in portfolio equity investment (from an inflow of $13.9b to an outflow of $1.5b). These three declines account for 72 percent, 15 percent, and 14 percent, respectively, of the decrease in private inflows to the five Asian countries. The severe reversal of commercial bank and other private lending, rather than the reverse flow of securitized international finance, thus predominantly explains the sharp declines in the exchange rates and in other asset values in these countries.

Financial and Capital Account Liberalization

In this section, we briefly summarize some of the recent work on financial and/or capital account liberalization both in general and that in Asia. We first note that liberalizations are often partial and incremental. Till the recent imposition of controls by Hong Kong and Malaysia, each year more and more emerging markets were moving slowly but steadily towards greater liberalization of their capital accounts and financial sectors.[3] Few emerging markets had full liberalization. Nevertheless, fairly large capital movements may take place even with partial and incomplete liberalization.

Demirglic-Kunt and Detragiache (1998) study a large panel data set covering 53 industrial and developing economies during 1980-95. During this period the banking sector was increasingly liberalized. Yet, the frequency of systematic banking problems markedly increased, raising the possibility that greater fragility is a consequence of liberalization. Although financial fragility is affected by a host of factors, financial liberalization can be seen to have a negative effect on banking sector stability. Their findings strongly suggest that institutional development and the regulatory framework needed for financial markets to operate efficiently should be emphasized early in the liberalization process. There appears to be a consensus that ending financial repression is a precondition for freeing capital accounts. Yet, few authors have investigated the interaction between these two sectors after they are liberalized. One exception is Goldfajn and Valdes (1997) who through a three-period, three-agents (investors, financial intermediaries, and central bank) model show that intermediaries' role of transforming maturities results in larger movements of capital and higher probability of crisis. Haggard and

Maxfield (1996), and Park (1994) also caution about rapid financial and capital account liberalization, particularly in a regime of fixed exchange rates. On the other hand, Bartolini and Drazen (1997) model a situation of foreign uncertainty about government's attitude towards taxation of capital. In this situation, a liberal capital outflow policy sends a signal of future favorable policies towards foreign investment and hence may trigger a capital inflow. This conclusion is supported by Mathieson and Rojas-Suarez (1993) who report that portfolio adjustments following capital account liberalization have often led to a net capital inflow and real exchange rate appreciation. To summarize, these studies tell us that though capital account liberalization generally leads to a net capital inflow, fixed exchange rates may not be viable when the capital account is liberalized. Nevertheless, financial and capital markets interaction causes a large movement of capital and a greater probability of crisis.

Asian Financial and Capital Account Liberalization

Now we turn to studies of financial and capital account liberalization in the five affected Asian countries. Binhadi (1994) reports that Indonesia had liberalized the exchange rates and the capital account in 1970 while tax reform and trade and industry deregulation began only in the second half of eighties. In June 1983, determination of interest rates was left to each bank's discretion. Before October 1988, the private banks and foreign banks were not permitted to enter the banking sector. Kiriwat (1994) finds that after achieving fiscal balance and export success, the financial authorities in Thailand removed all interest rate ceilings gradually between 1989 to 1992. At the same time, the authorities felt that the securities market needed to be strengthened to provide both a counterweight to the power of large banks and give corporate managers instruments to manage their cash flow and risk.

Zialcita (1994) studies external account liberalization in the Philippines. The Philippines had full current account convertibility in 1981-82, but capital account restrictions remained pervasive. Following the balance of payments crisis and debt moratorium of October 1983, a floating regime was established. In 1991, the Philippines permitted full inflow of capital and limited outflow capital to $1m per investor per year. Dooley (1994) notes that capital account liberalization in Malaysia and Indonesia (and in Chile and Mexico) was followed by large inflows of foreign capital. In addition to the usual 'pull' and 'push' factors, speculative bubbles and government policies were behind these inflows. Poorly informed private investors were merely following a 'follow the leader' game.[4] Government policies of maintaining fixed exchange rates obviated the exchange rate risk. Though private investors/creditors expected the bubble to burst, they expected the government or the IMF to bail them out since they (IMF or the government) would not like the depositors hurt. Thus, he had noted in 1994 that capital inflows in some Asian countries involved moral hazard.

Johnston, Darbar, and Echeverria (1997) provide detailed information on the sequence and incremental nature of reforms of domestic and external transactions in Indonesia, Korea, and Thailand (and Chile) for the 1985-96 period. This information is reviewed against the balance of payments developments and macroeconomic and exchange rate policies in these countries. They favor a coordinated and comprehensive approach to reforms of these two sectors. They also suggest that managing capital flows successfully depends critically on the overall incentive-structure causing these flows and the stage of development of the domestic financial system.

Thus, the affected Asian countries mostly retained fixed exchange rates and had fairly liberal financial and capital sectors in place by 1997. However, they lacked either awareness or will/expertise to adequately supervise or regulate the financial sectors.

Asian Crisis: Diagnosis and Prognosis

Asian countries' economic performance was being held up as a model for other countries as late as April 1997. For example, Ito (1997), using the 'flying geese' hypothesis, identifies Japan, flying in front, flanked by Hong Kong and Singapore, and followed by Korea and Taiwan as miracle economies. He noted that Malaysia, Thailand, Indonesia, and the Philippines were just behind them in economic success. For example, during the thirty years preceding the crisis, per capita real income levels increased tenfold in Korea, fivefold in Thailand and fourfold in Malaysia. All these countries had high savings and investment rates, were applying modern scientific thought and technology to industry, and had highly trained labor forces. A major crisis in these economies begs for answers. We present the following explanations.

Low Marginal Productivity of Capital

One reason for the Asian crisis is that marginal productivity of capital had fallen quite low in these countries by 1997. Young (1994, 1995), Kim and Lau (1994), and Krugman (1994) argue that most of East Asia's remarkable success preceding those years was attributable to factor accumulation (including capital accumulation) rather than to miraculous achievements in productivity. An implication is that East Asia had excessive investment who marginal productivity had substantially fallen. Investors' sudden realization of this low return on real investment in the affected countries was one cause of the Asian crisis. This structural problem was not widely recognized before 1997.

Minsky's Financial Instability Hypothesis

The Asian experience lends some support to Minsky's (1986) financial instability hypothesis that a country's economic success carries the seeds of a later financial crisis. Minsky argued that economic booms cause both lenders and borrowers to take risks they otherwise would not. Such risk taking results in financial instability as borrowers seek cash to finance acquisition of additional capital goods and lenders willingly provide it. Any shock to the system can easily push the borrowers into insolvency. Hardy and Pazarbasioglu (1998) find some evidence of this financial instability in Asia. Asian countries had a higher than average relationship between banking sector distress and credit growth. They also had excessive buildup in the foreign liabilities of the banking sector.

Fixed Exchange Rates and Un-Hedged Borrowings

Washington-institutions (IMF and the U.S. Treasury) have stressed the maintenance of relatively fixed exchange rates as one of the causes of the crisis. The exchange-rate confidence, solvency, and debt crises that erupted in the affected economies in mid-1997 was not a result of the usual macroeconomic imbalances. The fixed-exchange rates led banks and corporations in the affected countries to borrow large amounts of short-term, foreign currency denominated un-hedged foreign capital that was used to finance poor quality investments.

'Push' Factors and Rise in Country Risk

The preceding explanation raises the question why fully rational lenders/investors lent and invested in such low-quality investments. It appears that 'push' factors, viz. low rates of return available to financial institutions in Japan and the U.S., and vent of surplus of investible funds for whatever diversification existed, combined with optimistic expectations were responsible for flows to these countries. Yet, in the middle of 1997, the lenders/investors revised their return-expectations downwards and risk-expectations upwards and suddenly pulled their funds back.

Chinn and Maloney (1998) for Korea and Taiwan, and Maloney (1997) for Chile find that in spite of capital account liberalization, covered interest parity (CIP) did not hold for these countries. Covered interest parity has been used as a test of capital accounts' integration. These countries' capital markets therefore were not well integrated with world markets. However, CIP only adjusts for expectations of exchange rate depreciation. One should instead argue that these countries had higher 'country-risk.' In the middle of 1997, country-risk of the East Asian economies suddenly increased. Nevertheless, their real interest rates did not rise either speedily or sufficiently. The result was capital flight and currency and asset-value crises.

Regionalization and Contagion

The conventional wisdom is that the 1990s have been 'the decade of globalization.' This preconception does not recognize the simultaneous increase in regional linkages. During the past decade, regional economic links have intensified more than extra-regional ones. Trade among industrial countries in different regions has declined in relative terms while linkages between developed and emerging market economies within regions have increased. In addition, intra-regional trade among emerging market countries has been the fastest-growing category of all. For example, despite strong export to non-Asian trading partners, intra-Asian trade among developing countries has grown even more rapidly so that intra-regional exports as a proportion of total exports increased as illustrated by Table 6.4. The contagion to the other Asian countries can be partly explained by the recognition of these regional links by investors.

Institutional Factors

The Asian crisis shows that there are important differences between financial and other markets. These differences suggest that although there is a presumption that trade liberalization is welfare-enhancing, full liberalization of financial markets may well not be because it is associated with a higher probability of crisis. Financial markets will promote growth only if they have sturdy institutions to help them do their work, including strong government regulation, effective laws, and vigilant enforcement. The affected Asian countries had largely liberalized their financial and capital account sectors even though they lacked such sturdy institutions.

Comparison to the Chilean and Mexican Crises

Chile: Chile is one country where financial liberalization was taken to mean no regulation. Chile privatized its banks and liberalized exchange rates in 1974. Capital controls were completely removed by 1980. During this period several banks and whole saving and loan system collapsed. Some banks had no capital, and the incidence of connected lending within financial-industrial groups was high. Recession and serious deterioration in the terms of trade in early 1980s led to large reversals of capital flows. The bad debts of banks accelerated rapidly because of exchange rate and interest rate-lined losses.

The Chilean crisis of early 1980s, like the Asian crisis, was also manifested by a reversal of private capital flows. Still, it differs from the Asian crisis in the following ways: First, unlike the affected Asian countries, Chile's banking and financial sector was already on the verge of collapse before the crisis. Secondly, the Chilean crisis was triggered by events in the real sector, viz. recession and sharp deterioration in the terms of trade. On the other hand, the Asian crisis started with the sudden fall in confidence in Thai Baht's exchange value.

Mexico: Mexico was a large recipient of foreign capital in the period preceding its 1994-95 crisis. In fact, $104b of capital flowed into the country between 1990 and 1994 – it was 20 percent of total capital flows to developing countries during this period. However, most of this capital consisted of portfolio equity investment. None of the affected Asian countries experienced such large capital inflows preceding the crisis. Also, the dominant equity investment in these countries was direct rather than portfolio. Direct flows to Asian countries did not reverse during the crisis years. It was largely the reversal of short-term bank lending that characterizes the Asian crisis.

As stated above, one reason for the Asian crisis was the excessive boom in real investment in these countries. The boom had been going on for decades. The situation in Mexico was different. For ten years preceding 1989, Mexico experienced low or negligible growth and high inflation. From 1989 to 1994, Mexico's average GDP growth rate was 3.9 percent, and, inflation in 1993 fell to single digit levels for the first time in over 20 years. Thus, Mexico was not suffering from either a long boom in investment that had reduced the marginal productivity of capital in 1994 or from Minsky's financial instability in the last phase of a boom. Rather it was political (and suspected criminal) events revealed in December 1994) that caused the Mexican crisis. After the rescue package was put together, the crisis was quickly contained. The Asian crisis proved to be so enduring because it has demonstrated some structural problems of these economies.[5]

Conclusions

The return on financial investments in the U.S. (at least of the fixed income type) and Japan have been quite low. One source of these funds are prodigious Japanese savings coupled with its negligible (till recently) growth. For U.S., the wealth effects due to the 1990s boom, rising income inequality, and the maturing of the baby-boomers all provide a 'push' for new markets. These factors provide great opportunities for developing countries as a destination for capital flows. However, the Asian crisis, like the Mexican crisis of 1994-95, also shows the challenge of sustaining the confidence of foreign investors. Any unexpected development/shock can cause panic and 'run' on the country. Thus, developing countries ought to strengthen their institutions at the same pace as they liberalize their financial sector and open-up their capital accounts. The theoretical models discussed in this paper assume open economies, full information, and efficient global financial markets. The former two assumptions are particularly inappropriate for developing countries. In the 1980s, the information asymmetry between local firms/banks and foreign investors about local business conditions in Latin America was mitigated by government guarantees to foreign investors. Yet, as the experience of the 'lost decade' of 1980s showed, even sovereigns' may default. Imperfect information-models are needed as alternatives to the current full-information open-economy models. Furthermore there is a need for additional studies of the interaction of financial and capital account liberalization both to explain the Asian crisis and to understand this increasingly important part of modern economies.

Data

Table 6.1 Depreciation in Asian Exchange Rates

	Percent change from:		
	July 1, 1997 to Dec. 31, 1997	Dec. 31, 1997 to May 1, 1998	July 1, 1997 to May 1, 1998
Indonesia	−55.8	−31.2	−69.6
Korea	−47.5	26.7	−33.5
Malaysia	−35.2	5.7	−31.5
Philippines	−34.5	.6	−34.9
Thailand	−47.6	21.2	−36.5
Japan	−11.9	−1.9	−13.6
China	.1	.4	.5
Hong Kong	0.0	0.0	0.0
Taiwan	15.2	−.8	−15.8
Singapore	−15.4	7.0	−9.5

Note: Calculated from various issues of the IMF's International Financial Statistics.
Source: Bloomberg Financial Services, L.P.

Table 6.2 Depreciation in Asian Stock Indices

	Percent change from:		
	July 1, 1997 to Dec. 31, 1997	Dec. 31, 1997 to May 1, 1998	July 1, 1997 to May 1, 1998
Indonesia	−45.4	14.5	−37.0
Korea	−51.6	11.9	−45.8
Malaysia	−45.7	6.2	−42.3
Philippines	−32.4	16.7	−21.1
Thailand	−35.7	12.7	−27.5
Japan	−24.4	2.5	−22.6
China	1.5	13.7	12.0
Hong Kong	−28.6	−3.5	31.0
Taiwan	−9.5	1.9	−7.7
Singapore	−13.8	−8.9	−21.3

Source: Bloomberg Financial Services, L.P.

Table 6.3 External Financing in Five Asian Economies (Billions of Dollars)

	1995	1996	1997	1998	1999f
Current account balance	−40.6	−54.4	−26.8	69.4	46.3
External financing, net	89.0	103.2	27.5	−12.9	10.8
Private flows, net	86.4	106.4	−0.8	-38.6	5.1
Equity investment, net	15.3	18.6	4.4	14.2	25.2
Direct, net	4.2	4.7	5.9	9.9	11.9
Portfolio, net	11.0	13.9	−1.5	4.3	13.2
Private creditors, net	71.2	87.8	−5.2	−52.7	−20.0
Commercial banks, net	58.6	59.9	−17.2	−48.3	−18.7
Nonbanks, net	12.6	27.8	12.0	−4.4	−1.3
Official flows, net	2.6	−3.2	28.3	25.6	5.7
Int'l financial institutions	−0.4	−2.0	22.5	19.4	−3.3
Bilateral creditors	3.0	−1.3	5.7	6.3	9.0
Resident lending/other, net2	−34.3	−31.9	−31.3	−15.1	−13.5
Reserves (− = increase)	−14.1	−16.9	30.7	−41.3	−43.6

Source: Institute of International Finance.

**Table 6.4 Trade among developing countries (intraregional exports as a
        percentage of total exports)**

	1987	1998
Within Asia	27.4	38.3
Within Latin America	15.2	22.0
Within Europe	34.6	36.4
Within Africa	5.8	11.9

Source: IMF, Direction of Trade Statistics 1996-Yearbook and June 1999-Quarterly.

Notes

1. Other parts of the world have not been immune from contagion from the Asian
    crisis. The Russian economy was performing poorly in any case. But, Latin-
    American economies, including Brazil, arguably may have avoided their woes in the
    absence of contagion from the Asian crisis. This crisis has clearly exacerbated
    economic problems in many parts of the world. For example, the following
    economies (in addition to the five affected countries) have experienced recession
    (fall in output for two consecutive quarters) since the Asian crisis: Singapore, Hong
    Kong, Japan, Germany, Argentina, Brazil, Chile, Colombia, Venezuela, South
    Africa, Romania, Ukraine, Turkey, and the Czech Republic. See, the World Bank

(1999) and International Financial Statistics, various monthly issues. This crisis and its aftermath placed the global real economy to one of its greatest perils since the Great Depression.
2.   The decline in real estate prices in these economies is equally sharp.
3.   Please see various monthly issues of the International Financial Statistics for these data.
4.   The gradual liberalization from 1985 to 1996 of monetary controls and financial system, exchange system, trade and capital flows for Chile, Indonesia, Korea, and Thailand is brought-out very clearly by Johnston, Darbar, and Echeverria (1997).
5.   The 'push' factors (external or exogenous developments) like low rates of return in investing countries and investors' desire for diversification may be contrasted from 'pull' factors like policy reforms, regulatory changes, and a more attractive investment climate in the borrowing countries. See Calvo, Leiderman, and Reinhart (1993) for the use of these terms.
6.   Mexico overcame its structural problems by undertaking reforms during the 'lost decade' of the 1980s and during early 1990s.

References

Bartolini, Leonardo and Drazen, A. (1997), Capital-Account Liberalization as a Signal, *American Economic Review*, vol. 87, pp.138-154.
Binhadi, P. (1994), 'Financial Deregulation and Bank Supervision: The Case of Indonesia', in Faruqi, Shakil (ed.), *Financial Sector Reforms, Economic Growth, and Stability, Experiences in Selected Asian and Latin American Countries*, The World Bank, Washington, DC.
Bruno, Michael. (1996), *Deep Crises and Reform, What Have we Learned?*, The World Bank, Washington, DC.
Calvo, G. A., L. Leiderman and C. Reinhart. (1993), 'Capital Flows to Latin American: The Role of External Factors.' *IMF Staff Papers*, vol. 40, pp.108-51.
Chinn, Menzie D. and William F. Maloney. (1996), 'Financial and Capital Account Liberalization in the Pacific Basin: Korea and Taiwan During the 1980s,' *International Economic Journal*, 12, 53-74.
Demirguc-Kunt, Asli and Enrica Detragiache. (1998), 'Financial Liberalization and Financial Fragility,' presented at the *Annual World Bank Conference on Development Economics*, The World Bank, Washington, DC.
Dooley, Michael. (1994), 'Globalization, Speculative Bubbles, and Central Banking,' in Faruqi, Shakil (ed.) *Financial Sector Reforms, Economic Growth, and Stability, Experiences in Selected Asian and Latin American Countries*, The World Bank, Washington, DC.
Goldfajn, Ilan and Rodrigo O. Valdes. (1997), 'Capital Flows and the Twin Crises: The Role of Liquidity', *Working Paper*, 97/87, The International Monetary Fund, Washington, DC.
Haggard, Stephen and Sylvia Maxfield. (1996), 'The Political Economy of Financial Internationalization in the Developing World,' *International Organization*, vol. 50, pp.35-68.
Hardy, Daniel C. and Ceyla Pazarbasuoglu. (1998), 'Leading Indicators of Banking Crisis: Was Asia Different?' *Working Paper*, 98/91, The International Monetary Fund, Washington, DC.

Institute of International Finance (1999), *Capital Flows to Emerging Market Economies*, Washington, DC, April 25 and September 25, and detailed data for the five affected Asian economies provided by its staff.

International Financial Statistics, various monthly issues, Washington, DC.

International Monetary Fund (1999), *Direction of Trade Statistics*, 1996-Yearbook and June 1999-Quarterly, Washington, DC.

Ito, Takatoshi. (1997), 'What can Developing Countries Learn from East Asia's Economic Growth,' *Annual World Bank Conference on Development Economics*, The World Bank, Washington, DC.

Johnston, Barry R., Salim M. Darbar and Claudia Echeverria. (1997), 'Sequencing Capital Account Liberalization: Lessons from the Experience in Chile, Indonesia, Korea, and Thailand', *Working Paper*, 97/157, The International Monetary Fund, Washington, DC.

Kim, Jong-Il and Lawrence J. Lau. (1994), 'The Sources of Economic Growth of the East Asian Newly Industrialized Countries,' *Journal of Japanese and International Economics*, vol. 8, pp.235-71.

Kiriwat, Ekamol. (1994), 'Securities Market Regulations and Reforms in Thailand,' in Faruqi, Shakil (ed.), *Financial Sector Reforms, Economic Growth, and Stability, Experiences in Selected Asian and Latin American Countries*, The World Bank, Washington, DC.

Krugman, Paul. (1994), 'The Myth of Asia's Miracle,' *Foreign Affairs*, pp.62-78.

Le-Fort, Guillermo. (1994), 'The Financial System and Macroeconomic Stability: The Chilean Experience,' in Faruqi, Shakil (ed.), *Financial Sector Reforms, Economic Growth, and Stability, Experiences in Selected Asian and Latin American Countries*, The World Bank, Washington, DC.

Maloney, William F. (1997), 'Testing Capital Account Liberalization without Forward Rates, Another Look at Chile 1979-1982', *Journal of Development Economics*, vol. 52, pp.39-168.

Mathieson, Donald J. and Liliana Rojas-Suarez. (1993), *Liberalization of Capital Account, Experiences and Issues*, The International Monetary Fund, Washington, DC.

Minsky, Hyman P. (1986), *Stabilizing an Unstable Economy*, Yale University Press, New Haven and London.

Park, Daekeun. (1994), 'Foreign Exchange Liberalization and the Viability of a Fixed Exchange Regime,' *Journal of International Economics*, vol. 36, pp.99-116.

World Bank (1999), *World Development Report*, Washington, DC.

Young, Alwyn. (1994), 'Lessons from the East Asian NICs: A Contrarian View,' *European Economic Review*, vol. 38, pp.964-973.

Young, Alwyn. (1995), 'The Tyranny of Numbers: Confronting the Statistical Realities of the East Asian Growth Experience', *Quarterly Journal of Economics*, vol. 110, pp.641-680.

Zialcita, Edgardo P. (1994), 'Capital Account Liberalization: The Philippines Experience,' in Faruqi, Shakil (ed.), *Financial Sector Reforms, Economic Growth, and Stability, Experiences in Selected Asian and Latin American Countries*, The World Bank, Washington DC.

Chapter 7

Major Causes of the Korean and Asian Economic Crises

Chang Woon Nam

Introduction

During the past year myriad new reports appeared with accounts of the crash of the Asian economies. What began with the *panic* triggered by the failure of the Thai financial system led to the rapid economic downturn of some of the globe's most dynamic economies in 1997 and 1998. Especially for South Korea[1] the consequences of financial and economic crisis and the intervention of the IMF in overcoming the related problems were extremely painful, which include, for example,

- a large number of bankruptcies of industrial firms and private banks,
- the increasing pressure on industrial firms to carry out rapid structural change and specialization on a limited number of competitive areas including the so-called 'big deal' of exchanging business activities among large conglomerates,
- the massive dismissal of workers and the subsequent social and inner-firm unrest,
- the increase of production costs caused by the *won* devaluation and the change of relative prices of import goods such as semiconductors and natural resources like petroleum,
- the drastic decrease in domestic households' demand and firms' investment spending caused by income reduction and high interest rates, etc.[2]

These facts clearly indicate that the South Korean crisis has already turned out to be a real sector crisis rather than a financial crisis. According to the standard economic literature, a financial crisis is generally defined, for example, as a situation in which a significant group of financial institutions have liabilities exceeding the market value of their assets, leading to runs and other portfolio shifts, collapse of some financial firms and government intervention (Sundararajan and Balino, 1991). Additionally, it is also quite often characterized as a non-linear disruption to a financial markets in which adverse selection and moral hazard problems become much worse, so that financial markets are unable to efficiently channel funds to those who have the most productive investment opportunities

(Mishikin, 1996). According to Shin and Hahm (1998), the South Korean case not only demonstrates all the aspects of a financial crisis under the first definition but also fulfils the criteria posited by the latter definition. In addition, such type of financial crisis was accompanied by the currency crisis (i.e. strong depreciation of *won*) in the fourth quarter of 1997.[3] Their negative impacts rapidly led to the severe total economic break-down in South Korea as shown before. This abrupt crash was also partly triggered by the pressure of the IMF, which insisted on a domestic austerity package and on fundamental structural reforms in return for bail-out funds.[4]

Following the first big shocks of the crisis in South Korea and Asia, these standard questions have been raised repeatedly. After the lessons learned from the Latin American economic crisis, how could this happen again and especially to East Asia? How could such rapidly growing economies experience a sudden depression, one after the other? Why was the crisis not foreseen? And, of course, what can be done to prevent such types of unpleasant events in the future? In order to provide answers to these important questions and many others that follow, one must have thorough understanding of the origins of the Asian economic crisis. Many prominent economists have already made astute analyses of the major causes of the current financial and economic crisis. Yet, their arguments appear to be more strongly concentrated on the issues related to the *financial* sector, although they attempted to reflect in their hypotheses the crucial macro-, meso- and micro-economic conditions and other *real* sector problems in Asian countries which led to the crisis. In some cases, 'Western-made' explanations of the origins tend to be rather general and, consequently, do not adequately consider nation-specific differences in recent economic problems. Introducing the mainstream of theoretical explanations about the major causes of the crisis, this paper briefly suggests some (theoretically and empirically) controversial aspects as well as less well-known (Korea-specific) additional financial and real sector problems which assist in an understanding of the origins in the country.

Krugman's Hypothesis on the End of the Asian Miracle

According to Krugman's popular publication in 1994 entitled 'The Myth of Asia's Miracle' in *Foreign Affairs*, the Eastern European economies achieved rapid economic growth in the 1960s and 1970s.[5] The remarkable Asian economic development since the beginning of the 1980s could be very much comparable to the experiences of most Eastern European countries in this phase, which, however, was followed by collapse at the end of the 1980s.[6] One of the major reasons for the economic collapse in these Eastern European countries is the fact that the economic growth in the 1960s and the subsequent decade was mainly led by rapid growth in inputs (e.g. expansion of employment, increases in education levels and massive investment in physical capital) but unfortunately not accompanied by productivity growth (i.e. the growth in efficiency measured in terms of the 'output per unit of input'). Krugman (1994) additionally argued that the recent economic growth in Asian countries was mainly triggered by the increase in labor input (without achieving technological development) and that the labor productivity level in Asian countries was still quite low at the beginning of the 1990s when compared to those of developed countries. As a consequence, he made the rather pessimistic prophecy that Asian economies would gradually lose their growth dynamism caused by the continually diminishing returns, as was the case for Eastern European countries in the 1980s, and the so-called Asian miracle would eventually end in the long run.

Krugman's hypothesis remained influential, also in Europe. When the economy of East Asian countries started to crash in the wake of the failure of the Thai banking and financial system in mid-1997, many Europeans turned again to his 1994 article seeking an explanation for the origins of the current Asian financial and economic crisis. Is there a close comparability between the Eastern European and the Asian economic growth pattern? Is the low labor productivity level in Asia the major cause of the Asian crash? In order to examine these topics empirically, the changes in the level of (real) GDP per capita and GDP per hour worked (labor productivity) are investigated in a number of selected transformation and Asian countries (including South Korea) for the period 1960-92. For the purpose of this type of multilateral comparison, the GDP data expressed in so-called Geary-Khamis international dollars in 1990 are applied, which were recently estimated by the OECD (see appendix).[7]

Table 7.1 demonstrates the international comparison of GDP per capita development in the investigated years. In Eastern European countries such as the former USSR and Czechoslovakia as well as in Hungary and Poland, there was a gradual but moderate increase in the level of GDP per capita in the period of 1960-80 (see also below). Starting at the beginning of the 1980s, however, these countries' per capita GDP level stagnated (with slight fluctuations) and/or slowly declined, and significantly fell in the beginning of the 1990s when the so-called shock therapy was implemented to carry out the economic transformation. Compared to the Eastern European development in the 1970s, the growth of GDP per capita since the beginning of the 1980s was obviously more dynamic in the investigated Asian countries (South Korea, Taiwan and Japan). In 1960, Japan's per capita GDP level was comparable to those of Eastern European countries (3,879 Geary-Khamis dollars) but increased rapidly and reached around 20,000 Geary-Khamis dollars in 1992, which was far above the Eastern European level. Thanks to the remarkable growth that started in 1980, South Korea and Taiwan also easily surpassed the Eastern European GDP per capita in the second half of the 1980s and continued to grow rapidly in the subsequent years, although firstly in 1975 these two Asian countries were only able to achieve a per capita GDP similar to that of Eastern European countries in 1960 (see Table 7.1).

Table 7.1 Levels of GDP per Capita in Selected Asian and Eastern European Countries in the 1990 Geary-Khamis Dollars

	South Korea	Japan	Taiwan	Thailand	USSR	Poland	Hungary	Czechoslovakia
1960	1302	3879	1399	1029	3935	3218	3649	5108
1962	1348	4647	1518	1103	4130	3341	3963	5303
1964	1508	5514	1757	1191	4430	3600	4390	5370
1966	1738	6327	2013	1350	4796	3970	4646	5734
1968	1884	7757	2317	1464	5194	4281	4934	6206
1970	2208	9448	2692	1596	5565	4428	5028	6460
1972	2504	10378	3312	1647	5640	5005	5336	6854
1974	3021	10800	3645	1794	6175	5593	5716	7229
1976	3475	11309	4189	1982	6366	5885	5791	7444
1978	4124	12186	5044	2226	6565	6097	6253	7761
1980	4103	13113	5634	2384	6437	5740	6307	7978
1982	4553	13817	5971	2528	6544	5288	6580	8038
1984	5431	14602	6944	2730	6715	5649	6703	8300
1986	6426	15542	7932	2873	6924	5804	6693	8479
1988	7829	17028	9357	3449	7032	5790	6929	8675
1990	8977	18548	10324	4173	6871	5113	6348	8464
1992	10010	19425	11590	4694	4671	4726	5638	6845

Source: Maddison (1995), Monitoring the World Economy, OECD Development Centre Studies, Paris.

Table 7.2 shows that the recent rapid economic growth in Asian countries, particularly since the beginning of the 1970s, has been accompanied by a remarkable labor productivity growth, although the GDP level per hour worked of Asian countries (excluding Japan) remained – as Krugman (1994) already noted – far below the level of the US and Western European countries in the beginning of the 1990s. In general, one can easily see that the GDP growth of a country is closely correlated with the labor productivity growth in all investigated years. This was also true for those selected Eastern European countries, which had zero or negative annual average GDP (and also GDP per capita) growth rates in the period 1973-92, and also suffered from stagnating productivity growth. In addition, a significant catching-up process has recently taken place between the US, on the one hand, and Asian countries (like Japan, South Korea, Taiwan etc.), on the other. In the period 1973-92 the US had to be content with an average annual labor productivity growth rate of around 1 percent, while fast growing South Korea, Taiwan and Thailand achieved – from a rather low absolute level – an average annual growth rate of above 5 percent in the same phase.

Table 7.2 International Comparison of Economic Performance Measured in the 1990 Geary-Khamis International Dollars

	Annual average compound GDP growth rate (percent)		Annual average compound per capita GDP growth rate (percent)		Annual average compound growth rate of GDP per hour worked (productivity)		GDP per hour worked (absolute productivity level)	
	1950-73	1973-92	1950-73	1973-92	1950-73	1973-92	1973	1992
USA	3.9	2.5	2.4	1.5	2.7	1.1	23.45	29.10
Japan	9.2	3.8	8.0	3.0	7.7	3.1	11.15	20.02
Germany	6.0	2.2	5.0	1.8	6.0	2.7	16.64	27.55
France	5.0	2.1	4.0	1.6	5.1	2.7	17.77	29.62
Italy	5.6	2.5	5.0	2.2	5.8	2.4	15.58	24.59
UK	3.0	1.7	2.5	1.5	3.1	2.2	15.92	23.98
Czechoslovakia	3.8	0.2	3.1	-0.1	3.4	0.1	8.07	8.17
Hungary	4.1	-0.0	3.6	0.0	3.9	0.6	6.50	7.35
Poland	4.8	0.1	3.4	-0.6	3.8	0.4	5.74	6.14
USSR	4.8	-0.5	3.4	-1.4	3.4	-0.8	6.59	5.66
South Korea	7.6	8.3	5.2	6.9	4.1	5.2	3.22	8.48
Taiwan	9.3	7.8	6.2	6.2	5.6	5.3	4.13	11.06
Thailand	6.4	7.5	3.2	5.3	3.6	5.1	1.68	4.34
Indonesia	4.5	5.3	2.5	3.1	2.6	3.1	1.86	3.35
China	5.1	6.7	2.9	5.2	2.1	4.1	1.31	2.79

Source: Maddison (1995), Monitoring the World Economy, OECD Development Centre Studies, Paris.

In other words, although both Eastern European countries and Asian economies experienced sudden crashes – the former around ten years prior to the latter – there were significant differences in the general economic development and the productivity growth which led to the economic crisis in both types of countries. Krugman also admitted this fact in his 1998 home page article on '*What Happened To Asia*',

> It seems safe to say that nobody anticipated anything like the current crisis in Asia. ... There were some Asian skeptics – including myself – who regarded the claims of an Asian economic miracle as overstated, ... And some people – again including myself – raised warning flags a year or two before the Thai crisis, noting that the current account deficits of Southeast Asian countries were as high as or higher than those of Latin America in 1994, and ... [they] had no special immunity to financial crisis. ... What we have actually seen [in Asia] is something both more complex and more drastic [than a conventional currency crisis followed by at most a modest downturn and the gradual long-term slowdown in growth]: collapses in domestic asset markets, widespread bank failures, bankruptcies on the part of many firms, and

what looks likely to be a much more severe real downturn than even the most negative-minded anticipated (Krugman, 1998, p.1).

Some Additional Arguments to the Causes of the Korean Economic Crisis

More recently, many prominent economists voiced their opinions on the causes of the Asian crisis (including Bergsten, 1997; Krugman, 1998; Noland, 1998). According to them, the Asian crisis was initiated in the 1980s. The rapid appreciation of the Japanese *yen* against the US dollar in 1985 led to the relative increase in production costs in Japan, which triggered the movement of production facilities of Japanese firms to South Korea and Taiwan. In order to counteract its negative impact on the domestic economic development, Japanese authorities carried out an expansive monetary policy, which, in turn, increased asset prices in Japan and stimulated, due to the low domestic interest rate, capital inflow into South Korea and Taiwan. At the end of the 1980s, these Asian economies were forced to appreciate their currencies and to aggressively expand money supply. As was the case in Japan, the implementation of these political measures in South Korea and Taiwan created asset price bubbles at home and large capital flight to Indonesia and Thailand. On the other hand, the sharp devaluation of the Chinese *yuan* (by about 40 percent in 1994) and the Japanese *yen* (by over 25 percent in the period of 1995-96) put tremendous competitive pressure on the rest of Asia, eroding their trade positions and producing large trade deficits in South Korea and throughout East Asia.

Furthermore, it is also quite often argued that the rapid creation of bubbles in expanding production capacities and investment activities of (large) industrial firms (not only in the country but also abroad) were, to a larger extent, financially (in many cases also politically) backed by the government (the so-called moral hazard problem).[8] In this context, some industrial economists suggest that since the middle of the 1990s South Korean industrial firms have faced strong challenges in the Asian and world market, particularly from Chinese, Thai and Indonesian competitors. Furthermore, labor costs have also drastically increased in this country, which again made Korean products more expensive in the world market. In order to maintain their competitive position, South Korean industrial firms were forced to quickly carry out a structural change including large-scale investments in modern capital stock and to intensify their R&D activities (Bergsten, 1997). As a consequence, South Korean imports of modern investment goods have rapidly increased since the mid-1990s. In addition, the Korean *chaebols* also attempted a relocation of their production facilities to foreign countries. Although large South Korean industrial firms lacked their own financial means and suffered from the serious asset-liability mismatches,[9] argued Krugman (1998), they could well finance their (in some cases not adequately examined, risky and/or less profitable) long-term modernization and internationalization projects – thanks to government support – by taking short-term credits from domestic banks which played solely the role of 'cash box' in the country.[10]

To be sure, 'corporate sectors with high levels of debt are [generally] vulnerable to shocks that cause a fall in cash flow or an increase in fixed payment obligations – systemic shocks such as a fall in aggregate demand, a rise in interest rates, or devaluation of the currency (*when part of the debt is foreign*)' (Wade, 1998, p.698). In this context, it should also be noted that in South Korea there was asymmetry in the deregulation schedules regarding the foreign currency-denominated lending and borrowing of financial institutions in the country. In spite of the fact that in 1993 the Korean government expanded the positive list of usage for which financial institutions may provide foreign currency-denominated loans in the scope of the financial liberalization program, the quantity restriction on long-term borrowing was maintained, while the short-term borrowing (of banks) has always been freely allowed. As a consequence, the short-term foreign debts of the South Korean banks rapidly grew in recent years in order to meet the increasing investment demand of the corporate sector. For these reasons, the credit increase largely exceeded the growth of available domestic resources in the financial sector and the extra credit supply of banks was provided by the steady and strong expansion of external debts and foreign currency-denominated assets (Corsetti, Pesenti and Roubini, 1998; Leibfritz and Nam, 1998; Shin and Hahm, 1998; Chang et al., 1998).[11]

Such practices may be sustainable as long as the rate of economic growth remains high, as financial institutions compensate for the low effective rate of return on loans to these preferred borrowers with high rates of return on other loans. However, if the rate of growth slows, the bad loan drag begins to inhibit the ability of banks and non-bank lending institutions to supply credit to the economy. This is what transpired in a number of Asian economies in 1997, as some key export prices declined (computer chips, for example) (Noland, 1998, p.2).

Furthermore, Noland (1998) argued that such reductions in the export revenue in Asian countries rapidly created the expectation of declining corporate profits and equity prices. As a consequence, domestic and foreign investors started to transfer money abroad in search of higher returns. This, in turn, had a significant effect on the collapse of the domestic asset market and the exchange rate depreciation in Asian countries. In other words, apart from the large deficits in the balance of payments and the insufficient foreign currency reserves, the weakness of the real sector development such as the decline in economic and export growth, additionally makes the victims more vulnerable to the speculative attacks, panics and external financial shocks and leads to the sudden crisis, as is also shown in those monetary and financial crises in Europe and Latin America in 1992-93 and 1994-95, respectively.[12] However, for the Asian case some specific supplementary information and closer observations about such real sector problems appear to be necessary which support or partly reject such Western-style general hypotheses such as those made by Noland (1998). In the following, this task is carried out using South Korea as an example.

In the beginning of the 1990s South Korea experienced a sharp decline of real GDP growth rate from 9.1 percent (1991) to 5.1 percent (1992). However, this did not cause the crisis, in contrast to the more recent economic slow-down from

8.9 percent in 1995 to 7.1 percent in 1996. Even in 1997, the country was able to achieve a GDP growth rate of 5.5 percent, although its economy had already started to collapse in autumn. Under the additional consideration of the quarterly business climate index for the South Korean manufacturing sector provided by the Bank of Korea, one can easily identify that the rapid fall in the period of 1991-92 was accompanied by a decline in the index.[13] In spite of the increase in the real GDP growth rate from 8.6 percent to 8.9 percent in the period of 1994-95, however, the business climate index continued to gradually decrease since the 3rd quarter of 1994 and fell sharply in the 4th quarter of 1997. This fact clearly shows that South Korean manufacturing firms actually anticipated the decline in their economic activities since 1994, although the GDP growth rate was very high and its reduction was rather modest in the mid-1990s. Following the idea of Noland (1998), one can stipulate that in the middle of 1994 South Korean and foreign investors started to move money abroad in search of higher returns, and this process continued until 1997. This fact is also indirectly suggested in the recent development of the South Korean capital account deficits. Measured in terms of the 1990 won/US$ exchange rate, the amount of deficits accounted to approximately US$ 536 million in 1993, which was reduced by US$ 55 million in 1994. In both subsequent years, however, the sum of deficits increased rapidly and reached US$ 527 and US$ 704 million in 1995 and 1996, respectively.

More immediately, the sudden expansion of the trade deficit gap in 1996 appears to have made South Korea less immune to the financial crisis (Krugman, 1998; Shin and Hahm, 1998; Wade, 1998). Expressed in 1990 exchange rates, the amount of trade (goods and services) deficits increased between 1995 and 1996 from US$ 8 to 25 billion. Yet, it should be emphasized that this large gap was created not by the reduction in total exports but because the country's import growth was much faster than the export growth in the same year. Since computer chips have recently been the leading export components of South Korea, the decline in semiconductor exports in 1996 seemed to have created, to a certain extent, the expectation of declining corporate profits and equity prices, as Noland (1998) and Wade (1998) suggested. However, the percentage share of semiconductor export revenue amounted to around 15 percent of total South Korean exports in 1996. Partly thanks to the gradual export increase of items like cars, woven fabrics, ships, etc. South Korea was able to achieve a significant export growth also in 1996, although its rate was lower than that of 1995. By contrast, import growth was very dynamic between 1994 and 1996; particularly imports of petroleum and sophisticated semiconductors – the most important import item among investment goods – showed an above-average growth trend. In other words, the dependence of the South Korean manufacturing activities on the foreign-made semiconductors and petroleum imports had dramatically increased within two years. The percentage share of imports of the latter component reached around 10 percent of the South Korea's total imports in 1996, while that of the former product amounted to ca. 8 percent. In combination with the effects of a decrease in semiconductor exports on capital flight, these South Korean import performances made the country's economy more vulnerable to the financial crisis.

Especially imports of items like semiconductors and petroleum, which are compulsively required for the current manufacturing activities in South Korea, became obviously more expensive when the *won* was strongly devalued at the end of 1997. This was also one of the most decisive reasons why the domestic production system started to collapse in the country.

Arguments for the Asian Monetary Mechanism vs. the European Experiences

In the course of the long setting-up process of the European Monetary Union, the standard beliefs about the virtues of fixed exchange rate regimes remained unchanged. EU Member States believe that this exchange rate system imposes monetary discipline, removes uncertainty, limits speculation, and promotes international trade and investment within the EU. Underestimating the costs derived from the inability to conduct independent monetary policy which include loss of seigniorage, inability to select the most desired point on a shot-run Phillips curve, and inability to devalue or re-value for stabilization purposes (Karras, 1996), those Europeans who favor the establishment of such an international monetary mechanism (including the establishment of a monetary union[14]) argue this type of international co-operation has recently been required in Asia to reduce the disruptions of the financial system as well as to overcome and better react to such a crisis in a systematic way.[15] Apart from the unstable development of important Asian currencies in the last 15 years and related less-disciplined monetary policy practices of individual countries, the lack of regional co-operation in the fields of debt negotiation and expansion among Asian countries is quite often assessed as an important cause for the current crisis (Wade, 1998).[16] Moreover, many Europeans and Americans see the increasing economic integration among Asian countries as another crucial reason for the international macro-economic policy co-ordination in this continent, and, at the same time, assess the economies of East Asia as plausible candidates for internationally harmonized monetary policies as the EU Member States (Eichengreen and Bayoumi, 1996). For example, intra-Asian trade has been continuously increasing and the share of intra-regional merchandise trade (exports plus imports) in total trade had already reached 50 percent in the mid-1990s, while the same share accounted to approximately 70 percent in Western Europe (WTO, 1995; UNIDO, 1995). The cross-border investment has also been extensive in Asia. Particularly, flows of direct foreign investments from Japan, Hong Kong, Singapore, Taiwan and South Korea into China, Indonesia, Malaysia and Thailand have recently been pronounced (Nam and Nam, 1999).

However, apart from the fact that Asia has no single market yet and the degree of intra-labor mobility is still quite low at present – except the relatively high share of foreign workers in Singapore from Malaysia, Thailand, Indonesia and the Philippines and the emigration of Chinese workers in Hong Kong (Goto and Hamada, 1994), it should be noted that economic and structural disparities among Asian countries (e.g. Japan with highly diversified industrial structure vs. China with a large agricultural sector) are unfortunately more significant than those in the EU, which, in turn, appears to make policy co-ordination more difficult. Unlike the long-lasting integration process and political solidarity in Europe since the 1950s, the institutionalization process has always been weak in East Asia. For instance, countries in this area generally lack the political links and traditions needed to support a concerted exchange rate policy. Asian currency arrangements have widely varied from fixed to floating rates, and the trend toward greater exchange rate flexibility has recently been evident there. In addition, although the *yen* is increasingly used to invoice intra-Asian trade (and the Asian countries have gradually shifted the composition of their external debt away from the dollar toward the *yen*), the dollar has retained – also reflecting the intensive economic co-operation (e.g. bilateral trade) between the US and Asian countries – its important role in Asian exchange rate management (Eichengreen and Bayoumi, 1996). Furthermore, some financial markets in the Asian region (e.g. Hong Kong) are very open, while others remain (strongly) regulated and restricted (e.g. China).

More importantly, it seems to have been forgotten that, in spite of the strict exchange rate mechanism, the EU Member States suffered from the currency crisis in the beginning of the 1990s caused by the massive external speculative attacks,[17] as was the current case in Asia, and this event still makes the UK hesitant to join the Monetary Union. Furthermore, as a consequence, one of the strictest conditions (the continuous participation in the narrow 2.25 percent band of the ERM without devaluation for the last two years) required to become a member of the EU Monetary Union was abolished from the list of the so-called Maastricht convergence criteria. The major causes of the recent European financial crisis[18] well indicate possibilities that a kind of Asian monetary mechanism (with the fixed exchange rate system) and the efforts of the central banks in individual countries to maintain the agreed exchange rate could unfortunately be ineffective, when, for example, the currency of an economically dominant country such as the Japanese *yen* becomes strongly appreciated and other member states are – due to their slow economic growth – under severe speculative attack. At present, there are also intensive discussions in Europe about the long-term sustainability of the Monetary Union with one currency, the euro. One of the popular criticisms of its implementation is that such a strict monetary policy co-ordination in the EU should be carried out parallel to the supplementary co-ordination of other types of macro-economic (like fiscal, distribution and labor market) policy measures. This important aspect should also be adequately considered in Asia, if a similar style of monetary union is to be established in the future. For example, according to the traditional theory of an optimum currency area, a monetary union without fiscal and labor market policy co-ordination among member states appears to be rather unstable. An optimum currency area (OCA) is a region or a group of countries where it makes sense to employ one currency. According to Mundell (1968) and Mckinnon (1963), an OCA generally depends on four elements: the openness of the economies, the intensive intra-trade among the member states, the wage-price flexibility and the labor mobility.[19] The EU Member States – and also many Asian countries – satisfy two former criteria but wages and prices are not yet flexible enough in Europe, due particularly to the role of trade union in wage setting

(Tomann, 1997), and the intra-EU labor mobility is still low, partly also caused by the cultural and social barriers, the psychological cost of moving, etc. (Decressin and Fatas, 1994; Gros, 1996), which implies that even the EU is not an OCA at the present time (Eichengreen, 1991; De Grauwe, 1994; Karras, 1996; Walther, 1997). Because of these reasons, there is a fear that asymmetric shocks could lead to [recessions and increases in unemployment] which could create a social burden that is politically unacceptable to many governments.[20] These concerns are aggravated by the possibility that the introduction of a single currency and the process of economic integration increase the importance of national business cycles as countries become more specialized and, with the disappearance of exchange rates, they lose a stabilizing tool to mitigate the effects of nation-specific shocks (Fatas, 1997, p.744).[21]

Conclusion

The Asian miracle was real. It appears to be incorrect to make a prophecy about the end of the miracle in the long-run, taking the experiences of the former Soviet economies as an example. The development of Asian economies (tigers of the 1st and 2nd generation in particular) since the beginning of the 1980s was far more dynamic than that of Eastern European countries in the 1960s and 1970s. This remarkable Asian success was not only triggered by the increase in inputs but also associated with rapid productivity growth.

In other words, unlike the cases in transformation countries, these Asian economies did not suffer, prior to the 1997 crash, from the gradual long-term slowdown in GDP and productivity growth. The current Asian crisis which began with the panic triggered by the failure of the Thai financial system has already turned out to be a real sector crisis rather than a financial and currency crisis. Such an abrupt breakdown has particularly been evident and serious for the South Korean economy. The list of major causes for the current crisis in South Korea and in Asia is very long. The *financial* factors that led to the crisis generally include the serious asset-liability mismatches of domestic firms, the over-reliance on foreign debts partly caused by the badly designed government's financial liberalization schedule, the poorly-developed and less-transparent domestic financial system, the insufficient foreign currency reserves, the moral hazard resulting from the close relations between governments and large firms as well as from so-called cross-firm debt guarantee within a conglomerate.

In addition, some macro- and meso-economic conditions and weaknesses have not only made the Korean economy vulnerable to external shock but also contributed to the sudden capital flight of investors and the subsequent economic collapse in the country. Major *real* sector problems were, for example, the (expectation of) decline in economic growth rate since 1995 and the slow growth of export revenue in 1996 (due mainly to the world-wide decrease in price of the computer chips – Korea's most important export item), the sharp increase in trade deficit in 1995-96 caused by import increase of petroleum and sophisticated semiconductors, the intensive modernization efforts of Korean firms, and competitive pressure caused by the increase in labor costs and recent devaluation of *yuan* and *yen*, to name a few.

Furthermore, policy errors made by Asian governments and the IMF during the early stages of panic appear to have deepened the economic distress. For example, the increase in real interest rate combined with tax increases, cuts in government spending, etc. which were demanded by the IMF in return for bail-out funds depressed Korean firms' cash flow and raised their fixed-payment obligations, forcing them more strongly into insolvency.

The unstable development of important Asian currencies, the transmission of bubbles from one country to another and the related less-disciplined monetary policy practice of individual Asian countries since the mid-1980s were the initiators of the current Asian crisis. In this context, it is quite often argued that in Asia a more intensive co-ordination in the fields of monetary and exchange rate policy-making, debt negotiations and expansions appears to be necessary to prevent and to overcome the crisis. Yet, European experience with the EMS in the beginning of the 1990s shows that, in spite of the strict exchange rate mechanism, the EU Member States were not always able to remain immune to the self-fulfilling speculations (and panics) of international investors, when economic and financial fundamentals became weak. Although some economists and politicians support the idea of establishing a type of Asian monetary union (with a currency and a central bank), its realization is unlikely to take place in the near future, due to significant economic disparities, structural differences and varied financial systems in Asian countries. Additionally, the traditional theory of an optimum currency area suggests that the long-term sustainability of a monetary union can only be guaranteed when other types of macro-economic (e.g. fiscal, distribution, labor) policies are also coordinated at the same time. Moreover, Asia unfortunately lacks the kind of political solidarity and institutional process that have played an important role for the economic integration in the EU since the 1950s.

Appendix

The Geary-Khamis Approach for Converting Various Currencies into an International Common Unit

Although the use of exchange rates is the simplest way for converting currencies into a common unit, this method is no longer reliable for building internationally comparable indicators for measuring 'true' purchasing power and real product, mainly for the following reasons:

- Exchange rates mainly reflect purchasing power over the internationally tradable product items. In developing countries, where wages are generally low, the non-tradable goods and services such as haircuts, government services, building construction, etc. are significantly cheaper than those in developed high-income countries. Consequently, exchange rates generally understate real purchasing power.
- Exchange rates are often strongly influenced by their speculation and capital movement.
- Exchange rates have been very volatile in the past (see Maddison, 1995).[22]

The Geary-Khamis aggregation approach – initiated by Geary (1958) and amplified by Khamis (1972) – was first applied in practice in the context of the United Nations International Comparison Project (ICP) aimed at developing a reliable system of estimating and comparing real GDP and true purchasing power of currencies of a large number of countries (see also Kravis et al., 1978). In this multilateral aggregation method, international prices of various expenditure categories and purchasing power parities (PPPs) of countries are estimated simultaneously from a system of linear equations. These international prices are then employed to value the category quantities of individual countries in international dollars so that the category quantities can be added together to obtain total GDP.

As mentioned above, the Geary-Khamis equation system consists of two subsets. The international price of an expenditure category (IP_i) is defined as the quantity-weighted average of the purchasing-power-adjusted prices of the category in all the investigated countries, as shown in equation (a-1)

$$IP_i = \sum_{j=1}^{n} (p_{ij} / PPP_j)(q_{ij} / \sum_{j=1}^{n} q_{ij}), \qquad \text{(a-1)}$$

where i indicates expenditure category (i = 1, ..., m); j country (j = 1, ..., n); PPP purchasing power parities; p price and q quantity.

On the other hand, the purchasing power of a country's currency can be expressed as the ratio of the country's GDP valued at its own prices to its GDP valued at international prices (see equation a-2).

$$PPP_j = (\sum_{i=1}^{m} p_{ij}\, q_{ij}) / (\sum_{i=1}^{m} IP_i\, q_{ij}) \qquad (a\text{-}2)$$

As illustrated above, the calculation of international prices can be easily carried out when the PPPs are known. On the other hand, the PPPs are also easily computed if the international prices are known.

Geary (1958) observed and elaborated possibilities of solving these two equations to measure international prices for expenditure categories and PPPs of countries simultaneously. The Geary-Khamis approach gives a weight to countries corresponding to the size of their GDP, so that a large economy like the US has a stronger influence on the aggregation results than small ones do (see also Maddison, 1995).

Notes

1. The case of South Korea is of particular interest 'in that it grew so fast and so effectively up to 1997, and then fell so heavily. In the trauma of November and December 1997, the Korean economy, which had grown to become the eleventh largest in the world, was reduced to a wreck, tossed on the seas of international finance ...' (Mathews, 1998, p.747).
2. Therefore, any rapid economic recovery in Korea and other Asian victims appears to be led by an export increase, but this appears to require some time since Asia's economies also rely on intra-trade with each other. Additionally, the liquidity crunch and rather slow progress in corporate debt rescheduling has also limited the export response to currency depreciation.
3. On average, the *won* was devaluated from ca. 844 won/US\$ in 1996 to 1,415 won/US\$. In the middle of the currency crisis, its level reached approximately 1,850 won/US\$ in 1997 (Leibfritz and Nam, 1998).
4. Policy errors made by the South Korean and other Asian governments and the IMF during the first stage of panic appear to have contributed to the deepening of economic distress (Feldstein, 1998; Wade and Veneroso, 1998; Pincus and Ramli, 1998).
5. 'Once upon a time, Western opinion leaders [were] ... frightened by the extraordinary growth rates achieved by a set of Eastern [European] economies. Although these economies were still substantially poor ..., the speed with which they had transformed themselves from peasant societies into industrial powerhouses, their continuing ability to achieve growth rates several times higher than the advanced nations, and their increasing ability to challenge or even surpass American and European technology in certain areas seemed to call into question the dominance not only of Western power but of Western ideology' (Krugman, 1994, p.62).
6. 'It was simply not possible for the Soviet economies to sustain the rates of labor force participation, average education level, and above all the physical capital stock that had prevailed in previous years' (Krugman, 1994, p.63-64). He further notes: 'Once upon a time, Western opinion leaders [were]... frightened by the extraordinary growth rates achieved by a set of Eastern [European] economies. Although these economies were still substantially poor, the speed with which they had transformed

themselves from peasant societies into industrial powerhouses, their continuing ability to achieve growth rates several times higher than the advanced nations, and their increasing ability to challenge or even surpass American and European technology in certain areas seemed to call into question the dominance not only of Western power but of Western ideology' (Krugman, 1994, p.62). He observes:
'It was simply not possible for the Soviet economies to sustain the rates of labor force participation, average education level, and above all the physical capital stock that had prevailed in previous years' (Krugman, 1994, p.63-64).

7. Real GDP measures annual production of final goods expressed in base year prices and exchange rates. In many cases, however, the real GDP account overstates or understates the economic activities of a country.

8. 'This view is also reflected in the IMF programme for Korea, which demands that the [government] take measures that will weaken... the large, diversified, family-owned *chaebols*.

9. According to the Bank of Korea, the debt-equity ratio of Korean manufacturing corporations amounted to approximately 340 percent between 1973 and 1996, which is comparable to the Japanese ratio of 320 percent in the period of 1955-1973.

10. This type of arguments has been contested by Chang et al. (1998).

11. For example, in South Korea foreign currency-denominated assets of banks relative to nominal GDP went up to approximately 29 percent in 1996 from ca. 20 percent in 1992, while the ratio of total (short- and long-term) external debts to GNP rose to around 22 percent from 14 percent in the same period of time and reached around US$120 billion in September 1997 (Shin and Hahm, 1998; Chang et al., 1998)). The total sum of short-term foreign debt reached approximately US$95 billion in the mid-December 1997.

12. Furthermore, lack of transparency in balance sheets, foreign exchange reserves and foreign debt have had an important effect on the size of capital inflows in South Korean and other Asian victims and 'may have a significant role in explaining the magnitude of panic, and hence the extent of the outflows' (Wade, 1998, p.704).

13. The quarterly business climate index is calculated on the basis of business surveys conducted among South Korean manufacturing firms.

14. '... the institution of a single currency eliminates the *deadweight loss* due to currency transactions and to the need to collect and process information ... [Furthermore] benefits correspond to the *efficiency gains* from ... the elimination of the relative price distortions generated by the transaction costs, and ... exchange rate uncertainty ... It is ... difficult to identify the benefits deriving from a single currency, both theoretically and empirically. It seems reasonable, however, to assume that these benefits increase with the ... degree of openness [of involved countries]' (Ricci, 1997, p.9).

15. Regarding the benefits and costs of establishing the monetary union in the EU, 'the American school of thought appears to warn of the potential that the costs might dominate, while the Europeans sound more optimistic ...' (Karras, 1996, p.378).

16. 'The [Asian] region has the means to solve the crisis if only it could put them to work: some $700 billion of foreign exchange reserves between China, Hong Kong, Taiwan and Japan, growing current account surpluses in the crisis-affected countries, net creditor positions in terms of foreign asset ownership, and huge savings. ... These endowments could easily provide the basis for an Asian Financial Facility.' (Wade, 1998, p.702).

17. After this event, the view has been widely discussed in the economic literature that a currency crisis should be attributed not only to weak economic fundamentals

including also the large trade deficit, pre-existed resource misallocation and vulnerability of financial institutions to liquidity shocks but more strongly also to the realisation of a bad equilibrium triggered by the 'panic' (i.e. self-fulfilling speculation) of international investors (Obstfeld, 1994 and 1995).

18. The root of the European currency crisis is traced back to German unification, especially when the West German government agreed to a 1-to-1 swap of the East German Mark for the west German D-Mark. The result was a rapid increase in the German money supply after unification and a subsequent rise in inflation. The government's budget deficit also expanded, adding to the Bundesbank's alarm. In an attempt to control inflation and rein back money growth, the Bundesbank began to raise interest rates.

19. In addition, Kenen (1969) highlighted the importance of the degree of commodity diversification when there is an asymmetric demand shock, and argued that industrial countries with a high degree of product diversification are better candidates for a currency union than developing countries with a less diversified production structure. Since the exchange rate adjustment can only shift the whole price level of a country vis-a-vis that of foreign country, the application of this measure in a country with a highly diversified industrial structure to overcome the demand shock on a given product is associated with some negative side effects (Bofinger, 1994).

20. The major concept of an OCA can be easily shown on the basis of a simple example: Suppose, due to a change in tastes or some other non-cyclical factor, that France runs a trade deficit with Germany (i.e. when an 'external shock' hits France's economy), what can be done to eliminate this problem and its impact on the domestic economy? The devaluation of the French franc is not an option in the monetary union with one common currency. The only way to restore France's trade balance (i.e. to increase exports and/or to decrease imports) is to depress income and price levels in France and, at the same time, to expand them in Germany.

21. By contrast, emphasising the past experiences with the changes in export demand in the EU Member States, it is also argued that the impacts of such external shocks on the economic development and employment level would remain less significant and, consequently, the lack of exchange rate adjustments under EMU would not lead to major problems in this area (Gros, 1996).

22. Consequently, some caution is necessary when interpreting and comparing macro-economic data from different sources. For example, the World Bank indicated that, although China's GDP per head in 1990 was US$370 on a bilateral exchange rate basis, it rose to US$1,950 when adjusted to purchasing power parities. Other economists argue that it reached US$2,600 in the same year. According to the OECD's multilateral calculation based on the Geary-Khamis method, in 1990 China's GDP per head amounted to 2,700 in 1990 Geary-Khamis international dollars (Nam, 1997).

References

Bayoumi, T. (1994), 'A Formal Model for Optimum Currency Areas', *IMF Working Paper*, WP94/42.

Bayoumi, T. and B. Eichengreen. (1997), 'Ever Closer to Heaven? An Optimum-Currency-Area Index for European Countries', *European Economic Review*, vol. 41, Nos.3-5, pp.761-770.

Bergsten, C. F. (1997), *The Asian Monetary Crisis: Proposed Remedies*. Statement before the Committee on Banking and Financial Services, US House of Representatives, November 13, 1997, Washington DC.

Bofinger, P. (1994), 'Is Europe an Optimum Currency Area?', *CEPR Discussion Paper*, No.915.

Chang, H. J., H. J. Park and C. G. Yoo. (1998), 'Interpreting the Korean Crisis: Financial Liberalisation, Industrial Policy and Corporate Governance', *Cambridge Journal of Economics*, No.22: pp.735-746.

Cheney, D. (1997), 'Optimum Currency Areas: The Challenge for Policy', *IMF Survey*, January 13, pp.14-16.

Chowdhury, A. R. (1998), 'The Asian Crisis One Year Later', *WIDER Angle*, 1/98, World Institute for Development Economic Research.

Cohen, B. J. (1997), 'Optimum Currency Area Theory: Bringing the Market Back In', in: Cohen, B. J. (ed.), *International Trade and Finance*, Cambridge University Press, Cambridge.

Corsetti, G., P. Pesenti and N. Roubini. (1998), *What Caused the Asian Currency and Financial Crisis*, March 1998, mimeo, New York University.

Decressin, J. and A. Fatas. (1994), 'Regional Labour Market Dynamics in Europe', *CEPR Discussion Paper*, No.1085.

De Grauwe, P. (1994), *The Economics of Monetary Integration*. 2nd Edition, Oxford University Press, New York.

Dyker, D. (1992, ed.), *The European Economy*, Longman, London.

Eichengreen, B. (1991), 'Is Europe an Optimum Currency Area?', *NBER Working Paper*, No.3579.

Eichengreen, B. and T. Bayoumi. (1996), 'Is Asia an Optimum Currency Area? Can It Become One?', Regional, Global and Historical Perspectives on Asian Monetary Relations. *Center for International and Development Economic Research Working Paper*, No.C96/081. University of California Berkeley.

Eichengreen, B., A. K. Rose and C. Wyplosz. (1995), 'Speculative Attacks on Pegged Exchange Rates: An Empirical Exploration with Special Reference to the European Monetary System', *Working Paper of the Federal Reserve Bank of San Francisco*, No.95-04.

Fatas, A. (1997), 'EMU: Countries or Regions? Lessons from the EMS Experience', *European Economic Review*, vol. 41, pp.743-751.

Feldstein, M. (1998), 'Refocusing the IMF', *Foreign Affairs*, vol. 7, No.2, pp.20-38.

Frankel, J. A. and A. K. Rose. (1996), 'Currency Crashes in Emerging Markets: An Empirical Treatment', *Journal of International Economics*, vol. 41, Nos.3-4, pp.351-366.

Frankel, J. A. (1996), 'The Endogeneity of the Optimum Currency Area Criteria', *NBER Working Paper*, No. 5700.

Frankel, J. A. (1997), 'Is EMU More Justifiable ex post than ex ante?' *European Economic Review*, vol. 41, Nos.3-5, pp.753-760.

Geary, R. C. (1958), 'A Note on Comparisons of Exchange Rates and Purchasing Power Between Countries', *Journal of Royal Statistical Society*, vol. 2, pp.97-99.

Giavazzi, F. (1989), 'The Exchange Rate Question in Europe', In: Bryant R. C. et al. (eds.), *Macroeconomic Policies in an Independent World*, International Monetary Fund, Washington DC.

Goto, J. and K. Hamada. (1994), 'Economic Preconditions for Asian Regional Integration', in Ito T. and A. O. Krueger (Eds.), *Macroeconomic Linkage: Savings, Exchange*

Rates and Capital Flow, pp.359-385, Chicago: University of Chicago Press, Chicago.

Gros, D. (1996), 'A Reconstruction of the Optimum Currency Area Approach: The Role of External Shocks and Labour Mobility', *National Institute Economic Review*, No. 158, pp.108-117.

Hill, Ch. (1994), International Business: Competing in the Global Marketplace. Richard D. Irwin, Inc, Boston.

Johnson, C. (1998), 'Economic Crisis in East Asia: The Clash of Capitalisms', *Cambridge Journal of Economics*, No.2, pp.653-661.

Karras, G. (1996), 'Is Europe an Optimum Currency Area? Evidence on the Magnitude and Asymmetry of Common and Country-Specific Shocks in 20 European Countries', *Journal of Economic Integration*, vol. 11, No.3, pp.366-384.

Kenen, P. B. (1969), 'The Theory of Optimum Currency Areas: An Eclectic View', in: Mundell, R. A. and K. Swoboda (Eds.), Monetary Problems of the International Economy, pp.41-60, Chicago University Press, Chicago.

Khamis, S. H. (1972), 'A New System of Index Numbers for National and International Purposes', *Journal of Royal Statistical Society*, vol. 135, pp.96-121.

Kravis, I. B., A. Heston and R. Summers. (1978), *International Comparisons of Real Product and Purchasing Power*, Johns Hopkins University Press, Baltimore.

Krugman, P. (1994), 'The Myth of Asia's Miracle', *Foreign Affairs*, vol. 73, No.6, pp.62-78.

Krugman, P. (1998), *What Happened to Asia?*, January 1998, mimeo, MIT University.

Leibfritz, W. and Ch. W. Nam. (1998), 'Suedkorea: Baldige Ueberwindung der Rezession?', ifo Schnelldienst, vol. 51, No.11-12, pp.34-38.

Maddison, A. (1995), *Monitoring the World Economy 1820-1992*, OECD Development Centre Studies, Paris.

Mathews, J. A. (1998), 'Fashioning a New Korean Model Out of the Crisis: The Rebuilding of Institutional Capabilities', *Cambridge Journal of Economics*, No.22, pp.747-759.

Mishikin, F. (1996), 'Understanding Financial Crisis: A Developing Country Perspective', *NBER Working Paper*, No.5600.

McKinnon, R. I. (1963), 'Optimum Currency Areas', *American Economic Review*, vol. 63 (September) pp.15-30.

Mundell, R. A. (1968), 'A Theory of Optimum Currency Areas', reprinted in his *International Economics*, Macmillan, New York.

Nam, Ch. W. (1997), 'China's Recent Economic Performance in International Comparison', *International Quarterly for Asian Studies*, vol. 28, No.4, pp.345-360.

Nam, Ch. W. and I. S. Yoo. (1998), 'Changes in Korea's Competitive Advantage Revealed in the Recent Industrial Growth and Specialisation', *Ewha Management Review*, No. 16 (forthcoming).

Nam, Ch. W. and K. Y. Nam. (1999), 'Recent Industrial Growth and Specialisation in Selected Asian Countries', *Review of Asian and Pacific Studies*, No. 18, pp.13-39.

Noland, M. (1998), *The Financial Crisis in Asia*, Statement before the House International Relations Committee Subcommittees on Asia and Pacific Affairs, and International Economic Policy and Trade, February 3 1998, Washington DC.

Obstfeld, M. (1994), 'The logic of Currency Crisis', *NBER Working Paper*, No.4640.

Obstfeld, M. (1995), 'Models of Currency Crises with Self-fulfilling Features', *NBER Working Paper*, No.5285.

Oetker, I. and C. Pazarbasioglu. (1997), 'Speculative Attacks and Macroeconomic Fundamentals: Evidence from Some European Currencies', *European Economic Review*, vol. 41, Nos.3-5, pp.847-860.

Pincus, J. and R. Ramli. (1998), 'Indonesia: From Show Case to Basket Case', *Cambridge Journal of Economics*, No.22, pp.723-734.

Ricci, L. A. (1997), 'A Model of an Optimum Currency Area', *IMF Working Paper*, WP/97/76.

Shin, I. and J. H. Hahm. (1998), *The Korean Crisis – Causes and Resolution*, Paper presented at the East-West Center/Korea Development Institute Conference on the Korean Crisis, August 8, 1998, Honolulu.

Streifford, D. M. (1990), *Economic Perspective*. Richard D. Irwin, Inc, Boston.

Tomann, H. (1997), 'Is Europe an Optimum Currency Area?' *Discussion Papers in German Studies*, No. IGS97/18, The University of Birmingham.

United Nations Industrial Development Organisation (UNIDO, 1995), *Industrial Development – Global Report 1995*, Oxford University Press, Oxford.

Sundararajan, V. and T. Balino. (1991), 'Issues in Recent Banking Crises', in: International Monetary Fund, *Banking Crises: Cases and Issues*. Washington DC: IMF.

Wade, R. (1998), 'From 'Miracle' to 'Cronyism': Explaining the Great Asian Slump', *Cambridge Journal of Economics*, No.22, pp.693-706.

Wade, R. and F. Veneroso. (1998), The Asian Crisis: The High Debt Model vs. The Wall Street-Treaty-IMF Complex, March 1998, mimeo, Russell Sage Foundation.

Walther, T. (1997), *The World Economy*, John Wiley & Sons, Inc, New York.

World Trade Organisation (WTO, 1995), *Regionalism and the World Trading System*, Geneva.

Chapter 8

Questioning the Explanations
of the Asian Crisis

Partha Gangopadhyay

Introduction

Some East and Southeast Asian nations went into a tailspin in July 1997 with currency and banking crisis, regional financial panic whilst the crisis spread to financial markets around the world. These crises posed a serious threat to global economic expansion and caused a severe economic downturn. Krugman summarized the mood of the profession:

> What we have actually seen in Asia is something both more complex and drastic: collapses in domestic asset markets, wide spread bank failure ... and what looks likely to be a much more severe real downturn than even the most negatively-minded anticipated (Krugman, 1998, p.1).

The main explanations of the Asian crisis are couched in terms of serious policy errors committed by national governments. The purpose of this paper is to explain the dynamics of these errors. The Asian crisis has already triggered an avalanche of works on economic crisis. Sophisticated models have been developed to explain the high growth, high savings and high risks economies of East Asia (see Bai and Wang, 1999). It has been widely discussed whether or not these elements turned on efficiency (Krugman, 1994; Young, 1995). The sharp downturn of some these economies point to the possibility that they were exposed to high risks. The quality of governance has also been highlighted in this context.

Till the onset of the Asian crisis, the quality of governance in the East Asian model of development was the key to their economic success. It was worthy of emulation for other developing nations all around the globe. There is now a tacit consensus, led mainly by World Bank and IMF economists, that misgovernance and economic mismanagement played a major role in the Asian crisis. There is a gap in our collective understanding since we don't know the rationale behind such a wild swing in the quality of governance. The main goal of this chapter is to explain abrupt changes in the quality of governance. In so doing we extend the Kaldorian model (Kaldor, 1940) to capture the dynamics of the quality of governance in order to explain the crisis that engulfed some of the Asian nations in the recent past. The quality of governance varies across these nations and the chapter attempts to shed lights on the following stylized facts characterizing these nations: first, significant stability exists in the quality of governance in a nation. If a nation exhibits weak, or strong, governance, it persists for a while. Secondly, despite such stability the quality of governance has been fluctuating – some nations significantly improve quality of governance while others experience a marked deterioration. Finally, some of the nations with high quality governance quickly develop dynamics that leads to a sharp decline in their perceived quality of governance.

It has been widely argued that the quality of governance has had a strong influence in the growth as well as downturn in the Asian economies. We develop a simple model of changes in the quality of governance: it is argued that the quality of governance is an increasing function of domestic and foreign resources while these resources are an increasing function of the quality of governance. It is postulated that the relation between the quality and resources is non-linear with the typical S-shape production function relation bearing an initial increasing marginal increment in the quality of governance then declining as the resource availability increases. From these formulations we show that the stylized economy is characterized by stable multiple equilibria involving both low and high qualities of governance. The key point is that these equilibria can easily become unstable with a perturbation of resources that can, in turn, explain the dynamics in the quality of governance. We also develop a model to rationalize the S-shape wherefrom we establish the possibility of limit cycles that may characterize the quality of governance and economic growth of a nation.

Quality of Governance in Development

Governance typically represents political and administrative management in the process of economic development of a nation. In the basic tenets of neoclassical public finance theory, government is cast as a benevolent dictator tirelessly serving the welfare of its subjects. In the early literature on economic development, economists applied the neoclassical public finance theory to argue that a 'good' government looks after the welfare of people endangered by endemic market failure (see Bhagwati, 1984). In the traditional parlor of economic development, 'good' governance came to be equated with adoption of outward-oriented and 'good policies' creating dynamic comparative advantages. Along this train of thoughts, the strand of statist political economy emerged to argue that the quality of governance in economic development amounts to a careful manipulation of the competitive position of a nation in the international arena through an elaborate and sector-specific intervention by the national governments (Haggard, 1990). Industrial targeting in Japan and Korea was increasingly cited as an example of 'good' governance. International agencies also lent support to this view that market-friendly and 'good' governance impinges on economic progress of a nation

(Arndt, 1987; World Bank, 1993). Such a simplistic view of governance was heavily criticized by the positive public choice theory (see Mueller, 1989). The neoclassical paradigm was labeled as a 'caricature' while the positive public choice theory posits that a typical government is a self-seeking, malevolent Leviathan maximizing rents. In the context of developing countries, the case of rent-seeking is well-documented (Bhagwati, 1984). The costs of rent-seeking activities are enormous in the developing world. Naturally, the quality of governance, or 'good' governance as espoused by the statist political economy school, came under heavy fire. 'Good' governance is now characterized by the three elements to curb rent-seeking:

- Low level of predatory activities of governments (see Niskanen, 1971; Brenan and Buchanan, 1980 and Findley, 1988 among many);
- Weak influence of special interest groups and rent-seekers on bureaucracy (see Olson, 1982);
- Competent bureaucrats ably assisted by well-trained professionals.

It is indeed a moot point whether such stringency on governance is realistic. It prompted Roemer to express his dismay at 'good' governance,

> ... Strong, authoritarian government ... requires a configuration of bureaucratic competence and ruthless dedication to national economic success that is relatively rare and may be impossible to sustain (Roemer, 1993, p.88).

In the recent literature on governance, economists are turning their attention to the political microstructure of a system that puts forward the twin questions:

- How can be opportunistic governments be induced to act in the interests of their subjects?
- How to resolve or mitigate group conflicts among voters to put adequate pressure on the governments to act in public interest?

The Asian Crisis and Misgovernance

Till the onset of the Asian crisis, the quality of governance in the East Asian model of development was the key to their economic success. It was worthy of emulation. There is now a consensus that misgovernance played a major role in the Asian crisis. There is a gap in our collective understanding since we don't know the rationale behind such a wild swing in the quality of governance. Our main goal is to explain the abrupt change in quality of governance. Our model hence can explain:

- Why quality of governance varies across nations?

- Why significant stability in the quality of governance persists in nations?
- If a nation exhibits weak or strong governance, it persists for a while.
- Why has quality of governance been fluctuating – despite such stability?
- Some nations significantly improve their quality of governance while others experience a marked decline.

In the following we provide a detailed analysis of the factors held responsible for the onset and deepening of the Asian crisis.

Faltering long-term Government Policy

Indonesia, Korea and Thailand adopted an incorrect and uncoordinated sequence of reforms of domestic and external sectors. Especially, domestic sector reforms were not properly initiated when external sector reforms had been under way. These nations also chose incorrect exchange regimes that led to serious speculative attacks on their currencies. Most of these nations committed the error of retaining fixed exchange regimes during the liberalization of capital account that exacerbated the problem. Government-led moral hazard problems in investment became rampant in these nations. Poorly informed private investors followed the herd expecting the bubble to burst but also expecting relevant governments to bail them out.

Medium-Term Policy Errors: Emulating the Japanese Blunder of 1985

Japan adopted a series of policies in the 1980s that quickly weakened the economic status of Japan in the global economy. Japan engineered a policy-driven appreciation of yen against the US$ that caused capital flight from Japan to Korea and Taiwan in 1985. In order to boost the domestic economy an expansionary monetary policy was adopted that further intensified the flight of capital from Japan. In the 1990s Korea and Taiwan went the Japanese way by appreciating their currencies and expanding money supply leading to asset price bubbles and flight of capital from Korea and Taiwan to Indonesia and Thailand. Asset price bubbles also induced hectic expansion of production capacity of large firms on borrowed funds while these borrowings were backed by governments that eventually precipitated serious moral hazard problems in these nations.

Trigger Factor in the Crisis

Due to devaluation of Chinese currency by 40% in 1994 and devaluation of Japanese yen by 25% over 1995-96 many of the East Asian economies suffered an erosion of their competitive position in the world market. As a result, huge trade deficits appeared in South Korea, Taiwan and the entire Southeast Asia.

Major Policy Blunders

In order to alleviate these problems, governments of these Asian countries envisaged grotesque plan of industrial restructuring and unleashed ambitious plans for diversification of their production bases. The problem was that their large firms had inadequate means to undertake the diversification, and industrial restructuring. Naturally, governments induced domestic banks to lend credit for these grotesque programs. In some sense, banks were forced to take the role of the proverbial cash box. Lending soon exceeded domestic resources and resulted in expanding foreign debts.

Short-term Policy Errors

Austerity measures – cuts in taxes and government expenditures – were initiated to redress debt problems of domestic firms. Governments looked for a currency boost to improve cash flows problems for domestic firms to tide over debt crisis. To boost domestic currency, inflow of foreign capital was relied on. At the same time to attract foreign capital, interest rates were raised. This mix of policies backfired as increase in interest rates – accompanied by cuts in government expenditure and decline in export prices – exacerbated their cash flow problems of domestic firms.

Other Elements of Misgovernance

The IMF and the World Bank criticized these governments for inadequate financial sector supervision. It was highlighted that these governments spent little on auditing, monitoring and enforcement. It was also stressed that financial risks were poorly assessed by banking sectors. Rampant corruption in the bureaucracy seemed to have worsened the situation even further.

Transition from Governance to Misgovernance and the Onset of the Crisis

The crisis was preceded by declining corporate profits and equity prices, collapse of domestic asset markets, exchange rate depreciation and insolvency of big businesses. Investors started shifting capital being led by herd instinct. This soon caused a serious economic slump in the region. A wide range of work now highlights a critical transition in these economies in a histrionic fashion: in what follows we attempt to model such sharp turns in the quality of governance in these nations.

The Model

The point of departure is a two-way interaction between quality of governance and the available resources of the government: quality of governance, G, is an increasing and non-linear function of resources, T. On the other hand, T is an increasing linear function of quality of governance. We write them as:

$$G = G (T) \text{ with } G'>0 \qquad (1a)$$
$$T = T (G) \text{ with } T'>0 \qquad (1b)$$

This is a model of 'mutual causation' between two variables G and T (see Kaldor, 1940 and Swan, 1962). We postulate that G is S-shaped. For low values of T, $G''>0$ and for high values of T, $G''<0$. As resources increase, for low values of G, the government starts attracting high quality bureaucrats that in turn reinforce the quality till a limit – beyond which the traditional diminishing productivity sets in and the quality function G flattens out. We label this production function relation as G in Figure 8.1. We label the resource function as T in Figure 8.1 that linearly increases with increasing quality. We postulate that G and T mutually 'cause' each other: the greater the quality of governance, the greater the local and international revenues that the State can attract. The lower the revenues the lower is the quality of governance due to paucity of resources. The point of intersection between T and G characterizes an equilibrium as E_1. Why is this an equilibrium? At E_1 there is no tendency for either G or T to change, since the 'causal' relationships are simultaneously satisfied. Equilibrium E_1 is locally stable: in the vicinity of E_1, quality of governance and resources move in right direction to restore the system back to E_1.

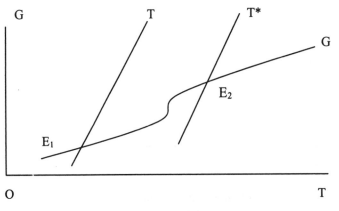

Figure 8.1 Equilibrium Quality of Governance

Now, from a simple comparative-static exercise one can easily establish that a shift in the T line will result in a change in equilibrium. For small shifts, the new equilibrium will be fairly close to the original one at E_1. However, if there is a significant shift of the T line, then the new equilibrium will go beyond the increasing productivity zone and the T line and Q functions will intersect at a new equilibrium E_2 at a high quality level. Such a movement from E_1 to E_2 can be very quick and if the T line is steeper than the slope of the Q function at E_2, then E_2 is also a stable equilibrium that will persist until further shocks to T. It is worth noting that the quality of governance is much higher at E_2. The increase in quality, following further increases in T, becomes sluggish. But a sudden and sharp decline in T can easily take the system back to the low-level equilibrium E_1. An extension is possible.

Now suppose that the T line is also non-linear and inverse S-shaped: the ability to raise resources of a government decreases at the outset till a critical quality is achieved. Once the critical quality of governance is reached, the government starts attracting larger resources beyond the critical level T_C. Thus:

$$T' < 0 \text{ for } T < T_C \qquad\qquad (1c)$$
$$T' > 0 \text{ for } T > T_C \qquad\qquad (1d)$$

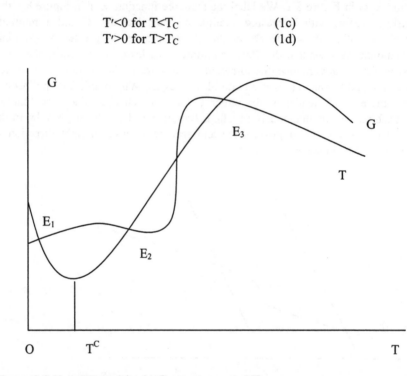

Figure 8.2 Non-Linearities in Governance and Taxes

It is possible that the system is now characterized by three equilibria E_1, E_2 and E_3. Equilibria E_1 and E_3 are stable and separated by an unstable equilibrium E_2. E_1 is the low quality equilibrium while E_2 is the high quality equilibrium. Any temporary perturbation from E_3 (or, E_1) beyond E_2 can lead to E_1 (or, E_3). Even more interesting cases arise when the equilibria are unstable: a small change leads to a 'vicious' or 'virtuous' cumulative process. Starting from an unstable equilibrium, any temporary improvement in quality of governance, or resources, will mutually reinforce each other to take the economy along a virtuous cumulative process. Similarly, a temporary decline in resources, or quality of governance, will mutually reinforce each other to engender a vicious cumulative process. In order to have unstable equilibrium, we need G and T to be strongly sensitive to each other near their intersection. The context of multiple stable equilibria can adequately explain the Asian developmental experience and crisis. The low-level equilibrium E_1 depicts a relatively stable position wherefrom the economic situation does not slide much. But this low-level equilibrium can be destroyed by a momentary, but sufficiently powerful, improvement in governance, or resource availability. Such changes can bring about a new era of high governance as captured by E_3. On the contrary, if the system is already at E_3, shocks cannot improve things, yet adverse shocks initiate changes that pulls the system back to the low-level equilibrium E_1.

The Full-Blown Model

We postulate that the quality of governance (G) is influenced by the level of economic development – as captured by the level of national income (Y) – and the quality of human capital (H). We similarly assume that government resources (T) are influenced by H and Y. It is further assumed:

$$G = G(Y, H) \text{ with } G_Y > 0, G_H > 0 \tag{2a}$$
$$T = T(Y, H) \text{ with } T_Y > 0, T_H > 0 \tag{2b}$$

We define E as the government expenditure that is influenced by the quality of governance (G) and the level of economic development (Y):

$$E = E(G,Y) \tag{2c}$$
$$E_G < 0 \text{ and } E_Y > 0 \tag{2d}$$

We write
$$E = E(G,Y) = E(G(Y,H), Y) \tag{2e}$$
$$= E(Y,H) \tag{2f}$$

with
$$E_Y > 0, E_H < 0 \tag{2g}$$

The Balanced budget requires (static sense):

$$E(Y,H) = T(Y,H) \tag{3a}$$

We know
$$T_H - E_H > 0 \tag{3c}$$
$$dY/dH = (T_H - E_H)/(E_Y - T_Y) \tag{3b}$$

Hence
$$dY/dH > 0 \tag{3d}$$
$$\text{If } E_Y > T_Y$$
$$dY/dH < 0 \tag{3e}$$
$$\text{If } E_Y < T_Y$$

The Simple Dynamic System

$$dY/dt = \beta[E(Y,H) - T(Y,H)] + b \qquad (4a)$$

Ignoring the balanced budget multiplies, it implies pump-priming.

$$dH/dt = \alpha E(Y,H) + h \qquad (4b)$$

Let us normalize by setting b=h=0. The locus along which national income growth is constant is given in the following. From (4a) and (4b) we know:
According as $E_Y > (<) T_Y$

$$\frac{dY}{dH}|_{\dot{Y}=0} = \frac{T_H - E_H}{E_Y - T_Y} > (<)0 \qquad (4c)$$

Postulate 1: At a lower level of development $E_Y < T_Y$ and hence

$$\frac{dY}{dH}|_{\dot{Y}=0} < 0 \qquad (4d)$$

Postulate 2: At an intermediate range $E_Y > T_Y$ and, hence,

$$\frac{dY}{dH}|_{\dot{Y}=0} > 0 \qquad (4e)$$

Postulate 3: Beyond a critical value of Y, say Y_C, $E_Y < T_Y$, and hence (4d) holds.

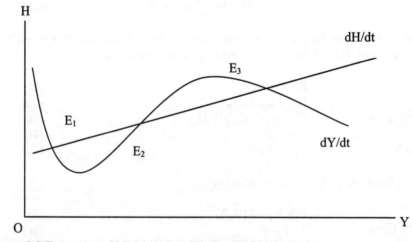

Figure 8.3 Existence of Multiple Equilibria and Limit Cycles

In the following case, when $E_Y > T_Y$ at the point of intersection, the focal point node E is unstable that will cause limit cycles. This can be seen from the characteristic roots of the dynamic system by applying the Poincare and Bendixson theorem.

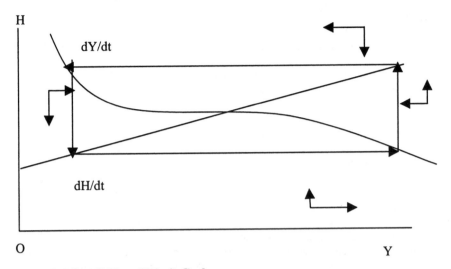

Figure 8.4 Possibility of Limit Cycles

From Bendixson's criterion, we know the cycle will exist if
$$\beta(E_Y - T_Y) + E_H \text{ cannot be of fixed sign (zero excepted).}$$
In terms of characteristics roots of the dynamic system:

Product of the characteristics roots
$$= \beta(T_H E_Y - T_Y E_H) > 0$$
Sum of the characteristics roots $= \beta(E_Y - T_Y) + E_H$

Thus, the equilibrium is stable or unstable depends on whether the sum of the characteristics roots are <0 or >0.

Concluding Comments

This chapter offers a simple model that is consistent with the stylized experience of the Asian economies. Some of these economies gathered tremendous economic momentum fairly quickly. National and international observers join their hands in the litany of good governance. Growth continued; so did the credo of good governance. Then, all of a sudden, the growth of these economies collapsed while some of these observers, and influential international organizations, started blaming bad governance for the crisis. This chapter is an attempt to explain the historic improvement in the credibility of some of the Asian governments that, all on a sudden, develops premature graying and quickly gets tangled with credibility problem leading to a reversal of fortunes at a lightning speed.

References

Arndt, H. (1987), *Economic Development: The History of an Idea*, University of Chicago Press, Chicago.

Bai, C. and Wang, Y. (1999), 'The Myth of East Asian Miracle: The Macroeconomic Implications of Soft Budgets', *American Economic Review*, Papers and Proceedings, vol. 89, No.2, pp.432-437.

Bhagwati, J. N. (1984), 'Development Economics: What Have We Learned?' *Asian Development Review*, vol. 2, No.1, pp.23-38.

Brenan, G. and Buchanan, J. M. (1980), *The Power to Tax: Analytical Foundations of a Fiscal Constitution*, CUP, Cambridge.

Findlay, R. (1988), 'Trade, Development and the State', in Ranis, G. and T. P. Schultz (eds), *The State of Development Economics: Progress and Prospects*, Basil Blackwell, Oxford.

Haggard, S. (1990), *Pathways from the Periphery: Politics of Growth in the Newly Industrialized Nations*, CUP, Cambridge.

Haggard, S. (1981), 'The Experience and Causes of Rapid Labor-Intensive Development in Korea, Taiwan, Hong Kong and Singapore and the Possibilities of Emulation, in E. Lee (ed.), *Export-Led Industrialization and Development*', ILO, Bangkok and Geneva.

Haggard, S. (1982), *Economic Development*, Basic Books, New York.

Kaldor, N. (1940), 'A Model of Trade Cycle', *Economic Journal*, vol. 50, pp.78-92.

Krugman, P. (1994), 'The Myth of Asia's Miracle', *Foreign Affairs*, November/December, 73(6), pp.62-78.

Krugman, P. (1998), 'Will Asia Bounce Back?', Speech for Credit Suisse First Boston, Hong Kong. <http://web.mit.edu/krugman/ www/suisse.htmal>.

Mueller, D. (1989), *Public Choice II*, Cambridge University Press, Cambridge.

Niskanen, W. A. (1971), *Bureaucracy and Representative Government*, Aldine-Atherton Press, Chicago.

Niskanen, W. A. (1992), 'The Case for a New Fiscal Constitution', *Journal of Economic Perspective*, vol. 6, No.2, pp.13-24.

Olson, M. (1982), *The Rise and Decline of Nations: Economic Growth, Stagflation and Social Rigidities*, Yale University Press, New Haven.

Roemer, P. (1993), 'Two Strategies for Economic Development: Using Ideas and Producing Ideas', *World Bank Proceedings*, W.E., Washington DC.

Swan, T. W. (1962), 'Circular Causation', *Economic Record*, vol. 38, pp.421-26.

Wolf, C. (1982), 'A Theory of Non-market Failure: Framework for Implementation Analysis', *Journal of Law and Economics*, vol. 22, pp.20-35.

World Bank (1993), *The East Asian Miracle: Economic Growth and Public Policy*, Oxford University Press: London.

Young, A. (1995), 'The Tyranny of Numbers: Confronting the Statistical Realities of the East Asian Growth Experience', *Quarterly Journal of Economics*, vol. 110(3), pp.641-80.

Chapter 9

China Beyond the Asian Financial Crisis: A New Path of Institutional Change

Leong H. Liew

Introduction

The Asian financial crisis had a profound effect on China. This is despite its economy largely avoiding the hardship that was inflicted by the Asian financial crisis on many other Asian countries. The Chinese economy still managed to grow at 7.8 percent in 1998 and 7 percent in 1999. The effect of the crisis on the immediate economy, however, is real. Exports and foreign investment to China were adversely affected. But the long-term significance of the crisis for China is its impact on the cognition of Chinese political leaders and state and party bureaucrats as to the appropriate paradigm for economic reform. The crisis devastated some Asian economies that not so long ago were the darlings of Western investors and had received high marks from the IMF for their macroeconomic management. The political fallout from the crisis has brought down a longstanding political leader in Indonesia (Suharto) and has weakened another in Malaysia (Mahathir). The economic and political fallout from the crisis has reinforced Chinese leaders' recent conversion to radical reform. More importantly, it has caused the bureaucracy to rethink and reshape their approach to reform, and secured their vital support for the successful implementation of radical reform.

The main theme of this chapter is that the Asian financial crisis has provided the exogenous shock that is likely to lead Chinese institutional change and reform on to a new path. The path of Chinese institutional change and reform that began with the ascendancy of Deng Xiaoping after the death of Mao Zedong had been heavily influenced by China's egalitarian Maoist past and the special position of workers in communist ideology. Although state and party leaders[1] might want faster reform, their desire was tempered by the knowledge that the state and party bureaucracy might not cooperate in such a reform. The Maoist legacy meant that party leaders had to give serious consideration to ensure that the reform program[2] chosen by them was broadly consistent with a Pareto-improving outcome. This did not mean that the program, in practice, made everyone better or at least no worse off as a result of reform. What it meant in practice was that reform policies were moderate and would endeavor to make no one worse off. In particular, because of the status of the state worker in a communist state, every effort was made to protect the state sector from the adverse effects of economic liberalization.

This chapter uses a simple game theory model to explain the evolution of Chinese economic reform, with a focus on the role of the Asian financial crisis in shaping this evolution. Chinese political leaders and state and party (S&P) bureaucrats play a 'game' where the initial equilibrium outcome (1978-92) was one of moderate reform. Even moderate reform policies, however, were unable to gain the cooperation of S&P bureaucrats. As the moderate reform polices, which retained an important role for the plan, proved unable to provide stable sustainable economic growth but instead caused high inflation and state-owned enterprises (SOEs) to run up massive debts, party leaders made a bold move and introduced radical reform measures in 1992. The sustainability of these measures was uncertain until the Asian financial crisis altered the perceived payoffs in the game and brought about a fundamental change in thinking of S&P bureaucrats to an acceptance of radical reform. This chapter explains how the equilibrium outcome of the game of Chinese reform strategy shifts from a moderate reform program without S&P bureaucratic cooperation to radical reform without S&P bureaucratic cooperation, and finally to radical reform with S&P bureaucratic cooperation.

Path-dependent Institutional Change and Reform

In explaining institutional change, path dependence means that what has happened in the past must shape what will happen in the future. In the words of North (1990, p.100),

> Path dependence means that history matters. We cannot understand today's choices (and define them in the modeling of economic performance) without tracing the incremental evolution of institutions'. He (North 1990, p.99) further points out that 'unproductive [institutional] paths can persist. The increasing returns characteristic of an initial set of institutions that provide disincentives to productive activity will create organizations and interest groups with a stake in the existing constraints.

As North sees it, institutions are the rules of the game that govern human interaction in a society and it is the high transaction costs to overcome the objections raised by organizations and interest groups to changes to these rules that allow unproductive institutional paths to continue to persist.

The expressed ideology underlying Chinese post-Mao economic reform from its beginning was socialism. Some analysts of China argue that 'socialism with Chinese characteristics' is now no more than 'capitalism with Chinese characteristics'. I would, however, argue that although many of the rules of the game in China today are counter to Maoist socialism, it is undeniable that socialist ideology is still used to justify many official policies in China, and that many official practices are legacies of China's Maoist past. The most enduring legacy of China's Maoist past is the former constraint on Chinese leaders of a Pareto-improving outcome–reform should leave no one, especially those in the state sector, worse off. China's Maoist past has created in North's words, 'organizations and interest groups with a stake in the existing constraints', and the promise of a Pareto-improving outcome is the price that Chinese leaders had to pay for overcoming the resistance of those with an interest in preserving the existing institutions.

Although history is given, the manner in which it affects public policy is not fixed. Public policy is influenced, but not predetermined, by history. I argue in this paper that Chinese history specifies a set of possible reform programs that may be acceptable to and workable in Chinese society. But the choice of a particular reform program and how the chosen program works out in practice is determined jointly by party leaders and the S&P bureaucracy. A particular path of economic reform is chosen not because it is ordained by history but as an equilibrium outcome of a game between the Chinese political leadership and S&P bureaucrats. This interpretation of the role of history in institutional change avoids a common criticism that studies relying on path-dependence explanation of institutional change are historicist–that some studies have treated path dependence as 'an overly deterministic concept'[3] and paid insufficient attention to the role and behavior of contemporary actors in determining institutional change.

In this chapter, I regard Chinese political leaders and S&P bureaucrats as the key actors in determining institutional change. Chinese political leaders are of course members of the state and party bureaucracy but their interests diverge. The distinction between Chinese leaders and S&P bureaucrats is based on their relative rank in the hierarchy. Chinese leaders are leaders in senior central leadership positions, while S&P bureaucrats include other leaders at local and other less powerful levels and remaining S&P bureaucrats. Managers of SOEs are part of these bureaucrats and the influence that workers in SOEs have on the reform process is exercised through them. Chinese political leaders are not of course united in their views on economic reform. But once they have reached a consensus, whatever policy direction they have decided is announced at a party plenum to the bureaucracy and population at large.[4] The implementation of the policy is then left to the bureaucracy, which decides how well it would carry out the policy. Thus the specifics of a given policy and the response of the bureaucracy to that policy would determine the value of the payoff of the policy to Chinese political leaders.

In this chapter, I describe the role of Chinese political leaders and S&P bureaucrats in determining the reform process by a simple game theory model of Chinese reform strategy. This model is based on the generic 2-party x 2-action non-cooperative game theory model and its application here is influenced by Tsebelis' work on the British Labor Party (Tsebelis, 1990, ch. 5). Table 9.1 presents the perceived payoffs at the beginning of reform to Chinese political leaders and S&P bureaucrats from their interactions in the economic-reform strategy game. These payoffs are the actors' own subjective evaluations, which may alter over time because of new or additional information available or changes in the environment. Chinese political leaders can choose a radical or moderate path of reform and S&P bureaucrats can either cooperate or withhold their support for the reform program chosen by their political leaders.[5] I define radical reform as reform that does not lead to a Pareto-improving outcome unless there is an explicit payoff transfer from winners (Chinese leaders) to losers (S&P bureaucrats).

Moderate reform is by definition Pareto-improving and an explicit transfer is not required.

Chinese political leaders prefer a radical program if they could be sure of support from the state bureaucracy, which is essential to effective reform policy implementation. Expressing it in another way, Chinese leaders would like to move faster in reform if they knew they could carry the bureaucracy with them. This support, however, is not guaranteed because of China's Maoist legacy. There are too many vested interests embedded within the bureaucracy that reduce the probability of cooperation. Without this support, Chinese leaders are better off with a moderate program of reform.

Table 9.1 Reform Strategy Game

S&P Bureaucrats

		Cooperation	Non-Cooperation
	Radical	R1, R2	S1, T2
Political			
Leaders	Moderate	T1, S2	P1, P2

Chinese political leaders can endeavor to ensure a Pareto-improving outcome in one of two ways. They can either adopt a moderate program of reform, which continues to subsidize state-owned enterprises implicitly through the plan and largely retains the administrative structure required to manage SOEs, or compensate losers in a radical program of reform that embraces comprehensive marketization, including privatization, of the state sector.

In the game between the political leaders and S&P bureaucrats, in the absence of compensation accompanying a radical program, the order of the payoffs is:

$$R1 > T1 > P1 > S1 \qquad \text{for the political leaders} \qquad (1)$$

$$P2 > S2 > T2 > R2 \qquad \text{for the S\&P bureaucrats} \qquad (2)$$

Regardless of the reform program, S&P bureaucrats will choose not to cooperate. If the reform program is radical, bureaucrats will lose most of their power and many will become redundant. It is therefore not in their interest to cooperate. If the reform program is moderate, their positions in the bureaucracy are secure, but the decentralization of the economy and bureaucracy that accompanies moderate reform gives them greater opportunities to rent-seek. Since S&P bureaucrats lose in a radical reform, their non-cooperation in a program of radical reform will produce a lower payoff to Chinese leaders than their non-cooperation in a program of moderate reform. S&P bureaucrats will work hard to impede a radical reform program.

Denote the value of compensation given to S&P bureaucrats in a radical program of reform as X. First assume that the compensation is not targeted and is given to all S&P bureaucrats, regardless of whether they cooperate or not. For a value of X to exist that can ensure that S&P bureaucrats will always be better off with a radical than with a moderate reform program, it is sufficient that (P2-R2) be not too large. The order of payoffs with non-discriminatory compensation is:

$$R1-X>T1>P1>S1-X \text{ for the political leaders} \tag{3}$$

$$T2+X> R2+X >P2>S2 \qquad \text{for the S\&P bureaucrats} \tag{4}$$

If compensation is targeted and is given to only S&P bureaucrats who cooperate, the order of payoffs with the compensation becomes:

$$R1-X>T1>P1>S1 \qquad \text{for the political leaders} \tag{5}$$

$$R2+X>P2>S2>T2 \qquad \text{for the S\&P bureaucrats} \tag{6}$$

No player in this game has a dominant strategy. Chinese leaders would be bolder in reform if they thought they could get the cooperation of S&P bureaucrats, and would choose a moderate program if they thought cooperation would be withheld. S&P bureaucrats would cooperate if radical reform is introduced with compensation that is targeted [equation (6) holds], but they would not cooperate if there is no compensation [equation (2) holds] or if compensation were granted to all without targeting [equation (4) holds]. S&P bureaucrats remain non-cooperative when Chinese leaders introduce a moderate program. S&P bureaucrats would take advantage of partial reform to rent-seek. The payoffs of the game where there is targeted compensation attached to radical reform dictate two Nash equilibria: radical reform with the cooperation of S&P bureaucrats and moderate reform without the cooperation of S&P bureaucrats. But if compensation were not targeted, the equilibrium outcome of the game would be moderate reform without the cooperation of S&P bureaucrats. If Chinese leaders choose not to compensate, the equilibrium outcome of the game would be moderate reform without the cooperation of S&P bureaucrats.

In an ideal situation, S&P bureaucrats who are adversely affected by a radical program of reform and cooperate in its implementation are identifiable. But in reality, actions of individual S&P bureaucrats are not entirely observable and difficult to monitor. The transaction costs associated with implementing a discriminatory compensating policy are therefore likely to be prohibitively large. In contrast, achieving a Pareto-improving outcome through a non-discriminatory compensating policy associated with radical reform or a moderate reform program does not have this problem. The associated transaction costs are likely to be lower. This meant that Chinese leaders would seek to derive a Pareto-improving outcome either by non-discriminatory compensation if they decide to choose radical reform, or choose moderate reform. But the payoffs of the game tell us that radical reform without compensation or with non-discriminatory compensation leads to the same equilibrium outcome of moderate reform and no S&P bureaucratic cooperation. Hence there is no reason for Chinese leaders to consider compensation if they were to choose radical reform. The equilibrium outcome of the game is therefore moderate reform and no S&P bureaucratic cooperation.

The irony is that S&P bureaucrats actually always prefer a radical to a moderate reform program when compensation is non-discriminatory. But unfortunately, non-discriminatory compensation does not provide the incentive for S&P bureaucrats to cooperate. In the absence of S&P cooperation, Chinese political leaders are better off with a moderate reform program. Although Chinese leaders and S&P bureaucrats strictly do not have a dominant strategy, the game where there is non-discriminatory compensation in radical reform can be considered as a form of prisoners' dilemma game. If S&P bureaucrats agree to cooperate in radical reform, both they and the Chinese leaders would be better off than their situation in the equilibrium outcome of moderate reform and non-cooperation.

The Folk Theorem states that, provided an iterative game is played an infinite number of times, or if the number is finite but sufficiently large, there is uncertainty about the opposite players' payoffs, the equilibrium outcome of each iteration of the game could be mutual cooperation (Fudenberg and Maskin 1986). In other words, radical reform with S&P bureaucratic cooperation could be the equilibrium outcome in the game where there is non-discriminatory compensation in radical reform if conditions specified by the Folk Theorem hold. The conditions are unlikely to hold, however, because of the requirement of a sufficiently large number of iterations. Chinese leaders cannot wait for the required number of iterations because compensation has to be paid out of fiscal revenues, and unless S&P bureaucratic cooperation is forthcoming quickly, compensation will have to cease due to insufficient fiscal revenues. The raising of adequate fiscal revenues for compensation is contingent on radical reform able to generate the necessary growth in GDP within the time constraint. Foreign borrowing is theoretically possible to provide the necessary funds for compensation but is unlikely to eventuate because of political uncertainty over reform and the amount of funds for compensation that is necessary. Foreign capital markets would be cautious, raising the cost of such funds, and Chinese leaders are reluctant to be overly dependent on foreign borrowing.

How well does the model just described help to explain post-Mao Chinese economic reform? An analysis of the history of Chinese economic reform from 1978 suggests that the model's equilibrium outcome–a moderate reform program without the cooperation of S&P bureaucrats does describe the actual situation in the period between 1978 to 1992. The model also lends support to North's argument that 'path dependency' is a consequence of the high transaction costs required to overcome the objections of entrenched interest groups.

The sections in the chapter below provide a narrative on the evolution of the Chinese approach to economic reform within the context of the model that was presented earlier. It explains how the initial conditions of reform changed in 1992 when the failure of the dual-track price system to insulate the plan from the market and accumulated large losses of state-owned enterprises altered the cognition of political leaders and forced them to change their perceived payoffs in the game. This led them to shift to a more radical approach to reform. Later the Asian financial crisis provided an exogenous shock that again altered the perceptions of the players and therefore the payoffs of the game. The new payoffs of the game shifted the equilibrium outcome of the game towards more radical reform by enhancing all players' perceptions that the Chinese radical reform program is unavoidable. Before the crisis, the question was whether the much-needed radical reforms would be carried through. After the crisis, the question has become when.

Chinese Reform 1978-1992: Pareto-improving Approach

Post-Mao Chinese economic reform from its inception in 1978 under Deng Xiaoping was moderate. As the narrative of Chinese reform below shows, the simple model presented above can explain the choice of this particular reform approach. The progress of post-Mao economic reform in the two decades from its genesis to the present, from the perspective of the relationship between the plan and the market and between the state and non-state sector, is presented in Table 9.2. The table shows that over the twenty years of reform, the Chinese economy has gone through no less than six major changes in reform policy direction. Reform began with an emphasis on following the 'law of value' in 1978 and by 1993 had swung into pursuing the 'Socialist Market Economy'.

Table 9.2 From Plan to Market

Period	Guiding Principle
1978-1979	Law of value
1979-1984	Planned economy as the core, supported by the market
1984-1987	Planned commodity economy
1987-1989	Greater use of market incentives
1989-1992	Integration of the plan and market
1993-	Socialist market economy

Law of Value

Reform in China began in 1978 with the decollectivization of agriculture. The decollectivization of agriculture resolved the free-rider problem and aligned agricultural incomes closer to effort. Although central control over much of agricultural marketing remained, agricultural procurement prices were increased and the overall result was a large improvement in agricultural productivity. McMillan, Whalley and Zhu (1989) estimated that total factor productivity in agriculture increased by 32 percent between 1978 and 1984. Of the total increase, 78 percent was attributed to the decollectivization of agriculture and the remaining

22 percent to higher prices. Between 1981 and 1984, average personal real income in China increased by 12.6 percent a year. This increase in real income occurred right across the board, with only a marginal rise in inequality (World Bank 1997, p.10).

The national plan remained the key instrument for allocation and distribution in the economy during that period. Reform on allocation and distribution was focused on ensuring 'plan prices reflect the law of value'. This means that in practice, the setting of plan prices would take greater account of their impact on demand and supply. Between 1979-1984, the guiding principle for the economy was to use the plan as the core instrument to coordinate the economy, with the market acting in a supporting role (*jihua jingji wei zhu, shichang jingji wei bu*).

Planned Commodity Economy

In 1984 the Communist Party of China (CPC), boosted by its success in reforming agriculture, introduced reforms to industry. At the same time, the Party expanded the role of the market. According to the then new guiding principle of reform, the economy was now a planned commodity economy (*you jihua de shangpin jingji*). Central to the new principle was the introduction of the dual-track price system. Under this price system, producers were allowed to sell all their production above the plan quota in the market and consumers and producers were allowed to purchase from the market any amount of commodities above what was allocated to them through the plan. The aim of the system was to quarantine the planned sector while allowing the market to coordinate economic activity in the rest of the economy and to provide incentives for above-plan production.

The dual-track price system was a key element in China's Pareto-improving approach to economic reform. By retaining the plan but allowing the market to operate around it, the Party had hoped to benefit from the advantages of the market while cushioning SOEs from market forces. The competition that SOEs would receive from the market was to be restricted to sales of their non-plan output and their purchases of non-plan inputs. Hence, it was thought, the state sector could enjoy some benefits of the market while avoiding its negative effects. Because the economy at the commencement of reform was well inside its production possibility frontier, Pareto improvements could be obtained through reform; the overall economy could be made better off without making the state sector worse off. This Pareto-improving strategy, by guaranteeing the interests of the state sector and the officials who managed them, was able to develop a constituency of S&P officials to support, or at least did not oppose, economic reform (Liew 1995). The existence of this constituency, however, did not mean that a majority of S&P bureaucrats cooperated in the implementation of the moderate reform program. As the narrative below describes, some of the institutions like the dual-track price system, introduced as part of a moderate reform program, led to perverse behavior of many S&P bureaucrats. What the Pareto-improving approach achieved was to induce sufficient number of S&P bureaucrats to make the program workable for a period of time.

The introduction of the dual-track price system expanded the role of the market in planning as well as in distribution. The CPC Twelfth Central Committee at its third plenum in 1984, which officially marked the shift in economic reform, announced that planning was to be divided into mandatory and guidance planning. Mandatory planning (*zhiling jihua*) was the old-style direct administrative planning by decree, while guidance planning (*zhidao jihua*) relied on indirect planning instruments or economic levers such as taxes and subsidies to guide production and distribution.

The 1984 plenum, like the one in 1978, was a watershed. At the Third Plenum of the Eleventh Party Congress in 1978, a socialist economy was defined as a planned economy. In his famous 1979 article (Chen, 1987, p.17-20), 'Issues regarding the plan and the market' (*Jihua yu shichang wenti*), influential party leader Chen Yun stated that 'only with a [planned economy] can socialism be built'. The 1984 plenum, in contrast, stated that the difference between a socialist and a capitalist economy 'lies ... in the difference of ownership' (CPC, 1984, p.14). Planning was no longer a prerequisite for an economy to be socialist.

In the period 1984 to 1987, greater weight was still placed on the plan than on the market, but from 1987 to 1989, more and more emphasis was placed on using the market. During that period, the focus was on the use of market incentives (in the state and non-state sectors) and foreign direct investment and the promotion of non-state township-village enterprises (TVEs) to spur faster economic development. The result was impressive. Total factor productivity in SOEs improved (Jefferson and Rawski, 1994; Jefferson and Xu, 1994) and there was a significant expansion of economic activity in the non-state sector.

The shift in emphasis toward the market during the period occurred despite an attack by leftists on the increasing market orientation of reform. Leftists had focused on the ideological orientation or 'surname' (*xing*) of reform policy – whether it is capitalist (*zi*) or socialist (*she*). The reformers, led by Deng Xiaoping, counter-attacked using the black cat, white cat analogy, arguing that it does not matter whether a cat is black or white as long as it catches mice–any policy that can improve the standard of living of the Chinese people is socialist.

The movement toward greater use of the market was severely tested in 1988 and 1989 when the center lost control of monetary policy to the regions. This was a consequence of the decentralization of economic power away from the center. The resulting high rate of inflation led to a sharp divergence between plan and market prices and encouraged massive rent-seeking by officials, who diverted production from the plan to the market. The diversion of production threatened many inefficient SOEs as they were unable to compete with the more efficient non-state TVEs in the market for supplies. Interregional trade barriers were set up in an attempt by regional governments to prevent the sale of in-region raw materials destined for in-region use through the plan to the markets of other regions that were offering higher prices. The high rate of inflation faced by urban residents and the loss of plan supplies by SOEs to the market through massive official corruption coupled with demands for political change led to the demonstrations in many cities in China, which culminated in the tragic military crackdown in Beijing on June 4, 1989.

Ironically, the amount of rents available under the dual-track price system was lower than the rents available under a centrally-plan system (Liew 1993). The reason was the gap between the black market price and the plan price under central planning is higher than the gap between the legal market price and the plan price under the dual-track price system. Because the market was illegal under central planning, it was difficult if not impossible for supply to respond to the higher black market price. This does not apply in a dual-track price system because the market in this system is legal and supply can respond relatively easily. In the freer post-Mao reform atmosphere, officials were able to flaunt their wealth earned from rent-seeking activities whereas in the politically austere Maoist period, rents were largely dissipated by law enforcement.

The World Bank (World Bank 1997, pp.10-11) using Chinese data estimated that between 1984 and 1989 average real personal incomes in China increased by less than 1 percent year. During this period GDP grew strongly but rural poverty increased and there was a rise in inequality. The World Bank suggested that Chinese data either underestimated personal income growth or overestimated GDP growth. This is because low growth in personal consumption could be consistent only with a significant growth in GDP if there were large increases in the savings of enterprises or the government, but the data do not support this explanation. There are reasons why personal income growth could have been underestimated and GDP growth overestimated during that period. Many personal incomes were earned from rent-seeking activities and many market activities, although legal, continued to face harassment from local officials. Hence, incomes from these activities were likely to be concealed. As well, the inflation rate was high and for political reasons, price deflators were likely to be underestimated. Many persons earning high incomes were beneficiaries of rent-seeking opportunities. The high rate of inflation affected those mainly on fixed incomes. They were mainly officials, and employees in SOEs that suffered from massive diversion of supplies away from the plan to the market.

Annual inflation reached a peak of 26.7 percent in the fourth quarter of 1988 (Khor, 1991, Table 3) and hit especially hard on cities, which have a high proportion of their residents working for the bureaucracy or in SOEs. The 1989 report of the Chairperson of the State Planning Commission pointed out that in 1988 a significant proportion of city residents experienced a fall in their standard of living (Liew, 1990, p.7). Pareto-improving welfare was obviously not achieved. The modeling of the game played between Chinese political leaders and S&P bureaucrats supports this conclusion–the game produced an equilibrium outcome of moderate reform without bureaucratic cooperation.

Integrating Plan and Market

Rent-seeking activities encouraged by the dual-track price system convinced the Chinese leadership that it was difficult, if not, impossible for the plan and market to coexist together. The dual-track price system was unable to guarantee a Pareto-improving outcome that Chinese leaders had hoped for. Many of the country's 'backbone industries' like coal and steel had great difficulty securing supplies guaranteed by the plan during the period of massive rent-seeking in 1988 and 1989. Workers from many SOEs that were adversely affected by the rent-seeking were among the many thousands who took part in the political demonstrations in 1989. A decision had to be made to resolve the dilemma between the plan and market. However, in a situation where neither the champions of the plan nor the champions of the market were able to gain a clear ascendancy within the CPC, the stated guiding principle of reform from 1989 until 1992 was a compromise of 'integrating the plan and market economies' (*jihua jingji yu shichang jingji xiang jiehe*). In practice, it meant the subordination of the market to the plan, with the authorities putting greater effort into preventing the leakage of supplies from the plan to the market.

The post-June 1989 switch of emphasis from the market to the plan by the CPC was an attempt to salvage the Pareto-improving reform policy that had been disrupted by the perverse behavior of S&P bureaucrats. The switch was formalized at the Fifth Plenum of the CPC Thirteenth Party Congress on 11 November 1989 (Liew 1990,p.9). The core of the new policy focus was to prevent the market from threatening SOEs by siphoning supplies away from the plan and sought to redress what was perceived to be imbalance in the relative growth rates of TVEs and SOEs since industrial reforms were introduced. Reflecting the new emphasis, the allocation of credit was recentralized and the specialized banks lost their autonomy in bank lending. Investment loans were brought back under mandatory planning and no investment loans were to be granted to TVEs, individual businesses and projects of SOEs that had not been approved by the plan.

The period 1989-92 saw an evaluation of the Party's reform program, in particular, its attempt at ensuring a Pareto-improving outcome through the dual-track price system. The main conflict among the political leadership was the appropriate place of the market in the economy. The attachment of the market on to the plan had created the problem of rent-seeking by officials. Moreover, the entry of non-state enterprises into the economy was providing competition to SOEs with unforeseen consequences. Even in the absence of plan evasion, as long as SOEs participated in the market, there was a probability of SOE failure; not all ventures into the market by SOEs could be successful. There was no guarantee that production above the plan-quota of state enterprises could automatically be sold in the market. Sales to the market, unlike sales under the plan, are not guaranteed. To be successful in the market, state enterprises have to produce goods of a reasonable quality at a competitive price, but the presence of non-SOEs in what was previously a closed market made the success of SOEs in the market difficult to achieve. The greater the involvement of SOEs in the market, the larger the potential amount of losses (and profits) in the state sector. In the first half of 1991, 36.7 percent of SOEs were in the red (Lam 1995, p.71). The market was proving to be more of a problem than an opportunity to many SOEs. To assist SOEs by winding back the non-state sector would be a major retreat from reform. Moreover, the TVE sector was the most vibrant part of the Chinese economy and was also its major earner of foreign exchange. But the market was difficult to control and made it difficult for the plan to protect SOEs.

In the northern spring of 1992, China's paramount leader, Deng Xiaoping broke the deadlock by giving a series of talks during his tour of South China (*nanxun*). His central message during his tour was that 'the difference between socialism and capitalism does not lie in [which system has] a higher proportion of planning or the marketplace'.[6] 'Planning and the market are both economic measures'. 'The essence of socialism is to liberate productivity and to develop productivity'. In a sense, his message was only a reaffirmation of the Party message at its 1984 plenum. However, it was significant because until Deng went on his tour of the southern provinces and added his voice to those of the pro-market forces, the reform process had looked to be stalled. The reassertion of central control over the allocation of credit had adversely affected many TVEs. Many of them could not gain access to the required raw materials and financial credit and had ceased operations.

End of Pareto-improving Approach

The negative experiences of the dual-track price system and continuing losses incurred by SOEs finally convinced the political leadership that the previous moderate reform program had reached a dead end and that the reform program needed change. Despite the likelihood of non-cooperation from the bureaucracy, a switch to a more radical program appeared necessary to Party leaders. In the context of the model specified above, Chinese political leaders believed that the payoff from radical reform without cooperation from S&P bureaucrats had increased relative to the payoff from moderate reform. Instead of $P1>S1$, the leaders now believed $S1>P1$. Chinese political leaders had re-valued their payoffs from a radical reform program upwards and re-valued their payoffs from a moderate reform program downwards. The revised payoffs for the political leaders became:

$$R1>S1>T1>P1 \text{ for the political leaders} \qquad (7)$$

The payoffs of the S&P bureaucrats remained unchanged. The change in the game's payoffs produced a new equilibrium outcome. Political leaders switched from a moderate to a radical reform program but the action of S&P bureaucrats remained non-cooperative because targeted compensation continued to be ruled out.

Socialist Market Economy

The decisive shift to the market was affirmed in 1993 at the CPC Fourteenth Committee at its Third Plenum, when it adopted the 'Decision of the CPC Central Committee on Some Issues Concerning the Establishment of a Socialist Market Structure'. The decision represented a victory for those who were pro-market. It signaled the replacement of the plan by the market and placed the need to clarify property rights at the top of the reform agenda. Accordingly, the market is 'to play the fundamental role in resource allocation under macroeconomic control by the state' (CPC Central Committee 1993, p.12). The dual-track price system was to be abolished as soon as possible and by 1994, only 4 percent of national production was to be subjected to mandatory plans drawn up by the State Planning Commission.

The 1993 decision not only replaced the plan with the market but it also sought to make the management of SOEs independent from government administration. An important part of the separation of government from enterprise management was the clarification and redistribution of the property rights of SOEs. The property rights of SOEs in China were too dispersed for economic incentives to work efficiently. SOEs had too many government agencies [mothers-in-law (*popo*)] interfering in their management and attempting to secure access to their residual cash flows. These government agencies sought to gain access to the residual cash flows of SOEs but sought to avoid being held responsible for their performance. It was difficult to hold the agencies individually accountable for the losses of the SOEs because control of the SOEs was dispersed and there was no clear line of responsibility.

According to the 1993 decision, most small state enterprises would be privatized, while the management of those not sold would be contracted out. Large and medium SOEs would be corporatized. Many would be turned into limited liability and stockholding companies, which would welcome the injection of non-state and foreign capital. A number of joint stock companies would be allowed to list their shares on the stock market. SOEs would be held accountable for their losses and enterprises continuously in the red or insolvent would be made bankrupt (CPC Central Committee, 1993, p.1).

The evidence of the adoption of a more radical reform program was immediate. Hundreds of thousands of SOEs' employees were made redundant as a result of the policy shift. According to Labor Minister Li Boyong, SOEs would lay off 6 million urban workers in 1997 and that between 8 to 10 million workers in SOEs would be retrenched in the next three years (Chan 1998). The regions worst hit were in northeast China, which is the center of China's heavy industry. By the time of the Fifteenth Party Congress in 1997, 25 percent of medium and large SOEs had become limited liability stockholding companies, with the state holding only 43 percent of their assets.[7]

While Chinese leaders had decided to shift to a more radical reform program, in practice, the shift in policy reform is more limited than what is suggested by the increase in unemployment numbers. Despite a revision in the payoffs for the political leaders, the equilibrium outcome of the reform strategy game still has S&P bureaucrats remaining non-cooperative. Many loss-making SOEs continued to be subsidized by banks because of local official pressure and loans continued to be granted because of personal connections than on the basis of potential rates of returns.

Chinese leaders saw that years of economic progress were wiped out in Indonesia by the Asian financial crisis because of poor corporate governance. This has had a significant impact on Chinese leaders. Chinese leaders were aware of the serious situation facing their country's banking system. Undisciplined lending to SOEs by China's banks have created a sizeable portfolio of non-performing loans, which according to various estimates is about 20-40 percent of total loans. The size of these non-performing loans would make many of the country's commercial banks insolvent.[8]

As a result of the Asian crisis, the perceived payoffs of the Chinese leaders from a radical reform program in the absence of S&P cooperation (S1) in the game increases. This does not change the fundamental relationship of the payoffs in equation (7). However, the crisis has also altered the perceptions of S&P bureaucrats about their payoffs from non-cooperation with Chinese leaders in a radical reform program. It is clear that subsidies to loss-making SOEs are only postponing the inevitable. Scarce capital is not put to efficient use. This has a negative impact on future growth. While subsidizing SOEs may preserve employment in the short-run, the inefficient use of capital will seriously undermine future employment generation. As the Asian financial crisis shows, the collapse of the banking system as a result of poor lending has real effects on the economy. As a result, S&P bureaucrats have become less antagonistic towards radical reform and more pessimistic about the outcome associated with moderate reform. Consequently, their perceived values of R2 and T2 have increased relative to the values of S2 and P2 as a result of the crisis. Moreover, they have become more cooperative in radical economic reform. Their perceived value of R2 also has increased relative to the value of T2.

Other recent developments as well have reinforced the shift in the perceived payoffs of Chinese leaders and S&P bureaucrats in the strategy game. As a result of China's success in international trade, in particular being the country that enjoyed the largest trade surplus with the US after Japan, China is now under pressure from the US and the EU to further liberalize its economy. China's continuing success in international trade is likely to be contingent on it liberalizing its economy further, which means less protection for China's SOEs. The consequence of this is that pro-export interest groups within the bureaucracy will support the radical reform program.

Although S&P bureaucrats as a group might still prefer a moderate program of reform, they prefer to cooperate once Chinese leaders adopt a radical program. S&P bureaucrats as a player in this game believe that a radical reform program might leave some of them worse off, but a significant number of them now believe that they would be better off cooperating with a radical reform program. Their number is sufficient to enable cooperation in implementing a radical reform program. Payoffs of S&P bureaucrats as a group become

$$P2 > S2 > R2 > T2 \qquad\qquad (8)$$

As a result of the change in payoffs, the game now has a new equilibrium outcome. Chinese leaders introduce radical reform policies and S&P bureaucrats now cooperate to implement them.

The Asian financial crisis and recent developments outlined above have changed the perceptions of an even greater number of S&P bureaucrats on the desirability of radical reform. This will change the payoffs of S&P bureaucrats as a group such that

R2>T2>P2>S2   (9)

The change will however not affect the equilibrium outcome. It will remain as radical reform with S&P cooperation. The significance of the Asian crisis in changing the equilibrium outcome of the reform strategy game is therefore not that it has necessarily convinced a majority of S&P bureaucrats that they are now better off with a radical rather than moderate reform program. Its significance lies in the fact that S&P bureaucrats are now convinced that they can benefit and be better off if they cooperate than if they do not in a radical program. Instead of obstructing privatization, for example, they would take part in the process and attempt to benefit from it. S&P bureaucrats in the past were concerned with personal compensation in a radical reform program; now, they are more likely to be concerned with how to take advantage of the opportunities that are potentially available to them from radical reform.

The equilibrium outcome of radical reform with S&P cooperation is manifested dramatically in the bankruptcy of the insolvent Guangdong International Trust and Investment Corporation (GITIC), the investment arm of the Guangdong government, which until its closure was thought to be untouchable by Chinese and overseas investors alike. The closure of GITIC followed the closure of CADTIC, the financial institution that belonged to the Ministry of Agriculture for corruption and property speculation, the Hainan Development Bank and Venturetech Investment Corporation.[9] Reform of SOEs does not appear to have slowed because of the financial crisis. In the first ten months of 1998, 70 million employees were retrenched from SOEs (Sender, 1999). Retrenchment of workers from SOEs is occurring in all parts of the country and its magnitude suggests that the policy must receive significant cooperation from the bureaucracy right around the country. The pertinent question of Chinese reform now is not whether radical reform will be implemented but when it will be successfully accomplished.[10]

Conclusion

'Path dependence', which claims that what happened in the past has determined the present, provides a powerful explanation as to why inefficient institutions continue to persist in China. It is easier to adapt to existing rules than to change the rules that govern a game. China's reform strategy is constrained by its Maoist past. A culture of egalitarianism and state dominance has created organizations and interest groups with a stake in the existing institutions. Path dependence in this paper is modeled as constraints that are reflected as payoffs in a two-party game where interactions between Chinese leaders and S&P bureaucrats determine equilibrium reform outcome. Payoffs in the game explain why China's previous reform strategy was moderate and aimed to produce a Pareto-improving outcome, which was designed to leave the state sector no worse off. Problems with such a strategy, which culminated in the tragic June Fourth Incident in 1989, started a process that altered the perceptions of Chinese leaders of their payoffs in the game. In 1993 this alteration led to a change in the action of the leaders and shifted the equilibrium outcome of the game to radical reform without the cooperation of S&P bureaucrats. The Asian financial crisis disrupted this equilibrium outcome in 1997. The crisis provided an exogenous shock to China's reform strategy game and altered the payoffs of S&P bureaucrats. The result is a new equilibrium outcome of the game to one of radical reform with S&P bureaucratic cooperation. The significance of the Asian crisis is not that it has necessarily made S&P bureaucrats favor radical over moderate reform. The new equilibrium outcome does not depend on S&P bureaucrats favoring radical over moderate reform. Its significance is that it makes S&P bureaucrats wanting to cooperate once radical reform is adopted.

Notes

1. There were, are and will continue to be differences in opinion among political leaders in China. In this chapter, party leaders are treated as a unified group and their decisions are collective decisions.
2. Programme is the word used here (and in some other parts of the chapter) instead of strategy to avoid confusing its meaning with the meaning of the game theory concept-strategy.
3. This was the explicit criticism made by Levi (1997: 29) of Putnam (1993), who argued that events in the fourteenth century produced a culture of civic engagement in Northern Italy and distrust in Southern Italy.
4. The bureaucracy would have been consulted before the decision is announced.
5. Bureaucratic cooperation or non-cooperation is of course not absolute. S&P bureaucrats are deemed to cooperate when sufficient of them cooperate to enable key components of a reform program to be implemented.
6. This and the following two sentences were quoted in Lam (1995: 75).
7. Wen Hui Bao, 12 May 1997, p.4 and 15 September 1997, p.3. Cited by Gilley (1998: 314).
8. A comprehensive treatment of China's financial sector is given in Lardy (1998).
9. In other related developments, in 1998, China's central bank, the People's Bank of China, announced a RMB270 billion bond issue to recapitalise its state-owned commercial banks, and ordered all commercial banks, except those exempted by the State Council, to divest their trust and investment business by the end of the year.
10. The market model that finally emerges from China's radical reform need not, of course, be the 'American model'. It will be a market model with Chinese characteristics. Just as the Japanese have their own market model, the Chinese will have theirs.

References

Chan, Vivien Pik-Kwan. (1998), '10 Million Jobs to Go in State Firms', *South China Morning Post*, 10 February.
Chen, Yun. (1979), 'Jihua yu shichang wenti' (Issues of plan and market), in CPC Central Committee Secretariat Research Office and CPC Document Research Office (eds) (1987), *Jianchi Gaige, Kaifa, Gaohuo*, (Persist in reform, opening up, and vitalize:

excerpts of key documents from the Third Plenum of the Eleventh Party Congress), Beijing: Renmin Chubanshe.

CPC Central Committee (1984), *China's Economic Structure Reform*, Beijing: Foreign Languages Press.

CPC Central Committee (1993), 'Decision of the CPC Central Committee on some issues concerning the establishment of a socialist market economic structure', *Beijing Review*, Nov. 22-28, pp.12-31. Original Chinese version in *Renmin Ribao*, 17 November.

Fudenberg, D. and E. Maskin. (1986), 'The Folk Theorem in Repeated Games with Discounting or with Incomplete Information', *Econometrica*, vol. 54, pp.533-554.

Gilley, Bruce. (1998), *Tiger on the Brink: Jiang Zemin and China's New Elite*, University of California Press, Berkeley.

Khor, Hoe Ee. (1991), 'China: macroeconomic Cycles in the 1980s', *IMF Working Paper*, WP/91/85, International Monetary fund, September.

Jefferson, Gary and Thomas Rawski. (1994), 'Enterprise Reform in Chinese Industry', *Journal of Economic Perspectives*, vol. 8, pp.47-70.

Jefferson, Gary and Wenyi Xu. (1994), 'Assessing Gains in Efficient Production among China's Industrial Enterprises', *Economic Development and Cultural Change*, vol. 42, pp.597-615.

Lam, Willy Wo-Lap. (1995), *China After Deng Xiaoping*, John Wiley & Sons, Singapore.

Lardy, Nicholas R. (1998), *China's Unfinished Economic Revolution*, Brookings Institution Press, Washington DC.

Levi, Margaret. (1997), 'A Model, a Method, and M map: Rational Choice in Comparative and Historical Analysis', in Mark Irving Lichbach and Alan S. Zuckerman (eds), *Comparative Politics: Rationality, Culture, and Structure*, Cambridge University Press, Cambridge.

Liew, Leong. (1990), 'Chinese Economic Reforms before and after June 4', Revised version of a paper presented at the *Asian Studies Association of Australia Eight Biennial Conference*, Griffith University, 2-5 July.

Liew, Leong. (1993), 'Rent-Seeking and the Two-Track Price System in China', *Public Choice*, vol. 77, pp.359-375.

Liew, Leong. (1995), 'Gradualism in China's Economic Reform and the Role for a Strong Central State', *Journal of Economic Issues*, vol. 29, pp.883-895.

McMillan, John, John Whalley and Lijing Zhu. (1989), 'The Impact of China's Economic Reforms on Agricultural Productivity Growth', *Journal of Political Economy*, vol. 97, pp.781-807.

North, Douglass C. (1990), *Institutions, Institutional Change and Economic Performance*, Cambridge University Press, Cambridge.

Putnam, Robert D. (1993), *Making Democracy Work*, Princeton University Press, Princeton.

Sender, Henny. (1999), 'Prolonging the Pain', *Far Eastern Economic Review*, 20 May, p.54.

Tsebellis, George. (1990), *Nested Game: Rational Choice in Comparative Politics*, University of California Press, Berkeley.

World Bank (1997), *Sharing Rising Incomes*, Washington DC.

Chapter 10

Problems of Globalization in India

Alok Ray

Introduction

Opening up the economy to forces of international competition – its timing, phasing, sequencing and exact mechanics – has been the most controversial component of the economic liberalization package in developing countries like India. This chapter seeks to clarify some of the major issues in external liberalization, with special reference to the recent Indian experience. What is true for India should be relevant for many other countries in the Asia-Pacific region.

Among other things, the chapter analyzes the logic (as well as the conditions for success) behind the standard external liberalization package as advocated by the 'Washington consensus'. It then critically examines a number of issues: (i) should stabilization and domestic liberalization necessarily precede trade reforms; (ii) can a 'big' country like India achieve international cost competitiveness by domestic liberalization alone; (iii) whether expansion must precede import liberalization; (iv) should import liberalization be restricted to capital goods and intermediate goods or should it be extended to consumer goods as well.

Faced with a severe foreign exchange crisis in 1991, India was forced to follow, almost step by step, the typical IMF-World Bank stabilization-cum-structural adjustment package. This package has three components:

1. stabilization which basically implies cutting down fiscal deficit and the rate of growth of money supply;
2. domestic liberalization which consists of relaxing restrictions on production, investment, prices and increasing the role of market signals in guiding resource allocation; and
3. external sector liberalization or relaxing restrictions on the international trade in goods, services, capital and technology.

Economists of all persuasions generally agree that central as well as state governments in India have been living beyond their means for a long time (Ray, 1987; 1990). Hence there is an urgent need for 'stabilization' or macro-economic balance. This is recognized to hold the key to keeping inflation and balance of payments (BoP) under control as both these problems basically arise from a mismatch between aggregate demand and aggregate supply. However, opinions sharply differ on the mechanics of how to reduce fiscal deficit – which expenditures and subsidies to cut, how tax revenues should be increased – and the implications of alternative measures for investment, growth and income distribution. Nonetheless, the general necessity of reducing fiscal profligacy of the government is not seriously questioned, though the exact measurement of fiscal indiscipline remains a problem area. There is also a broad consensus in favor of domestic liberalization as it is widely recognized that most of the bureaucratic controls on investment, production and prices have outlived their utility and have even become counter-productive. However, 'external sector liberalization' or opening up the economy to forces of international competition (particularly its timing, phasing and sequencing) is the most controversial and the least understood component of the liberalization package in India.

In this chapter, we shall try to clarify some of the major issues in external sector liberalization, with special reference to the Indian context. The Indian experience should be highly relevant for many other developing countries. Hopefully, this may also help to remove some of the confusion and misunderstanding which prevails in this area. Though some degree of overlap is unavoidable, we shall take up the issues one by one for the convenience of the reader. For a discussion on the nature and the implications of globalization from the perspective of developed countries, the reader may refer to the articles of Rodrik (1998) and others in the Symposium on Globalization in the *Journal of Economic Perspectives*, Fall 1998.

Contours of the Trade Liberalization Package

According to the conventional Fund-Bank wisdom, in order to achieve efficient resource allocation in line with comparative advantage, domestic price structure should be closely linked to international price structure or, more accurately, the marginal rates of transformation through foreign trade. Unless this adjustment is made, efficiency and ultimately BoP and growth will suffer. So, they generally advocate a three-pronged phased trade liberalization program.

1. First, quantitative restrictions (QRs) and import licensing should be converted to equivalent tariffs. This establishes a direct and transparent link of domestic prices to foreign prices. Some of the other advantages are:

    a. With tariffs, true protection is known to all concerned parties, including potential investors.
    b. Tariffs are more stable. Tariff-equivalents of quotas change as domestic or (ii) (ii) Tariffs are more stable. Tariff-equivalents of quotas change as domestic demand or supply curves shift.

c.   QRs imply an arbitrary, haphazard structure of protection with no clear rationale. Irrationality of an equivalent tariff structure will be more obvious and hence correction will be easier to make.

d.   Tariffs are less discretionary than QRs and hence involve less 'lobbying cost'.

e.   Since any one can import, tariffs imply less monopoly power to importers, as compared to quotas.

f.   Conversion of quotas into tariffs would imply more government revenue, unless import licenses were auctioned off to the highest bidder.

g.   If import licenses are allocated on the basis of installed capacity (as is sometimes done under 'Actual User' principle), this may lead to excessive underutilized capacity.

2.   Second, the average level of tariffs as well as the dispersion of tariff rates is to be gradually brought down. Reducing the average level of tariffs will cut down protection to more rational levels. Bringing tariff rates towards greater uniformity is designed to reduce 'distortion' of domestic prices since a uniform structure of effective protection (which, incidentally, is guaranteed by uniform nominal protection to all industries) implies the same relative prices and resource allocation as under free trade.

3.   Finally, export incentives are to be provided primarily through exchange rate adjustment. The real exchange rate has to be maintained at an appropriate level so that exporting becomes and remains generally more profitable than home sales. All successful exporting countries (such as South Korea, Japan) had their trade regimes somewhat biased towards exports relative to production for the home market (or import substitution). Unless this is achieved, new investment would not flow into export industries and no significant jump in exports is possible. Some marginal exports out of existing capacity may still take place, either to get rid of temporary surplus or to remove bottlenecks on home production by earning some foreign exchange (through import-replenishment licenses which are issued on the basis of export earnings of a company) to buy the required (imported) inputs from the international market. Available empirical evidence indicated that the policy regime in India was generally biased against exports relative to home sales, despite all the export incentives provided through the complicated system of duty drawbacks, cash compensatory support (CCS), replenishment licenses and other fiscal incentives. Apart from the well-known elasticity conditions etc. in connection with devaluation, a few points should be kept in mind while judging the effectiveness of exchange rate adjustment:

The relevant exchange rate is the real or inflation-differential adjusted exchange rate. The effect of a devaluation on the BoP depends on whether the competitors are also devaluing their currencies.

The distinction between gross and net devaluation is important. If 20 percent devaluation is accompanied by the removal of 20 percent import duty and 20 percent export subsidy, the net effect is zero. Any small or temporary real depreciation may not produce any effect on exports. It must be substantial and sustained to offset the bias against exports relative to home sales. Otherwise, the required resource reallocation will not take place. So, one should not expect a clearcut relationship between exchange rate depreciation and export earnings, apart from the problem of lagged response of exports for various reasons (the so-called 'J-curve effect'). In order to get the desired result, particularly on capital inflows, people must believe that exchange rate is not going to depreciate further. If there is expectation that it would fall, there may be capital flight rather than capital inflow. Here, some economists (like Paul Krugman) believe that there is an essential difference in terms of expectations formation between developed and developing countries. So, if the US dollar begins to fall, market participants (speculators in particular) believe that it would bounce back. But if the currency of a developing Asian ecⁱnomy starts to go down (as it happened in South-East Asia in recent times) the market begins to expect a free fall. Whether devaluation would be inflationary largely depends on the monetary-fiscal policy of the government, specially when devaluation is accompanied by customs duty reductions on basic capital goods and raw materials. Despite very substantial depreciation of the rupee over the last few years, the inflation rate has largely been kept under control in India.

Stabilization Before Trade Reforms?

There is a school of opinion, which suggests that stabilization and domestic liberalization should precede trade liberalization. Stabilization affects trade policy reforms in several ways. *Ceteris paribus*, greater macroeconomic balance implies less need for trade restrictions to maintain current account deficit at a given level, unless the exchange rate is allowed to float with all attendant consequences. Hence, it becomes easier to remove trade restrictions once the overall macroeconomic balance is restored. Moreover, to the extent the inflation rate is determined by the level of initial macroeconomic imbalance, the real exchange rate and the real interest rate (the two crucial variables in external sector reform) will be affected by the degree of stabilization achieved. Finally, the composition of expenditure cuts while attempting stabilization (such as whether infrastructure investment is reduced) will influence the effectiveness of trade reforms in generating an appropriate supply response. Granted that stabilization is necessary for effective trade policy reforms, the next question is: should they be pursued simultaneously?

The exchange rate has two basic roles. For generating adequate exports the nominal exchange rate must be sufficiently depreciated to ensure an appropriate real exchange rate to maintain international price competitiveness. On the other hand, the (nominal) exchange rate serves as a nominal anchor for domestic prices, since the depreciation of the exchange rate, apart from being an important direct determinant of the domestic inflation rate, generates expectations of future inflation. Hence, the exchange rate is frequently used in many countries with history of high inflation rates as a stabilization instrument for controlling inflationary expectations. In such cases, a conflict would arise between the two roles of the exchange rate and the export promoting role of the exchange rate may have to give way to the nominal anchor role. One may argue that under these situations stabilization and disinflation should proceed sufficiently before trade policy reforms are attempted.

However, unlike in Latin American countries with history of hyperinflation, this argument should not be given much importance in the Indian context. The inflation rate in India has usually been kept within the single digit range. Moreover, given the low ratio of trade to GDP, the inflation rate in India is more crucially related to bad monsoons, hikes in administered prices, expansionary fiscal and monetary policy than to exchange rate changes. So, the conflict between the real target approach and the nominal anchor approach should not be serious in India, provided fiscal and monetary discipline is maintained. Moreover, since in a democratic setting radical reforms and unpopular decisions can not be pursued long without inviting strong political opposition, it may be a better strategy to push external sector reforms along with stabilization in a generally perceived 'crisis' atmosphere.

Why Not Domestic Liberalization Alone?

Though Indian industrialists have received protection from foreign competition for more than 50 years since independence, there is now a renewed talk of giving them further protection for another five to seven years and even hiking import duties in some cases where the WTO 'bound rates' are above the existing ones. The advocates of continuing protection basically believe that free competition among Indian firms following domestic liberalization is enough to foster globally competitive indigenous players who would be able to withstand foreign competition even when protection is eventually removed, say, after 5 years. The question then boils down to whether domestic liberalization alone is enough for efficient industrialization in a 'big' country like India. In addition, how are consumers likely to be affected in the process.

The supporters of external liberalization would argue along the following lines. If controls on investment and production by domestic firms alone are removed without permitting foreign competition, the more efficient of the domestic firms would expand, leading to possible monopoly. The costs associated with monopoly as well as concentration of wealth would follow. One can, of course, find fault with this argument. In a globalized economy, domestic monopoly may simply be replaced by the monopoly of a giant international corporation reaping the cost advantage of global economies of scale. The global monopolist can then fleece the consumers just as well as a domestic monopoly.

A priori, the possibility cannot be ruled out. Whether it is likely to happen in practice is an empirical question. Consider the case of the soft drinks market in India, as a typical instance. A number of Indian companies were selling a fairly large variety of branded soft drinks even before the advent of Pepsi and Coke. But the bottle size increased from 200 to 250 ml only after Pepsi entered. The size further increased to 300 ml after Coke came in. The price remained the same which effectively meant a fall in price. Alongside, the dominant Indian soft drink company Parle's bottling plants and some of its brands were bought up by Coke. Through these devices, Coke quickly increased its market share. But the consumers, if anything, have gained. There has been no job loss as Indian workers are still working in the bottling plants even after the change of ownership. In fact, Coke and Pepsi are setting up new bottling plants along with the increase in the total market through vast promotional campaigns. This means more employment for ordinary Indian workers.

There was always an apprehension that after getting rid of Indian competitors Coke and Pepsi would collude and consumers would be subjected to monopolistic exploitation. But so far this has not happened. Coke and Pepsi are involved in a fierce Cola-war throughout the world. The same is happening in India. The picture would have been totally different if only Coke or Pepsi was allowed entry. The basic requirement for keeping monopolistic tendencies in check is to allow everyone – domestic and foreign – entry. This threat of competition from existing as well as potential entrants would prevent exploitation of consumers. Even in the global soft drinks market, there are other players like Cadbury Schweppes (the makers of Canada Dry), for instance, though they are not as large as Coke or Pepsi. So, the probability of monopolistic exploitation by global giants in an open economy is not that high. Moreover, the chances of this happening can be minimized by proper government policies, in particular by allowing entry of all players – domestic and foreign. Finally, even if a global monopoly results, the cost reduction through global economies of scale would usually mean a lower price or better quality for consumers because of potential competition from other global players than if the monopoly were a domestic one.

The Indian automobiles market has also gone through a similar experience. Toyota and Hindustan Motors began making cars at about the same time. The absence of competition as a result of government policy left no incentive for Hindustan Motors to innovate. With competition at home and abroad, Toyota became a global success story replacing American cars on their home turf. It is only after Suzuki was allowed collaboration with Maruti – and that too primarily because it was late Sanjay Gandhi's (Sanjay Gandhi was Prime Minister Indira Gandhi's son) pet 'peoples car' project – that Ambassador faced real competition. The arrival of Maruti cars revolutionized the Indian car market. Even here, the government allowed only one foreign company, Suzuki, to come in as collaborators in Maruti Udyog, a public sector company. No other foreign automobile company was permitted to enter. Maruti was given a virtual monopoly in the small-sized car segment. As a result, Maruti-800 cars were selling at a hefty monopoly premium and the consumers suffered. The government should have allowed all Indian and foreign companies to set up car making units in India a long time ago. Now, with Telco and several other companies bringing out cars in the Maruti-800 range, Maruti's monopoly and market premium have come under heavy pressure. Car prices have witnessed a sharp reduction.

The issue is not import substitution versus export promotion. Over the last fifty years, import substitution was carried to the extreme and imports were restricted to petroleum products and other basic necessities which were not domestically available. Yet, there was a chronic balance of payments problems. So, exports will have to have a quantum jump. For this to happen, as already emphasized, exporting has to be made more profitable relative to home sales on a sustained basis. All successful exporting countries achieved this, partly through market friendly reforms and partly through state intervention. India's complicated export subsidy schemes through duty draw backs, replenishment licenses, cash compensatory support etc. failed to neutralize the huge advantages of selling in the protected home market. The massive depreciation of the rupee since 1991 has generally solved the relative profitability problem for exporters. Now the major constraints for them are infrastructure and procedural bottlenecks (bad roads, congestion in ports, stifling customs regulations), poor quality of Indian products, absence of brand image, stigma attached to 'Made in India' label, credit terms and new forms of protectionism in the West. Some of these will take time to resolve. Meanwhile, one primary requirement for successful export efforts is that all existing and potential exporters need to have quick access to world standard inputs at competitive international prices. This can be ensured only with liberalization of import of inputs.

The successful Korean model of providing crucial inputs – including import licenses and bank finance at concessional terms – to a select group of exporters is sometimes advocated in this connection. The Korean President could call up a dozen chiefs of business conglomerates – the *chaebols* – in his chamber and lay down export targets for them. He could promise to provide them all special facilities to achieve the targets and take punitive action if they failed. But in a parliamentary democratic regime like India this is simply not possible. All incentives for exporters will have to be made generally available through the automatic market mechanism. Otherwise, there will be charges of discrimination and favoritism. Hence, we need to have a liberalized import regime for everyone.

In modern day world, exporting sophisticated industrial products would require a brand image or tie-up with multinationals of established reputation. But such MNCs would be interested in using India as a base for exports – rather than solely catering to the Indian market – only if they face strong competition from other foreign players in the Indian market. Further, foreign companies would not like to set up factories in India for exports abroad unless they are assured of a hassle-free regime of free imports of required materials from whatever global source they like. Specially, when there are countries with similarly lower labor cost advantages which are willing to offer a free-import regime to them.

Now that almost all major global players have established collaboration arrangements with Indian auto companies and they are all facing stiff competition in the Indian market, some of them would be forced to export their products for survival. They will also be compelled to indigenize their products to a large extent – otherwise importing all the major components at Rs. 48 per dollar would mean a near-prohibitive price in the Indian market. The companies to indigenize first will win. Greater indigenization would mean more jobs in the component manufacturing sector in India. Foreign partners would be induced to transfer technology and TQM (Total Quality Management) systems for manufacturing components in their own plants in India or to Indian companies with which they would work out sub-contracting arrangements. The process has already gained momentum in India. It is again competition which has induced Daewoo to pass the benefits of a depreciation of the Korean Won (against US dollar and hence Indian rupee) to Indian buyers of Cielo rather than fattening their profit margins.

True, the Indian industry suffers from certain handicaps relative to producers abroad. Many of them – particularly those who cannot access the global capital market – have to pay a higher real rate of interest. To some extent this is due to the subsidized credit to the priority sectors and the burden of non-performing assets (NPA) of the banking system which forces the banks to charge a higher lending rate to industry. They also have to put up with an inferior quality infrastructure, including the higher price of electricity. Again, this is mainly caused by the supply of power at highly subsidized rates to agriculture and the inefficiency of the State Electricity Boards. The advantage of a lower wage rate is often offset by even lower labor productivity and the absence of flexibility regarding deployment of labor. In addition, the Indian firms – specially those set up in the days of industrial licensing and MRTP regulations – suffer from small size and the resultant diseconomies of scale relative to the giant international corporations. Even though the constraints on increasing the size of the firm have been removed in recent years, the backdated technology embodied in the installed machinery and the difficulties of closing down non-viable units continue to serve as a drag on the profitability of many Indian business houses. A large section of Indian industry is arguing for an additional import protection – in the form of a higher countervailing import duty – to offset these coat disadvantages. But there is a major problem with this argument.

If an Indian producer is producing for the home market he can charge a higher price for the import-substitute as a result of the higher import duty. But if he is to export the product he cannot hike the price since the price in the world market remains the same. So, an exporter continues to suffer from the supposed handicaps, even when the import duty is raised. A bias develops against exports, relative to sales in the protected home market. Exports would shrink. The relative profitability of exports cannot be restored by additional subsidy to exporters either. The Western economies (EU and US, in particular), in all probability, would then be induced to impose an additional countervailing duty on Indian exports to offset the subsidy. Even WTO may uphold this. The solution to the resultant export and balance of payments problems can come only through a further depreciation of the rupee. Under a market-determined exchange rate this would come about automatically. However, under an adjustable peg or managed float system, this has to be enforced by conscious policy decisions.

Of course, the first best solution in such cases of general disabilities affecting Indian industry – irrespective of whether they are producing for the home market or exports – is to remove the basic causes behind the handicaps. But, steps like enhancing the efficiency of the financial sector through cutting down NPAs, improving the financial health of the State Electricity Boards, reducing power subsidies to agriculture or easing the process of closing down non-profit making units would take a long time. There are lots of political, legal and administrative hurdles along the way. Hence, in the short run and perhaps also in the medium run, the solution should best be attempted through a market-determined exchange rate. Depreciation would help the import-competing sector by providing additional (exchange rate) protection from foreign competition. It would also help exporters equally either by increasing the rupee realization from exports (assuming a 'small' country for which the export price in dollar terms is fixed) or by increasing the demand for Indian products abroad through a lowering of the dollar price in the world market (if India is a 'large' country in that specific export product and external demand is the binding constraint on exports).

If the Indian market for consumer goods remains highly protected, even foreign direct investment would come in only to 'exploit' the protected Indian market rather than to use India as a base for exports to other countries. Indian producers of consumer goods would then not be able to export their products, even with the help of foreign investors. It is not even necessary that domestic liberalization must precede external sector liberalization. China, for example, has been following a gradualist approach with regard to price, ownership and fiscal reforms while pursuing more radical trade reforms. Nonetheless, they are deriving significant benefits.

Export Expansion First, Then Import Liberalization?

Some Indian economists argue that import liberalization should take place only after exports pick up. They cite the examples of Japan, Korea and Taiwan in this connection. Their argument basically rests on the premise that exports take time to respond to reform measures (in particular, to a change in the bias of the regime towards export industries) whereas imports pick up immediately after import liberalization. This would lead to a BoP crisis, unless foreign assistance is available on a sufficient scale under favorable terms to bridge over the temporary crisis. Two counter-arguments may be considered here.

That immediate import liberalization would lead to a BoP crisis is true provided the government wants to peg the exchange rate. With full floating, imports can not exceed the current foreign exchange availability through exports, remittances and capital inflows. That is why the floating of the rupee should constitute the center-piece of external sector reforms.

As already noted, easy availability of international quality inputs at internationally competitive prices is a prime requirement for success in manufactured exports. In principle, a duty drawback scheme for exporters should achieve the same result, even within a highly restricted import regime. But, in practice, it does not work that way. Collecting duties and then giving them back is administratively more cumbersome, time-consuming and open to abuse than waiving duties. Further, duty drawbacks do not offset the effects of non-tariff barriers on imports. Moreover, the quick provision of inputs at world or near-world prices for specific exporters can be practiced more effectively by authoritarian regimes (such as they were in Korea or Taiwan) as compared to bureaucracy operating in a parliamentary democracy like India. So, ready availability of world class inputs at international prices can be assured to all existing and potential exporters in India only if imported inputs are generally available through the automatic market mechanism. This would be a particularly important consideration for potential foreign investors who would like to use India as a base for exports to other countries, using inputs purchased from the cheapest possible source in the global market.

Conclusion

Liberalization is expected to improve efficiency and international competitiveness, and after the initial adjustment phase, set the economy on a higher growth trajectory. However, if one goes by the Indian experience, India apparently moved to a higher growth path of more than 7 percent GDP growth for three consecutive years 1994-96 but then slid back to a lower growth rate of 5 percent. There are many reasons for the slow down, the global recession and a slump in commodity prices being the major causes. This is one of the prices of globalization. Global development (good, or bad) will affect an open economy. However, globalization of Indian economy will have a limited effect on rural poverty.

References

Ray, A. (1987), 'Economic Liberalization in India: BoP Implications', *The Economic and Political Weekly*, No. 4, pp.12-29, Bombay.
Ray, A. (1990), 'The Theory of Devaluation for Less developed Economies: Where Do We Stand?' B. Dutta (ed.), *Economic Theory and Policy*, pp.20-32, Oxford University Press, N. Delhi.
Rodrik, D. (1998), 'Symposium on Globalization in Perspective: an Introduction', *Journal of Economic Perspectives*, vol. 12, No. 4.

Chapter 11

Growth vs. Development: A Challenge to China for the 21st Century

Lilai Xu and (Late) J.C. Liu

Introduction

In development economics, development and growth are two related yet distinct concepts. Fascist states had higher economic growth than democracies, but, with the social wealth accumulated through economic growth spent on producing ammunitions, on building concentration camps and on developing other means to oppress its nationals, what they achieved was not DEVELOPMENT. Unfortunately until now, a major misunderstanding still remains concerning the nature of the postwar development challenge. People still widely believe that by simply raising the GNP growth rate, by an average of five percent for example, all their social problems will be solved in due course. Despite the academic consensus that the term 'development' has wider connotation than that of 'growth', as Arthur Lewis first pointed out in the early 1950s and as reiterated in the World Economic Survey for 1968, it is a great misfortune that many nations, standing at the threshold of the 21st century, still take the GNP growth rate as their main or even sole national goal.

Some politicians tend to abuse the GNP growth rate indicator for the political expedience, and pragmatic economists are also fond of this indicator, and build complicated economic models for achieving a faster growth. These have led to a rather disastrous misperception that, so long as the rate of economic growth is higher than that of population growth, all social and political problems in a society will be solved or disappear. However, one must face the fact that social and political problems happen all the time, regardless of the economic performance of any society. In addition, sometimes the faster the per capita growth, the more acute these problems would become. The reason may sound too simple: as the pie of national income becomes larger, some may find their slice bigger than, or even twice as big as, what they had before while many others may find theirs smaller. Such was a typical phenomenon in the process of Japanese industrialization, which succeeded at the sacrifice of agriculture and by exploiting the peasant.[1] Similarly, this is also commonly seen in the NICs, such as South Korea and Southeast Asian countries whose economies are taking off.[2]

Generally speaking, when measuring development level we must consider social conditions in the following three dimensions: poverty, unemployment and injustice. 'If all three of these have declined from high levels, then beyond doubt this has been a period of development for the country concerned. If one or two of these central problems have been growing worse, especially if all three have, it would be strange to call the result development, even if per capita income doubled. This applies of course to the future too. A plan which conveys no targets for reducing poverty, unemployment and inequality can hardly be considered a development plan.' (Seers, 1973, p.3) As society progresses, elements such as national education level, equality between genders, freedom of expression, national sovereignty and ecological environment should also be included in the scope of development. In other words, development is measured by the weighted average of a series of indicators although how to weight the indicators remains to be a challenge.[3]

Surely, a high economic growth rate during a certain period can provide a potential chance for further development. For example, country A and country B had same per capita incomes and unemployment rates at the end of the 1970s. While their unemployment rates remained the same in the 1980s, country A's per capita income was higher than country B, though its increased portion all went to the wealthy end of the population. Compared to country B, country A's economic power was stronger in the 1980s, but this was not a period of development. It should be noted, however, that tax system could transfer part of the income from the rich to the poor. And since the rich tend to save more, under specific policies their savings can also be turned into effective investment to create more employment and education opportunities. Therefore, country A's high economic growth in the 1980s can be taken as an indicator of development potential in the 1990s. Nonetheless, even under such circumstances, growth and development are not to be confused or lumped together, but remain two mutually related yet distinct concepts.

China's High Growth Rate and Relatively Low Development Level

Obviously, China's economic growth has been speeding up dramatically since the late 1970s when the goal of modernization was set up and followed by a series of economic reforms and open-door measures. From 1978 to 1997, the average growth rate of China's GNP was 9.9 percent and was 12 percent between 1991 and 1995 alone, far surpassing the world average growth rate of the same period. Data from the World Bank show that China ranks the seventh in the world in terms of GDP, with some of its major agricultural and industrial products even ranking first, such as grain, cotton, meat, peanut, rapeseed, fruits, steel, coal, cement, cloth, and television sets.[4]

However, although China's growth rate attracts the eyes of the world, its overall development is lagging. The ever-declining comparative advantage of farming can hardly keep the rural youth in the village. Every year around the time of Spring Festival there is a big surge of the 'wave of migrant workers' traveling between cities and their home villages. Even the continuous expansion of cities cannot keep up with the speed of the inflow of surplus rural labours.[5] Among the 1.5 million such migrant population in the city of Wuhan, about half a million or one third of them are whole families uprooted from their home villages. Among 3.29 million migrants in Beijing, 9.95 percent are children under the age of 14. In 50 major cities, about 65.7 percent of the immigrants live in their self-built huts. And in such rapid expanding 'hut neighborhoods', living facilities, hygienic conditions, and safety are, as expected, extremely undesirable, even to the extent of becoming sources of epidemic diseases and criminal activities. According to statistics, the ratio of criminal offenses by rural immigrants in Beijing raised from 25.5 percent in 1990 to 56 percent in 1995. This ratio is even higher, about 70~80 percent, in the neighbourhoods of high immigrant concentration.[6]

In terms of urban employment, China has experienced three unemployment cycles since the 1970s.[7] During the third cycle which began in 1995, a total of 13 million workers were laid off in early 1998, a figure which is expected to reach 20 million in mid-1999. In addition, among those still employed, more than 10 million are in the state of semi-unemployment with their wages suspended or stopped. It is estimated that the above two groups together account for 12.5 percent of the total urban labour forces.[8] Meanwhile, among those re-employed, because trade unions are either nonexistent or only decorative in many township enterprises and small foreign-funded enterprises, workers are reported to have very little work protection, and their individual dignity as well as legal rights, especially those of female employees, are grossly and widely violated.

Moreover, in the process of economic growth, neither the timely setting up of social security system nor improvement of national education have come hand in hand with vastly expanding production. Rather, the medical care policies under the old system have been greatly weakened, and government investment in education eroded. As a result, it hurts or threatens not only the interest of those in the labor forces, but also the basic needs of the retired. It even denies the school-aged children of what is called 'compulsory education'. For instance, the 'Hope Project' was originally initiated as a grassroots campaign to fund, with private donations from urban sympathizers, schooling for pupils in remote and poor rural areas. However, in recent years even some of the mid-sized cities, for lack of education funds, have resorted to the 'Hope Project' as a means to enroll urban school-aged children into schools. According to statistics of the State Education Committee published in February 1998, 57 cities of nine provinces/autonomous regions could not provide their school-aged children with necessary facilities for schooling.

Turning to environmental protection, official statistics are also dismal. The approach of 'pursuing economic growth only' is increasingly destroying the balance between useable natural resources and ecological conditions, creating and worsening noise and atmospheric pollution, water and waste-disposal pollution, and pollution generated by village and township enterprises. It is not surprising that, in some places, environmental pollution and ecological damage have become a constraint to further economic growth, and a threat to public health and social stability. Up to the mid-1990s, 78 percent of the city rivers could no longer serve as a source of drinking water, above 50 percent of the urban underground water was polluted, two thirds of the urban residents in the whole country were living and working under noises exceeding normal standard. The fact that the lung cancer is the number one cancer in China shows a direct connection to air pollution in cities. Meanwhile, China's arable land is shrinking year by year and species are drastically reducing. In some ecologically fragile areas, there is no drinking water for either human beings or livestock, and even no wild plants to survive, not to mention growing crops.[9]

From the social aspect, corruption among the party and governmental officials is at the center of many social problems now facing China. New development in recent years has been what is called 'collective corruption', in which the individual criminal is no longer the center of the crime, but part of a group committing and sharing the benefit of corruption collectively.[10] On top of all this, the public directs their anger most strongly and focally at those government bodies in charge of public security, judiciary, industrial and commercial regulation, as well as taxation. For it is here in these government bodies that law breaking by deliberation or by law enforcement personnel can be seen. This all leads to the rapid decline of public security, rampant criminal activities, the frequent comebacks of the repeatedly banned fake and poor-quality commodities, and all implicitly related to the corruption of these government bodies themselves.[11] Many people think that the malpractice in such government organs even exceed the worst period of the Nationalist Party rule in the 1940s.[12]

Going hand in hand with the worsening corruption is the intensifying polarization between the rich and the poor. The plight of the laid-off workers is pitiable enough, but conditions in rural areas are even grimmer. It is common that people die since they cannot afford medical expenses or get rejected by hospitals for insufficient medical down payment.[13] In years of poor harvest, more and more rural children have to leave school because their peasant families cannot manage to pay their tuition.[14] People's Daily admits that a bottle of foreign wine consumed by the privileged rich in their almost everyday dinner banquet can cost what would be enough to feed a whole peasant family.[15] From the above we can see that if economic reform serves only the purpose of high economic growth without or with very little contribution to development as defined in the first part of this article, with its tremendous social costs, this reform will cause a lot of confusions and even disasters to the society.

Theoretical and Practical Pitfalls

The key reason for the gap between China's high economic growth rate and its low development level is that, from the very beginning, China has slipped into a theoretical pitfall. This pitfall has been deepened dragging the country deeper and deeper in the mire. In the late-1970s, China raised the slogan of the realization of the Four Modernizations and soon specified its resolve to 'achieve the GNP doubling in ten years and then another doubling by the end of this century'. Deng Xiaoping's 'cats theory' laid down the ethical and behavioral code for achieving such a goal. According to his theory, it is unnecessary to get entangled in the endless debate as whether market economy is capitalism or whether planned economy is socialism by nature. No matter it is a white cat or black cat, it would be a good cat so long as it can catch the 'mice' of 'raising social productivity'. Deng also pointed out that, in order to promote social productivity, part of the population should be allowed to get rich first.

In retrospect, twenty years of Chinese reforms have actually been motivated by human desires and liberation of individuality, which reject the ethics and the entirety of society as an extrinsic force suppressing human nature. In Chinese intellectual history, except for the Mao era, human desires have never been fundamentally refuted, but got coordinated after being acknowledged. The concept of coordination is also called normalization in the form or by means of creating order.[16] Dr. Sun Yat-Sen, in elaborating his 'Three People's Principles', made 'getting wealthy' as the aim of his 'Principle of the People's Livelihood' and, at the same time, stressed that 'each individual's getting wealthy' can only be realized when 'everyone gets wealthy'. However, Mao Zedong thoroughly negated individual desires and advocated the idea of selflessness, leading only to relations in which 'everyone eats from one big pot', making each individual an appendage to the collective entirety. As a result, the public ownership did not bring about 'common wealth', but 'egalitarian poverty for all'.

China therefore began to explore a new way out. In carrying out economic reforms and the open door policy, long suppressed human desires finally got released amidst the cheering for a market economy. However, by taking advantage of the lack of institutional restraints and democratic ideas, the most evil side of capitalism has become a seriously erosive power. Lust for material gains is overflowing, corruption rampant, and the crime rate soaring. In its 30 years of seclusion and isolation, the socialist China had no chance and consciousness to absorb the merits of capitalism. When China finally embraced capitalism, the evils affected China even before the country can benefit from the merits. In comparison, it took capitalist countries a long process of about two hundred years to adopt the good elements of socialism, allowing it sufficient time to select, test and absorb them. More importantly, such a process in capitalist countries has been accompanied by and coordinated with the process of political democratization, which served to restrain the negative impact of capitalism. This accounts for the capability of capitalism to maintain its robust vitality.[17]

It is noteworthy that, covered by the 'theory of socialist first stage', the radical rightist school of thought advocates high economic growth and economic liberalization on the one hand, and adamantly opposes political democratization on the other. Yet an economic liberalization without political democratization would only become a market economy monopolized by bureaucrats. As a consequence, both protected and participated by the political establishment, wealth has been rapidly accumulated into the hands of the few in the name of 'socialist primitive accumulation'. Given that the 'primitive accumulation of capital' is a bloody and violent process, the radical rightists seem to suggest that it must also be a historical necessity to loot peasants through imposing various fees, and to loot the whole populace through high inflation. It also follows, according to that logic, that linking political power with money, and carving up state assets through corruption are all unavoidable or even fair and reasonable.[18] Consequently, when a small portion of people become richer and richer, a whole range of serious problems keep getting worse: urban unemployment, unchecked migration of rural population into cities, prostitution, school dropouts, no social security or medical insurance, environmental deterioration, and moral and ethical bankruptcy.

It is clear that China achieved its goal of doubling its national economy in the decade at a heavy social cost. Lacking a sober understanding of those potentially explosive and volatile factors hiding behind these heavy costs would bring about an immeasurable disastrous consequence to China. Since China includes one fourth of the world's population, a disaster for China would inevitably hit the whole world as well.

New Historical Turning Point

In recent years, China's top leadership has been insisting on politics taking the command, on guarding against economic disorders, and on seeking high growth while maintaining social stability. This is an indication of today's top leaders' awareness of the imbalance and the limit in the 'cat-theory' approach. In retrospect, the rash advances to brave the price raise in 1988-89 lit the fuses of Tiananmen incident, and the advocacy of 'becoming a bit bolder and striding a bit wider' in 1992 led to an overheated economy and the spread of corruption. The Chinese government is now faced with not only how to turn the money-losing state enterprises into profitable ones, nor how to keep the 8 percent GNP growth rate, but also the ever increasing environmental problems and a whole range of complicated social illnesses, too.[19] In a word, China has come to a crucial point where it must have a comprehensive reflection on its former priority of 'productivity increase only'.

During the past 20 years, China has always been regarding the process of modernization as economic development, and economic development has been further understood as one of the rate, scale and volume of economic growth, of GNP, and of national per capita income growth. Obviously, lacking the understanding of the differences between the modernization and development, China habitually confuses the two concepts by widely using them indiscriminately. Two negative consequences ensue. First, people are not theoretically prepared to reflect on the negative effects of 'modernization' or 'high economic growth' on social transformation. Second, without original studies on the essences of development and nature of modernization, the so-called 'economic development' research is usually reduced and limited to superficial studies of ad hoc counter measures to economic problems, often resulting in seeing the tree but losing the sight of the forest. It follows that decision-makers lose insight and wisdom when faced with various social issues.

It may well be said that the reform and 'open door' policy in the 1980s and 1990s has lifted China from an ideological vortex by liberating human desires and individuality of the Chinese from the stiff, traditional socialist principles. We may also say that, by achieving an unprecedented high economic growth, the reform and 'open door' policy has marked a historical turning point for China. We must further realize, however, that China is now faced with yet another turning point. That is, on the basis of justifying and legitimizing human desires and individuality, it must transform its 'development strategy' from one centered on economic growth to one aimed at sustained development of the society as a whole. Such a strategic transformation should be accomplished through setting up new harmonious orders by coordinating and normalizing relations among people, between people and society, and between mankind and nature. The gist of this transformation of development strategy will be: (1) only 'people', who are the subject of the society, rather than 'materials', which are the object of the society, would take the center position in development; (2) economic growth must be within the confine of the level at which the environment condition permits; (3) economic growth must be achieved without violating the principle of fairness both among a generation and between generations; (4) efforts must be evaluated and judged prior to policy implementation.[20]

In order to successfully accomplish this transformation of development strategy, China must take the rule of law and democratic government as essential common elements for both modernization and sustained development. Although 'capitalism' is a term in economics, it has long been regarded in western countries as the cornerstone of democratic government. Similarly, socialism, also being an economic term in the true sense of the word, often gets mixed up with authoritarianism in the realm of politics. In fact, while there are many socialist countries adopting authoritarian political system, there are also quite a few western democratic countries with strong socialist elements. It is just because that capitalism and socialism criticize and redress each other's weak points, the two of them can complement each other in some ways.[21]

Thus, one important reason why western capitalism can maintain a strong vitality is that it absorbs nutrients from socialism. By the same token, through linking reforms and the 'open door' policy to 'the first stage of socialism', China in fact openly admits that socialism must be supplemented by capitalist nutrients.

People cannot accept either capitalism or socialism in their pure forms for long. Although 'the essence of capitalism relatively goes along with human nature and, therefore, facilitates economic activities', competition among people for wealth will unavoidably destroy friendly relationship among them and harm the peaceful atmosphere of the society, leaving only desires for wealth reigning over everything. Socialism, on the other hand, is 'a system that, by nature, suppresses individual desires and freedom', but it nonetheless 'represents a realm of lofty morality and, therefore, has its own inherent value' (Zhang, B., p.49-50). The future of China's reform and development depends, to a great degree, on a successful coalition of its domestic moderates in both the rightist and leftist camps, rather than on the radicals, either on the right or left. The Radical right trend of thoughts does not have any positive impact on social development. Radical leftist trends of thought would probably stage a comeback and dominate if corruption becomes particularly serious and in times of great social upheaval. Therefore, in order to obtain a real development, China must simultaneously resist both the trends of radical thought, and avoid jumping from one extreme to the other.

Conclusion

Since its adoption of economic reform and the 'open-door' policy, China has achieved a high economic growth rate which has been acknowledged by the whole world. However, such an achievement has been accompanied with a very high social cost. Facing the 21st century, China must forsake the lopsided approach of 'productivity alone' that pursues solely economic growth rate, and replace it with a comprehensive development model centering on 'people/human being'. Such a strategic shift will enable China, while maintaining a reasonable growth rate, to alleviate rather than aggravate poverty, unemployment and injustice in the society, to guarantee rather than hinder education for its nationals and equality between genders, to protect rather than destroy ecological balance and environment for human living, and to promote rather than restrict freedom of speech and political democracy. Western countries and China's neighboring countries including the US and Australia, functioning either as moral supports or out of self-interest, should extend more concern and encouragement to the prospect of China maintaining its social stability and achieving sustainable development.

Notes

1. See Jansen, M. B., 1962; Sinha, R. P., 1969; Tsutomo, O., 1967.
2. See Adelman, I. and S. Robinson, 1978; International Labour Office, 1977.
3. On the problems of measurement, see Seers, D., 1973, pp.4-7.
4. Relevant data are shown in the table below:

	Product in 1996	Share in the world (percent)	Product per capita
GNP	6859.4 bn. Yuan		5634 yuan
Grain	451 270 thou. tons	22.2	370.6 kg
Cotton	4 200 thou. tons	21.7	3.4 kg
Meat	52 600 thou. tons	25.1	43.2 kg
Peanuts	10 140 thou. tons	35.2	8.3 kg
Fruits	46 530 thou. tons	11.3	38.2 kg
Steel	101 240 thou. tons	14.2	83.2 kg
Coal	1 397 000 thou. tons	30.0	1147.4 tons
Cement	491 190 thou. tons	35.1	403.4 tons
TV set	35 420 thou. tons	24.5	0.029 sets

Source: China's National Situation and Strength monthly, vol. 1, 1998, p.13.

5.   Refer to *Zhongguo Guoqing Guoli Yuekan* (China's National Situation and Strength monthly), vol. 2, 1998, p.26.

6.   See *Guang Ming Daily*, Beijing, Jan. 11, 1997, p.1.

7.   The first unemployment peak was in 1978-79 when the educated youth returned to the cities from the rural areas after the Cultural Revolution. The registered unemployment rate in the urban area reached 5.3 percent and 5.4 percent respectively in 1978 and 1979. The second unemployment peak took place in 1989 when employees were subject to the selection policy. The registered unemployment rate in the urban area was 2.6 percent in that year. The third period of unemployment started from 1995, resulting from 'achieving the two fundamental changes'. See *Liao Wang Zhoukan* (Liaowang Weekly), vol. 1, 1998, p.10.

8.   See *Liao Wang Zhoukan* (Liaowang Weekly), vol. 1, 1998, p.10; *Ming Bao Monthly*, vol. 1, 1998, p.92.

9   See *Zhongguo Guoqing Guoli Yuekan* (China's National Situation and Strength monthly), vol. 2, 1998, pp.9-10.

10.   This is identified as collective bribe, collective holding-back, collective smuggling, collective tax cheating taxing, collective graft, collective misconduct in office, collective arbitrage, collective falsification, and collective waste. See Chen Jian-xin (1998).

11.   The most notorious case of fake- and poor-quality commodities in the 1990s is the fake wine in Shanxi province. More than 120 people died after they have drunk the fake wine. See *Liao Wang Zhoukan* (Liaowang Weekly), vol. 10, 1998, p.13.

12.   *East China Times* (Australia), March. 26, 1998.

13.   See *Zheng Ming Monthly* (Hong Kong), No. 6, 1998, p.25.

14.   In August 1996, in a town near Zhengzhou City in Henan province, for example, 500 pupils from peasant families with tuition unpaid were forbidden to take class by the school. When the school year of 1997 started the next year, the same school demanded that every pupil should come to school with 200 kilograms of dried tobacco leaves in order to register for the new semester. See *Banyue Tan* (Journal of Half-monthly Comments), No. 21, 1997, pp.28-29.

15.   See   *Renming Ribao* (People's Daily), July 14, 1995.

16.   See Li Chang-li (1997), pp.37-38.

17.   See Zhang Bao-min (1998), pp.49-50.

18.   See Yang Fan (1996), pp.25-27.
19.   Prime Minister Zhu Rongji admit that his government had 12 difficult problems to deal with. See *Our task and current issues*, State Council Documents, 26 March 1998.
20.   See He Zhong-hua (1997); Yu Yuan-pei and Yang Jian-xiang (1997).
21.   See Zhang Bao-min (1998), p.49.

References

A. In Chinese

Chen, Jian-xin. (1997), 'Be on the Alert of Corruption', *Xinhua Yuebao* (Xinhua Monthly), vol. 2, pp.25-28.

He, Zhong-hua. (1997), 'The Urgent Difficult issues in Development Study', *Xinhua Yuebao* (Xinhua Monthly), vol. 6, pp.45-50.

Li, Chang-li. (1997), 'The Accordance and Coexistence Principle will Lead China into the Twenty-First Century', *Ming Bao Monthly*, vol. 6, pp.34-42.

Yang, Fan. (1996), 'A Detailed Analysis on the Newborn thoughts in China', *Ming Bao Monthly*, vol. 1, pp.22-27.

Yu, Yuan-pei and Yang, Jian-xiang. (1997), 'Discussing on the Continuous Development in Philosophical Meaning', *Xue Shu Jie* (Academic Circle), vol. 1.

Zhang, Bao-min. (1998), 'Did the capitalism defeat the socialism?', *Ming Bao Monthly*, vol. 1, pp.42-53.

B. In English

Adelman, I. and S. Robinson. (1978), *Income Distribution Policy in Developing Countries: A Case Study of Korea*, Stanford University Press, Stanford, California.

Green, R. H. (1978), 'Basic Human Needs: Concept or Slogan, Synthesis or Smokescreen?', *IBS Bulletin*, 9:4.

International Labour Office. (1977), *Poverty and Landlessness in Rural Asia*, ILO, Geneva.

Jansen, M. B. (1962), 'On Studying the Modernisation of Japan', *Asian Cultural Studies*, No. 3, International Christian University.

Seers, D. (1973), 'The Meaning of Development', in Wilber, C. K. (ed.), *The Political Economy of Development and Underdevelopment*, Random House, New York.

Sinha, R. P. (1969), 'Unresolved Issues in Japan's Early Economic Development', *Scottish Journal of Political Economy*, June 1969.

Tsutomu, Ouchi. (1967), 'Agricultural Depression and Japanese Villages', *The Developing Economics*, vol. 5, pp.14-20.

Chapter 12

Globalization, Growth and Fiscal Policy: Lessons from East Asia

Jocelyn Horne

Introduction

Fiscal policies have a benign role for economic growth in the region, namely to provide a stable macro environment for investment. The changed environment of liquidity constraints on external borrowing and slowdown in output growth has led to new attention being directed towards the role and contribution of fiscal policy to reviving growth in the region. However, there is considerable debate on this issue; as noted by Garnaut (1998, p.19) in a recent review of the Asian crisis, 'the main unresolved questions of macroeconomic policy relate to adjustments of the fiscal settings'.

This chapter discusses the lessons for growth-promoting fiscal policy for East Asia and, more broadly for developing market economies that are pursuing strategies of trade and financial integration. At the risk of a premature disclosure of the plot, three broad principles emerge from the analysis. First, an emphasis on single-period rather than the intertemporal effects of fiscal policy on current account balances is misplaced. Second, both external and public stocks and flows require monitoring in a medium-term framework even in countries with low measured debt. Third, the potential role for growth-promoting fiscal policy centers upon the overall fiscal composition of the fiscal policy package rather than the budget thrust. lithe above three principles are followed, the growth-promoting role of fiscal policy in the new environment faced by East Asia will be enhanced. However, the quantitative contribution of fiscal policy to growth remains small relative to that of capital accumulation and productivity. Consider a developing country that is fully integrated in the global economy and borrows from the world capital market to finance its output growth by running a current account deficit. It wishes to pursue a set of fiscal policies that are growth promoting and also consistent with macrostabilization objectives. What set of policy prescriptions are suggested in the literature and policy debate?

A recent review of literature on fiscal policy and growth by Tanzi and Zee (1997) attempts to provide a comprehensive answer to this question. Their analysis examines systematically the various ways that the main fiscal instruments (tax policy, public expenditure policy, budget policy) influence economic growth through their impact on the determinants of growth; productivity (including technical change and more efficient use of existing resources) and resource accumulation. The broad conclusion reached is a positive one; a well-designed set of fiscal policies that exploits all the above channels has a fundamental role to play in influencing permanent output growth, especially when viewed from the perspective of endogenous growth theory.

Three qualifications to their analysis give pause for thought. First, as recognized in their paper, the empirical evidence in support of each fiscal channel is not robust. Second, the analysis assumes implicitly either a closed economy or one without liquidity constraints as well as unrestricted access to technology. The analysis does not consider the implications of trade and financial liberalization for the conduct and effectiveness of fiscal policy in terms of the additional constraints placed upon fiscal instruments such as trade taxes and capital taxes as well as the removal of financing constraints that enable consumption-smoothing in the face of temporary output or fiscal shocks. Third, the analysis assumes well-developed market institutions that underpin fiscal, structural and financial policies.

A more pessimistic analysis of the role of macro policy in promoting growth is given in De Long and Summers (1992). The authors note that the productivity slowdown experienced by industrial countries in the 1970s and 1980s cannot be attributed plausibly to inferior macro policies in the 1980s. Within its circumscribed growth role, macro policy operates in two ways; through management of aggregate demand and through the intertemporal allocation of output between consumption and investment. Excluding extreme situations of hyperinflation and financial collapse, macrostabilization is a necessary but not sufficient condition for economic growth; its precise impact being dependant on additional channels such as policy credibility and central bank independence that link stabilization of output levels to economic growth. In regard to intertemporal resource allocation, the required high social net (of private) returns to investment also limit the quantitative contribution of macro policy to growth. The sole fiscal policy prescription proposed by the authors is tax incentives to public investment in machinery and equipment on the grounds of its high net social returns. However, other writers (see Dowrick, 1995) have questioned the robustness of this finding, arguing that the observed high returns may be the outcome of rapid economic growth rather than the reverse causation.

In terms of the East-Asian growth experience and role of fiscal policy, a striking feature is their high investment and national savings ratios. While the issue of causation is subject to debate, high output growth, savings and investment ratios tend to be positively related and self-reinforcing. Unlike other developing economies, the current account deficit reflects the gaps between these high ratios rather than public sector dissaving. This feature, combined with access to global capital markets is the main rationale for the prevalent view that fiscal policy was not a cause of the crisis nor were current account deficits necessarily a cause for policy concern. This interpretation is also supported by 'new' open-economy macroeconomics that builds upon rational, optimizing micro behavior to derive the current account as the outcome of intertemporal optimizing savings and investment decisions. The economic situation and global environment has altered for East

Asia. The growth slowdown has weakened the self-reinforcing mechanisms of growth, high savings and investment rates.

The altered macro environment of output slowdown and exchange rate depreciation has widened budget deficits, reversing the earlier trend. Restricted access to global capital markets, reduced output growth and exchange depreciation have forced a switch from current account deficits to surpluses. Finally, debt build-up, primarily of private sector external debt but accompanied by growing public debt places a solvency constraint on continued primary budget deficits and trade deficits. The debate on appropriate post-crisis fiscal policy reflects an uneasy mix of old and new views on the scope, role and effectiveness of fiscal policy in integrated economies. The 'old' view focuses attention on the macrostabilization role of the budget policy instrument as highlighted within a static Mundell-Fleming framework. This aspect of fiscal policy is demonstrated in the earlier emphasis by both governments and the IMF on the need for restrictive fiscal policy through budget surpluses for the purposes of macrostabilization and external adjustment. An alternative view, still encased within a static framework, is to argue for a fiscal stimulus by allowing the automatic stabilizers to operate and is reflected in the subsequent switch to more flexible fiscal policies and accompanying budget deficit. The 'new' view, as formulated in an intertemporal savings-investment approach is reflected in attempts to reconcile the ex-post unsustainability of current account deficits, as reflected in forced exchange rate regime switches with an interpretation of these imbalances as optimal consumption-smoothing behavior together with the question of appropriate fiscal response in the presence of liquid constraints.

Fiscal Policy Setting

Fiscal policy was neither a cause of the crisis nor a critical determinant of economic growth. Nevertheless, its role in both the pre- and post-crisis period has been seen as crucial, primarily in terms of its contribution to macrostability.

Pre-crisis

Measured overall budget balances in terms of GDP reflect surpluses or near-balance in the period 1990-95 (Table 12.1). The raw data on fiscal balances support the general perception of fiscal discipline and prudent or conservative fiscal policy, especially compared to other developing economies. As noted in Nellor (1998), the existence of a budget balance or surplus does not make fiscal policy appropriate from the perspective of macrostabilization nor growth. A number of factors suggest that the underlying fiscal balances were less tight than measured or headline balances. These factors include: (a) high economic growth combined with revenue elasticities exceeding unity; (b) a failure to include quasi-fiscal costs such as implicit subsidies of directed bank lending and (c) the exclusion of government contingent liabilities in the form of explicit and implicit government guarantees to banks. More fundamentally, post-crisis structural shifts in the composition of both the tax and expenditure bases, in part necessitated by the crisis also suggest that the underlying fiscal positions could not have been maintained. The shifts include increased expenditure outlays on the social safety net and financial restructuring.

Viewed from the perspective of contemporary debate in the pre-crisis decade, policy concerns focused on the perceived overheating of East-Asian economies rather than concerns with fiscal and external sustainability. Monetary not fiscal policy was the direct source of overheating through excessive growth in private credit and hence bore the main burden of policy adjustment through (unsuccessful) attempts to sterilize capital inflows. The impact of overheating on current account deficits was also not seen as a cause for fiscal policy concern given that the deficit reflected a gap between high private investment and saving rates with financing from private capital flows rather than from foreign reserves. Additional to economic growth and current account imbalances (Tables 12.2 and 12.3), the main indicator of macro performance is annual inflation that shows low rates, albeit above that of Table 1.

Table 12.1 Asian Economies: General Government budget balance (percent of GDP)

	1975-82	1983-89	1990	1991	1992	1993	1994	1995	1996	1997
Indonesia	–	–1.3	1.3	–	–1.2	–0.7	–	0.8	1.4	2.0
Malaysia	–	–4.0	–2.2	0.1	–3.5	–2.6	2.5	3.8	4.2	1.7
Korea	–2.7	–0.3	–0.6	–1.6	–2.6	–1.0	1.0	–	–	–
Thailand	–5.8	–3.0	4.4	4.2	2.6	2.1	2.0	2.6	1.6	–0.4
China	–1.0	–1.7	–2.0	–2.2	–2.3	–2.0	–1.6	–1.7	–1.5	–1.5
Taiwan	–	1.3	0.8	0.5	0.3	0.6	0.2	0.4	0.2	0.2
Hong Kong										
Singapore	0.6	4.8	11.4	10.3	11.3	14.3	13.7	12	8.4	3.0
Philippines	–2.0	–2.8	–3.5	–2.1	–2.2	–1.6	–1.6	–1.4	–0.4	–0.9
India	–10.2	–14.9	–13.8	–10.6	–9.8	–10.5	–9.9	–9.2	–9.2	–9.1
Japan	–4.0	–0.4	2.9	2.9	1.5	–1.6	–2.3	–3.7	–2.9	–2.9

Source: IMF (1997), World Economic Outlook, Table A1, pp.49-51.

Budget deficits were supposed to be within 1 percent of GDP for Indonesia and Korea and a balanced budget for Thailand. The targets were revised subsequently, primarily on account of a larger-than-expected worsening of the macro environment from slow output growth and exchange rate depreciation as well as larger-than-anticipated fiscal outlays for financial restructuring and the social safety net (see Lane and others, 1999).

Table 12.2 Macroeconomic Performance (annual percent Change)

	GDP Growth				Inflation (CPI)			
	1983-85	1990-95	1996	1997	1983-89	1990-95	1996	1997
Indonesia	5.5	8.0	8.0	5.0	8.1	8.7	7.9	8.3
Malaysia	5.4	8.4	8.6	7.0	2.0	4.1	3.5	3.7
Korea	9.6	7.5	7.1	6.0	3.8	6.6	4.9	4.3
Thailand	8.1	8.4	6.4	0.6	3.1	4.9	5.9	6.0
China	10.7	12.3	9.6	8.8	9.0	11.4	6.1	1.5
Taiwan	9.2	6.6	5.7	6.7	1.2	4.0	3.1	2.0
Hong Kong	7.2	5.5	4.9	5.3	6.7	9.5	6.0	6.5
Singapore	6.9	8.5	7.6	7.2	1.0	2.6	1.4	2.1
Philippines	1.1	2.3	5.7	4.3	15.4	11.1	8.4	5.2
India	6.0	4.4	6.9	5.8	8.4	10.2	7.3	5.9
Japan	4.1	1.3	3.9	1.0	1.4	1.7	0.1	1.7

Source: IMF (1997), World Economic Outlook Table A1, pp.49-51.

Table 12.3 Asian Economies: External Indicators (in percent of GDP)

	Current account					External debt		
	1983-	1990-95	1996	1997	1998	1990-95	1996	1997
Indonesia	−3.5	−2.4	−3.4	−1.8	2.5	47.7	49.0	0
Malaysia	−0.7	−5.9	−4.9	−4.8	6.5	32.0	38.0	−
Korea	2.5	−1.2	−4.8	−1.8	12.9	10.0	23.0	65
Thailand	−3.2	−6.8	−7.9	−2.0	10.7	22.1	59.0	50
China	−1.0	1.2	0.9	3.9	3.4	14.4	16.0	1250
Taiwan	12.9	4.1	3.8	2.7	2.0	0.3	0.1	
Hong Kong	8.3	3.4	−2.5	−3.2	0.0	−	21.0	−
Singapore	1.8	12.2	15.0	15.4	20.6	−	11.0	−
Philippines	−0.3	−3.8	−4.7	−5.2	−1.5	53.6	59.0	
India	−2.4	−1.6	−1.0	−1.6	−1.8	29.4	−	22
Japan	3.0	2.4	1.4	2.2	3.6	−	−	−

Source: IMF (1997 October; 1998 October) World Economic Outlook,
(Table A1, pp.48-51; Table 2.12. p.64); Garnaut (1998, Table 1.5. p.24).

The first factor (macro environment) is estimated to have contributed 11.1 percentage points to the worsening of the budget deficit in Indonesia by 9.2 percent of GDP from 1997/98 to 1998/99 (Table 12.4). Corresponding endogenous effects on changes in the budget balance are estimated to be 1.5 percentage points in Korea, accounting for about 60 percent of the change in the budget deficit in 1998 and 3.1 percentage points in Thailand, contributing to almost all of the worsened budget deficit balance in 1997/98.

Table 12.4. Budget Balances (percent of GDP)

	Indonesia		Korea		Thailand	
	1997/98	1998/99	1997	1998	1996/97	1997/98
Budget balance	−0.9	−10.1	−	−4.0	−1.6	−5.1
Budget balance change	−2.2	−9.2	−	−4.0	−4.0	−3.5
Change due to						
economic environment	−4.2	−11.1	−	−1.5	−0.3	−3.1
Exchange rate	−3.5	−6.4	−	−0.9	−0.2	−2.0
GDP growth	−0.5	−4.0	−	−0.6	−0.1	−0.9
Oil price	−0.2	−0.7	−	−	−	−
Policy changes	2.7	1.7	−	−2.5	−2.6	−0.6
Outlays	2.7	3.8	−	−0.8	−1.9	2.6
Safety net	−	−1.0	−	−2.1	−	−0.6
Bank restructuring	−	−1.6	−	−1.4	−0.7	−2.0
Statutory revenue change	−	0.5	−	1.8	−	−0.7
Residual	0.7	0.2	−	−	−1.1	0.1
Memorandum IMF targets (1998)						
Real GDP growth		3.5		3.0		2.5
Inflation		5.0		9.0		5.0
Budget balance Percent GDP)		1.0		1.0		0

Source: International Monetary fund (1998, October), p.51.

Subsequent shifts in fiscal policy targets from small surpluses to deficits allowed for the operation of automatic stabilizers. At the same time, policy-makers attempted to offset the projected increases in budget outlays from financial restructuring and social safety net outlays by cuts in other outlays, especially infrastructure projects and revenue-raising measures. In the event, additional budget costs were more than fully offset only in Indonesia, leaving a net widening of the budget deficit of 10.1 percent of GDP, well above the targeted deficit of 1.5 percent of GDP. The above pattern of fiscal balances support the interpretation (see

Garnaut 1998, p.360) that the subsequent shift in fiscal stance towards automatic stabilizers was a forced rather than a voluntary policy response.

Two further aspects of the fiscal debate also deserve comment. The first issue is the seeming conflict between so-called 'good policy', namely a widening of the budget deficit through the automatic stabilizers and the observed adverse market response of exchange rate depreciation. Further examination reveals that, at least in Indonesia, the adverse market response reflects more the government's failure to adjust the deficit targets in light of the altered economic environment. This interpretation suggests a forward-looking rather than irrational response by market agents. Second, in all three countries, the main burden of adjustment of cuts in budget outlays was borne by cancellation or postponement of infrastructure projects. As discussed before, this response is inconsistent with growth objectives. Negative longer-term growth effects on the budget and fiscal solvency mean that an even stronger fiscal adjustment will be required in the future.

Static and Dynamic Macro Modeling

Debate on appropriate fiscal settings in post-crisis East Asia has centered upon the issue of permitting the automatic budget stabilizers to provide a fiscal stimulus to the economy versus budget tightening to assist external adjustment. This debate has been conducted within a static analytical framework. As argued in this section, a static approach to fiscal policy in an environment of high financial integration gives misleading policy inferences because it ignores the dynamic welfare gains from intertemporal trade.

The standard analytical tool for macro policy prescription is the static Mundell-Fleming model. The key premise that underpins this model is its focus on the role of monetary and fiscal policy as short-run stabilization instruments for aggregate demand management. Prolonged deviations from internal and external stabilization targets require policy response; the specific policy mix being conditional upon the degree of capital mobility, given the exchange rate regime. A key and well-recognized policy prescription is that under conditions of high capital mobility and flexible exchange rates, an expansionary bond-financed budget deficit provides a very weak stimulus to the economy.

The initial fiscal stimulus to the economy is offset by the open-economy multiplier and resulting current account deficit reinforced by nominal (and real) exchange rate appreciation in response to a higher interest rate differential. Conversely, a fiscal stimulus to output under conditions of low capital mobility (and the relatively greater impact of monetary tightening on external imbalance) provides apparent theoretical support to the present macro policy-mix in East Asian programs.

A major shortcoming of the above approach is that it ignores the role of the current account as a means of optimally allocating resources over time. This function is highlighted in intertemporal savings-investment models in which the current account reflects the outcome of aggregate, dynamic behavior of individuals who seek to maximize their lifetime utility. A country that moves from financial autarky to full financial integration with the world capital market derives a dynamic gain from intertemporal trade. At the autarkic real interest rate, defined as the autarkic price of future consumption in terms of present consumption, is assumed to lie above the world interest rate. The resulting optimal intertemporal trade pattern is a current account deficit in period 1 that allows the country to exploit the pre-trade interest rate differential through 'imports' of present consumption from abroad in period 1 by borrowing externally and repaying its debt in the second period through a current account surplus.

The above story is a stylized picture of a core component of East Asian trade patterns viewed from a financial integration perspective instead of the usual static trade framework that focus upon exploiting the differential between autarkic and world terms-of-trade under trade liberalization. Viewed from an intertemporal perspective, the role of fiscal policy alters in three main respects. First, in the absence of liquidity constraints and market distortions and assuming optimizing, rational behavior, observed current account deficits are not of policy concern. In the event of temporary real shocks such as negative output shocks or a balanced budget expansionary fiscal shock, the induced Current account deficit enables individuals to smooth consumption without altering permanently expenditure patterns.

Second, the linkage between changes in budget balances and the current account depends upon whether Ricardian debt neutrality holds. Empirical evidence is mixed; the existence of a partial private savings offset to public debt accumulation weakens support for a fiscal stimulus to the economy through induced wealth effects (or alternatively stated, the argument that competition of public with private debt drives out private investment and lowers long-terms growth). Third, the role of fiscal policy shifts from an emphasis on macro stabilization to its medium-term role in ensuring solvency or sustainability, that is, the requirement that the present value of the debt stock at some future date is zero.

It may be argued that the above assumptions and especially absence of liquidity constraints are no longer valid for Asian economies. In the presence of liquidity constraints, the economy is constrained to the autarkic point. Under flexible exchange rates, this implies the economy runs a balanced current account. In this situation, no fiscal response is needed since the liquidity constraint forces import compression with a resulting dynamic welfare loss. In contrast, under fixed exchange rates, a current account deficit has to be financed from foreign reserves. If the source of the current account deficit is an expansionary budget deficit, the appropriate response is fiscal tightening as in the static model in order to avoid the problem of vulnerability to a speculative attack in the presence of forward-looking agents and finite reserves. In any event, whether or not the fiscal stimulus is growth promoting cannot be ascertained from the first-period output effects. It will depend upon the means whereby the budget expansion is achieved.

Even if an intertemporal framework is preferable on theoretical grounds for analyzing fiscal policy in open economies, the question nevertheless arises as to the apparent inconsistency with an interpretation of the current account deficit as optimal and the speculative currency attacks in crisis-affected Asian economies.

One (among many) plausible explanations is argued in McLeod (1998); namely that borrowing by Asian economies was undertaken in an environment of risk underestimation that progressively rose as the quality of investments fell. The first-best solution is not to tighten fiscal policy nor to introduce capital controls but to strengthen institutions and information transparency as is being currently undertaken in the reform process.

Stocks and Flows

Fiscal policy settings are usually formulated in terms of budget flows rather than debt stocks and flows. East Asian economies are no exception Prior to the crisis, East Asian economies were not viewed as 'debt problem' economies with total external debt in terms of GDP estimated at 22.1 percent for the entire Asian region at end-1997 compared with the corresponding ratio of 64.9 percent for Africa, 8 Past budget surpluses were also reflected in very low levels of public indebtedness. The situation has now altered. Is there a debt problem? What is the appropriate fiscal policy formulation that monitors both flows and stocks and ensures consistency of macrostabilization targets with longer-term fiscal and external solvency? Data on outstanding debt provide a useful but by no means sufficient starting point for answering the above question. Despite the shift to large current account surpluses in 1997, external debt ratios have risen sharply, reflecting the cumulated impact on debt dynamics of inflation, interest rates, exchange rate depreciation and economic growth. At end-1996, external debt ratios are estimated to be 49.0, 23.0 and 59.0 percent of GDP in Indonesia, Korea and Thailand, respectively (Table 12.3). By end-1997, the combined impact of the above set of factors are estimated to have shifted the debt ratios to 125,65 and 50 percent of GDP, respectively (see International Monetary Fund, 1998). Corresponding public debt ratios are estimated to be much lower; at end-1997, public debt ratios are estimated to be 50, 12 and 25 percent of GDP for the three countries (Table 5). The lower level of public indebtedness, which is mainly external, reflects the dominance of private sector domestic and external debt. Notwithstanding its low base level, the trend of public debt is on an upward path, reflecting the post-crisis switch to budget deficits and interaction with debt-dynamics parameters.

Assuming the public debt-to-GDP ratio rises progressively over the medium term with continued overall budget deficits and primary budget deficits, is there a problem of fiscal insolvency? Fiscal solvency requires that the discounted present-value of primary budget surpluses (in terms of GDP) equal the outstanding public debt ratio. Assuming the economy is dynamically efficient (that is the long-run real interest rate is projected to lie above output growth), this requires a switch at some future point to primary budget surpluses of sufficient magnitude to stabilize the outstanding public debt ratio. From a growth perspective, what matters is a perceived inconsistency between the path of present and projected budget policies and the debt-stabilizing primary surplus. A widening gap signals a future switch in either tax and/or expenditure policy or recourse to monetary financing and thereby underlines policy credibility. Both options have negative effects on economic growth; the first through increased uncertainty of regime switch on private investment and the second through efficiency distortions arising from the inflation tax.

It may be argued that, given the much higher external debt ratio and reliance of economic growth on financing from private capital inflows, the threat to growth prospects comes from external rather than fiscal solvency. External solvency requires that the discounted present value of trade surpluses (in terms of GDP) equal the outstanding external debt ratio. As illustrated below, an emerging problem of external solvency, assuming unchanged fiscal policies, is identified only in Indonesia.

Application to East Asia

An assessment of the consistency of fiscal policy settings and projected trade balances with the requirements of fiscal and external solvency is given in Table 5. Solvency indicators are measured as the gaps between the projected paths of primary fiscal and current account balances and those calculated as stabilizing the respective outstanding debt ratios, with assumed discount rates within the range of 5-8 percent per annum (Table 12.5). The exercise is illustrative and subject to all the well-known weaknesses of model-free solvency indicators, in particular, the assumed independence of fiscal policy, interest rates and economic growth (see Home, 1991).

As shown in Table 12.5, in order to stabilize end -1997 public debt ratios, the three countries need to generate primary budget surpluses within the range of: 2.5-4 percent of GDP (Indonesia), 0.6 to 1.0 percent of GDP (Korea) and 1.4 to 2.2 percent of GDP (Thailand), as compared to their (1998) primary deficits. From a longer-run perspective, the issue of fiscal solvency becomes more critical owing to adverse demographics. A recent analysis by Heller (1999) shows that the combined long-term (2010) budget impact of demographic effects combined with education, increased medical demand and expanded pension coverage would raise the 1995 share of government social expenditures by 4.6 percentage points (Korea); by 0.2 percentage points (Indonesia) and by 0.6 percentage points (Thailand). These increases are more than quadrupled if the time horizon is extended to *2050* (see Heller, 1999, Table 4, p.52).

Among the three countries, a continuation of the present expansionary fiscal policy in Indonesia presents the only major inconsistency between stabilization policy, fiscal and external solvency.10 The immediate threat to external solvency is temporarily obscured by the large current account surpluses presently being run. However, these surpluses reflect a forced adjustment to liquidity constraints. Once access to global capital market reopens fully, an emerging gap between national investment and investment is likely again to be met by borrowing abroad. Given Indonesia's high stock of outstanding external debt, a higher trade surplus of 6.7 to 10.5 percent of GDP (relative to the 1998 trade balance) would be required over the medium term in order to prevent further external debt accumulation in terms of GDP.

Table 12.5 Solvency Indicators (Percentage of GDP)

	Indonesia	**Korea**	**Thailand**
Fiscal Solvency			
Public Debt to GDP	50	12	27
Discount Rate (% p.a.)	5–8	5–8	5–8
Primary Budget Surplus	2.5–4.0	0.6–1.0	1.4–2.2
Projected Primary Budget			
Surplus	–7–(–)8	–2–(–)3	–1.5–(–)2.5
Solvency Gap	9.5–12	2.6–4.0	2.9–4.7
External Solvency			
External Debt to GDP			
Ration (end–1997)	125	65	50
Discount Rate (p.a.)	5–8	5–8	5–8
Primary Current Surplus	6.2–10.0	3.2–5.2	5–8
Projected Current Account Balance	–0.5	11.4	9.7
Solvency Gap	6.7–10.5	–	–

Fiscal Composition

This section examines the question of the appropriate composition of the fiscal package in terms of the level and structure of growth-promoting tax and public expenditure instruments. It also asks what constraints on fiscal policy arise under open capital regimes.

Tax Policy

In terms of static allocative efficiency, there is a clear-cut negative relationship between the levels of taxes and output, arising from tax-induced distortions in economic behavior. But what of the impact on economic growth? The answer necessarily comes from endogenous growth theory since long-run growth in the neoclassical model is policy-invariant. The general message from endogenous growth literature is to emphasize the significance of the stock of human capital as determining the rate of economic growth (see for example, Romer, 1990). The growth impact of the tax burden on different factors of production will be sensitive to the specification of production technology.

Any impact of changes in tax rates on savings incentives levied on physical capital will depend upon its degree of substitutability or complementarity with human capital in the production process. For example, a cut in the tax rate on physical capital will not necessarily promote capital accumulation if offset by shifts away from human capital.

In regard to the structure of taxation, a prevalent view is that the incentives to high technology in East Asia have been beneficial to growth. In particular, since future economic growth in the region lies more in raising productivity than in resource accumulation a continuation of this tax policy appears attractive. In principle, policies that promote free trade in knowledge are growth promoting by increasing the available stock *of* human knowledge. However, specific policy prescriptions such as subsidies to R and D are model-specific, dependent on the specification of technology and source of market failure.

For example, in the Romer (1990) endogenous growth model, a clear-cut directive for subsidies to encourage research (and superiority to a subsidy to physical capital) derives from the dual assumptions that research has positive externalities that cannot be fully appropriated and from monopolistic pricing of the research used as an input in intermediate production of differentiated capital goods. A blanket prescription for targeted tax incentives to encourage high technology even in the presence of market failure needs to be balanced against political economy costs of rent-seeking and the formation of special interest groups.

Public Expenditure

Static efficiency losses derive from crowding out of private sector investment of most public expenditure activities (an exception being infrastructure). But what of the growth effects of public expenditure policy? Endogenous growth theory highlights the significance of possible spillovers to private investment productivity from certain types of public sector spending, especially infrastructure and primary education. The role of both types of public spending in enhancing past growth performance in the Asian region is emphasized in World Bank (1993). On these grounds, the cancellation or postponement of infrastructure projects in present fiscal settings to achieve stabilization targets appears counter-productive.

Globalization

Globalization imposes constraints on fiscal policy conduct on both the revenue and expenditure sides of the budget. In particular, capital mobility limits the independent use of taxes on capital through tax competition. For example, a country that lowers its tax rates on capital income below that of trading partners may gain temporary revenue as well as static efficiency gains but creates incentives for beggar-thy neighbor retaliation. In general, the fiscal instruments that offer the most flexibility under-globalization are those that may be altered easily, for example, VAT rates and excises on goods and services.

Concluding Comments and Lessons

This section draws together the main conclusions of the chapter and lessons for growth-promoting fiscal policies in East-Asian economies. These lessons are grouped under three broad principles; the need for emphasis on intertemporal rather than single-period effects of fiscal policy; the requirement of monitoring stocks and flows of public and external debt for assessing fiscal and external sustainability and the need to shift the focus from the overall budget balance to the composition of the fiscal package.

The first principle concerns a misplaced emphasis on the first-period impact effect of fiscal policy on current account balances and output levels as reflected in the initial policy prescriptions of fiscal tightening to reduce current account deficits and support ant-inflationary monetary policy. This prescription reflects a static, analytical framework in which the primary role of policy is to stabilize with an implicit positive linkage between stability and growth. Under conditions of global financial integration, this framework is misplaced. It ignores the critical function of current account imbalances in optimally allocating intertemporal resources with dynamic welfare gains from intertemporal trade. Even under altered conditions of liquidity constraints in East Asia, fiscal tightening is not necessary under flexible exchanges rates since the required balanced current account will be achieved through forced private expenditure reduction and import compression with a consequent dynamic welfare loss to the economy. The subsequent shift in recommended policy stance to widened budget deficit through allowing the operation of automatic stabilizers also remains embedded within a static policy framework.

Whether or not the resulting fiscal stimulus exercises any permanent growth effects will depend primarily upon the means whereby it is achieved (the third principle). The second principle is the need to monitor stocks of public and external debt as well as flows. This principle underpins the requirement of medium-term consistency between macrostabilization targets, fiscal and external solvency. The altered debt situation in many East Asian economies is reflected in an external debt build-up from output slowdown, exchange rate depreciation and past current account deficits. There is also a low but rising level of public indebtedness arising from the post-crisis switch from budget surpluses to deficits. Rising debt ratios need not necessarily indicate fiscal or external insolvency. An illustrative application of indicators of fiscal and external solvency to Indonesia, Korea.

Thailand suggests a wide gap in Indonesia between present and projected primary budget deficits and that required to stabilize the outstanding public debt-to-GDP ratio. The third principle is the need to shift the focus from the budget stance to the composition of the fiscal package that takes into account the differential growth impact of tax and public expenditure instruments under globalization. Inconsistencies in the post-crisis fiscal settings in East Asian program countries are apparent in attempts to offset increased budget outlays on financial restructuring and the social safety net by cancellation or postponement of infrastructure projects. The scope and impact of fiscal policy instruments on resource accumulation and savings incentives is likely to become increasingly constrained with the return of East Asian economies to full financial integration with the global economy. Fiscal policy has a potentially significant growth-promoting role in reducing the productivity gap between East Asia and industrialized economies by increasing incentives to adopt technology, dependent on the specific market failure and political economy costs.

References

De Long, B. and L. H. Summers. (1992), 'Macroeconomic Policy and Long-Run Growth', *Federal Reserve Bank of Kansas Economic Review*, 4th Quarter, pp.5-25.

Dowrick, S. (1995), 'The Determinants of Long-Run Growth', in Reserve Bank of Australia, *Productivity and Growth*, pp.7-47, Ambassador Press, Sydney.

Heller, P. (1999), 'Aging in Asia; Challenges for Fiscal Policy', *Journal of Asian Economics*, vol. 10, pp.37-63.

International Monetary Fund (1998), 'Fiscal Balances in the Asian Countries: Effects of Changes in the Economic Environment versus Policy Measures', pp.50-52.

Lane, Timothy, Attish R. Ghosh, Javier Hamann, Steven Phillips, Marianne Schulze-Ghattas and Tsidi Tsikata. (1999), *IMF-Supported Programs in Indonesia, Korea and Thailand: A Preliminary Assessment*, International Monetary Fund, January, Mimeo.

McLeod, R. and R. Garnaut. (1998), *East Asia in Crisis*, Routledge, London and New York.

McLeod, Ross. (1998), 'Indonesia' in McLeod and Garnaut, pp.31-48.

Mundle, Sudipto. (1999), 'Fiscal Policy and Growth. Some Asian Lessons for Asian Economies', *Journal of Asian Economics*, vol. 10, pp.15-36.

Nellor, David. (1998), 'The Role of the International Monetary Fund' in McLeod and Garnaut, pp.245-265.

Romer, Paul. (1990), 'Endogenous Technical Change', *Journal of Political Economy*, 98, October, pp.871-902.

Sachs, Jeffrey. (1982), 'The current account and macroadjustment in the 1970s', *Brookings Papers on Economic Activity*, 1, pp.201-259.

Seater, John. (1993), 'Ricardian Equivalence', *Journal of Economic Literature*, XXXI, March, pp.142-190.

Smith, Heather. (1998), 'Korea' in McLeod and Garnaut, pp.66-84.

Tanzi, Vito and Howell Zee. (1997), 'Fiscal Policy and Long-Run Growth', *International Monetary Fund Staff Papers*, 44, pp.109-179.

World Bank (1993), *The East-Asian Miracle: Economic Growth and Public Policy*, Oxford: Oxford University Press.

Chapter 13

Globalization, Trade Liberalization and Economic Growth: The Case of Vietnam

Binh Tran-Nam

Introduction

Every era has 'vogue' words and in the 1990s these words were definitely 'internet' and 'globalization'. The term globalization has long been used by many writers in every conceivable occasion so that it now conveys a variety of meanings to different people or in different contexts. It is clear, however, that no single word has, in recent time, been capable of arousing such passion, expectations, apprehension and confusion as globalization. The recent vigorous demonstrations against the World Trade Organization (WTO) Ministerial Conference meeting in Seattle and the World Economic Forum in Melbourne graphically illustrate this.

This chapter aims to examine the relationship between the process of globalization and economic growth in Vietnam. As a low-income, transitional economy coming out of a long period of international isolation only about a decade ago,[1] Vietnam differs from other countries in many important respects. Politically, it belongs to a handful of nations that still officially adhere to the principle of socialism. The present Constitution does not yet permit a pluralistic, multi-party political system. Economically, it belongs to a group of the poorest countries on earth in terms of GDP per capita in purchasing power parity $.[2] It is still a largely agrarian society with 80 percent of the population living in rural areas.

Like China, Viet Nam has adopted an incremental, piecemeal approach to economic reform. Since launching *Đổi Mới* (renewal or reform) in 1986, it has achieved remarkable economic successes: stable macroeconomic environment, rapidly expanding private sector and foreign trade, and steady economic growth. For the ten-year period 1986-1995, Vietnam's real GDP grew by an average rate of 6.4 percent per annum, primarily due to its growing openness. This rate was highest among the 40 poorest countries (see World Bank 1996, pp.172-188). As a result of rapid economic growth, Vietnam has reduced income poverty by 35 percent (from 75 percent to 40 percent) during the same period (see United Nations Development Program (UNDP) 1997, p.38).

After a decade of speedy growth, Vietnam's economy slowed down considerably in 1998 and 1999 when growth rates of real GDP dropped to 5.8 percent and 4.7 percent, respectively (see General Statistical Office 2000). Although the growth rate has improved in 2000 (forecast to be 6.5 percent), it is unlikely that Vietnam will immediately return to the high-growth path in the near future. There have been two explanations regarding Vietnam's slowdown. The first blames Vietnam's poor performance in recent years on its failure to pursue on-going reform in a coherent and decisive manner. This is evident from the government's insistence on the leading role of the state sector and the slogan 'market mechanism under the state management, oriented toward socialism', often cited in statements by senior government officials. The second attributes Vietnam's slowdown to the external shock of the Asian financial crisis, which ended the unsustainable bubble economy elsewhere in the region. The truth is likely to lie somewhere between these two alternative explanations.

At the same time, there are factors that ensure that Vietnam's will be further integrated into the world economy. These include Vietnam's joining the ASEAN Free Trade Area (AFTA) in 1995 and the Asia Pacific Economic Cooperation (APEC) in 1998, its application to join the WTO in 1995 and the signing of the bilateral trade agreement with the US in 2000 (to be ratified by the US Congress and Vietnam's National Assembly). This paper seeks to analyze the effects of international economic integration on Vietnam's economic performance and how Vietnam can maximize the benefits arising from the process of globalization. The focus of the paper is on the qualitative change in Vietnam's national governance in the globalized world economy.

It is argued that Vietnam must find answers to several difficulties arising from the process of globalization. The chapter analyzes Vietnam's degree of globalization. It is shown that while the Vietnamese economy is highly open in a certain sense, its international economic integration has so far been regional rather than global. It then studies the relationship between Vietnam's economic growth since 1989 and its economic openness, and considers the future trends and effects of globalization on the economy. It is suggested that the estimated benefits to Vietnam will be larger the greater is its international economic integration. It suggests some general policies that Vietnam can adopt in order to maximize the benefits of international economic integration. Finally, some concluding remarks are offered.

What is Globalization and What Does it Mean to Vietnam?

The meaning of globalization appears to have several dimensions: economic, social and cultural. Basically it refers to the process by which the socio-economic units of activity becomes integrated in the rest of the world's affairs. From an economic perspective, it can be described as the evolution from a situation of 'economic autarky' to 'economic nationalism' and then to 'international economic integration'. Thus, globalization is concerned with the increasing openness of a country in terms of cross-border flows of goods, services, capital, labor and ideas.

Defining in this rather conventional manner, globalization is an old process that reached an early peak towards the end of the 19th century, mainly among countries which are today developed. For these countries, trade and capital flows relative to GDP were close or even higher than in recent years. That earlier peak was reversed in the first half of the 20th century and only in the last 50 years the trend once again favored greater international economic integration. In the 1980s and 1990s, the pace of globalization accelerated due to cheaper, faster and more reliable means of transportation and telecommunication,[3] reduced artificial barriers to trade, increasing integration of the world financial markets and the ascendancy of capitalism over alternative economic systems. More specifically, the current climate of economic integration can be attributed to the pro-market policies of the Thatcher Government and Reagan Administration in the early 1980s, and to the rise of the internet in the 1990s.

Many observers see globalization as the inevitable shift from a manufacturing-oriented industrial economy to a service-oriented information economy. This shift represents the replacement of the Second Wave by the Third Wave, which is comparable to that of agricultural civilization (the First Wave) by industrial civilization (the Second Wave). The industrial age can be characterized by mass production, with economies of scale that arises from manufacturing with uniform and repetitive methods. The information age displays the same economies of scale, but with much less regard for space and time. In many ways, the internet, which renders distance and geographical boundaries immaterial, epitomizes globalization. The information world is one in which intangibles (knowledge, intellectual property) will increasingly dominate over tangibles (physical capital).

There is a spectrum of views regarding the benefits or otherwise of globalization. At the extreme optimistic end of the spectrum are those who see it as a powerful means for promoting economic prosperity and job creation (in the long run), and thus reducing poverty.[4] Such a view is based on both theoretical and empirical considerations. Theoretically, partial support is derived from the classical gains-from-trade proposition. This proposition, which went back at least 250 years to the work of Montesquieu and then Smith and Ricardo, was formalized by Samuelson (1950) and later substantially extended by a number of authors, most notably Kemp (see, for example, Kemp and Wan 1972; Kemp 1995, 2001).[5] There is also a growing consensus in empirical studies that greater openness to international trade has a positive effect on country per capita income (see, for example, Frankel and Romer 1999).

At the other extreme, there are those who argue that globalization is an unmitigated disaster (see, for example, the International Forum on Globalization (IFG) 1998). This view considers globalization (especially the extreme volatility in global financial markets) as the main source of massive economic breakdown in some nations, growing income inequality between and within countries, deterioration of working conditions, and loss of wilderness and biodiversity.

According to this view, globalization will produce a '20:80' society, in which the benefits of trade openness will be enjoyed by the top 20 percent of the labor force, whose skills are valued by transnational corporations. For the remaining 80 percent, the outlook is bleak, alternating between insecure employment and unemployment.

A more neutral viewpoint regards globalization as being insufficient for economic growth. Proponents of this view point out to the fact that many of the assumptions of the gains-from-trade proposition may not hold true in reality. For example, globalization seems to give rise to oligopoly instead of perfect competition, and trade is gainful under oligopoly only in specific circumstances. Further, trade is not necessarily welfare improving in the presence of volatile speculative capital inflows and outflows. It is also shown that successful economies open to international trade, but open economies are not necessarily successful (see, for example, Rodrik 1999).

Whatever its benefits and costs, globalization has certain implications and presents many fundamental challenges, both political and economic, to Vietnam. Firstly, globalization is often associated with reduced national sovereignty. This is, in principle, not acceptable to the Vietnamese Communist Party (VCP) which came to government on the platform of national independence. After a long war and a long period of international isolation, the Vietnamese government is understandably very conscious of national security. This resolve appears to be further strengthened by the Asian financial crisis in 1997–8. It will be a challenging task for the Vietnamese leadership to balance between the often conflicting forces of national independence and global interdependence in its economic policy deliberation.

Secondly, international economic integration will be a difficult process for Vietnam in view of it uneasy relationships with the US and China, the two most important countries in the world economy. The significance of the US market to developing and developed economies in Asia is undeniable. Yet, after twenty five years since the end of the war and despite President Clinton's historic visit to Vietnam, much suspicion still remains on both sides. Many Vietnamese leaders believe that the US should pay reparations to Vietnam before the two countries can engage in free trade. By the same token, the US government often links Vietnam's human rights record to trade negotiations.

Vietnam also has a long history of struggle against its giant northern neighbor. In the last five years, the improving relations and settlement of some border issues between China and Vietnam have allowed freer trade, investment and tourism. However, the very strength of the Chinese economy presents a serious challenge to Vietnam as Vietnam tends to produce goods at the low end of China's manufacturing industries. In a globalized world economy, how can Vietnam try to avoid being practically an economic province of China? The interaction of China's and Vietnam's economic policies will be of strategic importance to Vietnam.

Thirdly, as a transitional economy, Vietnam does not have competent administrative and legal systems, and a reliable banking system to cope with global economic transactions. Vietnam will need to develop these infrastructures rapidly to capture the benefits of globalization.[6] In this regard, Vietnam can perhaps make use of the experiences of China whose economic renovation began about a decade a head of Vietnam. This is an example of 'learning by watching' at the government level. Fourthly and finally, as a developing economy, Vietnam has not yet developed a mature machine-tool industry. Should Vietnam pursue a laissez-faire policy based on static comparative advantage (according to which Vietnam will specialize on low-value adding labor-intensive production)? Or should it attempt an interventionist industrial policy that promotes high-value adding industries that generate positive externalities to the rest of the economy? These are just a few issues that Vietnam must consider and respond to in the face of globalization.

How Globalized is Vietnam?

To determine the degree of globalization of the Vietnamese economy, it is necessary to examine Vietnam's cross-border flows of goods and services, capital, labor and information. Before proceeding, it may be worthwhile to note that while Vietnam has become increasingly more integrated with the world economy, there are a number of areas where a move towards self-sufficiency has been seen as both feasible and desirable. This is largely based on concerns for national security and covers specific items such as:

- rice and sugar;
- cotton;
- cement and possibly fertilizer;
- steel; and
- refined oil products.

Self sufficiency is often achieved at the costs of high product prices and low (or even negative) returns to invested capital. In terms of conventional measures such as total foreign trade (exports plus imports) as a percentage of GDP, Vietnam is a highly open economy. This is illustrated in Table 13.1.

Table 13.1 Vietnam's Total Foreign Trade as a Percentage of GDP

	1991	1992	1993	1994	1995	1996	1997	1998	1999
Exports	24.0	26.2	23.3	26.1	26.3	29.5	34.1	34.4	40.1
Imports	26.9	25.7	30.6	37.5	39.3	45.3	43.3	42.4	40.4
Total Trade	50.9	51.9	53.9	63.6	65.5	74.7	77.4	76.9	80.5

Sources: General Statistical Office (2000) and the World Bank (1999).

The figures in Table 13.1 are subject to an important qualification. There are large differences between prices of traded goods and services (in $US) and domestic prices (in Vietnamese dông). Without appropriate price adjustments, the raw data in Table 13.1 tend to overestimate Vietnam's degree of openness. The aggregate figures also tend to hide various domestic regulations and barriers to international trade.

Furthermore, when the total foreign trade is disaggregated by country of destination, it is clear that Vietnam's international trade is fundamentally regional rather than global. This is demonstrated in Table 13.2.

Table 13.2 Destination of Vietnam's Total Foreign Trade (percent)

	1990	1995	1999
Asia	43.5	72.4	57.7
Europe	50.5	18.0	26.3
– Eastern Europe	42.4	2.8	2.0
– EU	7.1	12.3	21.7
Oceania	0.3	1.0	7.3
Americas	0.7	4.4	5.7
Africa	0.2	0.7	0.4

Source: *Vietnam Economic Times*, 1 June 2000.

Until 1990, many of Vietnam's main trading partners were member countries of the Council for Mutual Economic Assistance (CMEA).[7] The collapse of Vietnam's allies and termination of CMEA assistance in 1989 produced profound changes in Vietnam's external trade. In the last decade, most of Vietnam's major trading partners were either ASEAN or East Asian countries. The theory of international trade suggests that it would be more beneficial for Vietnam to engage in trade with highly dissimilar countries such as the US or the European Union. The recent signing of the bilateral trade agreement with the US and President Clinton's historic visit to Vietnam will accelerate the process of Vietnam's international integration and thus pave the way for global and more beneficial trade.

An examination of foreign direct investment (FDI) to Vietnam confirms the above view. Table 13.3 shows how FDI to Vietnam increased rapidly from 1991 and reached a peak in 1997. These capital inflows fell substantially in 1997 and 1998 due to the Asian financial crisis, but have again risen in 2000.

Table 13.3 Vietnam's Foreign Direct Investment

	1991	1992	1993	1994	1995	1996	1997	1998	1999
Commitments									
– US$ million	1,417	2,321	3,661	4,167	6,566	8,633	4,397	3,899	1,477
Disbursements									
– US$ million	206	380	1,112	1,936	2,672	2,607	3,250	1,960	1,520
– % of GDP	2.4	3.9	8.7	12.5	12.9	10.6	12.1	7.2	5.3

Sources: Ministry of Planning and Investment and World Bank (1999).

But, once again, most of these FDI inflows have come from nearby countries such as Singapore, Taiwan, Japan, Korea and Hong Kong. These five countries collectively contributed about 58 percent of Vietnam's total FDI commitments and 54 percent of its total FDI disbursements during the period 1988-98. Thus, Vietnam's FDI can be characterized as being regional rather than global.

In terms of labor movement, a similar story is observed. Most overseas workers come from Japan or the newly industrialized nations, reflecting the distribution of FDI to Vietnam by country of origin. Traditionally, Vietnam used to send guest workers to the Soviet Union and Eastern European countries for relatively low-skilled jobs. Since the collapse of the CMEA in 1989, this practice of labor export has practically ceased. In recent years, a smaller number of Vietnamese guest workers in the garment and footwear industries have been sent to work in factories (owned by foreign investing companies) in nearby countries. Again, the number involved is small and the foreign location is regional.

It is difficult to measure how open a country is with regard to information. By any standard, Vietnam is closed in terms of information flows in both directions. Perhaps the most revealing indicator is the level of internet usage within Vietnam. According to the Vietnamese government's estimates, by the end of 2000, the number of internet subscribers in Vietnam will reach between 200,000 and 250,000 (or between 0.26 percent to 0.33 percent of the total population). This compares very unfavorably with neighboring nations. Even China is expected to have 20 million people (1.6 percent of total population) connected to internet by the end of 2000.

In summary, despite its high degree of openness, Vietnam's international economic integration has been regional rather global. This is not surprising in view of the fact that geography is a powerful determinant of bilateral trade. However, as a result of its bilateral trade agreement with the US, Vietnam will be facing an increasingly more globalized world economy.

Vietnam's International Economic Integration

Evolution of Trade Liberalization and Trade Policy

Foreign trade liberalization had commenced in Vietnam long before the official launch of *Đổi Mới* in 1986. The first step towards trade liberalization, a crisis measured adopted in February 1980, allowed provinces and large cities to establish their own export-import companies and trade directly with the outside world. This had achieved the intended policy objective of stimulating exports, especially in Ho Chi Minh City where the nationalization of Southern trade had never completely supplanted direct trade. Direct regional trade was soon suspended by central authorities and only tentatively reintroduced in 1983. More systematic trade liberalization was an indispensable component of Vietnam's *Đôi Mói*. However, international trade was continued to be controlled by a relatively small number of state-owned enterprises (SOEs) until 1988. Since 1989, foreign exchange and trade rules have been gradually relaxed with more participation of private enterprises. From just 80 in 1987, the number of SOEs authorized to engage in foreign trade surged by 1990 to 212. Authorization in 1991 for private as well as state enterprises to set up direct links with foreign markets further decentralized the trade structure (see Riedel and Turley 1999, p.30). It is estimated that at the beginning of 1998, the number of enterprises that participated in foreign trade in Vietnam was about 2,400. In the early 1990s, the government attempted to control the trading of consumer and producer goods by imposing import–export license, shipment permission and minimum working capital requirement. In 1996, together with the elimination of the shipment permission, the number of imported goods that require import–export licenses was reduced to 16. In 1997, all enterprises with import-export licenses were encouraged to export goods beyond registered items, including goods not produced by themselves. Non-tariff barriers to international trade are stipulated in a Decision signed by the Prime Minister and issued at the beginning of 1999. These include:

- quantitative controls (export quotas for rice and garment and textile; and import quotas for petroleum, fertilizer, steel, cement, construction glass, paper, sugar and liquors);
- prohibited goods (for exports: arms and military equipment, toxic chemicals, antiques, narcotics, wood, and wild and rare animals; for imports: arms and military equipment, toxic chemicals, antiques, narcotics, firecrackers, poisonous toys for children, cigarettes, used consumer goods and right-hand driving automobiles);
- authorization by special agencies (e.g. to import medicine, permission from the Ministry of Health is required); and other non-tariff barriers such as quality inspection, etc.

To summarize, it may be worthwhile to mention two things:

1. In practice, many fields of trade in Vietnam are still closed to some enterprises, especially to the private sector. Some restrictive foreign exchange controls still exist.
2. Through a variety of policy measures (tariff and non-tariff barriers, taxation and regulation) the government has encouraged import-substitution rather than export-oriented industries.

Growing Openness and Economic Growth

The main driving force has been the tradable goods sector, especially the foreign-invested industry sector. Thus, Vietnam's economic growth is primarily due to its growing openness and can be characterized as FDI-led. The importance of FDI to Vietnam's growth is illustrated in Table 13.4.

Table 13.4 Relationship between Disbursed FDI as a Percentage of GDP and real GDP Growth Rate in Vietnam, 1991-99

	1991	1992	1993	1994	1995	1996	1997	*1998	*1999
FDI/GDP (percent)[a]	2.4	3.9	8.7	12.5	12.9	10.6	12.1	7.2	5.3
Real GDP (%) Growth Rate[b]	6	8.6	8.1	8.8	9.5	9.3	8.1	5.8	4.7

Sources: [a] GSO and UNDP; [b] Ministry of Planning and Investment. *: Provisional

The simple correlation coefficient between the two variables in Table 13.4 is 65.4 percent, indicating a close correlation between FDI and economic growth in Vietnam. This confirms the role of FDI as a primary determinant of economic growth in Vietnam in years to come. Table 13.4 also confirms the Chinese experience that the impact of FDI in terms of commercial activity – export growth, employment creation and cash flow – lags behind by about five years. In the case of Vietnam, non-petroleum FDI dates from around 1990–91.

FDI Climate in Vietnam

From a legal perspective, Vietnam's Foreign Investment Law (FIL), promulgated in 1987 and subsequently amended in 1990 and 1992, goes further than most other developing countries in protecting FDI, not only against outright expropriation, but also against subsequent changes in laws. However, a number of problems relating to FDI are apparent:

- *Low rate of disbursement*: From Table 13.3, it can de deduced that less than 43 percent of the approved FDI were implemented between 1991 and 1999. This low rate of disbursement is attributable to a number of factors which include a weak administrative system (which lacks experience, coordination and efficiency), an adequate legal system and an unreliable banking sector. However, the disbursement rate has improved in recent years.
- *Tax compliance costs are too high*: While Vietnam currently provides a very favorable corporate tax regime, foreign investors are confronted with complicated and inconsistently applied tax laws. In terms of dealing with government departments, foreign investors are faced with inexperienced administrators. changing requirements, hidden fees and very costly appeal procedures. Thus, the business costs of tax compliance in Vietnam are very high (see Heij 1995).
- *Expatriation of profits tend to be difficult*: Although the FIL guarantees foreign investors the right o repatriate capital and profits, Decree No. 18-CP

restricts these overseas remittances and subjects them to a withholding tax varying from 5 to 10 percent.

- *Dispute resolution is not regarded as satisfactory*: In dispute resolution, Vietnam has ignored the current worldwide trend towards international arbitration. Vietnam's dispute resolution provisions, via the Foreign Arbitration Committee, are needlessly restrictive.

The Vietnamese government have been consciously aware of these problems and introduced various measures to improve its FDI climate. These simplification measures have been met with approval from foreign investors but much improvement is still required.

Participation in the Regional and International Trade Groupings

As a member country of AFTA, Vietnam is committed to implement the Common Effective Preferential Tariff Scheme (CEPT) by 2006. The CEPT scheme is based on the reciprocal, product-by-product basis, and seeks to reduce the tariff within AFTA to 0–5 percent. The CEPT scheme also requires commitments to harmonize customs, investment, and standard regulations and procedures. The CEPT scheme uses four lists: Inclusion List (IL), Temporary Exclusion List (TEL), Sensitive List (SL) and General Exception List (GL) for determining the pace and scope of trade liberalization. Vietnam is also a member of APEC whose objective is open regionalism, that is, unlike AFTA, all reductions in trade barriers apply to all countries, not only members of APEC. However, APEC obligations are not binding as in the case of AFTA or WTO.

In 1998, Vietnam published the CEPT tariff reduction schedules for items in the IL (to be reduced to 0–5 percent by 2006) and TEL (to be transferred to the Inclusion List by 2003 in five equal installments from the beginning of 2000). These schedules indicate that by 2006, the average tariff rates for items in the IL and TEL will be 2.3 percent and 3.9 percent, respectively. The overall average tariff rate of items in both lists will be 3.0 percent. However, it is apparent that Vietnam is still facing several difficulties in meeting its AFTA obligations. Firstly, it is not clear whether the tariff reduction schedule in the IL and TEL is a formal notification, or just an attempt by Vietnam to protect domestic producers as long as legally possible. Secondly, Vietnam's GEL does not yet comply with the principle of the Article XX of GATT. The bilateral trade agreement between Vietnam and the US will also provide another set of pressures for trade liberalization.

Setting commitments and obligations aside, trade regionalization and globalization will present Vietnam with adjustment costs and overall benefits. Two obvious adjustment costs include short-term problems associated with increasing unemployment and revenue losses. A related issue is the distribution of economic gains. Without appropriate policy responses, increase in overall economic prosperity may be accompanied by deteriorating income inequality.

Le (1999) applied the Global Trade Analysis Project (GTAP) to quantify the benefits of international economic integration to Vietnam under four different trade reform scenarios: Vietnam unilaterally reduces its tariff rates for all imported commodities by 50 percent, ASEAN member countries reduce their tariff rates by 50 percent, other countries holding their tariff structure constant (AFTA), APEC countries reduce their tariff rates by 50 percent, other countries holding their tariff structure constant, and all countries in the world reduce their tariff rates by 50 percent. His results are summarized in Table 13.5.

Table 13.5 Impact of Various Trade Reform Scenarios on Vietnam

Change in	Scenario 1 (Unilateral)	Scenario 2 (AFTA)	Scenario 3 (APEC)	Scenario 4 (Global)
Exports (percent)	1.7	0.4	1.8	3.3
Imports (percent)	8.5	2.7	7.8	9.9
Trade Balance (US$ million)	−575	−198	−518	−577
GDP (percent)	2.9	1.6	3.2	4.0

Source: Le (1999).

The above results seem to be generally consistent with trade theory that suggests that the greater the freedom of trade, the larger is the benefit to the trading nations. However, the AFTA scenario is an exception. This is due to the fact that Vietnam and some ASEAN member countries (such as Indonesia, Philippines and Thailand) have similar comparative advantages in agricultural and marine products, textile and garment, and footwear. Thus, Vietnam and those countries are currently competing rather than complementing. As a result, trade liberalization within AFTA produces relatively small gains to Vietnam.

Vietnam's Governance in the Face of a Globalized World Economy

As discussed, globalization presents great challenges to the Vietnamese government. Despite the government's concerted attempts since 1986 to restructure its institutions in line with its policy of economic renovation, the existing institutions and political machinery are still geared for a centrally planned economy. Thus, the role of the government as a good governance provider is crucially important in maximizing the benefits of international economic integration. In this regard, it should be noted that, as indicated in Table 13.5, the benefits of globalization to Vietnam are not particularly large (ranging to a maximum of 4 percent growth in GDP). Thus, Vietnam's globalization policy must be seen as a part of its comprehensive, on-going structural reforms.

There is now a consensus in the economic development literature that not only macroeconomic stablization should precede trade liberalization, but also that goods markets should be liberalized before financial markets and microeconomic reforms, such as privatization, should be administered first. A quick examination of the Vietnamese economy since 1986 confirms that Vietnam has precisely followed this course of policy prescription. The country is now ready to accelerate trade liberalization, and financial markets and microeconomic reforms to capture the full benefits of globalization. But these broad economic directions should be complemented by a variety of other policies as discussed below.

A Compensation Scheme

The normative theory of international trade states that trade is gainful for all if the government implements a compensation scheme for those who are worse off as a result of trade. This idea can be generalized to economic reforms (including internal structural reforms) in general. It is recognized that the information requirements for full compensation are too prohibitive in practice. Nevertheless, the government should try to build a political context for reforms (including trade liberalization) based on the principle of compensation. Such a scheme can be administered through the tax-transfer system that may reduce income inequality between regions, and between cities and rural areas. New findings based on more accurate data suggest that a more even distribution of income may help to generate more growth in the long run (see Deininger and Squire 1997).

Accelerating Trade Liberalization and Privatization

The theory of trade, supplemented with empirical evidence, suggests that Vietnam should try to increase trading with complementary, rather than similar, economies such as North America and the European Union. Similarly, it will be necessary to privatize a high proportion of SOEs and create a level playing field for all enterprises, private or state-owned. These have already occurred but can be accelerated further.

Encouraging FDI but Avoiding FDI Competition

Vietnam's banking, administrative and legal systems must be quickly improved and simplified in order to encourage foreign investment, especially FDI. With respect to ASEAN countries, FDI competition is not a real problem because they are foreign investors in Vietnam. Further, as member countries of AFTA, they will ultimately have similar tax policies, which will reduce FDI competition. Thus, China will be Vietnam's main competitor for FDI, especially following the trade agreement between Vietnam and the US. In principle, China and Vietnam should conduct negotiations to reduce mutually harmful FDI competition.

Monitoring Short-term Debts

In the last few years, Vietnam's short-term debts have grown fairly rapidly. In the context of increasingly international financial integration, the Vietnamese government needs to monitor Vietnam's foreign debts, especially short-term and non-concessional debts. There is a variety of policy measures, including tax policy, that can discourage foreign borrowing and portfolio investment.

Concentrating on Light Manufacturing Industries in the Short Run

Vietnam should move away form its current import-substitution policy to an export-oriented policy. In accordance with the static principle of comparative advantage, Vietnam should focus, at least in the short run, to relatively labor-intensive industries such as food processing or light manufacturing industries (textile and garment, and footwear). These industries can help to alleviate partially the unemployment problems arising from the agricultural and state sectors. Export-oriented industries may also help to diffuse technology more rapidly.

Industrial Policy in the Long Run

Vietnam may have to devise a strategic trade policy in the long run, at least in response to China's industrial policy. It is very difficult for Vietnam to modernize and industrialize in the presence of strong competition from low-price (sometimes below production costs) manufactured products from China. Thus, Vietnam needs to develop a flexible industrial policy that can deals strategically with China's own policy. An alternative direction is to focus on some aspects of knowledge-intensive industries (that do not require to much production experience) such as software development (using the Indian model).

Human Resource Policy in the Long Run

In order to encourage FDI in the long run, the government must implement a well planned human resource program. A skilled workforce not only uses capital more effectively, but also attracts more capital inflows from overseas. Such a policy requires more resources to be allocated to the education sector. This may slow down the growth rate of real GDP in the short run, but will be beneficial in the long run.

Conclusion

Vietnam entered the 21st century as one of the world's poorest nations. Despite remarkable economic achievements in the last decade, its economy remains small and backward, and may of its population still live in poverty. Yet the country is not poor in many other human development dimensions. If the recent past record is any indication, Vietnam is capable of rapid growth. Globalization presents the country with an opportunity to accelerate its economic development. The Vietnamese leadership's good governance is crucial in minimizing the costs and maximizing the benefits of Vietnam's increasing international economic integration.

Notes

1. The US-led trade embargo against Vietnam was only officially lifted in 1994. Prior to that, Vietnam received very little aid and foreign direct investment. For example, in 1990, official development aid per capita to Vietnam was the second lowest among low-income countries, excluding India and China (see World Bank 1992, p.256). Also, while Vietnam officially embraced economic reform in 1986, there is a common consensus that marks 1989 the emergence of Vietnam's 'market economy'.
2. In 1995, Vietnam was ranked 152 in 174 countries in terms of PPP GDP per capita (see UNDP 1998).
3. For example, by 990 air transport costs per mile had dropped to 10 percent of their 1930 level. Between 1930 and 1996, the cost of a three-minute telephone conversation between London and New York fell from US$300 to US$1 (see Stalker 2000).
4. This is the view promoted by international institutions such as the WTO, the World Bank, the International Monetary Fund (IMF), etc and supported by the majority of economists.
5. The gains-from-trade proposition was first established under very restrictive assumptions. It has since been extended to more general situations in which (i) the trading country is small or big, (ii) markets are complete or missing, (iii) technology exhibits increasing returns to scale so that markets are not perfectly competitive, (iv) resources or renewable or exhaustible, (v) trade is by barter or money, (vi) economic agents are short-lived, and (vii) technology and preferences are trade dependent.
6. A number of Vietnamese legal officers and university academics have spent time in various Australian cities learning about the common law and observing Australian courts in practice.
7. In the sixth plenum in March 1989 (just months before the collapse of the Soviet Union), the VCP Central Committee still regarded the Soviet Union and the CMEA as the 'guide line for expanding foreign economic relations' (see Riedel and Turley 1999, p.21).

References

Deininger, K. and L. Squire. (1997), 'Economic Growth and Income Inequality: Reexamining the Links', mimeo, World Bank.

Frankel, J. A. and D. Romer. (1999), 'Does Trade Cause Growth?', *American Economic Review*, vol. 89, pp.379-399.

General Statistical Office (2000), *Statistical Yearbook*, Statistical Publishing House, Ha Noi.

Heij, G. (1995), 'Costs of Compliance: The Taxpayer's Hidden Tax Burden', *Asia-Pacific Tax Bulletin*, vol. 1, pp.22-24.

International Forum on Globalization (1998), *The Siena Declaration*, IFG, Siena.

Kemp, M. C. (1995), *The Gains from Trade and the Gains from Aid*, Routledge, London.

Kemp, M. C. (2001), *International Trade and National Welfare*, Routledge, London.

Kemp, M. C. and H. Y Wan. (1972), 'The Gains From Free Trade', *International Economic Review*, vol. 13, pp.509-522.

Le, Q. P. (1999), 'Assessing Vietnam's Trade Reform in the Regional an Global Context: GTAP Model', Paper presented to the *PhD Conference in Business and Economics*, Perth, November.

Riedel, J. and W. S. Turley. (1999), 'The Politics and Economics of Transition to an Open Market Economy in Viet Nam', *OECD Development Centre Technical Papers No. 152*, OECD Development Centre, Ha Noi.

Rodrik, D. (1999), *The New Global Economy and Developing Countries: Making Openness Work*, Overseas Development Council, Washington DC.

Samuelson, P. (1950), 'Evaluation of Real National Income', *Oxford Economic Papers*, vol. 2, pp.1-29.

Stalker, P. (2000), *Workers without Frontiers: The Impact of Globalization on International Migration*, Lynne Rienner, Boulder.

United Nations Development Program (1997), *Human Development Report*, Oxford University Press, New York.

World Bank (1996), *World Development Report*, Oxford University Press, New York.

World Bank (1999), *Preparing for Take-off*, Oxford University Press, New York.

Chapter 14

Decentralization and Capacity Building: Selecting Modes of Training for Indonesia

Koichi Mera

Introduction

The need for capacity building in developing countries has long been advocated. International organizations such as the United Nations, the World Bank, and the Asian Development Bank have been working on this issue. Many young people from developing countries are being trained in universities in advanced countries under the auspices of their own national governments, donors, and other international organizations. Many have gone back to their own country and, if they joined the public sector, are working for the central government rather than local governments. Behind successful national economic management of some developing countries, one can find highly trained bureaucrats, in some cases, they are called the Berkeley mafia or the Cornell mafia, depending on the university where many of these bureaucrats were trained. Capacity building of a select few might have been completed successfully for many countries. However, the developing countries are now demanding much more capacity building as they decentralize. Currently many developing countries are moving from a centralized system of governance to a decentralized one. It is reported that 63 out of the 75 developing countries with a population greater than 5 million have gone to a decentralized system since 1980s.[1] This is generally viewed as a desirable move. It is often said that decentralized governance will meet residents' desires more closely as decision-makers are very familiar with the conditions of their own areas. This will be true when certain conditions are met. But, the issue is not an academic one. Decisions to decentralize are decided politically and are not made on the basis of its merits versus demerits. There are many reasons for these political decisions. In some cases, it is a way of avoiding some responsibility by the central government, a means of obtaining greater amounts of foreign aid, due to pressure against dictatorship, or for improving the support for the political leader.

For whatever reasons, Indonesia has embarked on the road to decentralization in a grand scale. As a backlash to Soeharto's highly centralized control of the country, there was increased pressure on President Habibie, his successor, to decentralize. The Parliament hastily adopted two laws to decentralize the governance system of the country in the spring of 1999. These two laws require the government to implement drastic measures for decentralization within two years. The Law on Regional Governance (Law 22, 1999) specifies political and administrative responsibilities for each level of government, and the Law on Fiscal Balance (Law 25, 1999) delineates the new division of revenue sources and intergovernmental transfers, including sharing of oil and gas revenues. A notable aspect of the Indonesian decentralization is its magnitude and rapidity of change. Under these laws, all public service delivery functions except defense, foreign affairs, monetary and trade policy, and legal systems will be decentralized to district level governments that number about 350. Provinces, higher level of governments that number 26, are not given much responsibility except for coordinating district level governments. The district level governments, which comprise districts and cities, will become responsible for most public services such as education, health, infrastructure and local services. This implies that the share of spending by subnational governments will increase from 19 percent in 2000 to 40 percent in 2001.[2] It is not only a matter of increase in spending. In the past, local governments have been subjected to the directives from the Center. They have been accustomed to follow Central guidelines and financial allocation. Quite frequently, the Central Government provided consultant services during the preparation of investment projects. They have not been trained to think on their own. The need of capacity building at the local level is enormous because ways of thinking needs to be changed, and the present number of local governments is very large.

Alternative Approaches to Capacity Building at the Local Level

International agencies and donor organizations have given considerable attention to capacity building in recent years. The United Nations General Assembly requested an evaluation of operational activities in 1995. In response, the UN (1999) recently published a book evaluating capacity building activities supported by the UN system. The projects evaluated were mainly aimed at national organizations, and not for those at the local levels. UNDP (1998) publication introduces a large number of donor-financed projects in support of decentralized governance. Some projects are aimed at capacity building at the local level. However, each one is addressed to one community or a single organization. None of them is addressed to the overall strategy of capacity building at the local level. The Asian Development Bank (ADB) recognizes that 'subnational governance is the realm that has the most immediate impact for the majority of people living in the Asian and Pacific region' (ADB 1998, p.20). It derived a set of guidelines that are useful for developing capacity at the local level.

The newly issued Urban Sector Strategy of ADB (2000) lists capacity building as one important policy area. However, neither presents an overall strategy for capacity building at the local level. In determining a strategy for national capacity building at the local level, there is a need to identify modes of capacity building (supply methods) and also there is a need to identify the clients of capacity building (receivers). There are several alternative modes of providing capacity building in general. The most frequently used modes are:

1.   Enrollment in academic degree programs
2.   Enrollment in short-term training programs
3.   Training of trainers
4.   On-the-job training
5.   Consultant services for on-site training

Let me discuss the relative merits of each alternative.

Enrollment in academic degree programs is a useful way of training a selected few but only a few. In addition, it takes time to train. This mode alone does not meet the enormity and urgency of the need of the country. Already there are a number of programs that are providing funds for this purpose. Enrollment in executive programs would be a cost-effective way of training a sizeable number of persons in a relatively short period. Such programs can achieve a great deal. We need to keep in mind, however, that training one person out of a large number of a work group such as department is not so effective because frequently the person trained cannot train the entire group by him/herself. It is necessary to have a critical mass of trained groups.

Training of trainers is often considered a highly cost-effective way of propagating training. It is indeed a good way in the long-run. But, again this will take a long time. First, the first tier of trainers need to be well trained, often in academic degree programs. Then, the second tier needs to be trained in a similar ways or in shorter courses. Training of trainers will be more successful and faster if it is applied to those who have a significant level of experience and knowledge. Indeed, this method of training has been adopted in most countries. On-the-job training is an excellent way of training, but it requires a sizeable number of good training grounds. In addition, it requires significant length of time. This mode is not appropriate for the task at hand in Indonesia. Consultant services may be used to train civil servants as well as solving their own problems.

To be effective, consultants should be readily accessible. Thus, it is a good idea to have excellent local consultants who would be readily available to local governments. Intellectual leaders within their own region need to be trained as consultants if this approach is taken. On the receivers' side, the following groups can be identified at each level of the national hierarchy.

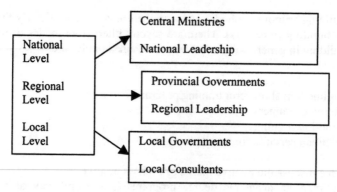

Figure 14.1 The Hierarchy of Decision Making

The Central ministries and national leadership do not decide on any specific issues, but set general guidelines and policies. The national leadership includes prominent professors and opinion leaders in the field. At the regional level, provincial governors and regional opinion leaders play major roles. In the case of Indonesia, the significance of this level is somewhat diminished. The leaders include professors in regional universities. They may function as opinion leaders, but also perform as consultants for local governments. At the local level, local governments play a major role. First, the political leadership, the mayor or district head and the members of the local council should be the main target of capacity building. Second, bureaucratic leaders should be targeted for capacity building. As the number of the targeted recipients of capacity building is large, there is a need of having a correspondingly large number of potential suppliers of capacity building. If there are consultants available from nearby, the objective could be achieved. Those could be consultants in the same local jurisdiction or within the same or nearby province. University faculty members may also perform this role.

CBDI – Approach

After considering the need for and supply capability of capacity building at each level of the country, a group of USC School of Policy, Planning, and Development faculty developed a multi-layer approach in response to a call for proposals by the United States Agency for International Development in 1999. The project which was approved late in 1999 is called Capacity Building for Decentralization in Indonesia or CBDI. In order to strengthen local administrative capacities, we need to strengthen such capacities at all levels in the country, e.g., at the national, the regional, and the local level. Unless these capacities are strengthened at the national level, local level capacities cannot be strengthened. Even if they are strengthened, they cannot be maintained.

The strengthening of such capacities is necessary at the regional level in order to spread knowledge and skills to individual local governments. Thus, our approach can be seen in Figure 14.2.

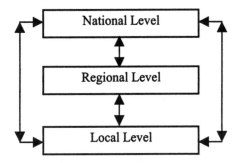

Figure 14.2 Flow Diagram of Our Approach

By addressing capacity building at three levels, we believe that capacity building can be strengthened and maintained.

At the national level, we have identified the prestigious Institute of Technology Bandung as the national academic institution. We also have chosen several Central Government organizations as the administrative institutions, such as the Ministry of Home Affairs, the Ministry of Finance, the Ministry of Settlements and Regional Infrastructure, and Central Planning Agency. All will have a leadership role in the building of capacities at the local level. At the regional level, we envisage regional universities as leaders within their respective region. At the local level, the local governments of the Kabupatens (districts) and Kotamadjas (cities) will be the focal points of capacity building. Thus, we have prepared a number of training and technical assistance activities designed to work at these three levels.

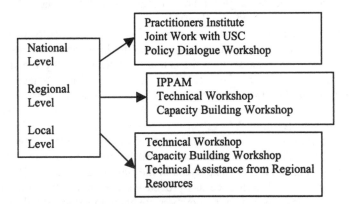

Figure 14. 3 Capacity Building at Different Levels

As shown in Figure 14.3, the first element is the Practitioners Institute (the Institute for Planning and Development Practitioners) that has been held every summer at the School of Policy, Planning, and Development of the University of Southern California. This two-week Institute is designed for high-level experienced professionals and academics who have been involved in local level management and development. The world's top experts in many fields are invited to speak at this Institute, and participants learn up-to-date knowledge and discuss new ideas for providing public services and managing infrastructure investment at the local level. A limited number of Indonesians are participating in the Institute as a part of this project. The participants will, upon return from Los Angeles, utilize the knowledge gained at the Institute for improving their guidance toward regional and local counterparts. During 2000, three ITB faculty members and a senior planner of Central Planning Agency were invited to participate in the Practitioners Institute as a part of CBDI activities.

The second element is the joint work of USC-ITB itself. Through the work with USC faculty, the ITB faculty will acquire and expand knowledge in the field of capacity building for local planning and management. The knowledge they acquire will mainly involve universal theories, techniques, general knowledge in the field, and specific solutions to specific problems based on the experience of the USC faculty. The USC faculty in turn will gain a great deal of Indonesia-specific knowledge. Through this process, the ITB faculty will become able to lead the field for the country more competently. The third element is the Policy Dialogue Workshop itself. This is an occasion for Central ministries to express their respective policies and filed questions and comments. By having this opportunity, various groups such as local government leaders, donor agencies and NGOs are able to communicate with national policy leaders to clarify issues and to influence their policies. Exchanges of views serve as a vehicle for expanding knowledge and for improving understanding. Through an exchange of views, policy makers are able to identify the areas that need more resources, opportunities for collaboration and cooperation, policy directions that require greater attention. Through discussion of one particular project, a host of issues related to capacity building at the local level will be reviewed and clarified.

At the regional level, particular attention is given to faculty members at regional universities. Because of an easy access to local governments in their respective region, and because they are intellectual leaders, they are invited to become leaders in the region for local level capacity building. Selected faculty members will be invited to participate in the Capacity Building Workshop that is held at Bandung in each of the two years in which this project will is implemented. When the Capacity Building Workshop is completed, they will provide technical assistance on certain issues on which an agreement will be made with each of the local governments. This technical assistance will be provided on site at the local government, with all high level employees in the field in attendance. This kind of on-site training/technical assistance has proved more effective than training of a few of the employees. These faculty members are encouraged to extend services to other local governments in the region.

At the local level, we will host two Workshops, Technical and Capacity Building. At the Technical Workshop, we will invite the heads of selected local governments and their associates to Bandung. The objective is to inform them of the coming changes in the administration, and of the need for capacity building at the local level. We will host presentations by the heads of local governments concerning current issues. These presentations will help to sharpen the contents of the next Capacity Building Workshop. Local government employees will participate in the Capacity Building Workshop along with university faculty members or other resource persons. These employees will be assisted by university faculty members when they need technical assistance. Another characteristic of our approach is our emphasis on administrative capacity. We will consider the capacity of administrative personnel, particularly with planning functions, since this is very important for the performance of local government in satisfying residents' needs. Under the general guidance of the local Council and of higher levels of the government, they should be the one preparing specific programs of service delivery and infrastructure investment. Even though some of the work may be contracted out to consultants and operating agencies, they must know what to contract out and how to supervise these contractors. We are targeting our ultimate effort at building the capacity of local government employees. These subjects are a high priority for capacity building at the local level:

1. Understanding the functions of local governments,
2. Priority setting in infrastructure development and service provision,
3. Setting infrastructure and service standards,
4. Infrastructure planning and capital budgeting,
5. Pricing of local services,
6. Managing private provision of local services, and
7. Community participation in decision-making and implementation.

On the basis of a training needs identification (TNI) survey, we were going to select several high priority subjects. Another characteristic of our approach is to help those that will be willing to help themselves. We shall be targeting all regions of Indonesia, but would like to help those who are willing to learn and want to improve their capacity. We planned to help all kinds of local governments, urban and rural, those on the outer islands or in Java, and the rich and the poor. In addition to the multi-level approach to training, our approach can be characterized by the following.

• *Orientation to Policy Makers*

We have given emphasis on the orientation of policy makers. One objective of holding a Policy Dialogue Workshop at the beginning was, not only for informing our project to those involved in decentralization of the country, but also to provide a proper perspective to national and local decision-makers such as the high and medium level government officials in the Central Government and the governors and heads of local governments. Another orientation Workshop was held in Bandung prior to the Capacity Building Workshop. Mayors and heads of district governments were invited to the Workshop, and listened to lectures by prominent speakers on decentralization, and they themselves presented 'the state of the local government' to the audience. They were briefed about the lessons their employees and resource persons were going to receive in the near future. In this way, co-operation by the local government leadership was requested. This method turned out to be effective.

- *Group Learning*

We are relying on group learning method in this project. In the Capacity Building Workshop, there are five persons from each local government, three government employees mostly from BAPPEDA and two resource persons appointed by the local government. These five persons work on all assignments and particularly on the study task selected for technical assistance following the Workshop. This group of persons working together, we believe, would give enough momentum to the decisions that the governments make. If only one person learns off-site, the person may not be influential enough to induce changes.

- *Training of Resource Persons for Wider Dissemination of Knowledge*

It is important to train government employees. But, at the same time, it is also important to train experts who would be available to a number of local governments on demand. Government employees, however capable, cannot concentrate on specific projects or tasks as they need to cover a wide range of issues. On the other hand, resource persons outside, whether professional consultants, university faculty members or NGO personnel, can concentrate on certain issues. In addition, they are available not only to one local government but also for a large number of local governments. Therefore, the capacity building of resource persons outside local governments has significant merits.

- *On-site Technical Assistance*

Another feature of this project is to employ on-site Technical Assistance. One subject was chosen by each local government for study. They have each chosen a high-priority task. For the study, technical assistance was provided by the resource persons chosen by the local government. They came to the local government to discuss the issues, collect information, and present their findings. Through this technical assistance, local government employees were able to learn from the resource persons. In addition, CBDI instructors provided guidance at the Workshop and through visits to the local governments. This type of real problem-solving will give them much greater learning experience than solving exercises in classrooms.

Progress to Date

We have made substantial progress in (1) the identification of training needs, (2) the selection of training subjects for two years, and (2) the selection of local governments for training in the first year, and have proceeded to complete all of the elements of the capacity building program for 2000. We sent a questionnaire to all local governments in 8 selected provinces. Out of 121 questionnaire forms, we received 56 responses. These responses indicate that the local government staff is fairly well trained in physical subjects of providing infrastructure and services, but is not well trained in financial, managerial, and economic matters. In addition, they are familiar with the current and ongoing changes in the functions of local governments. Most of the subjects we are going to offer fit very well with their demand. Most of the local governments demonstrated they are willing to participate in the training.

By considering that the fiscal relationships of the local governments with higher levels of governments are now evolving, it has been decided that the subject of local government borrowing will be offered in the second year. The subjects of training in the two years are given in Figure 14.4:

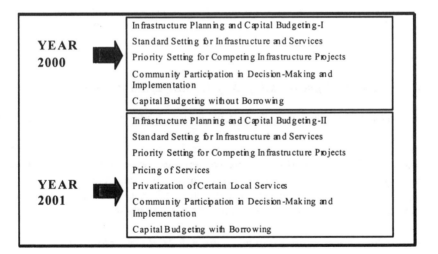

Figure 14.4 Training Subjects

We have selected 10 local governments on the basis of their geographic distribution, and diversity in characters such as urbanization and economic development. The linkage with ITB proved to be an important element in the selection process. The selected local governments are as follows:

Island	Province	Local Government
Sumatera	Sumatera Selatan	Kota Palembang
	Lampung	Kota Bander Lampung
Jawa	Jawa Barat	Kota Bandung
	Jawa Barat	Kabupaten Bandung
	Jawa Barat	Kabupaten Sumedang
	DI Yogyakarta	Kabupaten Bantul
	Jawa Timur	Kabupaten Bankalan
Kalimantan	Kalimantan Selatan	Kabupaten Banjar
Bali	Bali	Kabupaten Klungkung
NTT	Nusa Tenggara Timur	Kabupaten Timor Tenga Utara

These areas represent diverse local units. The three local governments in and around Bandung represents a large metropolitan economy, where as Timor Tengah Utara is a poor, isolated rural community. There are three Kotamadjas (cities) and seven Kabupatnes (districts). Each one of the ten local governments is highly committed to the training. Each of the selected local government chose two consultants from their own region who will come back later to provide technical assistance. This will be explained later in reference to Capacity Building Workshop. At the next higher level, the IPPAM program is held at the campus of the University of Southern California. The eleven Indonesian students enrolled in IPPAM's Urban Management Program have already completed their program in July 2000, and returned to their former organizations in Indonesia. They will be playing significant roles in their respective organizations. The following events were held:

- *Policy Dialogue Workshop, May 17, BAPPENAS, Jakarta*

We had a large attendance. Presentations were made by a representative of the Central Planning Agency, the Ministry of Finance, the State Ministry of Regional Autonomy, the Ministry of Settlements and Regional Development, and the State Ministry of Public Works. Serious concern was expressed about the possible consequences of implementing the scheduled decentralization and the need of capacity building was emphasized. Later in October, the Government announced its intention of going into the decentralized system in phases.

- *Practitioners Institute: June 13 through 23 at USC, Los Angeles*

This was held with the theme of Managing and Financing Local Development. 32 persons participated, of whom 16 were from Indonesia. The following topics were covered:
The role of local governments
Responsibilities for delivering infrastructure and public services
Central-local fiscal relationships
Local revenue generation

Community participation in local development
Borrowing for development
Privatization of service delivery
Pricing for services
Basic human needs at the time of decentralization
Participants presentations

- *Technical Workshop, May 22 through 24, ITB, Bandung*

The heads of the selected 10 local governments and their assistants gathered to hear the needs for capacity building to prepare for decentralization. The Director General of the Ministry of Human Settlements and Regional Development and a UNDP expert delivered speeches, the former giving a national perspective and the latter an international perspective. Each of the local government heads made a presentation on the state of the local government. During this workshop, specific subjects which require further technical assistance by regional consultants was determined through consultation.

- *Capacity Building Workshop, July 17 through 22, ITB, Bandung*

For each local government three employees and two regional consultants participated in this workshop. They went through 6 days of intensive training on the subjects selected for this year. These subjects were taught in teaching modules. Each session was conducted by a pair of USC and ITB faculty members. In addition to listening to lectures, each local government group was assigned to solve the issue identified in the Technical Workshop with the use of techniques learned during the Workshop. For example, each group was requested to organize community participation for promoting the project under consideration and to undertake a capital budgeting exercise.

- *Technical Assistance to Local Governments from Regional Consultants, Fall 2000*

Consultants trained at the Capacity Building Workshop of July will come back to each of the local governments that designated them for training. They will provide assistance to the task determined previously through discussion with USC-ITB faculty. It is our belief that government officials will be better trained at the job by engaging themselves in the tasks they are doing with help from nearby resource persons. In this case, consultants who have been trained in the same Workshop helped their tasks. This process was completed by the end of November. In each case, the local government produced an adequate report.

A Review and Prospect: Concluding Comments

A cycle of research and training events started in January. We have addressed capacity building needs at three levels in the nation. Each level was provided with a different set of programs. But, the largest effort was directed to the local government level. We have trained leadership and government employees of 10 local governments directly. But, at the same time, we have trained resource persons available for these local governments so that they will be available in the future for the same local governments and also for additional local governments nearby. It is hoped that the training of such resource persons will have propagating effects. Another characteristic of our system is that we place emphasis on real problem solving. Although we have provided concepts and techniques that are applicable to all local governments with lectures, we have used actual cases where each group was working at the office for training purposes. Trainees became 'consultants' for their own problems. By having significant representation from each local government (in our case, three persons) and having two resource persons who work for them, the Workshop has become a place for solving their own real problems. A critical mass of persons was there for each local government to make a difference. The learning effect must have been greater as a result. Site inspection revealed that each group was continuing the approaches they have chosen at the Workshop.

More gratifying experiences were gained when CBDI experts visited local governments at the conclusion of the study period. One after another, local governments expressed sincere appreciation for their participation in the project. One Planning Department Chief expressed the experience as reaffirmation of a paradigm change from the top-down to bottom-up. One Secretary to the District Head said that she learned two important points through this project: the importance of cash flows and of community participation. One consultant to a local government expressed his approach to find a 'win-win' solution. One local government leader said she would like to write a paper of her experience in a journal published by ITB. One Planning Department Chief mentioned that the combination of off-site lectures and on-site study worked very well for strengthening the capacity of the local officials. This cycle of training events will repeat itself in the second year. But, in the second year, we shall have another group of 10 local governments and a set of subjects that are slightly different from this year's. When the second cycle is completed, the system of capacity building at the local level will be further strengthened. In addition, teaching modules on key subjects will be left for replication elsewhere and for further development. Our teaching modules are shown in our website which is accessible to anyone. This success story does not necessarily imply that we were perfect. We have reviewed our activities during year 2000. In some areas we could have done better. For example, more extensive use of specific cases would have enhanced understanding of analytic techniques we taught. Also, we should have visited the sites more often during the period of technical assistance. These points will be taken into account in designing a program for this year. However, on the whole, we have been convinced that our approach is correct. We need to address capacity building at three levels as well as strengthening it at the local level.

Indonesia is a large country. Our effort is a small beginning. There is an immeasurably large need for capacity building as the local level. For example, we are covering at most 20 local governments out of nearly 350. However, we believe we have an overall strategy for building capacity at the local level that is suitable for the country for some time. With additional resources, the scale of operations may expand. But, it is also true that there are a large number of similar efforts going on within the country. We would like to work together with other similar works through exchange of information, and make joint efforts to the extent possible. For this purpose, we have established a website for providing detailed information about our activities. Through expanded operations and cooperation with other project activities, we are hopeful that we would be able to make a difference in the capacity of local governments in the near future.

Notes

1. Dillinger (1994), p.6.
2. The World Bank PREM, No. 43, September 2000, p.1.
3. Grindle (1997), defines 'capacity building' to include 'strengthening organizations' and 'reforming institutions' in addition to 'developing human resources', (pp.12-13). However, in this paper it is confined to 'developing human resources' only.
4. This is a special 13 months master's program called International Program for Policy and Management.
5. There was a massive reorganization of Central ministries after this date. The names of the organizations shown here are those at the time of the event.
6. In fact, we found after the fact that our approach resembles the one used by the World Bank for Africa Capacity Building Initiative (ACBI). Refer to James (1998), p.7.
7. www-rcf.usc.edu/~cbdi.

References

Asian Development Bank (1998), *Governance and Capacity Building in the Asian-Pacific Region*, ADB, Manila.
Asian Development Bank (1999), *Urban Sector Strategy*, ADB, Manila.
Dillinger, William C. (1994), *Decentralization and its Implications for Service Delivery*, World Bank, Washington DC.
Grindle, Merilee S. (1997). *Getting Good Government: Capacity Building in the Public Sectors of Developing Countries*, HIID, Cambridge: MA.
James, Valentine Udoh. (1998), 'Building the Capacities of Developing Nations through Empowerment', in Valentine Udoh James (ed.), *Capacity Building in Developing Countries: Human and Environmental Dimensions*, Praeger, Westport, CT.
UNDP (1998), *Decentralized Governance Monograph: A Global Sampling of Experience*, UNDP, New York.
World Bank (2000), 'Indonesia's Decentralization after Crisis', *PREM* No. 43, September 2000.

Chapter 15

Japan: Maturity and Stagnation?

Bill Lucarelli and Joseph Halevi

Introduction

Japan has now been mired in economic stagnation and recession for the past decade. What are the causes of this malaise? Is it merely the natural consequence of financial retrenchment after the collapse of the 'bubble' economy in the early 1990s, or does the present slump signify a more profound historical phase of industrial maturity and decline? The aim of this study is to provide several tentative hypotheses. In the first section, the onset of crisis and stagnation in Japan after the collapse of the 'bubble economy' in the early 1990s will be examined. The second section provides a more detailed exposition of Japan's oligopolistic role in the East Asian region from a Baran-Sweezy-Magdoff perspective.

The Era of Endaka

The result of the US pursuing an exchange-rate approach to the problem of trade with Japan was profound. They made no difference to the trade imbalance, but they stimulated Japan to undertake countermeasures to the high yen, which led to Japan's bubble economy, then to the collapse of the bubble economy, then to Japan's export of its bubble economy to South East Asia, and finally to the economic meltdown that confronts us today (Johnson, 1998, p.656).

Japan's current economic malaise has its roots in the chain of events that led to the expansionary monetary policies enacted after the September 1985 Plaza accords. The sharp appreciation of the Japanese yen failed to restore a balance of payments equilibrium with the US. The period of endaka, or the skyrocketing increase in the value of the yen, soon began to undermine the profitability of Japan's exports. By shifting a substantial proportion of their labor-intensive manufacturing offshore to the cheap labor zones of South East Asia, Japanese transnational corporations were able to restore their export competitiveness (Kriesler and Halevi, 1996). In order to mitigate the effects of an appreciating yen, the Japanese government embarked upon a program of monetary accommodation by reducing interest rates. Yet by pursuing relatively loose monetary policies, the government set in motion an unprecedented expansion of excess liquidity in the capital markets, most of which was channeled into what became known as zaitech operations, or speculative financial engineering (Yoshikawa, 2001). In retrospect, a financial mania was triggered in the real estate and equity markets.[1] The boom became self-fulfilling. As asset prices rose sharply, further borrowing only served to fuel the asset price spiral.

These events set in train the biggest build-up of excess liquidity in modern history. When the speculative bubble eventually burst in the early 1990s, the Japanese economy was effectively caught in a liquidity trap from which it has yet to recover. The current slump should also be viewed as the product of a severe crisis of excess capacity and over-accumulation. At the very core of this problem is the lack of effective demand. The structural propensity to build-up productive capacity while experiencing a concomitant and relative diminution of effective demand has led to a severe slump. Indeed, the only components of effective demand keeping the Japanese economy afloat are government spending and net exports. In the absence of a recovery of domestic consumption, both of these components will ultimately reach their economic and political limits.

Consequently, a considerable share of investment was also channeled into net capital formation, which in turn had induced a severe phase of industrial overcapacity (Itoh, 2000). Indeed, by the late 1980s, most of the large *keiretsu* began to generate internal funds for investment and curtailed their traditional reliance on the Bank of Japan (BoJ) and the big banks. In the early 1970s the large oligopolies relied on about 40 percent of their loans from the big banks. By the late 1980s, after the deregulation and liberalization of capital markets, this dependence had fallen to only 6 percent (Yoshikawa, 2001, p.57). Deprived of their traditional sources of investment, the banks began to engage in reckless speculation in real estate and the stock market. Japan's financial institutions injected about $US220 billion in new loans to the property sector alone between 1985 and 1990 (Whittaker & Kurosawa, 1998). In the aftermath of financial liberalization in the mid-1980s, speculation reached truly astounding proportions. The large *keiretsu* who had invested in extra capacity to meet the demand by the 1980s boom soon found that they were burdened with massive excess capacity. In 1989-90, the BoJ increased interest rates from 3.8 percent to 8.2 percent, which triggered the bursting of the financial bubble. Stock market prices tumbled by more than 60 percent from their peaks (Halevi and Lucarelli, 2002).

It can be argued, with considerable justification, that Japan had, in effect, generated a speculative mania in the East Asian region after the collapse of its own asset price bubble in 1990. This claim can be supported by the fact that Japan's commercial loans to the region had increased from only $US40 billion in 1984 to over $US265 billion in 1996 (Yoshikawa, 2001, p.9). The sharp fall in the volume of exports from East Asia just before the crisis had induced a series of balance of payments deficits, which were financed by short-term capital inflows, predominantly from Japan. At the same time, the collapse of Japan's speculative bubble led to a curtailment of their foreign direct investment (FDI) in the region from 1995 onwards. This process of retrenchment was also amplified by the sharp depreciation of the yen at about the same time. Between June 1995 and June 1997, Japanese claims in the Asian NICs fell from $US301 billion to $US180 billion (Hughes, 2000, p.229). Hence, it can be surmised that the crisis of over-accumulation in Japan had been regionalized before the onset of the financial meltdown of 1997-98. As soon as the East Asian countries encountered balance of payments deficits, spurred by problems of overcapacity, Japanese FDI was sharply curtailed, which would then act as one of the catalysts for the ensuing currency crises in 1997-98.

By the early 1990s, the Japanese economy was engulfed in a debilitating crisis of over-accumulation.

> The rate of capacity utilization in Japanese manufacturing in 1993 had declined by 17 percent from its peak of 1990, and it fell again after a feeble recovery in 1994. Continuing excess capacity certainly depresses investment in plant and equipment (p.27. With huge excess productive capacity, Japanese firms sharpened their competitive pressure in the market. Thus a vicious circle leading to a spiral of depression set in in the Japanese economy, comprising falling prices of shares and land, falls in workers' income, and depressant prices in the markets for products and services (Itoh, 2000, p.91).

To be sure, increases in productivity had outstripped wages growth by a large margin. The lack of effective demand in the domestic market only further encouraged outflows of capital, mostly destined to the East Asian region. By the early 1990s, East Asia had been transformed into a formidable export zone. Whereas in 1985, East Asia (excluding China) had only accounted for 12 percent of world exports, by 1993 this figure was 19 percent and reached as high as 23 percent before the outbreak of the financial crisis in 1997 (Hatch and Yamamura, 1996, p.189).

The high yen made Japanese wages simultaneously too high and too low. In terms of costs, wages were too high to compete against East Asian exports and sustain previous levels of manufacturing employment. From the standpoint of effective demand, however, wages were too low to absorb the excess capacity. Consequently, Japanese corporations accelerated their export strategies in order to resolve their problem of domestic surplus capacity and counteract a falling profitability. The high yen after 1985 therefore had a perverse effect in that capital could appropriate higher profits through a strategy of exporting capital to East Asia in order to export goods from these production zones to Europe and the United States. The domestic market could not act as the engine of growth as long as real wages lagged behind productivity growth in order to increase the level of oligopolistic profitability. FDI provided low cost production sites in East Asia that enabled Japanese corporations to export to the high wage markets in Europe and the United States (Steven, 1991, p.59). In essence, Japan sought to maintain its export-led growth by 'regionalizing' it (Gilpin, 2000, p.270).

As a large, industrialized capitalist economy with a relatively high level of per capita income, the role of effective demand in the dynamics of growth is critical. The investment of the large, oligopolistic *keiretsu* who dominate the Japanese economy will depend on the level of effective demand, which determines the degree of utilization of their productive capacity and their level of profits. In Japan, the phase of post-war development has encountered the limits to its growth in terms of reaching what Joan Robinson has described as the 'golden age' of the full employment condition of effective demand (Robinson, 1962, p.52). As soon as this state of 'maturity' is reached, the main problem that confronts the process of capital accumulation is the lack of effective demand (Halevi, 1992, p.468).

The Disarticulation of East Asia: A Baron-Sweezy-Magdoff Perspective

The evaluation of the process of accumulation in Asia should start from Japan, which constitutes the very core of capitalist development in the region. Japan represents the source of growth from the productive and technological side; it does not however represent the main source of effective demand. Markets external to the region provide the latter, in particular by the United States. In other words, if the balance of payments position of all the East and Southeast Asian countries, including China with Hong Kong, is consolidated we have an overall deficit with Japan which must be financed by borrowing from either Japan's and/or the world's financial institutions. The ability to sustain this situation depends on the capacity to generate net export revenues outside the area itself since the share of exports of those countries absorbed by Japan has been declining. By contrast the share of imports from Japan over those countries' total imports had been rising until the great collapse of 1997-98. For the area, excluding Japan, exports to the United States cover more than one third of total exports. Until 1995 the share of Japan's exports to the United States had been declining, but was still above one quarter which had been induced by the decline in the value of American dollar and the consequent shift of Japan's FDI towards Asia. Yet, as this shift generated an even higher deficit by Asia vis à vis Japan, the pressure to find export markets outside Japan became stronger. In this context, the following must be borne in mind.

A strong component of Asia's exports are in those products where price fluctuations are significant. Japan, by contrast, tends to focus on its exports in sectors where it has enough power not to be completely on the price taking side. This is also true in items such as microchips, whose production is highly cyclical due to the frequency of innovations. Precisely because it has all the structural inputs necessary to generate new machinery and equipment with which to produce new items, Japanese corporations can move on the upmarket side of price sensitive products, provided they are the outcome of technological innovations. Furthermore, Japan is the major supplier of capital goods to the region, including to countries where FDI is small such as South Korea. In addition to capital goods and systems used in production, a great deal of the infrastructure in East and Southeast Asia (power stations, electricity grids, bridges etc.), has been built by using Japanese companies and their technological systems. These two factors, capital goods used in production and capital goods used in infrastructure, tie the whole of East and Southeast Asia to Japan's input/output configuration. This gives Japanese corporations a structural and institutional oligopolistic position in the area without, at the same time, making Japan a major source of effective demand for the region.

The structural fault separating Japan from the rest of Asia is a specific feature of the capitalist development of the region after World War Two. It emerged especially in concomitance with the American war in Vietnam. The structural fault is due to the new positioning of the Japanese economy in the framework of the US presence which permitted Japan to pursue a strategy described by Kyoshi Kojima as that of *Full Range Industrialization* jumpstarted by the Korean war in 1950-53 (Calder, 1988; Schaller, 1985; 1997). Japanese exports rose quite rapidly through a strategy of industrial targeting (Nester, 1991), mostly because of high levels of domestic investment and output growth. Overall, however, Japan's share of exports over national income was quite moderate, never exceeding 13 percent. By contrast in the 1930s - when industrialization was accompanied by imperialist expansion into China and by a heavy preoccupation to generate external revenues in order to pay for the importation of strategic products exports exceeded 18 percent of GDP (Itoh, 1990; Nakamura, 1983). Thus, one of the characteristics of the post-war experience, especially during the *Era of High Speed Growth* (Kosai, 1986), is the absence of a structural balance of payments constraint for Japan.

The priority assigned to the capital goods sectors allowed the selection of export items without discriminating against the overall growth of the economy. Just the same, the softening of the balance of payments problem that obsessed Japan from the beginning of its industrialization until 1949, was facilitated by US transfers linked to the Korean War and by the additional spending engendered by the Vietnam War. Compared to Japan, the other major Asian countries of capitalist industrialization as South Korea and Taiwan did not follow the same pattern even when they aimed at a policy of significant self-reliance in relation to foreign direct investment inflows. Their industrialization involved a high share of imports over national income, a pattern that they had not changed once they reached higher levels of development and of per capita income (Maddison, 1985). In the fifteen years preceding the 1960s and the American war against Vietnam, these countries tended to be import-dependent on the United Sates and export-dependent on Japan, reflecting, in relation to the latter, a colonial pattern of trade. The situation was radically and abruptly changed with the rapid industrial spurt that began in the early 1960s in conjunction with the renewed American spending in the area connected to the intervention in Vietnam. The United States became the export market for the area as a whole, inclusive of Japan, while imports to South Korea and Taiwan now came mostly from Japan. This process, which crucially depended upon American policies, recreated a Japanese economic zone in Asia whose main feature was import dependency vis à vis Japan while the realization of profits, in the Marxian sense of Rosa Luxemburg and Michal Kalecki, was and continues to be sought in the United States.

This pattern has been reinforced by the growth of Japanese FDI in Thailand, Malaysia and Singapore. At a first glance, the People's Republic of China - which swiftly inserted itself, always via the American route, into a hitherto purely American-Japanese zone – appears not to follow the above pattern. Yet, if Hong Kong is included, and it must be since it is a major gateway for the trade of the

People's Republic, the combined current account position of China vis à vis Japan is negative. Furthermore, if the value of trade needed to sustain China's production aimed at the domestic market is subtracted, the trade in the export sector turns out to be fully dependent upon imports from Japan, confirming Japan's structurally based oligopolistic role in the area (Hochraich, 1999).

With *Full Range Industrialization* successfully completed the Japanese economy was in a position to export without needing many imports except for raw materials and food. By the end of the 1960s the economy was already approaching the maturity stage. Analytically such a stage can be identified as one in which the pre-existing warranted rate of growth is no longer sustainable. Surplus labor from agriculture is dwindling and the industrial sector becomes as a whole a modern sector with up to date capital stock (Sweezy, 1953). Under these conditions accumulation can be maintained by realizing profits abroad, or alternatively, profits and accumulation will have to give way to a higher share of wages and social consumption. This did not happen since the dynamic of real wages seldom outpaced that of productivity. Indeed, from 1973 onward real wages expanded always les; than productivity growth (Steven, 1996).

Since 1973, Japan has been trapped in a situation where the decline in the value of the American dollar compelled the enforcement of a tight wage policy in order to defend exports in the US and European markets. But such a tight wage policy stifled domestic demand and generated endemic unused capacity to which Japanese corporations responded by means of further investment and restructuring. Nixon's 1971 proclamation of the end the fixed parity system initiated a confrontation between the dollar and its rivals caused by the devaluation of the American currency (Parboni, 1981). That confrontation impacted more on Japan than on Europe. During the last years of the 1960s, Japan began to accumulate a balance of payments surplus. In Kaleckian terms this means that the external sector began to generate net profits for Japanese corporations2. The regime of financial instability caused by the American war in Vietnam with the demise of the fixed parity system and the ensuing speculative push on raw material and oil prices thwarted thereafter the ability of Japanese corporations to realize profits by means of exports.

In this context it is interesting to compare Japan and Germany during the period following the Nixon declaration. Both countries were affected by the breakdown of the long postwar boom and showed a marked decline in growth rates of GDP.[3] Japan's rate fell more than the German rate but nonetheless, stayed above it. Germany therefore gravitated more towards stagnation than Japan but only in terms of its internal demand. Sustained by a developed hinterland that was formed by the countries of the then European Common Market and also by Austria, Switzerland and Scandinavia, Germany was able to undertake a deliberate policy using the revaluation of the D-Mark in order to modify its pattern of capital accumulation towards multinational investment and net exports of advanced products (Halevi, 1995; Lucarelli, 1999). The material basis for the success of the policy lay in the fact that Germany was, and is, at the very heart of Europe's interindustry matrix. Thus German exports were essential for the normal functioning of every aspect of Europe's productive apparatus.

Japan, by contrast, suffered a significant decline in the share of its external surplus over GDP up to the point that in the 1973-79 period, the surplus averaged no more than 0.3 percent of GDP (OECD, 1986, 1996). In Kaleckian terms this meant that not much real profits were realized through foreign sales. Throughout the 1970s Japan had an endemic crisis of unused capacity making its economy more vulnerable than that of Germany. The external surplus shrank, while investment in machinery and equipment fell much less than the fall in the growth rate, leading to unused capacity and to a rise in the apparent value of the capital to output ratio.[4] Germany experienced a similar tendency but to a much lesser degree than Japan. Moreover, in the German case, the high level of profits realized abroad heavily mitigated such a rise. Although East Asia began to attract significant foreign direct investment from Japan precisely in those years, it could not as yet act as a hinterland sustaining the realization of profits because of the limited level of development of those countries during this period.

The temporary solution to Japan's over-accumulation crisis came from the United States' geo-strategic political economy. The Reagan years of renewed military spending and budget deficits, coupled with restrictive monetary policies and high interest rates, lifted in a selective manner, the level of demand in the United States, revalued the US dollar and enabled an overall expansion of exports from both Japan and East Asia. This is the period in which a virtuous circle was established. In addition to Japanese exports to North America, Japan's exports were needed to sustain East Asia's regional and, especially, extra-regional exports. The region rapidly became a sizeable Japanese hinterland and, by 1995, the majority of Japan's surplus in the balance of payments was realized within the region, although the relative majority of Japanese exports were still oriented towards the United States. In fact, the synergetic relation between Japan and East Asia increased during the second economic conflict with the United States triggered by the devaluation of the dollar after the Plaza accords signed in New York in September 1985.

This time the devaluation continued relentlessly for a good decade and it reflected the change in the United States perception of its role in world capitalism. Although seesawing since the beginning of the defeat of the intervention in Vietnam, Washington continued for nearly two additional decades to operate as a guarantor of the capitalistic and political interests of European and especially Japanese and Asian capitalism. Thus, in the mid-1970s the United States - whose international economic policies under President Ford and President Carter were bent on reconquering, via devaluation, portions of profits surrendered to European and Japanese companies – had to signal their willingness to undertake a fully fledged rescue operation of South Korea which was then mired in a deep financial crisis (Woo, 1991). Washington's attitude reassured a reluctant Japan who then lent money to Seoul. Japan's oligopolistic position in East Asia is not therefore independent from the geo-political and geo-economic strategies and perceptions of the United States. In this respect Hatch and Yamamura (1996) were wrong in viewing Japan's role in the area as moving towards a regional production alliance. During Reagan's first term in office another wave of concessions, intertwined with the deregulation policies pursued domestically (Nester, 1991), had favored both Japan, East Asia and China. And everything that stimulates production and exports in East Asia and China stimulates Japan's exports and direct investment to the region. In East Asia Japan is the oligopolistic power but it is not, however, the fulcrum of a regional system of production and coordination because the whole area, including Japan, is still anchored to the United States. Furthermore, the way in which it was anchored until 1995 was profoundly uneven.

Washington began to withdraw from political multilateralism, which implied an overall supportive attitude towards regional capitalisms, punctuated with attempts to correct imbalances when these raised concerns within the economic power groups in the United States. This became evident after the USSR intended to relinquish control over Eastern Europe as well as retreat from the Middle East.[5] Instead of continuing to be the Gramscian collective agent of the developed capitalist countries, the United States moved to a bilateral and eventually to a unilateral stance in international economic policies. Such a shift has been noticed especially by those economists who sincerely believe in the welfare gains stemming from free trade and globalization, as well as by those political scientists who put their faith in the stabilizing role of a hegemonic power (Krueger, 1996; Zupnick, 1999; Gilpin, 1987). The devaluation of the US dollar in the wake of the Plaza accords became an instrument for furthering the unilateralist strategy of opening up markets for American corporations and its main target was Japan. The automobile war, the telecommunication war (Motorola) and the microchips war, were the salient events during a decade of a seemingly unending devaluation of the American currency vis à vis the Japanese yen. Although the outcome of these confrontations is not so clear-cut, it did put the Japanese leadership on a constantly defensive basis thereby weakening the cohesion between the political, bureaucratic and business components of the ruling classes.

On the American front, the devaluation of the currency could not but have negative effects on the profits of Japanese corporations. Financially it devalued dollar-denominated assets; productively it put a further squeeze on the profit margins earned on those products exported to the United States for which there was an American competitor. In this case the full revaluation of the yen could not be passed onto export prices thereby giving rise to the phenomenon of Japanese wages being both too high and too low. Although the devaluation of the dollar stimulated the flow of FDI into the United States, its persistence did not help the links between Japanese transplants in the USA and the home base. The higher yen costs of intermediate products and technologies imported from the home company could not be fully passed onto final prices. Alternatively, Japanese corporations operating in the United States could become more or less autonomous units like the American multinationals in Europe. Yet one of the main features of Japan's multinational investment is the tight links it maintains with the homeland in engineering, productive and export bases.

In the end, East and Southeast Asia turned out to be the safest zone of oligopolistic hegemony for Japan. However, a safe zone can also become a stagnant area. The dynamism of the area was tied to its capacity to export, mostly to the United States. Exports, and expectations about exports, fuelled investment in the form of FDI, which meant imports from Japan as well as domestic growth which also required imports from Japan. Under the conditions of a depreciating dollar, the mechanism could operate successfully because of the particular position the US currency had in the monetary and exchange rate arrangements of the countries of the area. The pegging of the area's currencies against the dollar stimulated the pattern of expectations concerning exports and, consequently, the flow of Japanese FDI. Thus even the synergetic relations between Japan and its zone depended upon factors in which the United States political economy played a determinant role.

The reason why Japan could not become the hub of a regional production alliance, in the sense of Hatch and Yamamura, is due to two factors. First, the limited role it played as a source of regional effective demand. Second, precisely because Tokyo was a reluctant importer, evident by its rising surpluses with Asia, the synergetic relation between Japan and East and Southeast Asia depended on the circumstances that permitted those countries to generate extra-regional exports. While Japan successfully utilized its hegemony in order to realize net exports, it was both unable and unwilling to guarantee the stability of the region. In principle, its ruling classes should have understood that a depreciating dollar would have eventually prevented the Japanese national economy from squaring the circle. The disruptive effects caused by the devaluation of the dollar on the whole financial and productive system of Japan were understood instead by the American authorities who in June 1995 began to talk the dollar up. The following three years witnessed an appreciation of the American currency vis à vis the yen which ended the synergy with the Asian zone. In other words, from June 1995 Japan's export expansion came into conflict with the economic viability of its own direct sphere of hegemony. The Japanese monetary, government, and business authorities had supported the pegging of the area's currencies to the dollar. In the context of a long-term downward tendency of the American currency, the peg acted both as an anti-inflationary device and as a stimulus to exports. Japanese corporations literally built their regional power on the asymmetric movements of the area's currencies relative to the yen.

Commentators have pointed out that the peg was already being undermined by the recurrent devaluations of the yuan, the Chinese currency. Few stressed that Japan's exports and FDI to China were actually benefiting from the success of China's export drive and competitive devaluations. The oligopolistic position of Japan in the region increasingly used not as a process of integration like that of Germany within Europe, but to combat the disruptive effects of the devaluation of the dollar was oriented towards gaining as much as possible from the peg against the dollar as well as from the growth of China's export sector, itself not unrelated to the policies of abrupt devaluations pursued by Beijing's authorities. The relief represented by the 1995 revaluation did not materialize because of the collapse of the asymmetric synergy between Japan and Asia. In this context, Morishima (2000) has suggested a solution based on a sort of Asian Economic Community. Yet neither Japan nor the United Sates have the political will to initiate an East Asian Common Market, which would have to assign a major political role to the People's Republic of China and create within itself an Asian Payments Union. The international public expenditure generated by Cold War Keynesianism seems to have ended but the politics of the Cold War with its special armament programs (directed against China) is far from over. This political orientation is today accompanied by a greater struggle for the control over finance and liquid markets, which is what the ideology of globalization is all about. The Asian crash and the Japanese stagnation both turn out to be simply a new episode in the crisis of the regime that sustained the post-war period of capitalist expansion.

Concluding Remarks

At the time of writing, Japan was still caught in the quagmire of recession. Successive stimulus measures through public works programs and the bail-out of insolvent banks had blown out the budget deficit to over 10 percent of GDP, while the ratio of government debt was estimated at over 130 percent of GDP. The onset of a severe liquidity trap has led some economists, most notably Paul Krugman, to suggest that Japan should monetize its fiscal deficit in order to run a reflationary policy and thus stimulate domestic consumption (Krugman, 1999). This sort of panacea appears to be rather strange in the present context where banks are not lending and consumers are not spending. Indeed, the opposite effect might just as easily occur. A reflationary strategy could destroy the last remnants of consumer confidence: the purchasing power of household savings (Taggart-Murphy, 2000). On the other hand, if the Japanese authorities were to succumb to western demands from the OECD and the IMF and launch a neoliberal strategy of market liberalization, the short-term impact would be disastrous. A depressive spiral of bankruptcies and growing unemployment, not witnessed since the Great Depression, could be set in motion.

It would be more sanguine to declare that the banking crisis is symptomatic of a much deeper structural distortion. Severe excess capacity has been built up over the past decades regardless of profitability. The lack of effective demand is as much structural as it is cyclical. Domestic private consumption has been neglected over the decades because of a deliberate strategy to accumulate capital by investing in the capital goods sector. While this strategy of rapid industrialization has been successful in terms of a 'late-starter' in its efforts to catch-up with their western competitors, the downside has been a neglect of the development of the wage-goods sector. Quite simply, Japanese workers will not spend because of employment insecurity and the need to save for retirement in the face of a rudimentary social wage and a threadbare social safety net. It is precisely this dilemma that confronts Japan's policy makers.

Despite these domestic problems of deflation and a liquidity trap, Japan continues to accumulate a current account surplus, most notably with the United

States. A large proportion of this trade surplus has been accomplished by falling imports as a result of the stagnation of domestic demand. The problem of excess capacity will compel Japanese corporations to expand their exports in order to counteract a falling profitability on the domestic market. The burgeoning trade deficit in the US, however, could provoke retaliatory protectionist measures. The conditions are therefore quite favorable for the outbreak of a classical Keynesian trade war as each country pursues 'a desperate expedient to maintain employment at home by forcing sales on foreign markets and restricting purchases, which, if successful, will merely shift the problem of unemployment to the neighbour (Keynes, 1951, p.382-83).

Notes

1.   During the 1980s, the price of real estate rose by a factor of 5. At their respective peaks, the total estimated value of Japanese land was 60 percent of world property values, while Japanese equities accounted for almost 40 percent of world stock market values (Linge, 1997, p.62).

2.   From the national income accounting identity: $Y = I + C + (G - T) + (X - M)$ where the letters stand for investment, consumption, government expenditure, taxes, exports and imports. Assume that profits P are a given fraction of Y so that $P = \alpha Y$. Then: $P = \alpha[I + C + (G - T) + (X - M)]$. This means that for any given distribution of income between profits and wages, the higher the external surplus the higher the absolute level of profits. It is also evident that if income stagnates and $(X - M)$ rises, then α tends to rise unless the increase in the external surplus is offset by a decline in investment.

3.   GDP figures are important not for their welfare content which can be challenged on several grounds. Their relevance lies in the fact that they apply to a capitalist system whose dynamics and raison d'être are determined not by welfare considerations but by profitability. Hence to a given growth rate of GDP there corresponds a certain rate of profit over invested capital. At the limit – with Weberian capitalists who consume nothing and invest everything, and with Ricardian workers who must consume all their subsistence wages – the growth rate of GDP coincides with the rate of profit. Since in practice capitalists do consume some small fraction of their profits and workers do save some part of their wages, the growth rate will be equal to the rate of profit multiplied by the propensity to save out of profits. Indeed, after much theoretical debate this turned out to be the crucial determinant of the growth rate since if the propensity to save out of wages were to exceed that out of profits, accumulation would be positively related to a rising share of wages over national income. This scenario makes no sense since, at the limit, capitalists would disappear but a private investment system would still remain in place! (Pasinetti, 1974; Kaldor, 1996).

4.   The statistical growth rate of GDP is determined in an exact manner by the Feldman-Mahalanobis Harrod type equation $g = (i/v)$, where i is the share of investment over GDP and v is the capital-output ratio. The share of machines and equipment over GDP is a more reliable measure of investment since non residential structures are, as such, not productive being themselves the product of equipment such as cranes, trucks, etc. A rise in the capital intensity of production v is conducive to a higher rate of growth and accumulation only if it occurs

concomitantly with a still larger increase in the share of investment i. If this does not happen then, barring the case of technological regress, the system builds up unused capacity, which prevents the engineering capabilities of machinery (1/v) from being fully operational. A more complete version of the equation is that formulated by Kalecki (1972) in the context of planned development: $g = (i/v) + a - u$; where a are autonomous improvements and u is the share of output lost for junking older capital equipment. In the case of Japan the persistence of a high level of investment in equipment in the light of a fall in g cannot be explained only by a rise in u induced by restructuring, since this very process would lead to an increase in a offsetting in part the rise in u. As a consequence, the combination of a high share of investment and low growth points to systemic unused capacity.

5. [5]The support for regional capitalisms was not however uniform. India, for instance, the only functioning liberal-democratic regime in Asia and a completely capitalist mixed economy, never enjoyed the support that the United States gave to Japan, South Korea, Taiwan. It must be remembered that from the 1950s onward India was quite open to multinational investment as the Union Carbide accident in Bhopal sadly reminded us. By contrast, countries which were fully under the American umbrella and financial transfers were allowed not to permit foreign multinational investment, notably among them Japan and South Korea.

References

Calder, K. E. (1988), *Crisis and Compensation: Public Policy and Political Cold War in Asia*, Oxford University Press, New York.

Dixon, C. and Drakakis-Smith D., (ed.), (1993), *Economic and Social Development in Pacific Asia*, Routledge, London.

Dore, R. (1998), 'Asian Crisis and the Future of the Japanese Model', *Cambridge Journal of Economics*, vol. 22, No.7, pp.761-771, 1998.

Funabashi, Y. (1988), *Managing the Dollar: From the Plaza to the Louvre*, Institute for International Economics, Washington.

Gilpin, R. (1987), *The Political Economy of International Relations*, Princeton University Press, New Jersey.

Gilpin, R. (2000), *The Challenge of Global Capitalism*, Princeton University Press, New York.

Halevi, J., 'Asian Capitalist Accumulation: From Sectoral to Vertical Integration', *Journal of Contemporary Asia*, vol. 22, No.4, 1992.

Halevi, J. (1995), 'The EMS and the Bundesbank in Europe', in P. Arestis, and V. Chick (eds), *Finance, Development and Structural Change*, Aldershot, Hants, Edward Elgar, pp.263-291, UK.

Halevi, J. and Lucarelli, B. (2002), 'Japan's Stagnationist Crisis', *Monthly Review*, vol. 53, No.9.

Hatch, W. and Yamamura, K. (1996), *Asia in Japan's Embrace: Building a Regional Production Alliance*, Cambridge University Press, Cambridge; Melbourne.

Hochraich, D. (1999), L'Asie, du miracle à la crise, Bruxelles: Editions Complexe.

Hughes, C. H. (2000), 'Japanese Policy and the East Asian Currency Crises: Abject Defeat or Quiet Victory?' *Review of International Political Economy*, vol. 7, No.2, Summer.

Itoh, M. (2000), *The Japanese Economy Reconsidered*, Palgrave, New York.

Itoh, M. (1990), *The World Economic Crisis and Japanese Capitalism*, St. Martin's Press, New York.

Johnson, C. (1998), 'Economic Crisis in East Asia: The Clash of Capitalisms', *Cambridge Journal of Economics*, vol. 22, No.6, pp.653-661.

Kalecki, M. (1972), *Selected Essays on the Economic Growth of the Socialist and the Mixed Economy*, Cambridge University Press, Cambridge.

Keynes, J. M. (1936), *The General Theory of Employment, Interest and Money*, MacMillan & Co., London.

Kosai, Y. (1986), *The Era of High-Speed Growth: Notes on the Postwar Japanese Economy*, translated by Jacqueline Kaminski, University of Tokyo Press, Tokyo.

Kriesler, P. and Halevi, J. (1996), 'Asia, Japan, and the Internationalization of Effective Demand', *Economie et Societes*, Serie No. 10, 2-3.

Krueger, A. (1996), *The Political Economy of American Trade Policy*, University of Chicago Press, Chicago.

Krugman, P. (1999), *The Return of Depression Economics*, Penguin, London.

Kunio, Y. (1994), *Japanese Economic Development*, Oxford University Press, New York.

Kwan, C. H. (2001), *Yen Bloc, Brookings Institution Press*, Washington DC.

Linge, C. (1998), *The Rise and Decline of the Asian Century*, Macmillan, Melbourne.

Lucarelli, B. (2002), 'The East Asian Financial Meltdown', *Journal of Contemporary Asia*, vol. 32, No.4.

Maddison, A. (1985), *Two Crises: Latin America and Asia, 1929-38 and 1973-83*, Development Centre of the Organisation for Economic Co-operation and Development; Washington, DC, OECD Publications, Paris.

Morris, J. (ed.), (1991*)*, *Japan and the Global Economy*, Routledge, New York.

Morris-Suzuki, T. (1991), 'Reshaping the Industrial Division of Labour: Japanese Manufacturing Investment in S.E. Asia', in Morris J. (ed.), 1991.

Nakamura, T. (1983), *Economic Growth in Prewar Japan*, translated by Robert A. Feldman, New Haven: Yale University Press.

Nester, W. R. (1991), *Japanese Industrial Targeting: The Neomercantilist Path to Economic Superpower*, London : Macmillan.

Nordhaug, K. (2002), 'The Political Economy of the Dollar and the Yen in East Asia', *Journal of Contemporary Asia*, vol. 32, No.4.

OECD (1986), Historical Statistics, Paris.

OECD (1996), Historical Statistics, Paris.

Parboni, R. (1981), *The Dollar and its Rivals*, Verso, London.

Pasinetti, L. (1974), *Growth and Income Distribution: Essays in Economic Theory*, Cambridge University Press, Cambridge.

Pasinetti, L. (1981), *Structural Change and Economic Growth*, Cambridge University Press, UK.

Robinson, J. (1962), *Essays in the Theory of Economic Growth*, Macmillan, London.

Rowthorn, R. E. and Wells, J. R. (1987), *Deindustrialization and Foreign Trade*, Cambridge University Press, UK.

Schaller, M. (1985), *The American Occupation of Japan: The Origins of the Cold War in Asia*, Oxford University Press, New York.

Schaller, M. (1997*)*, *Altered States: The United States and Japan*, Macmillan, London.

Sheridan, K. (ed.), (1998), *Emerging Economic Systems in Asia*, Allen & Unwin, Sydney.

Sheridan, M. (1998), 'Japan's Economic System', in Sheriden, (ed.).

Steven, R., 'Structural Origins of Japan's FDI', in Morris (ed.), 1991.

Sweezy, P. M. (1953), The Present as History, New York: Monthly Review Press.

Taggart-Murphy, R., 'Japan's Economic Crisis', *New Left Review*, No 1(second series), Jan/Feb, 2000.

Whittaker, D. H. and Kurosawa, Y., 'Japan's Crisis: Evolution & Implications', *Cambridge Journal of Economics*, vol. 22, No.7.

Woo, J. (1991), *Race to the Swift: State and Finance in Korean Industrialization*, New York, Columbia University Press.

Woronoff, T. (1996), *The Japanese Economic Crisis*, Macmillan, London.

Yamazawa, I., (1990), *Economic Development and International Trade: The Japanese Model*, Resource Systems Institute, East-West Centre, USA.

Yoshikawa, H. (2001), *Japan's Lost Decade*, International House of Japan, Tokyo.

Zupnick, E. (1999), *V..ions and Revisions: the United States in the Global Economy*, Boulder, Colo, Oxford: Westview Press.

Chapter 16

Indicators and Trends in Economic Globalization

Stanislav Menshikov

Introduction

The term 'globalization' has been widely used in recent years, yet its exact meaning is still to be defined. In economic term 'globalization' has been used to describe rather close but still somewhat different phenomena:

1. the process of increasing mutual interconnections and interdependence of national economies on a world-wide scale meaning that this process also involves an increasing number (an absolute majority) of national economies and is accompanied by the liberalization of international economic flows;
2. the process of extending to other or all parts of the globe economic activities originating in certain countries or groups of countries (for instance, by way of transnational corporations – TNCs);
3. the progress in moving towards a united global economy without national barriers, the integration of national economies into one global economy.

While one could look at these definitions as reflecting different aspects and manifestations of basically the same set of processes, they do point to important differences in the treatment of such processes.

Indeed, the first definition, which puts the stress on interconnectedness and interdependence, seems to be purely descriptive of the progress in economic exchange between nations. Such exchange has existed since times immemorial, and hardly any nation, at any point in history has been immune to such exchange or completely isolated from it, at least for not very long historical time periods. Economic historians usually associate the beginnings of world (global) trade, world markets and the world economy with the Great Geographic Discoveries of the late 15th and early 16th centuries which established the first regular sea trade links between Europe and most other continents. Besides the fact that trade routes over land between Europe, Asia and Africa existed long before Christopher Columbus, this view is obviously Eurocentric, since it ignores the obvious fact that earlier civilizations might have contributed even more to global economic progress than ancient or feudal Europe. The new book by Andre Gunder *Global Economy in*

The Asian Age (University of California Press, forthcoming) is a brilliant analysis of the global economy as it existed in pre-Columbian times and provides (in the words of one reviewer) 'a compelling argument against Eurocentrism' and 'forces us to turn the telescope of world history around to see that the focus was, and is Asia NOT Europe'.[1]

Even so, the unprecedented rise in world economic exchange that occurred after 1500 (and particularly after 1800) is certainly correlated with and largely explained by the development of capitalism first in Europe, then on other continents, which, as a universal (all-embracing) form of market economy provides a natural mechanism for growing interconnectedness of economies, first local, then national, and finally global. Whatever economic progress under the Asian Mode of Production, it could not provide the underlying mechanism for economic interconnection to become global. Because capitalism rose in Europe first, and in North America and on other continents later, one can also see how important the second definition of globalization mentioned above which considers it as a process of extending certain economic activities to other parts of the globe. It is obvious that the predominant form of globalization so far (starting with 1500 and particularly after 1800) has been the extension of capitalism initially from Europe and later from Europe, North America and Japan to other continents and has the effect of partially or completely destroying other types of economic organization. At the close of the 20th century this process can be seen, *inter alia*, in the expansion of transnational corporations and in the spread of the American model of capitalism which claims superiority and dominance over other (European, Japanese, New Tiger) capitalist models. Another result of this process was the demise of communistic socialism in Eastern Europe and parts of Asia, the capitalistic transformation of this area and its painful integration into the dominant capitalistic world order. This raises the issue as to whether convergence of national economic systems to one model of socio-economic organization is the only and inevitable route in which globalization has to and will proceed, or rather economic interconnection and interdependence has the less painful alternative of mutual coexistence and adaptation of different models to each other.

This chapter does not pretend to suggest a solution for this issue. Obviously, the eventual winner in any race is the most efficient participant. A great deal depends, however, on which criteria of efficiency are used to choose the winner. It could be the rules of the market but, alternatively, also the principles of equity, compassion and human rights. It could be the simple rule of democratic choice between available alternatives, or, alternatively, the discipline of survival on a planet with limited resources. Whichever set of criteria one uses, it is not at all clear that the currently prevailing models of socio-economic organization are up to the task of providing humanity with the best solutions and that current patterns of globalization can guarantee sustainable development of the world economy.[2]

Abstracting ourselves for a moment from different economic models we have to admit that progress in economic interchange between nations is dependent on technology. Forgetting about feudalism, capitalism, communism, the Asiatic mode of production, the fact is that the absolute level and intensity of economic international interconnection is dependent on the level and availability of technology, particularly in transportation and communications, and also on the means of their production. Columbus could not have discovered America were it not for fantastic (for his times) progress in sea navigation. The virtual explosion of today's currency markets was impossible without the advent of computers and Internet. Whatever the future of globalization, progress in international interdependence cannot be turned around, at least not easily and not for long due to modern technology. Of course, the relation between technology and globalization is not simple and not necessarily linear. The basic framework and infrastructure that permits a given intensity of international economic interchange (and its maximum) is determined by technology. But prevailing socio-economic models will determine the actual rate of utilization of this technological potential. Because technology tends to generally develop faster than the ability of human beings and their socio-economic systems to adapt to new technologies, the latter will exert, as they have in the past, a revolutionary impact on socio-economic systems and push them towards adaptation and change. To be successful and even to survive, systems should, with time, become less rigid and more flexible.

Finally, I come to the third definition of globalization which puts the stress on movement towards one global economy, integrated and without national barriers. Insofar as historical evidence shows, there is no clear trend in this respect. Forces leading to integration and disintegration have worked in parallel to one another, one prevailing over the other in different periods of time. The immediate outcome of their interaction has largely depended on political, rather than economic forces. Thus one can think of a fairly closely integrated regional economy within the Roman Empire at a certain high peak period of its existence. Later it disintegrated into many independent feudal kingdoms, which were less economically interconnected. Early capitalism led to the emergence of new, relatively well economically integrated global colonial empires which, however, disintegrated in the 20th century leading to the new multiplicity of 150 or so sovereign national economies. In the second half of our century, there is a strong trend towards integration on a regional scale (EU, NAFTA, etc.). At the same time a large formerly economically integrated part of Eurasia, the Soviet Union, fell apart both politically and economically.

It is sufficient to observe that there is little likelihood of more integration (in the sense of eliminating national barriers) if coexistence of different socio-economic models prevails over convergence. Integration (in this sense) on a global scale will also depend on the continuing existence of the gap between nations in levels of economic development, productivity, incomes, and wealth. It is not reasonable to expect integration between nations that are divided by such a gap, at least not such integration that can avoid economic dominance of one nation over the other, i.e. new forms of colonization.

Statistical Indicators

Levels and intensity of international economic interchange are measurable with regard to most of its components, i.e. the movement between nations of goods, services, some factors of production (i.e. capital, labor, technology), migration of human beings, information, etc. For reasons of space this paper explores only statistics related to international trade, production, international capital investment, and international financial markets.

Trade and Production

We start with comparing two long time series from 1820 to 1992 reconstructed by Angus Maddison.[3] The two series are in constant 1990 dollars which makes it possible to calculate GDP and their individual growth rates. Any historical statistics of such length are subject to many doubts as to their accuracy. However, our aim is to look at big changes, not small variations generalized picture. In both the 19th and 20th centuries world trade was expanding substantially faster than world output. Growth in GDP in 1820-1900 was relatively slow, and it seemed easy for world trade to grow three times faster. Of course, the world output totals included the then very slow growing Russia and China whose combined share was pretty high. Output growth accelerated sharply in the 20th century (from 1.3 percent in 1820-1900 to 2.9 percent in 1900-1992, and to 4.0 percent in 1950-1992). World trade throughout the 20th century did not grow faster than previously (3.8 percent in 1820-1900 and 3.7 percent in 1900-1992) but it still expanded faster than GDP). In the second half of the century it accelerated to 5.7 percent increasing the difference to 1.7 percentage points.

On the whole, the ratio of trade to output grew about by the same number of percentage points – from only 1 percent in 1820 to 7.1 percent in 1900 and to 13.5 percent in 1992. This finding is certainly less than spectacular if we contrast it with widespread perceptions of the rate of globalization at the end of our century. We therefore have to compare the Maddison data with other sources, for instance, World Bank figures which are in current prices. While the ratio, according to these data, are substantially higher that the Maddison figures they, strangely enough, show no rise in last 15 years when globalization, in the general intuitive view, was accelerating and, at least progressing. To make a step further, we have to bear in mind that world trade measures only exchange in goods while GDP includes both goods and services. For the comparison to be more meaningful we have to look at the ration between trade and non-service GDP (we could also compare GDP with world trade in goods and services, but the latter data as a total for the world is either not readily available or non-reliable.[4]

Based on the Maddison date we have further estimated the share of service GDP in total GDP for the whole period of 1820-1992. The share of non-service GDP declined slowly in the 19th century, but later the decline accelerated bringing the ratio down to only 43 percent (as compared to 89.5 percent in 1820 and 70.9 percent in 1913). When we account for the much slower growth of non-service

GDP, particularly in the 20th century (as compared to total GDP), the ratio of trade in goods to output of goods makes a nearly threefold jump between 1950-1992 reaching 31.5 percent by the early 1990s. This looks like a more sensible estimate of the substantial, revolutionary increase in trade interdependence in the second half of the 20th century comparable in relative scope only to the historical periods between 1820-1870 and 1870-1913. The World Bank, conveniently enough, provides us with its own estimates of the share of non-service GDP in total world GDP -47 percent in 1980 and 37 percent in 1995. The latter figure is not too different from our own estimate based on Maddison. If we now relate world exports of goods to non-service world GDP, the ratio, based on World Bank figures, looks as follows.

According to the World Bank, the part of world goods output that enters world trade, has increased in the last 15 years from 40 to 50 percent. Both figures seem to be too high. This is perhaps due to the fact that trade flows are measured in full market values while data on non-service GDP are value-added figures. We have not tried to convert GDP figures to full market value or the trade figures to value added equivalents. Therefore the ratio should be seen as indicative more of the historical trend than of the exact share of output entering international commerce. Without passing a final judgment, we can assume that the real average measure of interconnectedness between nations via trade in goods is anywhere between one third and one half of world value added in goods output.

Investment

International movement of capital is another important indicator of economic interdependence. Investment in foreign assets takes various forms which can be roughly classified as belonging to four different groups:

1.   direct investment (associated with financial and management control over foreign business units);
2.   portfolio investment (which includes absentee foreign ownership of securities issued by both private and public entities);
3.   loans (extended by private financial institutions, governments or international financial institutions);
4.   short-term capital (which is mostly, but not exclusively, consists of deposits in foreign banking institutions).

In quantity terms, the relative importance of these forms can be illustrated by data showing the breakdown of US investment abroad and foreign investment in the US (this country is the largest world investor in other countries and also the largest market for investment coming in from foreign lands). At the end of 1989, US investment abroad totaled $1338 billion dollars, including $84 billion (6 percent) in government loans, $373 billion (28 percent) in direct investment, $190 billion (14 percent) in foreign securities, $33 billion (2.5 percent) in private commercial loans and $658 billion (49 percent) in short-term foreign assets and bank loans. In the same year, foreign investment in the US totaled $2075 billion, including $337 billion (16 percent) in foreign official assets (mostly US government securities), $400 billion (19 percent) in direct investment, $625 billion (30 percent) in private portfolio holdings, $39 billion (2 percent) in private commercial loans and $674 billion (32 percent) in short-term assets or bank loans.[5] The breakdown of total world foreign investments is not noticeably different from these figures, though country data may show substantial divergence from the general pattern.

In terms of quantity the three most prominent items on both sides of this balance sheet are obviously bank short-term assets, direct investment and portfolio holdings. In terms of relative stability (defined in this case as opposite to volatility) direct investment ranks first followed by portfolio holdings and short-term capital (which is largely speculative). Direct investment is also important in other ways since it is necessarily and directly linked to the international flow of goods, the transfer of managerial talent, information and technology. Direct investment is also increasingly affecting relative international income levels and income distribution. Direct investment. This is largely a 20th century phenomenon, which, unlike trade, was of little practical importance in the 19th century. Official estimates on a world-wide basis first became available with the publication in the 8ds of UN reports on the activities of transnational corporations, and later of the Annual World Investment reports by UNCTAD (United Nations Conference on Trade and Development). These estimates show a rapid rise of direct investment stock in the 80s and 90s. From $479 billion in 1980 they rose to $745 in 1985, $11726 billion in 1990, $2866 in 1995 and $3233 billion in 1996.[6] The average annual growth rate was 13.7 percent in the 80s and 11.0 percent so far, in the 90s.

But overall, the rise in direct investment stock in 1980-1995 (6 times in current prices) was well ahead of the rise in world trade and world GDP (both -2.6 times). The ratio of direct investment stock to trade changed from 25.0 percent in 1980 to 56.5 percent in 1995 and the ratio of direct investment stock to world GDP rose from 4.6 percent in 1980 to 10.1 percent in 1995. In both cases the ratio more than doubled. The ratios of world direct investment flows, rather than of stock, are much smaller (6.1 percent to world trade and 1.1 percent to world GDP in 1995). But then it is the stock of capital that (together with other production factors) acts to produce output and sales, rather than one-year investment flows. Direct investment flows remained around 5.2-5.4 percent of world gross fixed capital formation, both in the 80s and 90s. Gross product of foreign affiliates amounted to 5.2 percent of world GDP in 1982 and rose slightly to 6.0 percent in 1994. According to the 1997 World Investment Report, one dollar of foreign direct investment stock generates value added worth 64 cents.[7]

Direct investment is usually associated with the expansion of transnational enterprise, since in most cases the controlling and managing investor is a corporation based in a foreign country. Therefore, one can safely conclude that the share of transnational corporations in global output has more than doubled in the last 15 years. It is more difficult to correctly calculate the share of such corporations in world trade and global output. There is evidence to the effect that between 1971 and 1991 the combined sales of the world's 500 largest multinational corporations have grown sevenfold (from $721 billion to $5.2 trillion).[8] The latter figure is about a quarter of global GDP. The comparison is valid since the sales figure includes both domestic sales within the base country, exports from it and also sales in other countries by units belonging to the TNCs.

Comparisons with world trade are more difficult since this involves estimates of the volume of international interchange which is performed both outside the TNCs and related to regular export sales and import buying and also the flow of goods between the various units inside one TNC but situated in different countries. One report gave the following breakdown of such flows in the mid-80s: 18 percent of total sales of TNCs are exports from the base country, 39 percent are sales of units situated elsewhere around the world, and the remainder, 43 percent are domestic sales in the base country. The share of foreign subsidiaries of TNCs in their total sales increased from 30 percent in 1970 to 40 percent in 1980 and to well over 50 percent in 1990. Because wages abroad were usually lower than in the home base country, the share of labor employed in foreign subsidiaries (56 percent) and in net profits (60 percent) is even higher.

Formerly most foreign subsidiaries in manufacturing were set up for the purpose of capturing the local market and markets of neighboring markets making it possible to avoid tariff barriers for direct exports. Most of such investment was in other industrially developed countries, for instance, US and Japanese plants in Europe, or European and Japanese plants in the US. In these cases, a significant part of components for assembly in foreign subsidiaries would be imported from the home base of the mother country. Later on, TNCs also started setting up manufacturing subsidiaries in developing countries with the purpose of producing low cost components, which would be used in their base country's assembly plants. Therefore a growing part of the output of such foreign subsidiaries is now being shipped back to the country, which was the source of capital investment in the first place. Of course, foreign subsidiaries in mining were nearly always used to supply manufacturing with cheap fuel and raw materials.

According to various private estimates, major multinationals account for one third of all world manufacturing exports, three fourths of all commodity trade and four fifths of trade in technology. More than 40 percent of US exports and nearly 50 percent of its goods are flows which occur inside TNCs and are not regular trade in open markets between nations (though counted as such in trade statistics).[9] Assuming that the same shares apply to exports and imports of Germany, Japan and United Kingdom we come up with a total for 1995 of $1635 billion, or 32 percent of world trade. Adding in other countries with large home based multinationals, one could probably come up with a general estimate of 40 percent of total world trade accounted for by intra-TNC goods flows. There are at least, three ways in which the rise of such flows are important. (1) They obviously explain the big surge in the dependence of output on trade in the last 15 years. (2) These are not genuine market flows generated by competitive determination of supply and demand and conducted in market determined equilibrium prices. (3) They are an expression of a totally new phenomenon in international economic activity, i.e. international planning as well as output, investment, sales, price determination on a supranational level.

Portfolio investment. We have not been able to come across or attempt to compile statistics of world portfolio investment in stocks and bonds. Judging by US figures, world totals could easily exceed total direct investment and, perhaps, reach $6 or 7 trillion. Unlike direct investment where geographical location of plants, availability of markets and supplies, wage rates, business infrastructure at location and similar conditions are very important, portfolio investment is largely guided by securities' yield, growth prospects, liquidity and speculative considerations. The country of issue is important but not overwhelmingly so. The best markets are, of course, those that are long established and easily accessible. For instance, annual trade in US bonds grew from $50 billion in 1983 to $500 billion in 1993, a tenfold increase in a decade, twice faster than the rise in world direct investment.

The dependence of governments on foreign buyers of public bonds differs from country to country and from one type of bond to another. Foreign holdings of US public debt securities of all kinds is relatively stable at 20 percent of their total value. In Russia, which is an emerging market with little experience and relatively unstable political climate, foreign investors now own up to 30 percent or more of outstanding Treasury bonds (so-called GKOs and OFZs). Eurobonds issued by various countries are held largely by foreigners, and this is a rapidly expanding market. All in all, world markets in government bonds have become a significant source of financing and re-financing rising public debt around the world. This trade is not only an outlet for relatively non-risk investment for institutions, firms and individuals, but also a means for speculation. World markets in government bonds are estimated to have reached a daily turnover of $200 billion every day (data for 1993), which translates into an annual figure of $60 trillion. This is more than twice larger than world GDP and nearly 12 times larger than world trade in goods.

World trade in stocks has also expanded rapidly but is substantially smaller than trade in bonds -$25 billion per day, or close to $4 trillion per year. Even so trade in stocks is only slightly smaller than world trade in goods. Because of the technical revolution in communications and liberalization of international capital flows, investors in most countries are now able to invest and trade in practically all stocks quoted in leading stock exchanges around the world either directly or through mutual and other investment funds. For instance, a typical offshore mutual fund run out of New York and with customers around the world would have diversified investments in stocks of companies in more than 30 countries, from the US, Japan and Hong Kong to Australia, Russia and China. Private savings in dozens of countries are being internationalized as one big pool available for investment in private companies on a world-wide scale. Short-term capital. This is represented mostly by foreign deposits in commercial banks. The world total in these assets is estimated at approximately $10 trillion in 1993. This is the most fluid and volatile part of international investment for the simple reason that most of such assets are constantly migrating from country to country in the endless process of cross-currency and interest rate arbitrage.

Total turnover in currency exchange markets has increased from $10 billion per day in 1973 to $1.3 trillion in 1993 an increase of 130 times in 20 years. Initially currency exchange was mainly meant to serve international exchange of goods and services. Today, annual trade in currencies exceeds $400 trillion, a staggering amount that is 80 times larger than world trade in goods (it was only twice as large in 1973). Obviously, the basic material foundation of currency trading has been lost in the last two decades together with the crossover to floating exchange rates. The total daily volume of currency exchange has exceeded total world official gold and foreign currency reserves countries and is much larger than the combined reserves of the G-7 central banks. Obviously, governments and central banks are not in a position to influence exchange rates by monetary interventions and have to rely largely on psychological stimulants to perform their duty of exchange rate stabilization.

Another effect of exploding short-term foreign capital is the rise of transnational banks. Most leading commercial banks have become multinational, followed by investment banks, insurance companies and other financial institutions. Without internal multinational networks of branches equipped with modern computer and Internet linkages the banks could not be able to physically perform these staggering volumes of operations. But also because of their involvement in securities speculation, servicing short-term capital movements, financing foreign clients, their stability has been reduced, if not undermined. As the experience of the last decade shows, bankruptcies of large banks are not as remote a possibility as they were just a few decades ago.

Trends

There are a few controversial issues arising from economic globalization. The issues for discussion in this section are:

1.   Are national economies still mostly self-contained or are they already mostly dependent on the world economy?
2.   Does globalization necessarily go step in step with trade and other economic liberalization?
3.   Is globalization promoting economic stability or is it working towards larger cyclical and other fluctuations?

Level of self-containment and globalization. It is obvious from the above statistics that the level of globalization is very different depending on which particular indicator is considered. International labor mobility is the least developed despite its apparent strong rise in recent decades. Trade interdependence is much higher than dependence on foreign labor though their exact comparison would have to take into account the impact of globalization on national wage rates. Capital mobility is the most developed part of international exchange, particularly in portfolio investment and short-term capital movements. Output interdependence can be rated to enjoy an intermediate position between these extremes.

UNCTAD has suggested an index of transnationality which is the average of ratios of foreign assets to total assets, foreign sales to total sales and foreign employment to total employment.[10] However, this index has so far been applied only to data for transnational corporations, not to the whole economy. If the top hundred TNCs are considered, then the index is 51 percent in 1995 for all industries and ranging from 38 percent for metals to 68 percent for construction. The industries that are known to be highly globalized-automotive, electronics and petroleum-carry indexes of 44 percent, 49 percent and 50 percent, while the seemingly more domestic oriented food and beverages industry has a much higher index of 61 percent.

The high rate of globalization characteristic of the top TNCs is, of course, related to the fact that they account for the predominant share of total outward-going foreign direct investment. This share for the top 50 TNCs in ten major capital-exporting countries is estimated between 52 percent for Germany and 63 percent for the US to 96 percent for Australia. What it means is that national economies are today a combination of two sectors-one represented by a small number of TNCs and oriented largely towards the outside economy, and a majority of smaller enterprises with a predominant domestic orientation. Part of them are subcontractors for the TNCs and therefore also indirectly integrated into the transnational network but their share, to our best knowledge, has so far not been estimated.

Because of this duality it is easy to both exaggerate and underestimate the actual level of globalization of national economies. For instance, when the NBER indicates that foreign branches of multinational corporations account for about 15 percent of the world's industrial output, while 85 percent is produced by domestic corporations in single geographical locals,[11] It is probably right. But such branches should be seen as parts of much larger companies in which output in their home country is largely integrated or at least coordinated with output, sales and investment in their foreign affiliates. Assuming an average transnationality index of 0.48,[12] this implies a rough doubling of their figure. Now, 30 percent of the world's industrial output directly associated with globalization and not counting TNCs subcontractors, is a very high ratio of output interdependence.

There are other subtle globalization effects that are not captured by statistics. As indicated before, the overall share of services in total GDP has increased substantially in recent decades. Since most of them remain non-tradable (albeit more tradable than previously thanks to modern computer-tele-communications systems), the geographical scope of their immediate markets remains national or even local. However, as correctly indicated in the latest World Investment Report, some non-tradable services are being increasingly standardized. International hotel chains or transnational fast-food companies provide more or less the same product to consumers around the world while they are not necessarily linked through trade. It is true that most international trade and capital flows are accounted for by exchange among the most industrially developed countries. The share of trade between them in total world trade is increasing. High-income economies accounted for 69.6 percent of world exports and 74.2 percent of world imports in 1980. Their shares expanded to 77.7 and 76.8 percent respectively in 1995.[13] The share of developed countries in world outward stock of foreign direct investment was 97.8 percent and 77.8 percent in world inward stock in 1980. These figures changed to 91.0 and 70.2 percent respectively in 1996.[14] The trend towards more investment integration between the developed and developing countries is clearly seen but the interflow of capital among the richer nations remains by far predominant.

Both country groups have increased their dependence on external trade and capital flows. Goods exports were on the average 42,9 percent of the non-service GDP of high income countries in 1980 rising to 52,1 percent in 1995. The same ratios for the rest of the world changed from 33,7 percent in 1980 to 40.3 percent in 1995.[15] The developed countries are on the average more dependent on external trade than developing countries. The ratio of inward stock of foreign direct investment to GDP has become more important for both groups of countries rising from 4.8 percent in 1980 to 9.1 percent in 1995 in the developed countries and from 4.4 to 15.4 percent in the developing countries.[16] It is probably correct to conclude that both international trade flows and foreign investment have become significant factors affecting overall economic performance of most parts of the world.

However, the extent of global interdependence should not be exaggerated. While production in TNCs is about equally divided today between the home country and foreign markets, overall economic activity, on the average, within national boundaries remains the dominant part of total economic activity. In section we consider in more detail country and regional deviations from this general proposition. Interdependence and liberalization. National and concerted policy measures to enhance freer movement of trade and capital flows across borders have been on the rise in the recent decade leading to a much higher degree of liberalization than at any time in the past. While this progress has been uneven in various countries and regions there have been no significant instances of regress towards official protectionism. However, this does not necessarily mean that trade is becoming less subject to various other constraints and that competition in international goods and capital markets has become more open. In fact, there are serious indications to the contrary.

The increasing share of world trade performed within transnational corporations is for all practical purposes isolated from open markets and direct competition. When Boeing (the largest world producer of aeroplanes) or Seagate (the top world producer of hard-disk drives for computers) import hundreds and thousands of components for their final assembly from different affiliates in different countries or sells its products to oligopolistically organized airlines, computer companies and governments around the world, there is next to no free competition since all such flows are either determined by intra-firm plans or by co-operative arrangements with other firms and governments.

Because the upsurge in globalization has largely taken the form of TNC expansion, in has led to increasing concentration on a global scale not only in terms of rising shares of top TNCs in total output and sales but also in rising collusion between potential competitors, mergers and acquisitions with a monopolizing effect, exclusionary vertical practices and predatory behavior.[17] As a result, entry of new producers in world goods markets is more restrained and competition is mainly restricted to oligopolistic rivalry between the giants of the industry. In such conditions relative advantages already gained and dominant positions acquired in the past by leading countries and companies tend to become ossified and even stronger-to the detriment of newly emerging competitors.

This trend is supported by the relative weakness or absence of competition law and competition policies regulating trade and investment flows and TNC practices. It is not clear to what extent such anti-monopoly policies could be effective in the face of strong technological inducements to concentration and collusion. The need for such policies on an international level is clear. Yet most of the necessary institutional and legal infrastructure has yet to be created.

Globalization, Growth and Instability

There is no evidence that rapid globalization has so far resulted in faster overall growth of the world economy. In fact, the evidence is quite to the contrary. World growth fell from the relatively high rates of 1950-1980 to much lower rates in 1980-1995, particularly in the 1990s and was more in line with the previous low rates of the first half of the century. If one correlates this change with the fact that 1950-1980 were the decades of flourishing Keynesian-type intervention of national governments in the economy and that the latter period was one of the demise of national state intervention and the rapid growth of neoliberal policies in line with globalization, then the conclusion leaps to the eye: globalization (at least in its present form) has certainly been a factor in seriously slowing down world economic growth. Whether other factors not directly tied to globalization were important in bringing about this result is a subject for further research. One would assume that rapid technical progress associated with privatization should have been a significant addition to the growth potential. However, if it did, it was certainly overcome by other factors working for deceleration.

The other effect is the growing economic instability that is more pronounced in the highly volatile capital and foreign exchange markets but which is also beginning to affect some sectors of the real economy. The world-wide stock market crash of October-November 1997 is one manifestation of this trend. Unlike the previous crash of 1987, which was mostly Wall Street rooted, the latest panic originated in Southeast Asia and was directly connected with speculative international capital entering the region in quantity in previous years and then leaving in a rush in response to local financial tremors. Something similar occurred in Mexico in 1994. But the main question this time around is why did the relatively small bourses of Hong Kong and neighboring countries so seriously affect the much larger markets in Japan, Europe and the US. Why was the tail able to wag the dog?

One reason is that the crises in Southeast Asia were caused in part by serious troubles in their real economies and particularly in the sectors that are strongly integrated with the world economy via the TNCs. The companies most seriously hit in New York and elsewhere in the rich countries were TNCs with high-tech component producing affiliates in Thailand and Malaysia. Also hit were leading transnational banks with large and sometimes questionable assets in the same region. Underlying the crisis were overproduction and sales problems of these industries accentuated by wide currency fluctuations which tended to undermine their competitive position in world markets.

This leads us to a hypothesis first suggested to our knowledge by William Greider[18] in 1997 but well before the recent crisis. Greider believes that the rapid expansion of foreign affiliates of TNCs tends to create overcapacity in the relative industries since it adds new capacity in new countries without the compensatory elimination of old capacity in the richer part of the world. This over-expansion can be financed only by higher profit margins which are based on utilizing low-cost labor in the poorer countries as well as eliminating high cost jobs and pressuring wages to stagnate in the richer countries. As a result, consumer demand tends to lag behind rising output which should eventually lead to an overproduction crisis of major proportions. Unlike Keynesian policies, neoliberal and monetarist policies are not equipped to prevent or mitigate overproduction problems. Effective anti-crisis intervention has been long rejected by national governments and concerted intergovernmental action in areas not related to exchange rates and short-term financial fire-fighting is all but absent.

Countering Greider's thesis is the claim that the richer countries are not too dependent on new countries where most of the overproduction is bound to concentrate.[19] However, as the recent crisis has demonstrated, some richer countries, like Japan and Korea, are more dependent than others on trade with the regions and recessions in these countries would inevitably also *affect* the US and Europe. Globalization tends to increase the exposure of stronger economies to crises in weaker economies. The linkage in trade and other goods flows is magnified by linkages in intra-TNC finance and short-term capital volatility. A combination of these could reach a critical mass sufficient to set off a chain reaction. These hypotheses are new and not tested by either practice or by economic theory. There is room for additional serious academic research in this area.

Has globalization reached its top limits? How much room is there for further economic integration? Are national economies bound to disappear giving way to one integrated world economy? Definite answers to these questions will be known only in the next century, something we can only hypothesise about. As pointed out above, apart from the TNCs, domestic economic ties in the world as a whole (and in most countries) are still larger than the flows between nations. This conclusion is true on the average and for most national economies. In large countries with large populations, the share of external ties tends to be smaller, all other factors being equal. Thus, in the group of high income economies, Japan and the US are the two countries with the lowest ratios of exports of goods and services in total GDP (9 and 11 percent) while the two countries with the highest shares are

Singapore and Hong Kong (207 and 147 percent). All these countries, as well as the ones with average shares (Germany and France), are highly integrated with the world economy by any modern criteria.

It is not believable that most countries in the high-income economies group would tend to converge in statistical trade dependence to figures cited for Hong Kong or Singapore. But it is quite possible for them to tend to come closer to the average level and even exceed them in future decades. This movement, if the past is any indication of the future, will probably be rather slow. In 15 years between 1980 and 1995 the share of exports of goods and services in US GDP has increased by a meager one percentage point (from 10 to 11 percent) and for Japan it even fell (from 10 to 11 percent) and for Japan it even fell (from 14 to 9).

The practical absence of any pronounced correlation between per capita income and trade dependence is well documented. Average shares are practically the same for all the country groups. Countries with very different economies in development level and structure tend to have approximately the same level of foreign trade dependence. It is therefore hard to believe that in the future, trade dependence will increase (at least substantially) in line with the rise in productivity and income per capita levels. As manufacturing industries and modern services develop in the lower-income economies, a substantial part of their output/ not necessarily linked to foreign TNCs, will tend to be oriented towards domestic markets before it is able to compete in international trade. This means that we do not expect dependence on foreign trade to rise very much in the coming decades. It is more probable that further economic interdependence will be shown in capital movements between countries. As demonstrated above, average ratios of inward foreign direct investment stock to GDP have risen substantially between 1980 and 1995 in both developed and developing economies. These ratios for 1995 in different country groups are interesting. Among the developed countries Japan and the US are, as in trade, among the least dependent. Yet in absolute value the US is by far the largest world attractor of foreign direct investment. One can hardly expect the US to integrate much more that it already has. On the other hand, Japan has a huge potential for attracting more direct foreign capital. As an international financial center it is already much more integrated. Some developed countries with relatively small economies tend to attract rather large foreign capital ranging from 28 to 44 percent on the ratio (Benelux, Australia, New Zealand). But other small developed countries, like Finland and Iceland lag far behind. Reasons for the difference are largely historical and geographical.

In the developing economies group many important countries are highly dependent on foreign capital, probably up to the limit (Singapore, Malaysia, Saudi Arabia), while many others are relatively less involved (Brazil, Thailand) but with a potential for further involvement. Still others are practically out of the picture. One country setting an example is China with its substantial stock of foreign capital that looks relatively moderate only in relation to its huge GDP (18.2 percent-most of it accumulated in the 1990s). Russia (with a ratio of only 1.1 percent) is still at the beginning of its integration in terms of direct foreign investment while its dependence on foreign trade (both exports and imports) is already fairly large for a big country.

Conclusion

One can hardly expect globalization to lead to the demise of the national economies within the observable future. The European Community is, of course, a special case. The success of EC integration (despite its many problem) underlines one of the most important barriers to further globalization and integration, i.e. the large differences in incomes in different groups of country. Integration has been more successful between developed countries with relatively close per capita incomes (and wage levels). Where the income gaps are large, integration proceeds but without any attempt at eliminating national economic barriers between countries. This relates first and foremost to TNC expansion in the developing countries. The problem, in a theoretical setting, is that in a world economy (were there are no national frontiers) labor should ideally be as mobile as capital in order for the system to reach maximum efficiency. In such a world, labor mobility would in the long run lead to a convergence of national wage rates as well as unit labor costs and profitability levels. Wage rates need not be exactly the same but the wide gap that exists today would have to be largely eliminated. In the long run that would probably mean a substantial rise in wage rates in the developing countries and a reduction of wage rates in the developed world. While in the developing world there should not be too much difficulty in raising wage rates from their current low levels, at least not in the near future, reducing wages or even keeping real wages stagnant in the richer countries is a process leading to social controversy.

These controversies are already evident even though national economic boundaries still very much in existence. This is particularly true in those richer countries were governments are permitting real wages to stagnate while local jobs are lost to foreign affiliates of large corporations. The US is one example of the erosion of trade union power that has gone along with the rise of TNCs. The resulting negative reaction is finally being felt. The recent lack of support in US Congress for 'fast-track' trade negotiating is largely due to pressure from organized labor on democratic congress members from large labor constituencies that are displeased by closed factories, lost jobs and stagnant wages as a result of production having been moved to low-wage countries.

While national governments are in existence, conflicts such as these will gain force unless some way is found to resolve the issue in a smoother manner than the current downsizing. The latter is generally accepted in the richer countries as a progressive 'reform' that should be modeled on the US example. It is doubtful that it is, in fact, the best way of resolving the problem. On the other hand, the TNCs are vitally interested in retaining national borders in the developing countries which serve as natural barriers to absolute labor mobility and thus help keep wages in these countries from rising too fast. To make the point clearer (and, perhaps, closer to reality), consider the case of two former communist countries in Europe that are being integrated into the world system, albeit in two very different way. These two countries are East Germany (former German Democratic Republic) and the Czech Republic. Both were roughly comparable in industrial structure, wage rates and per capita incomes prior to the fall of communist regimes in 1989. But one was integrated into a larger Germany, as part of that country while the other retained its sovereignty.

In Eastern Germany wage rates were substantially increased and brought up to about 70 percent or more of their level in Western Germany though output in the eastern lands is still way below its pre-unification peak and unemployment there is much higher. This had a controversial effect on the economy of the united country and has created financial and political problems for the German government. In Czechia real wages were reduced by market reforms, but mass unemployment was avoided and output levels have exceeded the pre-reform peak. The reason for raising wages in East Germany was that the government in Bonn was now responsible for the residents of that region who were equal in voting rights with other Germans and thus had a claim on the resources of a united country. But the Czechs had no 'rich big brother' to care for them. Their integration into the EC is delayed. Lower wages (perhaps four or five times lower than in Germany) are the 'price' paid for retaining their national identity. Of course, unlike East Germany, Czechia had no other choice. The moral of the story is that retaining national borders is in the interests of TNCs because it helps sustain barriers to international labor mobility. When borders are eliminated, the gap in income levels is reduced too fast and this will never happen unless there is an overriding political or other non-economic benefit to be gained by political integration.

Therefore, while economic and even political integration between the richer countries might proceed in the foreseeable future at a respectable rate, integration between the richer and the poorer parts of the world will remain restricted to certain trade and capital flow liberalization measures but will not extend to elimination of national borders, either economically (common market, free flow of goods, labor and capital, common currency etc.) or politically (common government institutions).

Notes

1. Andre Gunder Frank, ReOrient: Global Economy in the Asian Age, University of California Press, forthcoming.
2. I quote here from the Prospectus of the Gorbachev Foundation's Research Project on Globalization: 'Our initial hypothesis is that the survival and development of mankind is increasingly dependent on its ability to effect a profound spiritual reformation, to be followed by a dramatic reordering of the social, economic and cultural patterns of its development. The Project is, in fact, an attempt to verify this hypothesis'. Let me say directly that this approach is very different from the approach taken by Francis Fukuyama in his 'End of Civilisation' who, for all practical purposes offers one and only one model for the future of humanity.
3. Angus Maddison, Monitoring the World Economy, OECD, Paris, 1995.

4.   The World Bank provides most figures for individual countries but fails to calculate and publish world totals.
5.   Source: Economic Report of the President of the US, 1990. Interestingly enough, in 1972 direct investments were 52 percent of total US assets abroad (as compared to only 28 percent in 1089) while short-term capital was a meagre 8 percent of the toml compared to 49 percent at the end of the 80s. The trend is clear.
6.   The source is 'World Investment Report 1997', UNCTAD, Geneva, pp.4-313.
7.   Ibid., p.16.
8.   From the 'World Investment Report 1993' as cited by William Greider, 'One World, Ready or Not? The Manic Logic of Global Capitalism', Simon & Schuster, New York, 1997.
9.   Ibid., pp.21-22.
10.   World Investment Report 1997, pp.33-34.
11.   R. E. Lipsey, M. Blomstrom, E. Ronstetter, 'International Production in World Output', National Bureau of Economic Research, Working Paper 5385, 1995.
12.   World Investment Report, p.28.
13.   World Development Report, 1997, p.243.
14.   World Investment Report, 1997, pp.313-319.
15.   Calculated from data in World Development Report, 1997.
16.   World Investment Report, 1997, pp.339-341.
17.   For a detailed discussion of these aspects see World Investment Report, 1997, pp.133-178.
18.   William Greider, 'One World, Ready or Not? The Manic Logic of Global Capitalism', Simon and Schuster, New York, 1997.
19.   This thesis has sounded not only in Mr. Greenspan's public statements but also (among academic economists) by Paul Krugman as quoted in the 'New York Times', November 17, 1997.

Chapter 17

Some Theoretical Foundations of Russian Economic Policies

A. Nekipelov

Introduction

A large number of publications has been devoted to the theory of economic transformation, and experiences accumulated by a large group of countries, which have embarked upon the issue of transition from command to market economies. However, though we know today much more about this process than ten years ago there are still serious difficulties in understanding the nature of this process, optimal economic policies and even assessments of economic transformation efficiency in different post-socialist states. Moreover, in a sense, we can speak now of a kind of 'ossification' of basic approaches to market transition, which is manifested in a clear division of scholars between the proponents and opponents of the Washington consensus paradigm.

To a certain degree such a state of affairs can be explained by natural and, in essence, inevitable differences in value judgments between scholars. Those of them who appreciate most of all individual freedom are expected to be more to rant towards proliferation of poverty, which often accompanies reforms, than those who place much more importance to the principles of social justice and solidarity. From purely scientific point of view division of scholars with regard to optimal strategy of post-socialist transformation is based on their attitude towards main currents of economic thought – monetarism, on the one hand, and (neo) Keynesianism and institutionalism, on the other. As a result, the discussion is centered on issues relating to the expedient speed of economic liberalization, privatization of state property, management of aggregate demand and formation of market institutions. Doing so researchers often overlook the fact that the post-socialist states confront some problems, which do not exist in a mature market economy. Evidently, neither monetarist, nor Keynesian approaches should be expected to be efficient in dealing with such issues. The list of these specific transition problems includes massive reallocation of resources and formation of genuine market agents.

Reallocation of Resources

There are no scholars who doubt that huge reallocation of resources should accompany transition to market from planned socialist economies. Perhaps, because of the evident character of the general conclusion some important aspects relating to the nature of this process remain unobserved. To simplify the analysis let us suggest that a post-socialist economy has no other differences from a mature market economy than specific allocation of resources it inherits from a command economy. In other words, we shall now examine a model, which could emerge in practice only if all institutional changes needed to transform a command socialist economy in genuine market economy were carried out 'overnight'.

The reasons why immediate start of full-fledged market mechanism in formerly command-type economies provokes serious redeployment of the factors of production are obvious. First, the decisive factor determining allocation of resources between competing uses radically changes: it is now rather demand (both private and public) that dictates allocation rather than state-established plan targets. Secondly, state priorities themselves undergo significant changes as compared to old system (renunciation of excessive militarization of the economy, hypertrophied development of heavy industry, changes in principles of integration in the global economy). As a result, introduction of market mechanism sends, under these conditions, numerous waves from prices to costs and, back, from costs to prices. These waves necessitate an adequate adjustment of production to follow. The situation is further complicated by the fact that economic units themselves undergo restructuring of their productive assets in conformity with a change in motivation. New goals are profits and net worth as opposed to fulfillments of plan targets of the precious era.

It should be noted that all these processes are of microeconomic character; they are directly related to modifications in the structure of demand and output rather than to their aggregate dimensions. The mechanism of these changes is well known: it is similar to microeconomic shifts in production under the influence of evolving consumer preferences. The major difference is that of scale: one thing is a change in production as a result of shift of consumer preferences from, say, chocolate to ice cream, another redeployment of productive assets under the influence of a set of new motifs pursued by economic agents.

No doubt, the process of transition has macroeconomic dimensions as well. However, their analysis is accompanied with methodological problems, which are often overlooked in the literature. The latter are linked to the fact that macroeconomic notions of market economies cannot be applied directly to a command economy. Let us examine the problem of consumer expenditures and savings. Under socialism households make their own decisions with regard to current expenditures and savings and, from this point of view, there is no difference between their behavior in a command economy and the behavior of households in mature market economies. At the same time non-equilibrium prices and resulting shortages of many consumer goods created distortions in the division of household incomes between consumption and savings as compared with market conditions.

Differences in the sphere of production are even greater. Under a command economy the fact that an enterprise has money on its current account with a bank by no means implies that it can freely buy any goods it needs. Significant amounts of money are effectively blocked on bank accounts until these enterprises succeed to receive the so-called 'funds' (permission to buy fixed amount of commodity from a particular producer). This means that respective sums of money, in fact, cannot be regarded as 'universal equivalent', and therefore as genuine money – as a medium of exchange. During the transition to market economy the situation changes radically. Socialist pseudo-money becomes genuine means of payment, pseudo-prices and pseudo-interest rates transform respectively to genuine prices and genuine interest rates. The formation of equilibrium prices and interest rate takes place under the influence of (and in conformity with) money supply, aggregate demand and output. As a result markets adjust levels of consumer, investment and government spending.

It should be noted that though the general price level has to increase within a transition framework, this is rather a result of the transformation of these so-called 'socialist commodity-money instruments' into real market-regulators. The rise in price levels is not due to growing aggregate demand. It is necessary to control this inflation and one can easily see that it is qualitatively different from inflation in a market economy. To do so it is sufficient to freeze a part of household and enterprise deposits at the outset of market reforms; later on they should be gradually unblocked.

Another phenomenon with macroeconomic consequences, which is often overlooked, is the presence of a friction in the economic system, which puts obstacles in the way of quick adaptation of the economy to a radically new demand structure. In particular, one has to take into account the fact that possibilities of resource reallocation are limited due to a physical specificity of factors of production used in different sectors of the economy. Thus, changes in individual and public preferences resulting from market transition leads to under-utilization of existing productive assets (human capital being one of them), at least in the short-run. This means that the short-run aggregate supply schedule finds itself far to the left from the potential output curve, being at the same time inelastic wi'h regard to the price level. Its gradual shift to the right can proceed parallel to market induced resource reallocation and without any relationship to price level. In this respect one can assert that the transition is accompanied by a kind of supply-side shock, which is the major reason for stagflation – encountered by all post-socialist states during initial years of transition. It is noteworthy that in this case the increasing price level is rather a result of falling output than growing aggregate demand. Similarly, emergence of excess productive capacities and structural unemployment is a consequence of changes in the structure of efficient demand. A big danger for an economy suffering from this kind of structural shocks is to drag the process of adaptation for so long that a significant part of physical and human capital gets completely lost. This phenomenon can be called 'systemic hysteresis' using the term aimed to describe the well-known macroeconomic situations when current market variations result in adverse changes in the long-term path of economic development. The nature and problems of market reallocation of resources should be taken into account when devising economic policy. Several things have to be discussed here.

On the Efficiency of Keynesian Recipes for Economies in Transition

Let us cast a look at the expediency of effective demand stimulation in Russian economy. My point is that the relevance of Keynesian recipes may be weak. Existence of excess capacity under these circumstances is a result of changes in the structure of aggregate demand and not due to a reduction in its level. One should not also confuse a lack of aggregate demand with a lack of money experienced by some economic agents. Keynes, as is well known, understood by demand deficit the situation when economic agents did not want to spend money they had. That is why proposals to pursue expansionist monetary and fiscal policy are fraught with adverse economic consequences as well as with discredit of Keynesianism in Russia. I believe, therefore, that under normal economic environment it would be expedient for the Russian State to carry out pragmatic fiscal and monetary policies targeting steady economic growth with acceptable, from macroeconomic point of view, level of inflation (up to 15-20 percent a year). It should be noted that in the period of mass reallocation of resources some inflation could be even useful, as it would act as a kind of lubricant helping the economy to get adjusted to new systemic conditions.

On the Mitigation of Structural Shock

The second problem, also being a subject of sharp polemic, relates to the expedient use of structural-shock mitigation. The need for some kind of 'anesthesia' in some degree is acceptable to everybody. Representatives of the mainstream argue the relevance of creating a social safety net. They are skeptical about a passive (that is aimed exclusively on amortization of structural break-up) industrial policy, as they believe, that such a policy is fraught with a preservation of inefficient production activities. They also highlight the arbitrariness of the civil officers and proliferation of corruption with a passive policy. Though such dangers do exist, they should not be considered fatal. Mechanisms, ensuring gradual, but stead pressure of the market upon restructuring production brunches, as well as the methods of reforming civil services, need to provide for qualitative improvement of its efficiency. At the same time, placing the burden of adaptation on tools of social policy can lead to a serious loss of potentially effective industries. It will also lead to excessive financial costs of creating such an overwhelming social safety net. That is why the best method to adjust Russian economy to the requirements of the market consists, in my opinion, in combining the tools of (passive) industrial, and social policies.

On Activist Government

The third problem also has a normative character and can be formulated as follows: does society always agree that an allocation of resources takes place in strict conformity with the requirements of the market?

As is well known, perfect competition leads to an efficient use of economic resources and thereby posits the economy on the so-called production possibility frontier. In this rather narrow sense the market system is desirable. But it is also known that the particular point on this frontier will not necessarily conform to the equity that churns serious issues concerning social justice, desirable structures of production and roles of nations in the global economy. That is why a society can consciously prefer Pareto-inefficient state of the economy.

What is good, and similarly what is bad is a 'question of taste'. From the point of view of a society as a whole, it is a question of prevailing preferences. The revelation of preferences is a function of political system. But an aim of positive economic research consists in describing results of realization of different economic policies and in this regard economists with different value judgments should not differ very much in their conclusions.

One can hardly deny the fact that liberal economic policies are a tool of reaching production frontier with income differentiation that depends on the initial distribution of properties, knowledge and abilities among members of a society. In today's Russia such policies would freeze huge inequality in wealth distribution and cause further shift of the industrial structure towards extraction of natural resources. If the society is not happy with this perspective it simply has no alternative active social and industrial policies within a sound market framework. Only by correcting (not undermining!) the action of market forces it can, under these conditions, grope for desirable social relations, realization of dynamic comparative advantages and ambitious economic and social. Of course a loss of a part of the current income and consequent human hardship may well be the price of such policies.

I am sure that there are few people in Russia who would be satisfied with the loss of human capital and technological potential along with further shift towards specialization on production of raw materials, which results from the country's static comparative advantages. This is quite understandable especially if one takes into account the fact that simple regrouping of human and production resources could produce a major market effect in the future according to dynamic comparative advantages of the country.

Russia also needs to take clear position with regard to the production of social goods. The necessity to do so is related to the fact that the supply of merit goods cannot be determined by the market, whereas the outcome of market forces for non-merit may not be accepted by the society as socially optimal. Under these conditions the spelling out of ecological, social and other standards becomes one of the main tasks of the government. Similarly, it is very important to take into account the prevailing opinions on social justice when formulating the strategy of socio-economic development. No doubt, social targets cannot be independent of the amount of resources at the society's disposal. Theoretically speaking, to ensure optimal use of the latter one needs a 'map of social indifference curves' and a discount rate to compare the results achieved in different time-periods. The respective set of parameters, reflecting social preferences, can only be provided by a political system. Many 'mainstream' Russian economists seem to believe that adjusting economic policies to value judgments of population (which they think in Russian case are outdated or even soviet-type and, therefore, 'wrong') has nothing to do with economic approach. They do not notice that this kind of reasoning is in contradiction with basic notions of modem economic thought: the latter rather examines the results of these or those individual preferences for allocation of limited resources than makes judgments with regard to their quality. Consumer choice theory considering individual tastes as an exogenous factor is a good example. Are there really any reasons to treat group preferences differently?

Thus, the necessity of government intervention in economic matters is predetermined by the fact that some problems, in principle, cannot be resolved by the market, whereas in other cases market outcomes do not conform to social preferences. It is important, however, that introducing corrections in resource allocation in accordance with national interests the government does not undermine the workings of the market mechanism.

While collecting taxes governments get an opportunity to affect allocation of resources. At the same time it has numerous indirect methods, rducing taxes or extending subsidies, introducing export promotion measures, setting up import limiting tariffs, creating stimuli for formation of competitive corporations concentrating both production and finance activities, making steps aimed at attracting foreign capital etc. The government is also entitled to establish price control for those goods and services produced by natural monopolies.

To choose optimal tools of industrial policy is, by no means, a simple thing, because the same tools can be attained differently. For example, one can defend national production both by creating tariff barriers and extending subsidies to indigenous producers. It is also not easy to decide whether it is better for Russian to stimulate the manufacturing sector by keeping energy prices at low level; or by directly subsidizing manufacturers while allowing energy prices to attain the world level. It is, however, important that the respective decisions be taken on the basis of concrete analysis rather then on simplified and ideological notions on what is the realm of 'market' and what is not.

It is very important to design the industrial policy in such a way that the market pressure upon the priority sectors grow in a gradual but steady fashion. It is not a good idea, for instance, just to introduce high tariffs for defending selected industries. The schedule of their reduction to normal level should be adopted simultaneously, thus pushing national producers rather to adapt to than to isolate from the world market.

No doubt, the implementation of an industrial policy is linked to a significant redistribution process, which can only be carried out by the executive power (both federal and regional). Thus, to pursue such policy, it is necessary to keep the level of government spending (and revenues) rather high. For a long period in Russia government revenues have been rather low (about 35 percent of GDP). It is only recently it has achieved the 40 percent mark as a result of hike in oil prices on the world market. It should be noted that in most successful post-socialist countries this indicator varies between 40 and 50 percent while in OECD countries as a whole it equals approximately half of their GDP. Of course, the aim is not to artificially 'inflate' this indicator in Russia taking resources from entrepreneurial sector of the economy. One has to understand that pursuing an active industrial policy is impossible with concentration of significant funds in government coffers.

One can often hear that an industrial policy is something like a philanthropic donation of funds by a government to all those who need it. This is a deeply erroneous idea. Now in Russia an implementation of active industrial policy is also linked to the admission of harsh realities: For Russia the prospect for being in the backwater of the world economic community for many decades is now very realistic. That is why conditions should be created to concentrate very scarce resources in well-selected areas, which provide the country with a chance to return in foreseeable future in the ranks of developed nations. Tough market laws have to be given opportunity to carry out 'natural selection' among the remaining, non-priority industries.

It is true that pursuing industrial policy is accompanied with different risks. One can make a mistake in the selection of prospective directions of technological progress and economic development. It is not always easy to envisage reaction of other countries and international organizations to these, or those, measures in the economic sphere. This is important given the fact that not only firms, but states and even big regions compete today in the global economy. But the conclusion of all this is that the factor of uncertainty should be taken into account when designing industrial policy. There is nothing especially new in this requirement for both economic theory and policy. It looks very strange, however, when liberal policies are associated with the present conditions of the Russian economy with its modernization and with mitigation of inequalities in wealth distribution. To my mind, this line of propaganda, chosen by the Russian proponents of liberalism (in its European meaning), indirectly supports the well-known fact that the country's population is quite unsusceptible to purely liberal values.

Formation of the Market Agents

Up to the present moment we recognized that a post-socialist economy works according to the standard market laws. Whether this conclusion is consistent with the reality is extremely important from the point of view of both directions of further research, and policy recommendations. We shall consider this question using the example of Russian economic system as it has emerged during the 1990s. If we come to conclusion that a normal market economy has developed in Russia during this period, then scientific and political discussions should concentrate on the standard set of problems for this type of economy: e.g. which kind of monetary and fiscal policy should be carried out? Do we really need an active industrial policy? And if so, how should it be realized?

Some thoughts are available to support this approach. In Russia the mechanism of command management have been done away with completely and significant liberalization of economic activities has taken place. The basic institutions of market economy (private property, main infrastructure for commodity and factor markets) have been laid down; and market signals (prices, interest and exchange rates etc.) are being formed in the market sphere. At the same time there are some circumstances that raises questions about the efficacy of markets. As an example, an unprecedented split between financial and industrial spheres is only one of them. It is also impossible to explain the long-term absence of the link between the interest rate and the yield of capital in the real sector of economy. Attempts to explain high interest rates – which dominated the Russian economy up to 2000, by references to high risks of investments in production, to my mind – explain little. Not only the question on nature of such risks, which make all industrial activities unprofitable, it also remains unclear what is the explanation. No answer is given to the obvious question relating to the sources from which payments of those extraordinary interests were made. The explanation of 'demonetization' of the real sector of the economy is not convincing. First of all, it begs a question of why in normal market economies nothing of the kind occurs. A standard result of toughening monetary policy is a deflationary shock. In Russian it led to a situation with an obvious split between the domain of price and output levels, on the one hand, and the domain of money supply on the other. Secondly, statistical data quite definitely testify to the absence of a positive correlation between money supply rates of growth and 'degree monetization' of the economy.

One also witnesses an inadequate reaction of the Russian economy to market signals and standard measures of economic policy. To characterize the first phenomenon it is enough to refer to weak dependence between employment and demand for production. Second one can be demonstrated on an example of fiscal policy. An attempt to characterize the Russian fiscal policy, pursued till 1999, with the aid of standard approaches leads nowhere. On the one hand, the presence of high budget deficit, as it may seem, testifies to a softness of financial policy. But on the other hand, during this period the constant reduction of government spending had been going on. In other words, budget deficit remained at a high level not because expenditures were inadmissibly high, but because reduction in government spending was accompanied by even faster fall of budget incomes. In my view, these and other similar phenomena testify to the emergence in Russia of a 'quasi-market' economic system that functions in conformity with the laws – rather different from those of a normal market economy. But if one agrees with this conclusion, then the following questions arise: should Russia go on with this current economic system? Should Russia take more measures aimed at transforming it into a genuine market economy? The answer to these questions are to shape further discussion concerning particular measures of economic policy. Absurdities of the economic model, which emerged in Russia, are so obvious, that no one, in my belief, will insist on its perpetuation. But to force a national economy to function in conformity with the market laws, it is necessary first of all to understand the reasons of today's distortions.

Distortions in Behavior of Economic Agents and their Consequences

Banal is the statement that economic agents behave differently in conditions of market economy, than under a command socialist economy. First, what strikes one's eye when comparing two systems is freedom of decision-making by enterprises in the first case and the absence of that freedom in the second. This fair observation leads to a correct conclusion that it is impossible to start the market mechanism without a dismantling system of command management of economy. Therefore it is imperative to take steps aimed at liberalization of economic activity.

But the specific behavior of market agents is linked not only to freedom of decision-making, but also to their motivation. The originality in formulating this idea in connection with the problems of market transformation should be given to J. Kornai. In a famous book Kornai convincingly showed how completely decentralized system can function according to the rules, which are qualitatively different from those of market economy. The ten-year experience of post-socialist transformation provides us with sufficient materials to make further theoretical generalizations in this regard. First, the experience gained during Russian reforms testifies to the fact that the problem of market motivation may not be satisfactorily resolved with privatization of state properties, at least such privatization, which took place in Russia. Secondly, countries such as Hungary, Poland, Slovenia (let alone China and Vietnam) have clearly demonstrated, that the switch of economy in more or less normal market mode of functioning is possible with conservative approaches to privatization of state assets.

The fact is, the motivation and action of an economic agent depend directly on property rights rather than the form of ownership. The former relates to the character of mutual relations between owners of the capital and enterprise managers. This nuance becomes essential in conditions of separation of management from the property on capital. First, enterprises can now have many owners, and, second, a problem of subordinating their activity to the interests of capital owners appears.

In the Russian model of privatization there existed a whole number of elements, which led to the formation of a highly distorted system of corporate management within large and medium-size enterprises. Deficiencies in legislation referring to joint-stock companies, which did not provide for due protection of the rights of minority shareholders, resulted and continue to result in orientation of the so-called 'strategic investors' on pumping out enterprise assets in their own pocket rather than on maximizing firm's net worth. High dispersion of shares, which resulted from voucher privatization, made it possible to engage in this fascinating business with a very small share of the firm's capital. The situation was aggravated by the fact that during privatization the problem of management of assets still remaining in state property was completely ignored. Given a rather significant share of state-owned capital in many privatized enterprises it is easy to understand how their managers and/or some shareholders have succeeded to subordinate the activity of such enterprises to their own purposes. I am convinced, that the distortion of property rights represents rather a systemic factor than an individual defect of the Russian economic system; ultimately, it is what determines all specific features in functioning of Russian economy.

From what has been told it follows clearly that an absence of an effective control by the owners of capital of enterprise activity the respective firm tends to become rather an object of primitive asset-stripping on the part of enterprise management and/or individual shareholders than an object of application of creative efforts. The mechanism of this asset-stripping takes the form of market transactions, wherein financial sphere is involved. In these conditions the level of equilibrium interest rate is being determined not so much by demand for capital, needed for creative production activity, as by demand for credits, used in diverse schemes of capital withdrawal from real sector enterprises. In many respects it is here that we have to search for final causes of an unusual separation of financial sphere from the real economy in Russia, as well as of a surprising, on the first sight, discrepancy between low yield of investments in real sector of the economy and exorbitant interest rates.

This is not to say that the demand for credits, used in diverse schemes of withdrawal of capital from enterprises, was a unique factor, determining an unusually high level of interest rates in Russia. Liberalization of a command economy results in huge differences in profitability between various branches of economic activity. Accordingly, some of them receive an opportunity to attract additional capital paying very high interest rates. As a good example, an unusually high profitability of imports of consumer goods in Russia immediately after opening our retail market can be cited. However, in any case it is important to take into account the fact that it is impossible to fully understand dynamics of interest rates in Russia without paying attention to that part of demand for credits, which was determined by, so to say, destructive purposes. That is why the assertion that high interest rates were provoked by high yields of GKO (state short-run bonds) seems doubtful. Rather the inverse is true: the state had to admit so high profitability of investments in GKO because it had to compete in markets of loanable funds with other borrowers, who were ready to pay high interests.

It would have been very strange if people engaged in cannibalizing joint-stock capital in to their own pockets, had admitted the introduction of transparent systems of financial accounting and reporting at enterprises. But in the absence of authentic documents characterizing firms' financial position in securities markets inevitably turn into a kind of casino. Their quotations have practically no relation to efficiency of capital in this, or that, area of real economy. Property rights distortions are, to my mind, also directly related to 'demonetization' of Russian economy, though plenty of other factors are at work here as well. The absence of due control by shareholders over firm's management results in the latter engage rather easily in transactions fraught with damage for the former. In other words, one of the important obstacles in the way of inefficient decision-making has been eliminated and, as a result, even privatized enterprises are characterized by soft budget constraints. Of course, the question remains: why should managers need to supply their output to insolvent consumers, even if they personally do not suffer any special losses as a result of these transactions? The answer is not unequivocal.

On the one hand, in conditions of production restructuring there exists a significant degree of uncertainty concerning the prospects of demand for a commodity. Such a situation encourages managers to supply firm's output to enterprises, which at a particular moment do not have money, but which, probably, will receive them after selling their own products. Proliferation of similar expectations among managers, who, in effect, do not take any risk upon them, results in fast accumulation of mutual debts. As the number of insolvent enterprises rises barter transactions become more and more common. Thus, soft budget constraints at a micro level produce a split between money supply and price level. On the other hand, it is known, that arrears and barter are frequently used for tax evasion. However, it should be noted that appropriate schemes frequently result not only in low tax incomes for the government, but also in a redistribution of the capital between shareholders of appropriate enterprise and its managers. It is obvious; therefore, that improvement in corporate governance (that is rationalizing property rights) would eliminate, from the enterprise's opportunity set, the use of such schemes of tax-evasion.

Proliferation of in-kind transactions in the real sector of the economy makes it impossible to collect taxes in a normal way, contributes to budget deficit, state non-payments and thereby back-fire at the further demonetisations of the economy. The loop gets closed: the state does not pay for its own orders, as it cannot collect the taxes, and financial position of enterprises gets worse because some of them fail to receive payment for the goods they supplied to the state.

From what has been said about distortions of Russian economic system it follows, that to switch it in a mode of normal market system it is necessary, first of all, to introduce such changes in property rights, which would make enterprises maximize profit in the short-run and net worth of the firm – in the long run. Creation of effective mechanism for management of state assets (including their privatization) is an important part of this problem. At last, in order to make the market mechanism work, it is necessary to clean balance-sheets of all economic agents (including the state) off all overdue debts; otherwise enterprises, even after rationalization of property rights, will be simply blocked financially. Such restructuring of balance sheets will inevitably produce some increase in money supply.

It is sometimes specified that the formation of 'virtual economy' in Russia is a way of its adaptation to market shock. True, arrears do soften current structural problems, but they realize this with great cost degradation of scientific and productive potential of the country. The consequences of such treatment appear to be more dangerous than the disease itself.

Improving Behavior of Economic Agents

Errors made by Russian reformers in the transformation of property rights resulted in the emergence of an extremely distorted system of corporate governance in a majority of big and middle-sized enterprises. The main issue here is to undertake measures, which would place the management of enterprises under a control of owners of capital and would thus reorient joint-stock companies towards profit maximization in the short-run and net-worth maximization of the firm in the long-run. Once implemented this would offer the basic prerequisites for adequate reaction by economic agents to market signals, create an efficient system of corporate governance, make it possible to introduce financial transparency in Russian enterprises. This will thus pave the foundation for efficient stock markets in Russia.

There are two main directions of actions here. First, it is necessary to complete – as soon as possible – the institution of the practice of legal mechanisms that will enable all shareholders to perform the functions as genuine owners a firm with sufficient protection for minority share holders. Secondly, given the fact that the state in Russia continues to remain a big owner, it is important to establish a system, which would guarantee a market type of management of the bulk of public assets. Such a mechanism based on setting up a state investment and holding company (or several companies) was designed and proposed by the author.

Introducing Changes in Economic Behavior of Authorities

An eradication of anti-market instruments of control, frequently used by Russian authorities at all levels, is of extreme importance for normalizing economic activity. To a significant degree an achievement of this goal is enmeshed with a consolidation of the rule of laws in the Russian society. At the same time it is necessary to reduce the tool-kit for economic management at the disposal of authorities.

A complete elimination of state arrears (including coercion to accept as a means of payment all kind of money surrogates) is especially important. To realize this aim I find it justifiable to introduce a law according to which the federal government should print money if it cannot fulfill its contractual obligations; or securitize them in a civilized manner. It is essential also that such facts become publicly known and regarded as an evidence of government's failure. It is also important that an inclusion of an organization by the government in the list of those consumers, to which supplies, say, of electricity, gas etc. may not be stopped under any conditions, be automatically accompanied by extension of government guarantees for the suppliers of the respective goods and services. Obviously, such measures are meant to improve responsibility of authorities for their contractual obligations rather than stimulate inflation.

As was mentioned, the emergence of in-kind economy in Russia is rooted in distortions in property rights and anti-market behavior of authorities. But a feedback also exists: solvency of the real sector of the economy constitutes an insurmountable obstacle for the normal workings of the market mechanism. That is why the task of monetizing the Russian economy is referred to here as a systemic one, absolutely essential for enforcing the standard behavior of economic agents. It is possible to settle this problem gradually, on the basis of a responsible attitude of authorities to their contractual obligations and resolute application of bankruptcy procedures to insolvent enterprises. These issues seem to be naïve, however they have gone beyond the stage when it could be successfully dealt with. To me there is no alternative today to the general overdue debt set-off. The idea is to clean balance sheets of all economic agents including that of authorities. Current accounts of all those economic agents, which have a surplus of overdue accounts receivable over overdue accounts payable, should be automatically credited with respective amounts of money. Net debts of those economic agents, which run deficit with regard to overdue financial obligations, have to be transferred to the government. The latter should make final decisions with regard to the destiny of such firms, major options being debt-equity swaps, extension of credit and initiation of bankruptcy procedures. It should be stressed that this overdue debt set-off can bring lasting results only if it is synchronized with realization of other systemic measures; otherwise its effect will be temporary.

On Other Structural Reforms

It is certainly good that after years of unilateral emphasis on issues of financial stabilization the proponents of the Washington consensus began to pay attention to the problem of institutions. As a result, the notion of 'structural reforms' emerged.

However, to my mind, the concept of structural reforms is still far from perfect, at least when applied to the economy. Two things have to be mentioned in this regard. First, there is a list of partial reforms without clear indication as to what is urgent and what is not. This approach is implicitly based on an understanding that transition economies are effectively normal market economies with partial deficiencies in some institutions. As I tried to demonstrate above, this is not true for Russia. Secondly, there is an obvious drive to use the concept of structural reforms to impose liberal ideology upon the respective states. My point is that the market system in transition economies should be adjusted in such a way as to address the concrete problems facing these countries and to the prevailing preferences in these societies.

Land Reform

Land (in broad meaning of the word, including all natural conditions of production) is by all means the most important production factor and, therefore, the existence of efficient mechanism of its allocation is a substantial prerequisite for an efficient economic outcome. It is also true that this mechanism should be based on market principles. The problem is whether it may be constructed exclusively on the basis of private ownership and free trade of land.

It is not true, as many Russian and foreign proponents of free land market claim, that there is no other way to introduce rationality both in agriculture and economy as a whole. It is a well-known fact that a market allocation of land can be carried out in conditions when public-owned land is leased out on a competitive basis to its users. Moreover, there exists a strong argument in favor of such leasing arrangement.

First, lease payments for the use of natural resources can, in the case of Russia, replace a significant part of traditional taxes. It is difficult to overestimate this fact: in contrast to standard taxes lease payments for natural resources ('rent') do not lead to distortions in resource allocation. Secondly, world experiences demonstrate that a free market of land based on private ownership is fraught with transformation of land into a speculative asset, the price of which can deviate from the level associated its real value. Financial bubbles, which develop on land speculation, can play a fatal role in provoking deep financial crises. This is one of the main reasons why in majority of states numerous restrictions on the use of private land have been enacted – often as a result of accumulating negative experiences.

It is hence much more important today to concentrate efforts on establishing an efficient system of leasing out public land (and other natural resources) to competitive uses than to engage the country in a new privatization campaign. After all a privatization of land (if considered necessary) will be much easier and fraught with fewer social conflicts after equilibrium lease rates have been formed in the market.

Reforming Financial Infrastructure

By all means, an introduction of unlimited convertibility of currency, inflexibility in regulation of money supply (introduction of currency board being the most logical proposal with this respect), provision for complete freedom of capital movement in and out of the country (including short-term capital), introduction of rigid measures of prudential supervision for banks – all this, according to formal criteria, perfectly corresponds to the process of globalization of the world economy. But alongside with the positive aspects of financial liberalization the risks, associated with it, are well known: national financial system become ideal conductor for external shocks. There is no secret also in the fact that resulting dangers are especially serious for the countries with weak financial institutions. But one should not forget that in Russia the situation is further aggravated by the possibility of financial shocks superimposing upon above described structural shock. That is why today it seems expedient rather to strengthen the financial sphere than to loosen it, to take restrictive measures with regard to transfers of short-term capital in and out of the country.

Existing experience shows that market economy is compatible with quite a broad range of models of monetary and financial infrastructure. This makes it possible to shape this sphere in accordance with particular problems encountered by the respective country. In the Russian case the latter are: weakness of financial institutions and the government's need of foreign exchange to meet foreign debt obligations. The proposals put forward in the next paragraph take account of these particular issues.

It should be admitted that in 1990-s the ruble has performed the money functions in a very limited degree. On the one hand, it was to a great extent replaced by barter transactions and non-payments in servicing exchange of goods in the real sector of the economy. On the other, foreign exchange has nearly substituted for the ruble as a means of wealth preservation (or as an asset) and, to a significant degree, as a means of circulation. The ruble has been nearly transformed in a kind of 'representative' of US dollar, in the sense that paper money used to be a symbol of gold in the era of gold standard. Proposals to introduce in Russia the so-called 'currency board' are aimed at leading this process to its logical end.

I am sure that Russia should not unilaterally give up its sovereignty in the monetary sphere. On the contrary, under certain conditions it may count on transforming the ruble in the reserve currency for CIS countries. That is why Russian authorities have to aim at achieving the following two-in-one target: to extend the ruble's sphere of action to the whole economy and to create favorable conditions for the ruble to perform all money functions.

The above-mentioned general overdue debt set-off would provide for the solution of the first part of the problem. Realization of the second part is linked to the elimination of demand for foreign currency as an asset. Under conditions of immaturity of financial infrastructure and significant debt burden it seems logical to limit domestic convertibility of the ruble for legal entities to current account transactions. In other words, the Central bank proposal of the beginning of 2000 to introduce obligatory sale by the exporters of all their foreign exchange proceeds in the foreign exchange market is totally justified. As in the Polish case, existing foreign exchange accounts might be preserved, but their replenishment excluded. The right to buy foreign currency In the market would have to be granted against Import contracts or foreign debt obligations.

However, nowadays an opposite idea is quite fashionable: with reference to the 'money overhang', resulting from mass inflow of foreign currency in the country, reduction in or even removal of obligatory sale of the currency is proposed. I think that the problem of excess liquidity can be resolved efficiently without such measures, which put additional obstacles in the way of the process of transforming the ruble in genuine money. The executive power should initiate creation of a special fund for meeting official foreign debt obligations. Using part of budget incomes for replenishing this fund the government would increase demand for foreign currency, thus assisting in keeping exchange rate at a desirable level, from a macroeconomic point of view, without printing additional money.

The sphere of financial institutions has been in bad shape during all period of reform/and has not fulfilled its main function of transforming savings in investment. The Russian securities market has been rather a 'decoration' than an efficient tool of resource allocation; the interbank money market has not been able to recover since its 1994 collapse, short-term credits to the real sector of the economy have been extremely limited, whereas long-term credits – nearly absent. Asset-side activities of commercial banks have been, in a significant degree, reduced to investments in government securities and foreign exchange. Basic weakness of financial infrastructure has clearly manifested itself in August 1998, when its effective collapse provoked huge losses by corporate and individual clients, nearly destroyed the payments system and put the country on the eve of the economic chaos.

Such a state of affairs is to a significant degree a result of various factors – many of whom are outside the financial sphere; as was argued above, separation of the latter from the rest of the economy is rooted in basic distortions of the economic system. One can hardly imagine a normal bank, which would extend credits to illiquid clients. However, complicated issues linked to financial recovery of this sector, rational division of function inside it, its interaction with international financial system and others do remain. Under current conditions the following algorithm of actions within this particular sphere seems expedient.

Policy aimed at financial recovery of the banking sector, introduction of its transparency and toughening of prudential requirements to its activity should be continued. General overdue debt set-off could significantly support this policy because it would remove confusion linked to uncertainty with regard to financial position of numerous economic agents (banks included), radically improve situation with their liquidity.

A set of measures aimed at orienting commercial banks mainly towards provision of firms with credits for financing their working capital requirements is needed. As far as long-term investments are concerned such financial intermediaries as investment, pension and insurance funds should play the major role in financing them. In particular, it seems expedient to reconsider the attitude towards commercial bank investments in stock of domestic and foreign companies. As is well known, shares are not part of liquid financial instruments because their quotations are susceptible to broad variation.

In July 1999 under strong IMF pressure, the Russian government assumed responsibility to undertake a set of measures aimed at further liberalization of both current and capital transactions of the balance of payments. Under current circumstances this decision does not lead to reduction of capital outflow from the country, recovery of Russian industry. August 1998 crash clearly demonstrated importance of imposing strict controls over short-term capital inflows and outflows. That is why the government has to examine with attention the expediency of introducing this or that kind of Tobin tax. In classical case it represents a special tax on all foreign exchange transactions; its other forms were used, for example, in Chile and Israel where foreign investors had to deposit significant additional funds in case of short-term investments.

The necessity of government intervention in economic matters is predetermined by the fact that some problems, in principle, cannot be resolved by the market, whereas in other cases market outcomes do not conform to social preferences. It is important, however, that introducing corrections in resource allocation in accordance with national interests the government does not undermine the workings of the market mechanism. A good mix of governments and markets is a necessary pre-condition for sustained economic progress.

Reforming Natural Monopolies and Utilities

Russian mainstream economists and international financial organizations consider a restructuring of natural monopolies and utilities as most urgent challenges facing Russia now. They argue that disintegration of natural monopolies should be aimed at creating and separating potentially competitive production structures thus providing the base for higher efficiency and more transparency. Reforming utilities, on the other hand, is important, according to their view, because it alleviates the burden borne by the state budget and contribute to the creation of a well functioning labor market. It is correct that separating competitive and monopolistic structures from current natural monopolies (for instance production of gas and electricity, on the one hand, and their distribution, on the other) could be economically efficient. The problem, however, lies in the way these reforms should be implemented. To my understanding financial order should be introduced within the current natural monopolies and their balance sheets 'cleaned' from overdue accounts receivable and payable.

Of course, this cannot but lead to lengthening of time needed for these reforms. But to begin working from the opposite end, first disintegrate and only then impose financial order, is fraught with arbitrary redistribution of shareholders' property. There is no surprise that minority shareholders of the Russian united electrical systems are very nervous with the proposals of restructuring put forward by its management.

The same is true with regard to utilities. There is no doubt that the current situation when the government subsidizes significant part of rent payments distorts the situation on labor markets and inhibits labor mobility. The problem, however, is that it is very dangerous to change this state of affairs immediately just by removing subsidies. Ensuing readjustment of labor markets needs a long time and, therefore, drastic complication of the situation in social sphere can emerge. This means the reforms of utilities should be well designed and gradual.

Of course, one can accept the necessity to act cautiously and without hurry in carrying out structural reforms in the field of natural monopolies and utilities only if s/he does not think that any price should be paid for an urgent realization. My point is that Russia faces now much more serious challenges. Moreover, introducing corrections in property rights, changing economic behaviors of authorities, monetizing the real sector of the economy would create favorable conditions for implementation of other structural reforms.

Concluding Comments

Issues concerning transition to market economies are terribly complex. Despite the accumulation of our collective experiences on this transition over the ten years, there seems to be a little progress in our understanding. The progress has been thwarted by ongoing ideological wrangling that led to a clear division of scholars between the proponents and opponents of the Washington consensus paradigm. To a certain extent such a rift is acceptable as our views are tainted by the political judgments, which depend on value judgments. This rift represents a re-emergence of a classic cleavage between Keynesian and Monetarist approaches to macroeconomics. Evidently, neither monetarist, nor Keynesian approaches should be expected to be efficient in dealing with these complex issues associated with transitions. The list of these specific transition problems includes massive reallocation of resources and formation of genuine market agents.

There are no scholars who doubt that a huge reallocation of resources should accompany transition to market from planned socialist economies. Perhaps, because of the evident character of the general conclusion some important aspects relating to the nature of this process remain unobserved. Such reallocation of resources can cause structural shocks. A big danger for an economy suffering from this kind of structural shocks is to drag the process of adaptation for so long that a significant part of physical and human capital gets completely lost. This phenomenon can be called 'systemic hysteresis' using the term aimed to describe the well-known macroeconomic situations when current market variations result in adverse changes in the long-term path of economic development.

Simple recipes of Keynesian economics may not be suitable. Existence of excess capacity under these circumstances is a result of changes in the structure of aggregate demand and not due to a reduction in its level. One should not also confuse a lack of aggregate demand with a lack of money experienced by some economic agents. Keynes, as is well known, understood by demand deficit the situation when economic agents did not want to spend money they had. That is why proposals to pursue expansionist monetary and fiscal policy are fraught with adverse economic consequences as well as with discredit of Keynesianism in Russia.

Any such transition will inevitably evoke serious problems regarding short-term shocks. Mitigation of these shocks is typically accorded primacy. That is why the best method to adjust Russian economy to the requirements of the market consists, in my opinion, in combining the tools of (passive) industrial, and social policies. It is important to realize that the process of transition creates distortions within the economic system. Successful reforms must adequately address these distortions. Errors made by Russian reformers in the transformation of property rights resulted in the emergence of an extremely distorted system of corporate governance in a majority of big and middle-sized enterprises. The main issue here is to undertake measures, which would place the management of enterprises under a control of owners of capital and would thus reorient joint-stock companies towards profit maximization in the short-run and net-worth maximization of the firm in the long-run.

An eradication of anti-market instruments of control – frequently used by Russian authorities at all levels – is of extreme importance for normalizing economic activity. To a significant degree an achievement of this goal is enmeshed with a consolidation of the rule of laws in the Russian society. At the same time it is necessary to reduce the tool-kit for economic management at the disposal of authorities. Land (in broad meaning of the word, including all natural conditions of production) is by all means the most important production factor and, therefore, the existence of efficient mechanism of its allocation is a substantial prerequisite for an efficient economic outcome. By all means, an introduction of unlimited convertibility of currency, inflexibility in regulation of money supply (introduction of currency board being the most logical proposal with this respect), provision for complete freedom of capital movement in and out of the country (including short-term capital), introduction of rigid measures of prudential supervision for banks, all this, according to formal criteria, perfectly corresponds to the process of globalization of the world economy. But alongside with the positive aspects of financial liberalization the risks, associated with it, are well known: national financial system become ideal conductor for external shocks. There is no secret also in the fact that resulting dangers are especially serious for the countries with weak financial institutions. Therefore, reforming the financial sector is an important part of the reform process. Russian mainstream economists and international financial organizations consider a restructuring of natural monopolies and utilities as the most urgent challenges facing Russia now.

Chapter 18

Characteristics of Small Firm Managers: Evidence from Sri Lanka

Jonathan Batten and Samanthala Hettihewa

Introduction

The advent of globalization has posed serious challenges to regional economies and small businesses. Yet it is widely admitted that small businesses in Asia and Europe have provided significant boost to the local economy. Various studies highlight the strong performance of small businesses in South and Southeast Asia. Small businesses have performed very well in Sri Lanka and this chapter offers a detailed study of small businesses in Sri Lanka. A number of authors, including Chua, Chrisman and Sharma (1999), have highlighted the concern of incumbent presidents, or principals, of family owned firms in maintaining the loyalty and involvement of family members and non-family managers. These concerns arise from the principal's inability to observe the actions of agents, which include both family and non-family managers, or to mitigate the asymmetries of information, which arise when the agent runs the business instead of the owner. The objective of this study is to investigate and explain, using the principal-agent framework, cross-sectional variation in the managers of small firms in Sri Lanka[1], by determining the relationship between key firm-specific variables and the characteristics of small firm managers. A countrywide, random survey is used as the basis for identifying cross-sectional variation due to differences in industry, size, ownership, and the relationship of the manager of the firm to the owners of the firm. The characteristics of firm managers include the age, education, management experience and employment background of the managers. Since most managers surveyed were male, we were unable to establish cross-sectional variation on the basis of gender.

Thus study extends an earlier study by Batten and Hettihewa (1999), which investigates cross-sectional variation in Sri Lankan small firm management practice. This earlier study found significant cross-sectional variation in the small firm practice and attributed these results to the cost of acquiring new technology, asymmetries and opacity in financial information and the non-value maximizing behavior of firm owners who were also firm managers. This study is based upon a sample of 73 responding firms which comprise family owned firms (61.6 percent), firms managed by owner managers (52.0 percent), although a significant proportion (62.2percent) of family owned firms are managed by employed managers. These results are largely consistent with other studies in the U.S. (Berger and Udell 1998), and Asia (Moore 1997) where family owned and owner managed small firms tend to be the norm. The results also highlight the differences in small firm management between countries. The high level of professional management in Sri Lankan small firms is more consistent with the business structures of the Japanese and Korean firms (see Redding 1990, p.205) than the firms of overseas Chinese who tend to be family managed.

Also, having a high proportion of non-family managers in family firms is inconsistent with some studies in other developing countries that suggest family owned firms may attempt to 'block the mobility' of non-family managers to ensure employment for family members (Levinson 1987). The results suggest that though ownership and management structures of small firms vary (due to differing cultural and social factors), management behavior may still be explained in terms of existing agency theories where conflicts exist between management and old and new stockholders of the small firm. Statistical analysis highlights significant cross-sectional variation between the set of firm variables and characteristics of individual managers. The cross-tabulated results suggest (using chi squared and correlation statistics) that larger firms have older and more experienced managers, sole-owners tend to be more educated and that the primary industry have managers with the least management experience, while the tertiary sector have managers with the most industry experience.

Economic Policy and Small Firms in Sri Lanka

Sri Lanka, with a population of 17.4 million people in 1997, maintained strong economic growth through the 1990s despite the well-documented ethnic crisis which resulted in a culturally based civil war, high defense expenditures and increased levels of foreign debt (Hettihewa, 1993). Economic growth peaked in 1993 at 6.9 percent and remained between 5 percent and 6 percent thereafter, while per capita gross national product (GNP) grew from $US375 in 1988 to $US640 in 1995, an increase of 71 percent over the period. Unemployment was recorded as 12.5 percent in 1995, while inflation fell from 15 percent in 1988 to 7.7 percent in 1995.

These economic indicators understate the significant positive changes in the social fabric of Sri Lanka in recent years. Alternate measures of the well-being of individuals (e.g. the Human Development Index, see ul-Haq (1995)) highlight the significant positive changes in the real living standards of Sri Lanka where there has been a high level of satisfaction of basic needs although GDP per capita is relatively low.

A feature of Sri Lankan economic policy in the 1960s and 1970s was its focus towards the management of the deterioration in the terms of trade. Safeguarding local industries using trade restrictions and promoting 'infant industries' were popular concepts[2]. Inefficiencies and reduced competitiveness in these export industries were partly offset by ongoing devaluation of the local currency (the Sri Lankan Rupee SLR). However, while providing some benefits in the form of more competitive exports, negative impacts were increases in the cost of manufactured imports essential for the longer-term development of the secondary and tertiary industry sectors. Other negative impacts were the failure to diversify exports and to develop technical expertise in the production process. Consequently by the 1980s, Sri Lanka was still largely agricultural and dependent on three major agricultural export products namely, tea, rubber and coconut, although policy initiatives had begun aimed at developing small and medium scaled industry (e.g. the formation of the Industrial Development Board in 1969).

During the late 1970s economic policy became more outward looking with strategy directed towards achieving higher levels of exports and liberalizing trade. This was highlighted by the Five-Year Plan 1972-1977 where the small firm sector was given priority in the development policy agenda. Specific policy objectives were directed towards saving foreign exchange through the introduction of the dual exchange rate (Foreign Exchange Entitlement Certificates) scheme, creating new employment, encouraging the location of secondary industry to rural areas, and diversifying the agricultural base to higher-value crops. There were also attempts at promoting price stability and equity for producers and consumers using schemes such as the food crib system (Ellis et al., 1997). Nonetheless, the trade imbalance could not be solved due mainly to lower prices for traditional agricultural and gem exports, and the low productivity level of manufactured products compared with the newly emerged Asian countries.

The failure of Sri Lanka to achieve stated economic objectives might be compared with the success of the newly industrialized Asian economies and other Asian nations such as the Philippines and Thailand during this period. However the situation is changing. In the late 1980s some favorable signs were seen in terms of export diversification, with manufacturing exports counting for more than 50 percent of total trade exports. Although there is still an obvious need for the government to ensure competitive and fair pricing in subsidized and protected industries (Rajapakse 1996), and to maintain the pace of microeconomic reforms, in particular by withdrawing from its involvement in food marketing channels (Ellis et al., 1997).

One implication of this survey is that the low productivity level of industry may be due to the difficulty small business experiences when trying to expand activities, particularly through the acquisition of new technology. The uniform perception among survey respondents that government is not doing enough for small business needs to be addressed. Clearly the government has provided various incentives, however it appears that these policy initiatives are not sufficiently targeted to 'small' firms. An example includes the support schemes in place to acquire new technology.[3]

Development of Key Propositions

The key proposition being investigated is that the characteristics of small firm managers vary with different types of firms. There are a number of reasons why cross-sectional variation may exist between different types of small firms. Firstly, government policy may have been directed towards the establishment of a particular status quo in one industry group, over other industries. For instance the primary sector in Sri Lanka has been singled out for special treatment by government through its infant industries policy. The separation of ownership and control of the firm, between family and non-family members, may result in agency problems associated with corporate governance and in choosing the optimal capital structure for the firm. Owner managers may also engage in non-value maximizing behavior to reduce risk, or exhibit expense preference behavior for lifestyle reasons (Berger and Udell 1998). Asymmetries in information may also exist between non-family and family members, small firm owners and firm managers, and between small firms and financial intermediaries. The following five Propositions examine these issues from the perspective of the small firm manger:

Proposition 1: Firm classification will be associated with the age of the small firm manager. Specifically larger firms are expected to have older managers.

The capital structure of the small firm varies with its life cycle (Berger and Udell, 1998). That is, as the firm ages and becomes larger the financial mix will change. In the U.S., small innovative start-up firms (high-risk, high growth) are mostly reliant upon the entrepreneurs (or family's) equity. These young firms would be expected to have younger managers. However, firms as they mature may suffer from information asymmetries particularly with regard to accessing additional capital, and so will rely upon older managers who are more likely to have the informal networks and skills necessary to convey the firm's credibility to the various stakeholders. Smaller and newer firms with low initial wealth endowments are also expected to better control the expense preference or risk reduction behavior of management. Knowing this, older managers who may be looking for an easy life will not be attracted to smaller (and younger) firms.

Proposition 2: Firm classification will be associated with the level of education of the small firm manager. Specifically owner managed and smaller firms are expected to have more educated managers.

Structural change in economies encourages the development of small business in niche industry areas where barriers to entry, based on size, may be reduced by the rapid pace of technological change. However, while the cost of acquiring the appropriate technology is also important and may create a hurdle to industry entry, outside contracting and industry downsizing provide other opportunities for small business, particularly in service areas (Keeble, 1990). Thus entrepreneurs with sufficient initial wealth to acquire the appropriate technology, and knowledge to use this technology may create a comparative advantage over other firms in niche service areas. Information is likely to be more transparent the larger the firm and larger firms enjoy economies of scale in the generation of the information that potential stakeholders require. Larger firms will therefore attempt to use the cost of information as a hurdle to prevent new firms achieving a market position. New start up firms, which are smaller and tend to be owner-managed, may be able to overcome this hurdle by using new skills to gain a comparative advantage. A measure of the potential skills of the manager is the education of the manager. Consequently to maintain or gain comparative advantages smaller firms, and owner-managed firms, will rely upon having more educated managers than larger firms.

Proposition 3: Firm classification will be associated with the management experience of the small firm manager. Specifically, larger, family-owned and tertiary sector firms are expected to have more experienced managers.

Sri Lankan government policy has encouraged industry consolidation; while subsidization has discouraged changes in management practice preventing much needed structural adjustment, or improving competitive practice and fairer prices. Dunham (1993) therefore concludes that these policies have tended to be unfocused, poorly coordinated and to have a dubious welfare impact. This is illustrated by the primary sector where minimum price schemes and government policy was directed towards establishing high value-added horticultural exports as a major industry (e.g. spices such as vanilla). Managers in such an environment are likely to be older patriarchs and are likely to exhibit expense preference behavior, and to block the mobility of younger skilled managers who are not family members (as suggested by Levinson (1987)), or other family members should the firm be a family-owned firm. Firms when they hire managers incur agency costs since managers are likely to put their own welfare above the welfare of the owners of the firm. The simplest way of controlling these agency costs is to allow management incentives to be linked to the financial well being of the firm. Family owned firms are less likely to impose these governance structures since they may wish to engage in expense preference behavior. Older managers in family owned firms (who are also likely to be family patriarchs) would maintain loose incentive structures to ensure control is maintained. Expense preference behavior may also take the form of the firm maintaining the employment of family members who should otherwise be sacked. This is consistent with Covin (1994) who observes that family owned firms are less likely to have formal written policies to guide employees, and to use performance based criteria. Thus larger firms and many family owned firms

Proposition 4: Firm classification will be associated with the employment background of the manager. Specifically, tertiary sector firms are expected to have specialized firm managers and owner managers are expected to have more technical skills.

Firms operating in the primary, or agricultural sector, tend to rely on individual, unskilled, contingent contractors (e.g. day laborers) to accommodate the seasonalities of production. Firm managers will generally not require specialized skills to manage such a labor force, whereas the reverse would be the case for tertiary sector managers. Evidence from developed countries has also suggested that recruiting, motivating, and retaining skilled employees is one of the main problems for small firms (Hornsby and Kuratko 1990). Thus secondary and tertiary firms would attempt to retain skilled labor that had been difficult to acquire and so require that managers have more specialized skills (e.g. human resources experience).

The knowledge and the facilities to set up clear plans, to implement and carry out those objectives and to establish monitoring and controlling methods, are essential for firm success. However the inability to establish clear plans and the lack of these facilities may make it extremely difficult to maintain the viability of the firm's activities. Under these circumstances having managers with more specialized administrative skills solves information opacity. Owner managers are more likely to be innovators and specialists and may be poor administrators or managers. Non-owner managers presumably have been hired for their management skills, and should be more adept at performing these key functions. Government sponsored development of selected industries would be expected to generate rapid growth in small firms in the selected industries. Wynarczyk et al., (1993) observed that in fast growing small firm, management policy will be continuously developing and the skill set required to conduct the firm will change. Tertiary sector firms which face rapid growth and competition from other service providers are therefore likely to require specialized firm managers, while owner managers in these firms are expected to have more technical skills.

Data and Methodology

This chapter reveals the findings of a mail survey of small firm management of Sri Lankan firms. The firms surveyed are derived from the Sri Lanka Small Firm Database, which is a complete listing of small firms. The evidence presented in the chapter is the response to the survey from the listed managers of three hundred (300) randomly selected small firms. Anonymity was assured to the respondents by sending an unmarked reply-paid questionnaire. Interested respondents were also promised a copy of the findings. From an overall mail-out of 300 firms, 73 questionnaires were returned and processed. This resulted in an effective response rate of 24.3 percent (i.e. 73/300), which is considered a good response rate for a mail survey of this nature. Given the limited statistical information available on small firms in Sri Lanka it is not apparent whether a response bias has been introduced into the sample. However the results suggest a good mix of respondents by the various small firm variables. Also, given the large sample size and the significant level of response it is fair to infer that the information considered in the chapter accurately represents the practices of the small firm sector in Sri Lanka.

The 73 respondents were generally male (67 or 91.8 percent); above 40 years of age (59 or 80.8 percent); generally secondary school educated with only 17 (23.3 percent) having tertiary education; generally well experienced in managing firms with 53 respondents (72.6 percent) having a minimum of 5 years management experience; and generally from a sales background with 38 respondents (52.1percent), with 13 (17.8 percent) from financial administration, 9 (12.3 percent) from marketing, 10 (13.7 percent) from production and 3 (4.1 percent) from human resources. The survey was structured to record the various firm-specific characteristics and management practices of the 73 respondents. The firm-specific characteristics are:

1.   Firms classified by industry. There are eleven (11) industry categories. These are later consolidated into 3 groupings, primary (25 or 34.2 percent), secondary (23 or 31.6 percent) and tertiary sectors 25 (34.2 percent).

2.   Firms classified by ownership. There are two categories whether the firm was not a family owned firm (28 or 38.4 percent), or whether it was a family owned firm (45 or 61.6 percent).

3.   Respondent classified by ownership. There are two categories, whether the respondent was not an owner manager (35 or 48.0 percent), or whether the respondent was an owner of the firm (38 or 52.0 percent).

4.   Firms classified by size. There are six categories that are consolidated into 2 groupings, whether the firm had sales less than Sri Lankan Rupees (SLR) of 80,000 per annun (US$1480), or whether the firm had sales greater than SLR 80,000 per annum. (The exchange rate was 1US$ = 54SLR). There are 27 or 37.0percent of firms with sales < 80,000 SLR, while there are 46 firms (63.0 percent) with sales > 80,000 SLR. While the smallest of these firms are very small in terms of turnover compared to western firms, it should be pointed out that many of the 'small' small firms had twice in sales the average Sri Lanka GNP per capita.

After undertaking an analysis of the data which included a correlation (ρ) and chi-squared (χ^2) analysis of each of the sets of variables, a more complex analysis was undertaken by constructing two-way tables of the four firm characteristics and the five management practice variables. Cross-tabulations between the various firm characteristics and the manager's characteristics were examined using chi-square tests since the survey was based upon categorical data. The null hypothesis for these tests was that the firm variable and the management practice variable are independent.

Results

1.   *Analysis of Manager's Characteristics*
      The respondent profile is generally consistent with other surveys of south Asia where firms tend to be managed by patriarchs who have extensive personal connections (Redding 1990). The correlations between the manager's characteristic variables were low. Significant correlations were also tested using was χ^2 tests. The significant relationships included:

(a)   Management experience and the age of the respondent (χ^2 = 21.483, degrees of freedom (df) = 4, p = 0.000 and ρ = 0.357). As one would expect the most experienced managers were also the oldest (experience was positively correlated with the respondent age). However most managers (9/14 or 64.2 percent) who were less than 40 also had less than 5 years management experience. This suggests that most small firm managers are not managers until they are at least 35.

(b)   Management experience and the education of the respondent (χ^2 = 5.183, df = 2, p = 0.075 and ρ = 0.287). Management experience was also positively correlated with education, that is, most of the managers with higher education (16/17 or 94.1 percent) also had more than 15 years management experience. This result is consistent with managers undertaking higher education later on in their careers.

(c)   Employment background and education (χ^2 = 3.131, df = 3, p = 0.372 and ρ = -0.287). Though the chi-squared result was not significant, the high negative correlation does suggest a tendency for managers from sales backgrounds to only have secondary education (34/38 or 89.5 percent) whereas other areas (e.g. financial administration with 5/13 or 38.5 percent) tend to have more highly qualified managers.

(d)   Employment background and management experience (χ^2 = 10.167, df = 6, p = 0.118 and ρ = -0.252). The chi-squared result was almost significant at the 90 percent level of confidence, however there was a strong positive correlation between the two variables. The result suggests that most financial administrators (9/13 or 69.2 percent) have more than 15 years management experience. This may be compared with sales that had a more even distribution of the manager's experience.

(e)   Gender and education (χ^2 = 2.611, df = 1, p = 0.106 and ρ = -0.270). Though the result must be qualified due to the small sample size and the small number of female respondents, education and gender were definitely negatively correlated. That is female managers (3 of the 6 respondents) tended to be better educated and have higher education. These 3 female respondents were also financial administrators. This suggests that education may still be the major form of organizational mobility for women in developing countries in small business. This single issue warrants extensive investigation.

2.   *Analysis of Firm-Specific Variables*
The primary industry sector was the highest single industry category accounting for 25 (34.2 percent) out of 73 enterprises. This group included 13 (16.7 percent) from the agriculture and plantation sector, and 12 (15.4 percent) from the mining and processing sector. The secondary sector came as the second highest category with 8 (10.2 percent) enterprises from the

garment industry, and 10 (12.8 percent) from other manufacturing industries. There was no response from the construction and finance industries. The large capital requirements in establishing firms in those two sectors may have precluded them from the original mail-out to small firms. Transport and storage counted for only one enterprise among the 73 responses. This result was also likely to be due to the presence of significant establishment costs, a form of industry entry barrier, for small firms in this industry. The majority of the firms indicated that they were not family firms (45 or 61.6 percent), while most firms were sole owner operators. Most firms (46 or 63.0 percent) had annual sales above SLR80, 000 though there were three very small firms whose annual sales were less than SLR20, 000.

The correlations between the firm-specific variables were all low. The two correlations that were statistically > 0 include the negative correlation between the family ownership and owner manager variables (-0.362), and the negative correlation between the owner manager variable and size (-0.224). Cross tabulations of the four dependent variables, with the significance tested using χ^2 statistics, provides an insight into these relationships. These two pairs of variables were also the only statistically significant χ^2 relationships: the cross tabulation between the family and owner manager variable (χ^2 = 9.582, p = 0.002); and the owner manager and size variable (χ^2 = 3.666 p =0.056). The first result reflects the greater proportion of family owned firms using non-owner managers (28/45 or 62.2 percent) than family members (contrary to expectations of constrained mobility). The second result was due to the greater proportion of the largest firms using non-owner managers (26/35 or 74.3percent). That is, owner managed firms tend to be smaller than the other firms in the sample, although there are no other significant relationships with any of the other variables (such as industry).

3. *Analysis of Cross-Tabulations of Managers Characteristics and Small-Firm Specific Variables*

Table 1 presents the results from the cross-tabulations of the firm-specific variables and the characteristics of the small firm managers. The statistical significance of these relationships was determined using chi-squared tests and correlation statistics. Collectively the results provide support for the proposition that different manager's characteristics are associated with different types of small-firms:

(a)   older managers were associated with larger firms (due to a greater proportion of managers who are older than 40 in larger firms (41/59 or 69.5 percent) than smaller firms;

(b)   owner-managers tended to be more educated (due to a great proportion of owner managers (12/17 or 70.5 percent) who have tertiary qualifications than non-owner managers);

(c)   tertiary sector firms had more experienced managers (due to a greater proportion of managers with more than 15 years experience in tertiary firms (11/29 or 37.9 percent) than primary sector firms (7/29 or 24.1 percent).

These results were all significant at the 90percent level of confidence. There was also a slight tendency (ρ = -0.205) for primary sector managers to have a sales/marketing background, while tertiary sector managers tend to have a financial administration background though the chi-squared result was not significant at the 90 percent level. There was insufficient data to use gender as a dependent variable. These results collectively support the earlier propositions and may be interpreted in the context of existing theories on agency and asymmetries in information.

Conclusion

The objective of this study was to investigate the cross-sectional variation in the characteristics of small firm managers by investigating the small firm sector in Sri Lanka, and determining the relationship between key firm-specific variables and management practices. A countrywide, random survey was used as the basis for identifying cross-sectional variation in small firm management practices. The results suggest industry classification is associated with specific manager's characteristics. In addition, the results suggest a number of potential areas for further research, in particular the changing role of women, as small firm managers, in developing countries.

Notes

1.   The Central Bank of Sri Lanka (1998: 107-128), 'Economic Progress of Independent Sri Lanka' defines small firms as cottage and small scale industries, where the capital stock in plant and equipment is less than Sri Lankan Rupee 4 million (approximately US$74,000), and where the total number of employees is less than 50. There are approximately 100,000 such entities in Sri Lanka.
2.   For example see the tea industry (Ali, Choudhry and Lister, 1997) and rice, see Gunawardana and Oczkowski (1992).
3.   The 1997 Budget extended tax and import concessions on the acquisition of advanced technology to animal husbandry, fisheries, and tourism and community development projects. However the minimum investment varied from SLR 1 to 4 million (US$18,500 to US$74,000) subject to various criteria. The size of these potential investments placed these concessions outside the reach of many smaller firms (News Letter from the Sri Lankan High Commission, Canberra Australia).

References

Ali, Ridwan, Choudhry, Yusuf A. and Lister, W. Douglas. (1997), *Sri Lanka's Tea Industry: Succeeding in the Global Market*, Discussion Paper no. 368, World Bank, Washington DC.

Athukorala, Premachandra and Sarath Rajapatirana. (1993), 'Liberalization of the Domestic Financial Market: Theoretical Issues with Evidence from Sri Lanka', *International Economic Journal*, 7(4), pp.17-33.

Berger, Allen and Gregory Udell. (1998), 'The Economies of Small Business Finance: The Roles of Private Equity and Debt Markets in the Financial Growth Cycle', *Journal of Banking and Finance*, (22), pp.613-673.

Central Bank of Sri Lanka (1998), 'Economic Progress of Independent Sri Lanka', in *Annual Report*, Colombo, pp.107-128.

Covin, Jeffrey. (1994), 'Perceptions of Family-Owned Firms: The Impact of Gender and Educational Level', *Journal of Small Business Management*, July, pp.29-39.

Dunham, David. (1993), 'Crop Diversification and Export Growth: Dynamics of Change in the Sri Lankan Peasant Sector', *Development and Change*, 24(4), pp.787-813.

Ellis, Frank, Piyadasa Senanayake and Marisal Smith. (1997), 'Food Price Policy in Sri Lanka', *Food Policy*, 22(1), pp.81-96.

Finegold, David and David Soskie. (1988), 'The Failure of Training in Britain: Analysis and Prescription', *Oxford Review of Economic Policy*, 4(3), pp.21-53.

Garlick, Peter. (1971), *African Traders and Economic Development in Ghana*, Clarendon Press: Oxford.

Gunawardana, Pemasiri, J. and Eddie A. Oczkowski, (1992), 'Government Policies and Agricultural Supply Response: Paddy in Sri Lanka', *Journal of Agricultural Economics*, 43(20), pp.231-242.

Hettihewa, Samanthala. (1994), 'The Economic Implications of Sri Lanka's Debt Problem', *Indian Journal of Applied Economics*, 2(3), pp.12-35.

Hornsby, J. S. and D. K. Kuratko. (1990), 'Human Resource Management in Small Business: Critical Issues for the 1990s', *Journal of Small Business Management*, July, pp.9-18.

Keeble, David. (1990), 'Small Firms, New Firms and Uneven Regional Development', *Area*, (22), pp.234-245.

Levinson, Richard. (1987), *Problems in Managing a Family Owned Business*, in *Family Business Sourcebook*, editors, C. Arnoff and J. Ward, Omnigraphic Inc.

Lewis, Arthur. (1955), *The Theory of Economic Growth*, George Allen & Unwin, London.

Moore, Mick. (1997), 'Societies, Polities and Capitalists in Developing Countries: A Literature Review', *The Journal of Development Studies*, 33(3), pp.818-830

Rajapakse, Purinima. (1996), 'The Implications of the Emerging Trade Environment for Sri Lanka', *Asian Development Review*, 14(2), pp.116-151.

Redding, Stephen G. (1990), *The Spirit of Chinese Capitalism*, Walter de Gruyter: Berlin and New York.

ul Haq, Mahbub. (1995), *Reflections on Human Development*, Oxford University Press: Oxford and New York.

White, Howard and Ganeshan Wignaraja. (1992), 'Exchange Rates, Trade Liberalisation and Aid: The Sri Lankan Experience', *World Development*, 20(10), pp.1471-1480.

Wynarczyk, Pooran, Robert Watson, David Storey, Helen Short and Kevin Keasey. (1993), *Managerial Labour Markets in Small and Medium Size Enterprises*, Routledge: London.

Table 18.1   Cross Tabulations: Managers' Characteristics and Small Firm-Specific Variables

	X_1	X_2	X_3	X_3
	$\chi^2= 1.977$	$\chi^2= 2.751$	$\chi^2= 9.247$	$\chi^2= 7.021$
	df = 2	df = 2	df = 4	df = 4
	p = 0.372	p = 0.253	p = 0.055	p = 0.135
Y_1	$\rho = 0.081$	$\rho = 0.161$	$\rho = 0.243$	$\rho = -0.205$
	p =0.494	p = 0.174	p = 0.038	p = 0.081
	p = 0.700	$\chi^2= 0.770$	$\chi^2= 1.394$	$\chi^2= 0.402$
	$\chi^2= 148$	df = 1	df = 2	df = 2
	df = 1	p = 0.399	p = 0.498	p = 0.818
Y_2	$\rho = -0.030$	$\rho = 0.060$	$\rho = -0.090$	$\rho = -0.033$
	p = 0.802	p = 0.614	p = 0.449	p =0.783
	p = 0.308	$\chi^2= 3.05$	$\chi^2= 0.111$	$\chi^2= 0.668$
	$\chi^2= 1.038$	df = 1	df = 2	df = 2
	df = 1	p = 0.081	p = 0.946	p = 0.716
Y_3	$\rho = -0.112$	$\rho = 0.237$	$\rho = -0.035$	$\rho = -0.135$
	p = 0.346	p = 0.044	p =0.766	p = 0.256
	p = 0.019	$\chi^2= 0.167$	$\chi^2= 5.600$	$\chi^2= .698$
	$\chi^2= 5.539$	df = 1	df = 2	df = 2
	df = 1	p = 0.683	p = 0.061	p = 0.705
Y_4	$\rho = 0.383$	$\rho = -0.126$	$\rho = -0.141$	$\rho = 0.018$
	p = 0.001	p = 0.287	p = 0.233	p = 0.882

Source: Computed from a Sample

This table records the cross-tabulations between the five manager's characteristics and the four firm-specific variables. Since the responses are categorical, chi-squared tests (χ^2) are used to determine the significance of association between the two sets of variables. The null hypothesis for these tests was that the two variables were independent. A significant χ^2 (determined using the p-values beneath each value) indicates the firm-specific variable may have a significant effect on the management practice. The table also reports the correlation coefficient (ρ) between the manager's characteristic and the industry variable. The p-value beneath each value is the significance that the correlation coefficient is not zero.

X_1= Age, X_2=Education, X_3=Management Experience, X_4=Employment Background
Y_1=Industry, Y_2=Family Ownership, Y_3= Owner Manager, Y_4=Annual Sales

Details of Manager's Characteristics:

Sample Size: 73

Age Composition: Age<40 (19.2%), Age>40 (80.2%),
Education: Secondary (76.7%), Tertiary (23.3%).
Experience: Experience <5 Years (27.4%), 5 Years <Experience<15 Years (32.9%),
Experience >15 Years (39.7%).
Employment Background: Financial =17.8%, Marketing =12.3%, Production= 13.75,
Human Resources=4.1%, Sales= 52.1%.

Firm-Specific variables:
Industry Classification: Primary (34.2%), Secondary (31.6%), Tertiary (34.2%)
Ownership Pattern: Not Family Owned (38.4%) Family Owned (61.6%)
Annual Sales: Sales <Rs. 80,000 p.a. =37%, Sales Rs.>80,000p.a =63%

Chapter 19

The Political Economy of Rural Health Care in India

Amit S. Ray and Saradindu Bhaduri

Introduction

Public investment in health in India has been miniscule compared to the demand for health care in the country. The rural sector, in particular, has suffered gross neglect with regard to public health services and facilities.[1] Micro studies have shown an overwhelming dependence of the rural population on private providers, even for common minor ailments.[2] This is perhaps true for most developing countries. The proportion of private expenditure in overall spending on health is fairly high for LDCs, and often higher than that in many developed countries.[3] Although the need to provide free health care is fairly well-recognized, we do not observe any initiative in that direction reflected in terms of greater public spending on health in most LDCs, including India.

On the contrary, with economic liberalization and structural adjustment, compression of public expenditure has been an important goal. Accordingly, there has been an intensified effort to reduce the role of the Government in every sphere of economic activity. Even in case of merit goods like education and health, which have traditionally been provided by the State in many welfare nations, the government is now seriously considering reducing its expenditure and involvement. However, 'the success of liberalization and closer integration with the world economy may be severely impaired by India's backwardness in basic education, elementary health care'[4] Accordingly governmental under-activity in these sectors could prove to be self-limiting for the process of economic liberalization and globalization. The proponents of 'privatization' would argue that the vacuum created by the Government in the domain of merit goods would be immediately occupied (and much better served) by the private sector.[5] But this could be a matter of debate.[6] Our paper is an attempt to contribute to this debate from a theoretical as well as an empirical perspective, focusing on the case of rural health care in India.

In this study, we present a micro-theoretic model of rural health care to explain the choice between private and public health care by rural households belonging to different socio-economic strata. The results obtained from this model will be placed against some empirical evidence from rural India. Finally, we discuss the policy implications emerging from our results, particularly highlighting the implications of privatization of rural health care as part of India's liberalization process.

The Model

Our model of rural health care revolves around the concept of quality of service. The choice of public versus private health care by rural households will depend on the quality of service obtained from each of them in equilibrium. Our model posits that each set of provider offers a range of quality associated with varying costs and benefits. In equilibrium, the household equates its marginal benefits with marginal costs to arrive at its optimum quality. We expect the quality of health care to raise the probability of getting cured (Pr). The benefits (B) obtained by the rural households is a monotonic transformation of this probability (Pr), which in turn is a function of quality (Q) of health care service. Thus

$$B = F\{Pr(Q)\} = B\ (Q) \qquad (1)$$

We expect B to be an increasing function of Q but at a decreasing rate, i.e. $B'\ (Q) > 0$ and $B''\ (Q) < 0$. It simply means that the marginal gain in benefits from an increment in quality at the lowest end of the spectrum[7] is likely to be much higher than that obtained from an incremental quality at the upper end of the spectrum[8]. For simplicity, we assume the following quadratic functional form:

$$B = a + bQ - cQ^2, \text{ where } a, b, c > 0 \qquad (2)$$

It is depicted as BB in Figure 19.1. Since the benefits derived from quality operates via the probability of getting cured, there is a matter of perception and judgment involved in the specification of the benefits. Not all individuals will be able to perceive and judge quality of health care equally. In order to be able to distinguish between good and poor quality of medical care and appreciate good quality health care, one requires some degree of education and enlightenment. In this regard, we distinguish between two sets of households: (1) educated and enlightened (socio-economically advanced) and (2) uneducated and non-enlightened (socio-economically backward). The latter's B (Q) function will be more flat (B'B') than the former (BB) as their perceived probability of cure does not alter much with the quality of care. In other words, they are unable to make much distinction between medical care of different quality. More specifically, they fail to appreciate high quality medical care. As a result, they will overestimate benefits from low quality and underestimate benefits from high quality. Accordingly, the benefits functions for the two groups of households (enlightened and non-enlightened) may be specified:

$$B_e = a + bQ - cQ^2, \text{ where } a, b, c > 0 \qquad (3)$$
$$B_{ne} = a' + b'Q - c'Q^2, \text{ where } a', b', c' > 0 \qquad (4)$$

Furthermore, $a < a'$, $b > b'$ but $c < c'$.

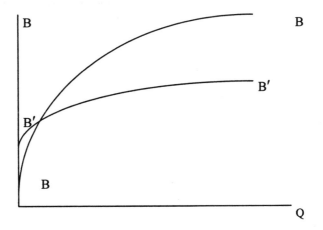

Figure 19.1 Benefits Functions of Households

From (3) and (4) we may derive the marginal benefits functions for the enlightened and non-enlightened households as:

$$MB_e = b - 2cQ \tag{5}$$
$$MB_{ne} = b' - 2c'Q \tag{6}$$

These are depicted in Figure 19.2.

The Cost Functions

We assume that the quality (Q) of health care services supplied by rural providers has two principal dimensions: (1) the quality of medical attention or consultation (including clinical evaluation, diagnosis and treatment) (Q_c) and (2) the quality of medical accessories like medication and diagnostic tests (Q_m).

$$Q = Q_c + Q_m \tag{7}$$

The cost of health care (C) will depend on its quality (Q). We assume

$$C = C(Q) = C(Q_c + Q_m) = C_1(Q_c) + C_2(Q_m) \tag{8}$$

We have two classes of health care providers: private (P) and Government (G) each characterized by distinct cost functions, $C_p = C_p(Q)$ and $C_g = C_g(Q)$ respectively.

In the private sector, there exists a whole range of providers, beginning with 'non-qualified' providers (quacks) of varying quality to 'super-specialized consultants'. Most of them offer a package deal of consultation (clinical check-up, diagnosis) plus medication (and diagnostic tests, if required) to the patients at a composite rate and it may be reasonably assumed that quality of consultation and the quality of medication vary directly (and proportionately) with each other i.e.,

$$Q_m \propto Q_c \qquad (\text{i.e. } Q_m = \lambda \, Q_c) \qquad (9)$$

The first component of the cost function $C_1 (Q_c)$ is assumed to be quadratic as a rise in Q_c is expected to raise costs more than proportionately.

$$C_{1p} (Q_c) = \alpha_c + \beta_c \, Q_c + \gamma_c \, Q_c^2 \qquad (10)$$

The second component, $C_2(Q_m)$, is assumed to be linear.

$$C_{2p} (Q_m) = \alpha_m + \beta_m \, Q_m \qquad (11)$$

From (7), (8), (9), (10) and (11), we obtain the following cost function for private health care services:

$$C_p (Q) = \alpha + \beta.Q + \gamma \, Q^2 \qquad (12)$$

Turning to the cost function for government health services, we note that it is supposed to come free of charges irrespective of the quality. The only cost of using such services would be the opportunity cost of their time spent on visiting the facility and waiting for the services, which is assumed away for simplicity. However, given the resource constraints faced by the public health system, patients are now treated free of costs but they are prescribed medication and diagnostic tests, which they obtain from the market. Accordingly, Q_c is held constant at a given level, say K, (which is fairly high since most doctors employed by the public health system are qualified professionals but may not be specialists).

$$C_{1g} (Q_c) = C_1 (K) = 0 \qquad (13)$$

But Q_m will vary considerably, ranging from spurious to cheap generics to branded products. $C(Q_m)$ is assumed to be linear in Q_m as before.

$$C_{2g} (Q_m) = \alpha' + \delta.Q_m = \alpha' + \delta.(Q - K) = (\alpha' - \delta K) + \delta.Q$$
$$= \mu + \delta.Q \qquad (14)$$

Accordingly the cost function for government health services will be

$$C_g (Q) = \mu + \delta.Q \qquad (15)$$

From (12) & (15), we can derive the respective marginal cost functions as:

$$MC_p (Q) = \beta + 2\gamma Q \qquad (16)$$

$$MC_g(Q) = \delta \qquad\qquad (17)$$

These are depicted in Figure 19.2.

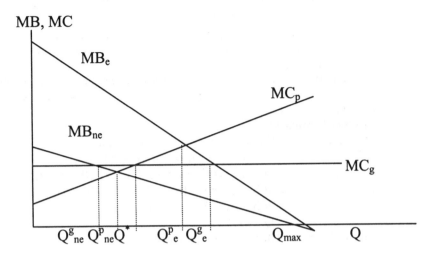

Figure 19.2 Equilibrium Quality of Service

The two marginal costs intersects at quality Q^* which may be solved by setting $MC_p = MC_g$:

$$Q^* = (\delta - \beta) / 2\gamma \qquad\qquad (18)$$
$$\delta > \beta > 0, \text{ and } \gamma > 0 \text{ ensure } Q^* > 0 [1,2] \qquad\qquad (19)$$
$$MC_p > = < MC_g \text{ according as } Q > = < Q^* \qquad\qquad (20)$$

Lemma 1A: In equilibrium, the enlightened household obtains higher quality of service than the non-enlightened household, if both opt for private health care, $Q^p_e > Q^p_{ne}$.

Lemma 1B: In equilibrium, the enlightened household obtains higher quality of service than the non-enlightened household, if both opt for government health care, $Q^g_e > Q^g_{ne}$.

Proof of Lemma 1A: Equating MC_p with MB for the two sets of households, we obtain the equilibrium Q for each of them to be

$$Q^p_e = (b - \beta) / 2(\gamma + c) \qquad\qquad (21)$$
$$Q^p_{ne} = (b' - \beta) / 2(\gamma + c') \qquad\qquad (22)$$

Since $b > b'$ and $c' > c$, the result follows.

Proof of Lemma 1B: Similar to Lemma 1A.

(Note: $Q^g_e = (b - \delta)/2c$, $Q^g_{ne} = (b' - \delta)/2c'$).

Assumption: We assume that the equilibrium quality from private health care for the two sets of households lie on two sides of Q^*, i.e.,[7]

$$Q^p_{ne} < Q^* < Q^p_e \tag{23}$$

Further assuming that Q^*, Q^p_e, Q^p_{ne}, Q^g_e, Q^g_{ne}, are all positive, we have:

$$\beta < \delta < b' < b \tag{24}$$

Lemma 2A: For the enlightened household, equilibrium quality obtained from government health care is higher than that obtained from private health care in equilibrium i.e. $Q^p_e < Q^g_e$.

Lemma 2B: For the non-enlightened household, equilibrium quality obtained from government health care is lower than that obtained from private health care in equilibrium, i.e. $Q^p_{ne} > Q^g_{ne}$.

Proof of Lemma 2A:

From assumption (23), we have $Q^p_e > Q^*$ which implies

$$\{(b - \beta) / 2(\gamma + c)\} > \{(\delta - \beta) / 2\gamma\}$$
$$\Rightarrow \{(b - \beta) / 2(\gamma + c)\} > \{(b - \beta) / 2\gamma\} - \{(b - \delta) / 2\gamma\}$$
$$\Rightarrow \{(b - \delta) / 2\gamma\} > \{b - \beta)/2\gamma\} - \{(b - \beta) / 2(\gamma + c)\}$$
$$\Rightarrow \{(b - \delta) / 2c\} > \{(b - \beta) / 2(\gamma + c)\}$$
$$\Rightarrow Q^g_e > Q^p_e$$

Proof of Lemma 2B: Similar to Lemma 2A.

Principal Results of the Model

1. In equilibrium, the enlightened household always ends up with higher quality of health care compared to the non-enlightened household, irrespective of their choice of private versus government health care.
2. Since $Q^p_{ne} > Q^g_{ne}$ for the non-enlightened household, they would in equilibrium prefer private over government health care on quality grounds.
3. Likewise, for the enlightened household $Q^g_e > Q^p_e$ and they would in equilibrium prefer government over private health care for quality reasons.

Empirical Evidence

The empirical evidence for this paper largely draws upon a survey-based Report (Ray 2000) prepared under the auspices of the Voluntary Health Association of India, New Delhi. It is based on surveys of rural households and medical practitioners in the state of *Uttar Pradesh*. We present the major conclusions of this empirical investigation juxtaposed against the results of our model. We find two distinct clusters of rural households. On one hand, there are households belonging to the lower castes[7] of the society, which are by and large characterized by low income and lack of education. The second cluster contains affluent, better-educated and high caste households. The two clusters roughly correspond to the non-enlightened (NE) versus enlightened (E) households described in our model. Curative health care practices of the rural households can be broadly classified into two types: (a) informal treatment, and (b) formal medical treatment. While the former includes home remedies as well as *ojha-tona*,[8] the latter implies use of modern medicines (mainly allopathic, but also homeopathic and ayurvedic).

Informal Treatment

Informal treatment in the form of home remedies is very common in UP, particularly as a first curative step. We find that 52 percent of patients (62 percent of upper caste patients) report to a medical practitioner only when home-remedies fail. Being a cheap substitute for modern medicines, home remedies are widely used among the economically and socially backward households not only as an immediate step but also in subsequent steps. Often they can not continue to afford the medicines prescribed by doctors in the first step and they are forced to revert back to home remedies. Alongside home-remedies, the traditional concept of faith-healing with the help of *ojha-tona* continues to be a popular curative measure among non-enlightened rural households in UP. *Ojha-tona* can be either pursued at home by knowledgeable elderly family members or neighbors free of cost or conducted commercially by 'professional' ojhas, at nominal costs. The idea of *ojha-tona* is to get rid of any possible evil spirit causing illness. Although it rarely yields any result, it continues to remain a first step towards cure as it comes free and it is believed to have no 'side-effects'. In fact, it is often simultaneously pursued with other forms curative measures. Surprisingly, some patients perceive to get cured by ojhas, where we have no other explanations to offer but the power of faith healing. Indeed, we found evidence of patients visiting ojhas even in the second or third steps after medical practitioners failed to cure them. We could identify three main reasons why patients using *ojha-tona* mostly belong to scheduled castes. First, their lack of enlightenment makes them rely more on faith healing and traditional rituals than on modern medicines. Second, poverty forces them to rely on cheap methods of treatment. Finally, ojhas are themselves people from scheduled castes and therefore they naturally attract patients from their own communities.

Formal Treatment

Formal medical care can be obtained from either from Government providers through the network of primary health centers (PHC) or from private providers of different types.

In UP, the entire network of PHCs are almost on the verge of collapse. Most of the centers are by and large non-functional due to lack of supplies, equipment and para-medical staff. However, the doctors posted at the PHCs are mostly qualified and competent, but most of them do not attend clinics.[9] Only a handful of government doctors are available in the PHCs. They examine patients clinically with some degree of competence and dispense medication, if available,[10] otherwise prescribes. Indeed, despite good clinical evaluation by PHC doctors, the quality of medical care obtained from PHCs ultimately depends on the quality of medication that the patients are able to obtain from the market.

Against the backdrop of this pathetic condition of the PHC network in UP, private practitioners have a roaring practice in rural UP. Doctor's clinics and chemist shops are found in every nook and corner. Regrettably, however, many of the private practitioners have no formal medical training or qualification. Some of them have experience of working in a chemist shop. Others are novices. There are a few practitioners who are trained either in the Indian System of Medicine (*Ayurveda*) or in homeopathy, but they do not treat patients according to Homeopathic or *Ayurvedic* traditions. All practitioners use allopathic treatment. Prescribing over-dosage of medication is very common, as their objective is to provide immediate relief to patients. Their focus is on treating the symptoms rather than curing the disease.

The cost of treatment varies with the degree of competence of these 'unqualified' practitioners. At the top end of the quality spectrum, there are a handful of qualified private doctors in the area maintaining full-time or part-time clinics in the villages. They are extremely competent but expensive and cater to the rural rich.

Our household survey indicates that the overwhelming majority of patients visit private providers and only a handful of cases opt for PHCs as a curative step. The reasons for not visiting PHCs are reported in Table 19.1. The most commonly cited reasons are: unsatisfactory facilities and services (32 percent), lack of information (17 percent), non-availability of staff (17 percent), private providers offer fast relief (17 percent) and long distance (11 percent). We delved deeper into this question and came up with interesting insights regarding the socio-economic dynamics of the use of PHC versus private health care.

Table 19.1 Reasons for not Visiting PHCs

Reasons Code	Freq.	Percent	Cum.
1	2	0.35	0.35
2	100	17.33	17.68
3	1	0.17	17.85
4	185	32.06	49.91
5	100	17.33	67.24
6	25	4.33	71.58
7	67	11.61	83.19
8	96	16.64	99.83
11	1	0.17	100.00
Total	**577**	**100**	

Codes: 1=gives same medicine, 2=lack of information about PHC, 3=PHCs are crowded, 4=lack of facility, 5=non-availability of staff/doctor, 6=misbehaviour of staff/doctor, 7=long distance, 8=quick relief from pvt. doctor, 9=cleanliness of pvt clinics, 10=anybody has prevented from going to PHC, 11=any other

Households belonging to the upper castes, which are mostly affluent, educated and enlightened, do appreciate the competence of PHC doctors and regard them as medical consultant with no fees. They can afford to buy the medicines prescribed by the PHC doctor. Some of them visit the PHC for all their medical treatment whenever there is a functioning PHC close-by.[11] Only in odd hours, they are often constrained to visit a local private provider (often non-qualified) in emergency, but invariably follow it up with a check-up by the PHC doctor at the earliest. But given that most PHCs have become virtually defunct in UP, many of the upper caste affluent households rely on private doctors at the upper end of the quality spectrum.

Low caste uneducated households, on the other hand, are unhappy with PHCs for many reasons. Most of them complain about the low quality of service obtained from PHCs. Since medicines are mostly unavailable, they are constrained to buy it from the market and hence they prefer a private provider offering a package deal. They cannot appreciate the merit of a proper clinical check-up and diagnosis without dispensation of medicines. These people appreciate quick relief provided by private providers, which minimizes their wage loss. Moreover, being uneducated, they have peculiar notions about what constitute good medical treatment. For instance, they often insist on injections, which are liberally applied by private 'quacks' but seldom by PHC doctors. Sometimes, private providers offer credit to poor households to build up a long term relationship. Also, some of them perceive a clear bias in treatment by PHCs in favor of high caste, educated and powerful (socially, politically and economically) people.

The Model and the Empirical Findings

By and large, the empirical observations from rural UP match with the overall outline and structure of our model. Broadly speaking, there are two sets of households, enlightened (E) and non-enlightened (NE) with distinct marginal benefit curves MB_e and MB_{ne} drawn according to their perception and appreciation of quality treatment. These intersect the MC_p on two sides of Q^*, such that the non-enlightened households prefer private providers over PHC as per Lemma 2B and the enlightened households prefer PHC over private providers as per Lemma 2A. It is somewhat counter-intuitive that the non-enlightened and less discerning households consider PHC to offer lower quality than private while the enlightened holds an opposite view. This is partly because the quality of PHC service is ultimately determined by the quality of medicines that the patients can afford to obtain from the market. Moreover, in making the quality comparison, it is the equilibrium quality (determined by equating MC with MB) obtained from each set of providers which is compared. For the non-enlightened households the marginal cost of quality from PHC exceeds that from private (essentially unqualified) providers, whereas for enlightened households the marginal cost of quality from PHC is lower than that from private (essentially qualified and competent) doctors.

The quality segment to the left of Q^* ($Q < Q^*$) is largely served by the private non-qualified practitioners catering mostly to the non-enlightened households. The quality segment $Q > Q^*$ is expected to be served by the PHCs serving the enlightened households. But, since there are not many PHCs in rural UP which are fully and effectively functioning, the qualified and expensive private providers have taken up this space catering to the affluent rural population.

Policy Implications

Our study shows that the government-run PHC network fails to provide quality health care to the rural poor. These households prefer to go to non-qualified private providers rather than visiting PHCs although the latter is free of cost.[12] Bhat (1993), Sundar (1995), Ray (1997) and World Bank (1994) also arrived at similar conclusions. There is, thus, little evidence to believe that the demand for health care service is indeed highly price elastic and hence the argument for providing free health care gets diluted. Accordingly, World Bank (1994) prescribes that the government should focus on preventive and promotive health services and create an environment to 'encourage the private sector to provide cost-effective services of acceptable quality'. Rural health care thus appears to be a perfect candidate for privatization.

However, such a move towards hasty privatization of rural health care could prove to be detrimental. Our model presents a case for public provision of health care on grounds of acceptable quality. We have shown that the 'cost-effective' private providers are essentially the low quality 'non-qualified' practitioners. The rural poor continue to depend on them and perhaps succeed in getting some immediate relief but at the cost of long-term damage to their health. Of course, one way of circumventing this problem would be through effective monitoring of health practitioners by the Government and through complete abolition of quackery. But then we are effectively left with the high quality expensive providers in the private sector and no Government provision. We must not forget that the large bulk of the rural poor will never be able to enter the domain of high quality health care market. As a result they will be left vulnerable with no access to health care of any quality.[13] Thus India would continue to remain backward in elementary health care and can never succeed in its efforts towards liberalization and globalization.

The policy objective should, therefore, be to ensure that quality health care is provided to the entire rural population, the non-enlightened segment in particular. Our model has clear policy prescriptions to achieve this goal. One way of achieving this would be by creating awareness among the non-enlightened masses (through education, for instance) and thereby causing an outward shift of their MB curve. If this curve intersects MC_g to the right of Q^*, these households will also opt for PHCs as per Lemma 2A and would end up with higher quality of medical care by rejecting the local 'quacks'. A second alternative would be to strengthen the PHCs by providing them with adequate supplies of good quality medicines and equipment. This will reduce the marginal cost of PHC health care from δ to 0. The MC_g will then coincide with the horizontal axis and in equilibrium both sets of households will obtain quality level Q_{max} from PHC, rejecting private providers. Both would require substantial government investment in the social sectors. Since India's public expenditure on health is abysmally low,[18] it is not unrealistic to increase India's public health expenditure, the standard efficiency arguments notwithstanding. This would go a long way in making India's efforts towards globalization a success.

Notes

1. See Duggal (1995).
2. See, for instance, Bhat (1993), World bank (1994), Sundar (1995), Ray (1997).
3. Parker (1986), Lerman et al (1985), Laurent (1982).
4. Sen (1998), p.82. See also Dreze and Sen (1995) and Dreze and Sen (1996).
5. World Bank (1994).
6. Romer et al (1984) argue that private medical practice is an obstacle to *Health For All*, favoring the affluent over the poor, cities over rural areas, treatment over prevention, and specialization over general practice.
7. If this is not true, only one provider will remain in the market.
8. Caste is a historical classification of the Indian society into socio-economic hierarchies.
9. Similar to the concept of witchcraft.
10. The doctors feel that without adequate supplies, equipment and staff, they cannot practice their profession effectively. As patients stop visiting the PHC, the doctors get more de-motivated. They also stop visiting the PHC and begin private practice so that they do not lose their clinical acumen for lack of practice.
11. However, PHC supplies of medicines are often of very poor quality.
12. Another study by Sanyal (1996) finds that more than 50 percent of the rural rich use public health facilities in states like U.P., Assam, Haryana, M. P., Orissa and Rajasthan.
13. If at all, the PHC network has been partially successful in serving the rural rich who can anyway afford to obtain quality medical care from the private sector.
14. In a study of Chile, Long (1986) also warns that undue policy emphasis on private health sector may endanger the quality of and access to health care services in countries with unequal income distribution.
15. It is only 1.7 percent of its total public expenditure, in contrast with 16.9 percent in US, 14 percent in UK, 5.9 percent in Brazil, 5.6 percent in Malaysia and 5.6 percent in Kenya. See World Development Report (1997).

References

Bhat, Ramesh. (1993), 'The Private-Public Mix in Health Care in India', *Health Policy and Planning*; vol. 8(1), pp.43-56.
Dreze, J. and Sen, A. (1995), *India: Economic Development and Social Opportunity*, Oxford University Press. Delhi.
Dreze, J. and Sen, A. (eds) (1995), *Indian Development: Regional Perspectives*, Oxford University, Delhi.

Duggal, Ravi. (1995), 'Health Expenditure Pattern in Selected Major States', *Radical Journal of Health*, vol. 1, pp.1-15.

Laurent, A. (1982), Health Financing and Expenditure: Rwanda and Togo, *Sandoz Institute for health and Socio-Economic Studies. Third World Series 2*, Geneva.

Lerman, J. L. et al. (1985), 'Treatment of Diarrhoea in Indonesian Children: What it costs and who pays for it', *The Lancet II*, pp.651-654.

Long, A. V. (1986), 'Changes in Health Financing: The Chilean Experience', *Social Science and Medicine*, vol. 22(3).

Parker, R. L. (1986), 'Health Care Expenditure in a Rural Indian Community', *Social Science and Medicine*, vol. 22(1).

Ray, A. S. (1997), 'The Economics of Health Care in India: A Case Study of Sewapuri Block in Uttar Pradesh', Chapter XXIb in *Report of the Independent Commission of Health in India*, VHAI, New Delhi.

Ray, A. S. (2000), *Utilisation of Curative Health Care by Rural Households*, Mimeo Report, VHAI, New Delhi.

Roemer, M. J. et al. (1984), 'Private Medical Practice: Obstacle to Health For All', *World Health Forum*, vol. 5(3).

Sanyal, S. K. (1996), 'Household Financing of Health Care', *Economic and Political Weekly*, May 18.

Sen, Amartya. (1998), 'Theory and Practice of Development', in Ahluwalia and Little (eds), *India's Economic Reforms and Development*, Oxford University Press, Delhi.

Sundar, R. (1995), 'Household Survey of Health Care Utilisation and Expenditure', *NCAER Working Paper*, No. 53, New Delhi.

Tulasidhar, V. B. (1993), 'Expenditure Compression and Health Sector Outlays', *Economic and Political Weekly*, November 6.

World Bank (1994), *India: Policy and Finance Strategies for Strengthening Primary Health Care Services*, Mimeo Report, Washington DC.

World Development Report (1997), *Selected Indicators on Public Finance*, World Bank, Oxford University Press, New York.

Index

Adverse Selection 89-90
Aggregate Demand 94-5
AFTA 33-4, 171, 178-80
Anti-dumping 20-1
APEC 56 171, 180
Appreciation of Life 65
ASEAN 25-40, 171, 175, 180
Asia
  East and Southeast 1-14, 90-4,
  108-110
  Economic community 205-6
  GDP 65-9
  Growth 70-15
  Fiscal settings 158
  Inequality 70-1
  Monetary mechanism 97-9
  Poverty 67-71
Asian Crisis 64-9, 78, 81, 89-94,
  108-118
Asian Crisis
  Financial 47-49
  Financial crisis 119-21
  Financial meltdown 204-7
  Lessons, fiscal policy 156-60
  Managerial signals 25-8
  Misgovernance 111-17
Asian Economic Crisis 24, 31, 35
Asian Economic Meltdown 1, 9
Asian Governments 32
Asian Integration 97-8
Australia 31

Bagehot W 59
Baht 9
Bank Run 52-3, 199-01, 207
Bank Supervision 51
Barron-Sweezy 202-7
Bubbles 94, 199
Business
  International 1-14

Small 248-60
Bhagwati, J 49

Capital
  Inflows 51-2,
  Account Liberalization 83-4
Chaoebols 33-6, 94, 172
China
  Growth and development 146-56
  Growth with stability 151-55
  High growth and low
  development 147-52
  Institutional changes 120
  Reforms 119-28
  Reform strategy 120-30
  Reform strategy game 122
  Rent seeking activities 128
  SOEs 121, 129, 131, 134
Chomsky, N 27
Cohen, J 1,5
Competitive Advantages 8
Complex Adaptive System 1-14
Complexity Theory 1-14
Conner, D 4
Contagion 52, 82-3
Contractionary Policies 58
Coordination of Macro Policies 97-8
Core Value of Development 67
Country Risk 82
Currency Board 57
Cycles
  Limit 116-7
  Vicious 114-5

Demand Side 21, 29
Demand Shocks 52
Diamond, D 53
Diamond, P 52
Dirigiste 32
Dunning, J 15-18, 21

Dybvig, P 53

Eastern European Countries 91
Economies of Scale 16
Eichengreen B 99
Eigen values 29, 116-7
Emerging markets 25, 51-3
Equilibrium
  Multiple 113-117
  Pareto-improving 120-2, 125-6
  Quality 112-7, 262-6
  Equilibrium and Stability 26, 47
Equilibria 26, 47, 53, 109,112-7, 124
EU 97-9
Excessive Leverage 51

FDI 15-21, 24-7, 30-5
FDI
  Barriers to Asia 33-4
  FDI from Japan 19-21
  FDI from South Korea 19-21
  Japanese 205-6
  L-Advantage 18
  O-Advantage 17-18
  OLI-Advantage 18
  Vietnam 175-9
Financial Intermediation 80
Financial
  Integration 176-80
  Market liberalization 80-2
  Market moral hazard 90, 95
  Market non-linear disruption 90
  Openness 177-8
  Reforms 243-6
Financial Issues
  Financial breakdown 48
  Financial crisis 48-50
  Efficient financial system 48, 50
  Eurobonds 48
  Financial intermediation 49, 50
  International financial integration
  48-50
  Intertemporal trade 49
  Risk-sharing 49
Fundamentals 51-3
Fundamentals-driven Crisis 52-3

Galbraith, K 57
GDP 67, 75, 92
GDP Growth 96-97
Gini Coefficient 70
Global
  Contagion 51-54
  Crisis prevention 52-7
  Crisis response 53-7
  Economic theory 47
  Economy 142, 180-2, 212-6
  Eurocentric 214
  Efficiency 48
  Financial integration 47-8
  Financial stability 58
  Forces 76
  Growth & instability 225-6, 237-8
  IMF crisis response 59-61
  Investment 216-7, 219
  Interconnectedness 212-29
  Portfolio investment 218-20
  Trade 55
  Trade Gap 97
Governance
  Activist 233-5
  Behavior 236
  Industrial policy 234-5
  Intervention 234-5
  Land reforms 241-2
  National level 189-91, 196
  Privatization 237-8
  Quality 110-4
  Re-allocation of resources 230-2
  Reforms of natural monopolies
  245-7
  Sub-national 186-9
  Vietnam 180-1
Greenspan, A 49
Grounded theory 1-14
Growth
  Crisis 81-2
  Development 64-5,146-55
  Education 71-3
  Environment 73-5
  Export-led 206-7
  Fiscal policy 156-69
  Inequality 70, 243

National income 120-2
Poverty 67-8

Happy Life 66
Happy Life Expectancy 66
Harberger Triangle 61
Harmonization 98
Hong Kong 6
Human development index 67, 76
Hymer 17

ILO 69
IMF 56-7, 59, 78, 80, 82, 90, 91,
    100, 108
Immiserization 69
India 136-48, 260-72
Indian
    BoP crisis 144-5
    Domestic liberalization 137-39
    Export expansion 144
    External sector liberalization 137-
    9
    Health benefits and cost 263-4
    Health care 262-71
    Health services 266-7
    Public expenditure 261-71
    Public and private health providers
    266-9
    Stabilization package 139
Indonesia 10-1, 77, 185-9
Instability
    Bankruptcies 89-90
    Banking sector instability 79, 82
    Banking liberalization 79
    Current account liberalization 79,
    81, 82
    Capital account liberalization 79,
    80, 82
    Financial crisis 81
    Financial fragility 79
    Financial repression 79
    Financial sector liberalization 79,
    83-4
    Fixed exchange rates 80-81, 82
    Panics 84
    Portfolio adjustment 80

Insufficient Capitalization 51
International Business
    Adidas 8
    Catastrophe 1
    CEOs 2, 3, 7
    Chaos 1
    Complexity Theory 1, 3-4
    Development 12, 13
    FAC 1
    Grounded Theory 1
    Presidents 8, 10
    Radical Paradigm 7
    Rupiah 8-9
    Vice-Presidents 2, 7
International Crisis
    Adverse Selection 50
    Brazil 51
    Capital Account Deficit 51
    Currency Crisis 50
    Current Account Deficit 51, 54
    Debt-servicing 50-1
    Devaluation 52, 58
    Emerging Markets 47-8 50-2, 54
    56
    ERM 47
    Global Integration 47
    Herd Behavior 34, 50-1
    Interbank Market 50
    International Financial Crisis 50
    Mexico 51
    Moral Hazard 50, 54, 56
    Russia 51
    Signaling Difficulties 34, 47
Ito's flying geese 82

Japan 10, 11, 15-16, 19-20, 32, 35
Japan vs China 203-7
Japanese FDI, 199-02, 205-6

Kaldor 108
Kindelberger 26-7
Kojima 17-8
Krugman 25, 79, 141, 90, 94, 96,
    102-3, 108
Krugman's Hypothesis 91-98
Kuznet's Cycles 26

Labor Mobility 99
LDCs 17-18, 21

Macro Issues
  BoP crisis 150
  Budget flows 164-5
  Currency depreciation 52
  Debts 166-8
  Devaluation 52
  Dissaving 157
  Exchange rates decline 82
  ERM 51-52
  Fiscal composition 166-8
  Import liberalization 150
  Inflation, debt and growth 81
  Keynesianism 232, 234
  Mundell-Fleming framework 160
  Overaccumulation 201-4
  Stabilization 158-60,
  Static and dynamic models 164-7
  Yellow Fever effect 52
Malayasia 1, 6, 9-1, 79
Management Issues 1-14, See Sri
  Lanka
Mandelbrot, B 4
Market Illiquidity 52
Market Mechanism 16
Market Failure 16
Marshall Plan 47
Merit goods 233, 261-2
Minsky's Instability Hypothesis 81-4
Mintzberg, H 5
Misgovernance 109-12, 238, 240-1
MNEs 8-10, 11, 24 –35
MNCs 16-18
Moral Hazard 56, 90
Mulitple Equilibria 47, 53, 114-5
Mutual Causation 113-5

Nash Equilibrium 53

O-Advantages 17-19
OLI Advantages 18-20
Optimum Currency Area 54, 98

Path Dependency 120-1, 133

Philippines, the 79
Policy Errors 100, 111
Product Differentiation 16
Production 215-6
Productivity Growth 100

Quality of National Policies 56

Ranis, G 17-18, 21
Regionalization 83-4, 187-99, 203-7,
  259
Rummel, R 27
Russia 212-47

Seigniorage 98
Single Markets 34
Small Business, See Sri Lanka
SMEs 33, 34
Smith, A 67
Social Development 66
Social Policy 58
Soeharto Era 58, 64, 76
South Korea 10, 11, 32, 35
South Korea
  Crisis 25, 91, 109-11
  Economy 15, 25, 92
  FDI 15
  Growth 15
Sovereignty 1
Sri Lanka 248-60
Stewart, J 1, 4-5
Strauss, A 4, 5
Subsistence Affluence 68
Sunspots 53
Supply Side 21, 29
System
  Capacity building 87-99
  Command to market 229-34
  Dual track price 127
  Socialist market 130-3
  Structural reforms 241-52
  Structural shocks 232-5
  Transition 232-3

Tequila Effect 52
Thailand 10-1, 81

TNCs 218
Todaro, M 67-68, 76-77
Tolstoy, L 50
Trade
  Distortions 247
  Formation of markets 235-7
  Groups 179-80
  Intermediate products 16
  Investment 216-20
  Liberalization 136-41, 171
  Production 215-6
  Trade Gap 100
  Trade policy 55

UNCTAD 26, 35
Underdeveloped Capital Markets
  55

Underdevelopment 67
UNDP 67, 71
Unhedged Borrowing 83
US 15, 16

VCPs 173
Veronon, R 16, 26
Vietnam
  Globalization 172-86
  Growth 177-80
  Trade liberalization 176-7
  SOEs 177-80

Wah, L 5
Washington Consensus 138
Well-being 64-6
World Bank 31, 70-1, 73-4, 79, 170